This book is dedicated to Manette, Elaine, Jan, and all of the current, past, and future ladies of WIT, with gratitude and love for their support and caring. And, of course, to my kids, their kids, and, as ever and always, to Sandy.

And, a bit of special thanks for his support, encouragement, and the "Marty button" to Marty Matthews. It's an honor to have a colleague with his capabilities, great humor, and attitude!

Contents

Part Two   Banking

Part Three   Managing Your Investment Accounts

Part Four   Tracking Your Financial Position

Part Five   Forecasting Your Financial Future

Acknowledgments

This book, like most others, is the end product of a lot of hard work by many people. Among them are

- Megg Morin, acquisitions editor at McGraw-Hill, for her encouragement, support, great humor, and always positive outlook! She is a delight!
- The folks at Intuit, especially Eddy Wu for his technical expertise, willingness to answer questions, and quick responses.
- Patty Mon, the wonderful editorial supervisor, and the project manager, Patty Wallenburg, both of whom are colleagues of the highest caliber and who make each day a joy when we get to work together!
- Our terrific technical editor Mary Higgins, the best copyeditor on the planet, Lisa McCoy, proofreader Paul Tyler, and indexer Jack Lewis for their wonderful skills!

Introduction

Choosing Quicken Personal Finance Software to organize your finances was a great decision. Quicken has all the tools you need to manage your personal finances. Its well-designed, intuitive interface makes it easy to use. And its online and automation features make entering transactions and paying bills a snap. But if that isn't enough, Quicken also offers features that can help you learn more about financial opportunities that can save you time and money—two things that often seem in short supply.

This introduction tells you a little about the book, so you know what to expect in the chapters to come.

About This Book

This book tells you how to get the most out of Quicken. It starts by explaining the basics—the common, everyday tasks that you need to know just to use the program. It then goes beyond the basics to show you how to use Quicken to save time, save money, and make smart financial decisions. Along the way, it shows you most of Quicken's features, including many that you probably didn't even know existed. You'll find yourself using Quicken far more than you ever dreamed you would.

Assumptions

This book makes a few assumptions about your knowledge of your computer, Windows, Quicken, and financial management. These assumptions give you a starting point, making it possible to skip over the things that are assumed you already know.

What You Should Know About Your Computer and Windows

To use this book (or Quicken 2012, for that matter), you should have a general understanding of how to use your computer and Windows. You don't need to be an expert. As you'll see, Quicken uses many standard and intuitive interface elements, making it easy to use—even if you're a complete computer novice.

At a bare minimum, you should know how to turn your computer on and off and how to use your mouse. You should also know how to perform basic Windows tasks, such as starting and exiting programs, using menus and dialog boxes (called just *dialogs* in this book), and entering and editing text. Chapter 2 gives you a few basic computer usage tips and conventions. If you are fairly new to computing, there are some how-tos and explanations that may be useful to you.

If you're not sure how to do these things or would like to brush up on them, get *Windows 7 QuickSteps* from McGraw-Hill. This resource will provide all the information you need to get started.

What You Should Know About Quicken and Financial Management

You don't need to know much about either Quicken or financial management to get the most out of this book; it assumes that both are new to you.

This doesn't mean that this book is just for raw beginners. It provides plenty of useful information for seasoned Quicken users—especially those of you who have used previous versions of Quicken—and for people who have been managing their finances with other tools, such as Microsoft Money (welcome to Quicken!) or pencil and paper (welcome!).

Because the book assumes that all this is new to you, it makes a special effort to explain Quicken procedures as well as the financial concepts and terms on which they depend. New concepts and terms first appear in italic type. By understanding these things, not only can you better understand how to use Quicken, but you also can communicate more effectively with finance professionals, such as bankers, stockbrokers, and financial advisors.

Quicken Updates

One of the terrific things about computing in 2012 is our Internet connectivity and capability. Quicken's team, like all program developers, is working to improve the software throughout the year, not just when a new version is released. That means that Quicken can send small changes to their program each time you update the program. Because of this, you may see illustrations in this book that differ from the ones you see on the screen. The procedures haven't changed, only small changes have been made to make the program more user-friendly.

Organization

This book is logically organized into six parts, each with at least two chapters. Each part covers either general Quicken setup information or one of Quicken's financial centers. Within each part, the chapters start with the most basic concepts and procedures, most of which involve specific Quicken tasks, and then work their way up to more advanced topics, many of which are based on finance-related concepts that Quicken makes easy to master.

It is not necessary to read this book from beginning to end. Skip around as desired. Although the book is organized for cover-to-cover reading, not all of its information may apply to you. For example, if you're not the least bit interested in investing, skip the chapters in the Investing part. It's as simple as that. When you're ready for the information that you skipped, it'll be waiting for you.

Here's a brief summary of the book's organization and contents.

Part One: Learning Quicken Basics

This part of the book introduces Quicken's interface and features, and helps you set up Quicken for managing your finances. It also provides the information you need to test Quicken's online features. If you're new to Quicken, the first three chapters in this part of the book may prove helpful.

Part One has three chapters:

- **Chapter 1:** Getting to Know Quicken
- **Chapter 2:** Computing with Quicken
- **Chapter 3:** Working with Accounts, Categories, and Tags

Part Two: Banking

This part of the book explains how to use Quicken to record financial transactions in bank and credit card accounts. One chapter concentrates on the basics, while another goes beyond the basics to discuss online features available within Quicken. This part of the book also explains how to automate many transaction entry tasks, reconcile accounts, and use Quicken's extensive reporting features.

There are five chapters in Part Two:

- **Chapter 4:** Recording Bank and Credit Card Transactions
- **Chapter 5:** Using Online Banking Features
- **Chapter 6:** Automating Transactions and Tasks
- **Chapter 7:** Reconciling Your Accounts
- **Chapter 8:** Examining Your Bank Activity

Part Three: Managing Your Investment Accounts

This part of the book explains how you can use Quicken and Quicken.com to keep track of your investment portfolio and get information to help you make smart investment decisions. The first chapter covers the basics of Quicken's investment tracking features, while the other two chapters provide information about online investment tracking and research tools. You'll see how the features available at Quicken.com can help you evaluate your investment position.

There are three chapters in Part Three:

- **Chapter 9:** Entering Your Investment Transactions
- **Chapter 10:** Using Transaction Download and Research Tools
- **Chapter 11:** Evaluating Your Position

Part Four: Tracking Your Financial Position

This part of the book concentrates on assets and liabilities, including your home and car and related loans. It explains how you can track these items in Quicken and provides tips for minimizing related expenses.

There are two chapters in Part Four:

- **Chapter 12:** Monitoring Assets and Loans
- **Chapter 13:** Keeping Tabs on Your Net Worth

Part Five: Forecasting Your Financial Future

This part of the book tells you how you can take advantage of Quicken's built-in planning tools to plan for your retirement and other major events in your life. As you'll learn in this part of the book, whether you want financial security in your retirement years or to save up for the down payment on a house or college education for your children, Quicken can help you. It includes information on using Quicken's financial calculators and provides a wealth of tips for saving money and reducing debt.

There are four chapters in Part Five:

- **Chapter 14:** Planning for the Future
- **Chapter 15:** Using Financial Calculators
- **Chapter 16:** Reducing Debt and Saving Money
- **Chapter 17:** Planning for Tax Time

Part Six: Appendixes

And, to help you even more, three appendixes offer additional information you might find useful when working with Quicken:

- **Appendix A:** Managing Quicken Files
- **Appendix B:** Customizing Quicken
- **Appendix C:** Converting from Microsoft Money

Conventions

All how-to books—especially computer books—have certain conventions for communicating information. Here's a brief summary of the conventions used throughout this book.

Menu Commands

Quicken, like most other Windows programs, makes commands accessible on the menu bar at the top of the application window. Throughout this book, you are told which menu commands to choose to open a window or dialog, or to complete a task. The following format is used to indicate menu commands: Menu | Submenu (if applicable) | Command.

Keystrokes

Keystrokes are the keys you must press to complete a task. There are two kinds of keystrokes.

- **Keyboard shortcuts** are combinations of keys you press to complete a task more quickly. For example, the shortcut for "clicking" a Cancel button may be to press the ESC key. When instructing you to press a key, the name of the key is in small caps, like this: ESC. If you must press two or more keys simultaneously, they are separated with a hyphen, like this: CTRL-P. Many of Quicken's keyboard shortcuts are explained in Chapter 1.
- **Literal text** is text that you must type in exactly as it appears in the book. Although this book doesn't contain many instances of literal text, there are a few. Literal text to be typed is in boldface type, like this: **Checking Acct**. If literal text includes a variable—text you must substitute when you type—the variable is included in bold-italic type, like this: ***Payee Name***.

Icons

Icons are used to flag specific types of information.

Sidebars

This book also includes "New to Quicken 2012" and "In My Experience" sidebars. These sidebars are meant to put a specific Quicken feature into perspective by either telling you how it is used or offering suggestions on how you can use it. You'll learn a lot from these sidebars, but like all sidebars, they're not required reading.

About the Author

Bobbi Sandberg has long been involved with computers, accounting, and writing. She is a retired accountant currently filling her time as a trainer, technical writer, and small-business consultant. As a Quicken user and teacher since its inception, she knows the questions users ask and gives easy-to-understand explanations of each step within the program. She teaches at several venues, offering step-by-step instruction in a variety of computer applications. Her extensive background, coupled with her ability to explain complex concepts in plain language, has made her a popular instructor, consultant, and speaker. She has authored and co-authored more than a dozen computer books, including *Quicken 2011 The Official Guide*.

About the Technical Editor

Mary Higgins is a long-time Quicken user, having used each version since 1999. She enjoys pushing the limits of what the software is intended to do—clicking every button, navigating every menu path, reading the help files, etc. She reads and posts on the Quicken forums and finds it interesting to see how others are using Quicken and the different approaches to resolving issues.

Learning Quicken Basics

This part of the book introduces Quicken Personal Finance Software's interface and features. It begins by explaining how to install Quicken and showing you the elements of its user interface. It offers an entire chapter with instructions for setting up Quicken for the first time. Then it tells you all about Quicken's accounts, categories, and tags. Finally, it explains why you should be interested in Online Account Services and how you can set up Quicken to access the Internet and download information from your financial institutions. The chapters are

Chapter 1:   Getting to Know Quicken

Chapter 2:   Computing with Quicken

Chapter 3:   Working with Accounts, Categories, and Tags

Getting to Know Quicken

In This Chapter:

- *Exploring Quicken's uses*
- *Installing Quicken*
- *Starting Quicken*
- *Preparing a data file*
- *Registering Quicken*
- *Exploring the Main View*
- *Understanding other windows*
- *Learning Quicken's features*
- *Finding help in Quicken*
- *Exiting Quicken*

If you're brand new to Quicken Personal Finance Software, get your relationship with Quicken off to a good start by properly installing it and learning a little more about how you can interact with it.

This chapter provides a brief overview of Quicken, explains how to install and start it, takes you on a tour of its interface, and shows you how to use its extensive Onscreen Help features. Although the information provided in this chapter is especially useful to new Quicken users, some of it also applies to users who are upgrading. If you are a former Microsoft Money user, see Appendix C for some Microsoft Money–specific comparisons and explanations.

Chapter 1

What Is Quicken?

On the surface, Quicken is a computerized checkbook. It enables you to balance your accounts and organize, manage, and generate reports for your finances. But as you explore Quicken, you'll learn that it's much more. It's a complete personal finance software package—a tool for taking control of your finances. Quicken makes it easy to know what you have, how you are doing financially, and what you should do to strengthen your financial situation.

Exploring Quicken's Uses

At the least, Quicken can help you manage your bank and credit card accounts. You can enter transactions and have Quicken generate reports and graphs that show where your money went and how much is left.

Quicken can help you manage investment accounts. You can enter transactions and have Quicken tell you the market value of your investments. Quicken can also help you organize other data, such as the purchase price of your possessions and the outstanding balances on your loans. It can even store a copy of the warranty that came with your purchases.

With all financial information stored in Quicken's data file, you can generate net worth reports to see where you stand today. You can also use a variety of financial planners to make financial decisions for the future. And Quicken's tax features, including export into TurboTax and the Deduction Finder, can make tax time easier on you and your bank accounts.

With Quicken's online features, much of your data entry can be automated. Online banking enables you to keep track of bank account transactions and balances, and to pay bills without writing checks or sticking on stamps. Online investing enables you to download investment transactions. You can also read news and information about investment opportunities and advice offered by financial experts.

Quicken Versions

Intuit offers several versions of Quicken 2012 for Windows for managing personal finances: Starter, Deluxe, Premier, Home & Business, and Rental Property Manager.

Quicken Starter is an entry-level product designed for people who are new to personal finance software. As its name suggests, it includes basic features to track bank accounts and credit cards. It also enables you to use Online Account Services and Online Payment, and shop for insurance and mortgages. This version is sometimes included in computers you purchase from the manufacturer.

You can also import your files from previous versions of Quicken Starter edition, but not from other versions.

Quicken Deluxe is more robust. Designed for people who want to take a more active role in financial management, investments, and planning, it includes all the features in Quicken Starter plus the financial alerts feature, money-saving features for tax time and debt reduction, and free access to investment information.

Quicken Premier has all the features of Quicken Deluxe, plus additional features for investing and tax planning and preparation.

This book covers Quicken Deluxe and Premier editions. Although much of its information also applies to Quicken Starter, this book covers many features that are not included in the Starter version and a handful of features that are not included in the Deluxe version. If you're a Quicken Starter or Deluxe user, consider upgrading to Quicken Premier so you can take advantage of the powerful features it has to offer. One more thing—Intuit also offers two special versions of Quicken. If you're a small-business owner, Quicken Home & Business can handle all of your personal and basic business financial needs, including the business expenses you need to track for your tax return's Schedule C. If you manage one or more rental properties, Quicken Rental Property Manager can handle transactions and other information for tenants, rental income, and related expenses that you need to track for your tax return's Schedule E. As you can see, Intuit has you covered with a Quicken product for all facets of your financial life.

System Requirements

Quicken 2012 is designed to work with Windows 7, both 32- and 64-bit machines. It also works with Windows Vista and Windows XP SP2 and later. You'll need at least 1 gigabyte (GB) of random access memory (RAM) and a minimum of 450 megabytes (MB) of free space on your hard drive. You'll need a monitor that has a resolution of 1024 × 768 or higher as well as a CD/DVD drive. Internet access is needed for online work as well as program updates. You'll also need a printer if you want to print reports and graphs.

Getting Started

Ready to get started? This section explains how to install, start, and register Quicken.

The instructions in this section assume you're installing Quicken on a computer running Windows 7. Although Quicken will run under Windows XP or Windows Vista, the pathnames mentioned in this section may be different if you are installing Quicken on a computer running an operating system other than Windows 7.

Installing Quicken

Quicken uses a standard Windows setup program that should be familiar to you if you've installed other Windows programs.

Insert the Quicken 2012 CD into your CD or DVD drive. A dialog should appear, asking if you want to install the program to your hard drive. If so, click Yes to start the Quicken installer.

If this dialog does not appear automatically, you can start the installer by double-clicking the Computer icon on your desktop and then double-clicking the icon for your optical drive in the window that appears.

The installer displays a series of dialogs with information and options for installing Quicken. Read the information in the Welcome screen as seen here, and click Next to continue. When asked to agree to a software license agreement,

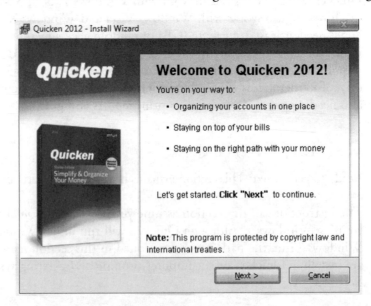

select the I Agree To The Terms Of The License Agreement And Acknowledge Receipt Of The Quicken Privacy Statement option. (If you select the other option, you cannot click Next and cannot install the software.)

You can click the Quicken Privacy Statement link to open this important document in a web browser window and read it; close the browser window when you're finished to return to the installer. You may clear the anonymous usage message check box if you choose. This option allows Quicken to collect information about how you use the program so that Intuit can make the program even more user-friendly. Click Next in the Install Wizard window.

In the Destination Folder screen, the installer tells you where Quicken will be installed—normally C:\Program Files(x86)\Quicken. You can click the Change button and use the screen that appears to change the installation location. To keep the recommended, default location, just click Next.

In the Ready To Install The Program screen, the installer displays a summary of what it will do. If this is a first-time Quicken installation, all it will do is install Quicken 2012 and any updates to the program. But if you're upgrading from a previous version, the installer will begin by uninstalling whatever version is currently installed. (You can have only one version of Quicken installed on your computer at a time.) Only the Quicken program files will be deleted; your data files will remain intact so you can use them with Quicken 2012. Click Install.

For upgraders, the data file you most recently used in the previous year's version will be converted to the Quicken 2012 format. A copy of the previous year's version data file will be placed in a folder called Q*xx*Files, where *xx* is the previous year's version.

Wait while the installer uninstalls the previous version of Quicken (if necessary), copies the Quicken 2012 files, and downloads any updates to your hard disk.

As part of the installation process, the installer uses your Internet connection to check for and download Quicken updates. This ensures that you have the most up-to-date version of Quicken installed. When the update is complete, the Installer displays an Installation Complete screen. Click Done.

Quicken should start automatically. Skip ahead to the section titled "Preparing a Data File." If Quicken does not start automatically, follow the instructions in the next section to start it.

Starting Quicken

You can start Quicken in several different ways. Here are the two most common methods.

Opening the Quicken Shortcut

The Quicken installer places a Quicken 2012 shortcut icon on your Windows desktop. Double-clicking this shortcut opens Quicken.

Opening Quicken from the Task Bar

You can also use the Start button on the Windows task bar to start Quicken and other Quicken components. Choose Start | All Programs | Quicken 2012 | Quicken 2012 to start Quicken.

Preparing a Data File

Quicken stores all of your financial information in a Quicken data file. Before you can use Quicken, you must either create a data file or convert an existing data file for use with Quicken 2012.

New User Startup

If you're a brand-new Quicken user, a Welcome To Quicken 2012 dialog appears. You have two options.

I Am A New User, Or I've Used Quicken Before But I Want to Start Over

When you select this option and click Get Started, Quicken creates a new data file called *yourname's* Quicken Data in a Quicken folder in your Documents folder. It opens the file and displays the Main View screen of the Home tab. This screen includes information and buttons that help you set up your Quicken data file. If you're following along and would like to set up your data file now, skip ahead to Chapter 3 and follow the instructions there. Then, to learn more about how Quicken works, read the section titled "The Quicken Interface," later in this chapter.

I've Used Quicken Before, And I Want To Open An Existing Quicken File

When you select this option and click Get Started, Quicken displays the Select Your Data File dialog. Continue following instructions in the section titled "Existing User Startup," next.

If you have just installed Quicken on a new computer, have selected the I've Used Quicken Before, And I Want To Open An Existing Quicken File option, and want to move your files from your old computer, click the How Do I Move A Data File From Another Computer link. This link, with your Internet connection, opens an explanation of how to move your files.

Existing User Startup

If you upgraded from a previous version of Quicken, when you first start Quicken, the Select Your Existing Data File To Get Started window appears. It offers three options:

- **Open A File Located On This Computer** displays the Open Quicken File dialog, which you can use to select a file on your hard disk. After selecting and opening a file, continue following the instructions in the section titled "Converting a Data File as Part of an Upgrade."
- **Restore A Quicken Data File I've Backed Up To CD, Disk, Or Online** enables you to open a backup file for use with Quicken 2012. (This option works only with files you created using Quicken's Backup command, which is discussed in Appendix A.) When you select this option and click Next, Quicken displays the Restore From Backup File dialog so you can select the type of backup file, locate it on disk, and open it. Along the way, it prompts you for a location in which to save the file; normally this will be in the Quicken folder inside your Documents folder. If a dialog appears telling you that you have to convert the data file, continue following the instructions in the section titled "Converting a Data File as Part of an Upgrade." When restoration is complete, Quicken opens the data file.
- **Start Over And Create A New Data File** displays the Create Quicken File dialog, which you can use to enter a name for your new Quicken data file. It then opens the file and displays the Main View screen of the Home tab. This screen includes information and buttons that help you set up your Quicken data file. If you're following along and would like to set up your data file now, skip ahead to Chapter 3 and follow the instructions there.

Converting a Data File as Part of an Upgrade

The Convert Your Data File To Quicken 2012 dialog appears any time you indicate that you want to update an existing Quicken data file for use with Quicken 2012. Clicking the Convert File button converts the data file named in the dialog to the Quicken 2012 format and saves the original file in C:\Users\ *yourname*\Documents\Quicken\ QxxFiles. The path for the saved copy of the original file may vary depending on which previous version you are upgrading from.

Registering Quicken

Sooner or later Quicken's Product Registration dialog will appear. It tells you about the benefits of registering Quicken and displays two buttons:

- **Register Later** lets you put off the registration process. Use this option if you don't have the few minutes it takes to register or your computer is not connected to the Internet. Keep in mind, however, that certain Quicken features will not function until you register.
- **Register Now** begins the registration process. You'll need Internet access to complete this process.

   To start the registration process, click the Register Now button. Then follow the instructions that appear on screen. When the registration process is complete, you can continue working with Quicken.

The Quicken Interface

Quicken's interface, which has been reworked for Quicken 2012, is designed to be intuitive and easy to use. If you are starting Quicken from scratch, after you have installed and registered your program, Quicken opens to the Quicken Home page as seen in Figure 1-1. This interface puts the information and tools you need to manage your finances right within mouse pointer reach. You never have to dig through multiple dialogs and menus to get to the commands you need most. You'll see how to get started using this Home page in Chapter 3.

   This section tells you about the components of the Quicken interface and explains how each feature can help you manage your financial life.

Exploring the Main View

The main Quicken window gives you access to most of Quicken's features and your financial information, as seen in Figure 1-2.

Account Bar

The Account Bar lists each of your Quicken accounts on the left side of the main Quicken window (refer to Figure 1-2). At the top of the Account Bar is a link to the All Transactions register, which shows the transactions for all of your accounts in one register.

   There are three main sections to the Account Bar: Banking, Investing, and Property & Debt. If the Account Bar is not displayed (refer to Figure 1-2), you

Figure 1-1 • The Quicken Home page helps you get started quickly.

can display it by clicking the small arrow beside the Accounts button on the left end of the main window's tabs.

If you can't see all of the accounts in the Account Bar, you can use the scroll bar on the right side of the Account Bar to scroll through its contents. You can also click the downward or right-pointing arrow beside a section heading on the Account Bar to hide or display, respectively, the list of accounts beneath it.

By default, account balances appear in the panel; however, you can right-click anywhere in the Account Bar to open a context menu. Choose Hide Amounts to hide amounts from view. (This also makes the Account Bar narrower so more information appears in the window beside it.) This contextual menu offers

Figure 1-2 • The Main View in the Home tab allows you to easily understand your financial information.

additional options for the display of the Account Bar, such as displaying cents in the amounts. You can also change the width of the Account Bar by dragging its right border.

The account names in the Account Bar are links; click an account name to view its register. You can customize the Account Bar to move accounts from one section to another or to hide an account from the Account Bar totals; learn how in Chapter 3.

You can add or hide other items in the Account Bar from the Account List, as explained in Chapter 3. Click View | Account Bar to open a menu that allows you to choose where the Account Bar appears, as seen here.

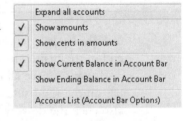

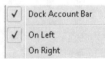

Tabs

Tabs occupy the main part of the Quicken program window. Some tabs, such as the Spending and Investing tabs, provide information about your financial status, as well as links and buttons for accessing Quicken features. Other tabs, such as the Home tab seen in Figure 1-2, enable you to view and customize Quicken settings for your financial situation. Use the Tabs To Show option from View in the Quicken menu to specify which tabs to display or hide from view. Chapter 3 explains how.

A tab exists for each major area of Quicken:

- **Home** displays customizable views of your Quicken data. Learn how to work with and customize the Home tab views in Chapter 8 and Appendix B.
- **Spending** provides information about your income and expenditures for all accounts or one of your choosing, for all dates, or for a custom date that you choose. You can use the drop-down lists to customize the information in both graphical and list formats. See Chapter 8 for more information about the Spending tab.
- **Bills** provides information about your upcoming bills and offers tools for working with bills and reminders. Chapter 6 discusses the Bills tab options.
- **Planning** gives you access to Quicken's financial planners, as well as the assumptions you need to set up to use the planners effectively. Part Five discusses Quicken's financial calculators and the Planning tab. In Quicken 2012, the Planning tab also includes tax-related options, such as projected taxes, a tax calendar, and your year-to-date income and tax-related expenses. Part Six includes Quicken's tax features.
- **Investing** provides information about your investment and retirement accounts and any stocks or mutual funds you've asked Quicken to watch for you. Part Three covers investing and the Investing tab.
- **Property & Debt** provides information about asset and debt accounts, including your home, car, related loans, and auto expenses. Part Four discusses the Property & Debt tab and its related features.
- **Tips & Tutorials** displays information about additional Quicken services. Learn more about this tab in Chapter 3.

The buttons in each tab indicates the current view or other options within each tab section. If there's more than one button or a menu in either of these areas, you can click a button or choose a menu command to switch to another view or account.

Understanding Other Windows

Quicken uses other windows to display information, depending on what you want to see or what task you are trying to perform.

List Windows

A list window, such as the one you see in Figure 1-3, shows a list of information about related things, such as accounts, categories, tags, or scheduled transactions. You can use a list window to perform tasks with items in the list.

Report Windows

Quicken's report windows (see Figure 1-4) enable you to create reports about your financial matters. You have the option to change date ranges, create comparisons, and customize reports. You can also use options and buttons at the top of the window to work with, customize, and save reports. Chapter 8 explains how to create and customize reports and graphs.

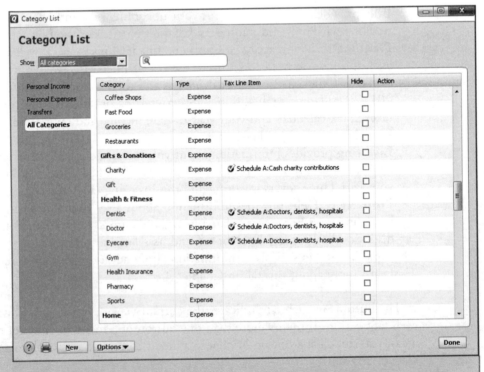

Figure 1-3 • The Category List window displays a list of categories you can use to identify your transactions.

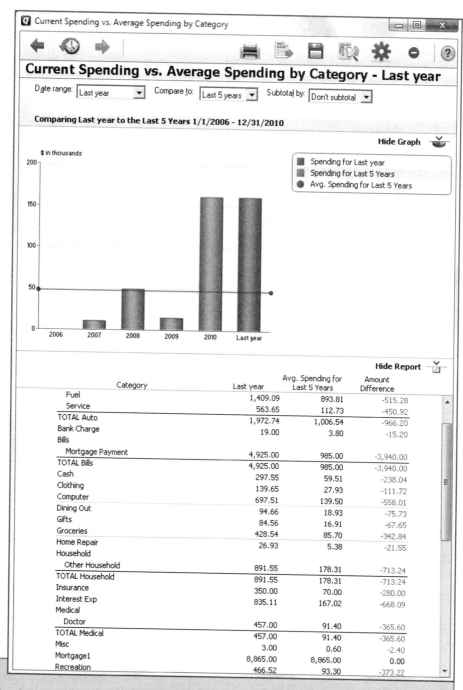

Figure 1-4 • Quicken's reports tell the story visually.

Learning Quicken's Features

Quicken offers a number of ways to access its features and commands, including standard Microsoft Windows elements, such as menus and dialogs, and Quicken elements, such as the Tool Bar, button bar, and links and buttons within Quicken windows.

Menus

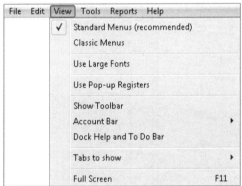

Quicken has two ways to display menus. The recommended Standard display shows six items on the menu bar, as seen here. If you choose Classic Menus, you have an additional seven from which to choose. You can choose commands from the menus as follows:

- Click the menu name to display the menu. If necessary, click the name of the submenu you want, and then click the name of the command you want.
- Press the shortcut key combination for the menu command that you want. A command's shortcut key, if it has one, is displayed to the right of the command name on the menu. An extensive list of Quicken's shortcut keys can be found in Appendix A.
- If your Windows program is set up to have keyboard access keys underlined, you can press ALT to activate the menu bar and press the keyboard key for the underlined letter in the menu that you want to open. If necessary, press the key for the underlined letter in the submenu that you want to open, and then press the key for the underlined letter in the command that you want.

Shortcut Menus

Shortcut menus (which are sometimes referred to as context or context-sensitive menus) can be displayed throughout Quicken. Point to the item for which you want to display a shortcut menu and click the right mouse button. The menu, which includes only those commands applicable to the item, appears at the mouse pointer.

NEW IN QUICKEN 2012

You may have noticed an item on your View menu called Use Large Fonts. This option enlarges the standard Quicken fonts in every tab, as well as in registers and on-screen reports. The menu bar, however, stays the normal size.

Dialogs

Like other Windows applications, Quicken uses dialogs to communicate with you. Some dialogs display a simple message, while others include text boxes, option buttons, check boxes, and drop-down lists you can use to enter information, similar to the one shown here. Many dialogs also include a Help button that you can use to get additional information about options. The Help button is often a small question mark inside a yellow circle. Note the Help button in the following illustration.

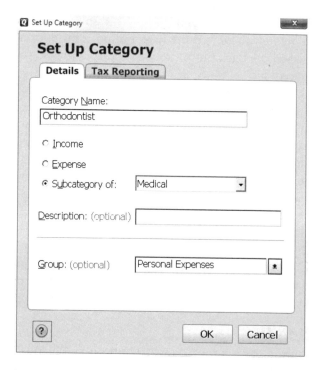

 The Use Large Fonts option was activated in the illustration.

Tool Bar

The Tool Bar is a row of buttons along the top of the application window, just beneath the standard menu bar, shown next, that gives you access to other navigation techniques and features. The Quicken Tool Bar appears by default, but can be turned off and customized. Learn how to customize it in Appendix B. Here's a quick look at the default Tool Bar.

- **Back** (an arrow pointing left) displays the previously opened window.
- **Forward** (an arrow pointing right) displays the window you were looking at before you clicked the Back button. This button is only available if you clicked the Back button to view a previously viewed window, otherwise it is grayed out.
- **One Step Update** (the blue curling arrow that points to the right) opens the One Step Update menu, so with your Internet connection you can update all of your online information at once. Clicking the triangle that's part of this button displays a menu of commands related to the One Step Update feature, including Update Settings, Manage My Passwords, Update Summary, and Schedule Updates. Chapter 6 discusses the One Step Update feature in depth.
- **Search** is a global search feature you can use to search for transactions entered into Quicken. Just enter the search criteria in the field, and press ENTER.
- **Customize Tool Bar** (the small gear icon) at the end of the Quicken Tool Bar allows you to make changes and additions to the Quicken Tool Bar. Learn more about customizing the Tool Bar in Appendix B.

Button Bar

The button bar is a row of textual buttons and menus that appears just above the contents of many Quicken windows. Most items on the button bar, which vary from window to window, are buttons; simply click one to access its options. The items with triangles beside their names are menus that work just like the menu bar menus.

   Keep in mind that Quicken's Onscreen Help may refer to the button bar as the Tool Bar. Throughout this book it is called the button bar to differentiate between it and the Quicken Tool Bar.

Finding Help in Quicken

In addition to the question mark option in many Quicken windows and the Help button in dialogs, Quicken includes an extensive Onscreen Help system to provide more information about using Quicken while you work. You can access most Help options from the Help menu, which is shown here.

Quicken's Onscreen Help uses a familiar Windows Help interface. You can use it to browse or search Help topics or display Help information about a specific window.

Help
Getting Started Guide
Quicken Help F1
Quicken Live Community
Quicken Support
Submit Feedback on Quicken
Join the Quicken Inner Circle
Privacy Preferences
Log Files
About Quicken
Add Business Tools
Add Rental Property Tools

Getting Started Guide

The Getting Started Guide link and your Internet connection take you to the Quicken website where you can download a .pdf file that gives you information on getting started with your Quicken program.

Browsing or Searching Help

Start by choosing Help | Quicken Help or pressing the F1 key. A Quicken Help window appears. The left side of the window has two tabs for browsing Help topics:

- **Contents** lists Help topics. Clicking a topic link displays information and links for accessing additional information in the right side of the window.
- **Search Quicken Help** enables you to search for information about a topic. Enter a search word in the tab's search field, and then click the Ask button. Click the title of a topic in the search results list to display information about it in the right side of the window.

IN MY EXPERIENCE

These days, any decent software program offers on-screen help. So what's the big deal about Quicken's? Quicken's Onscreen Help is especially ... well, helpful. It covers every program feature and provides step-by-step instructions for performing many tasks. Clickable links make it easy to jump right to a topic you want to learn more about. And as you'll discover while using Quicken, Help is available throughout the program—not just in the Quicken Help windows.

Onscreen Help also gives you, a Quicken user, the opportunity to help make Quicken a better software program. At the bottom of most Help windows, you'll find Yes and No buttons that you can use to tell Intuit whether the Help topic gave you the information you needed. Click the appropriate button as you use Onscreen Help to help the folks at Intuit make Onscreen Help more useful to you.

Quicken Live Community

With your Internet connection, the Quicken Live Community command takes you to Quicken's online user-to-user forum, where you can ask questions, get answers, and share information with other Quicken users. Click links or use the search feature to get the information you need to make the most of Quicken. In addition, Intuit is currently consolidating its customer feedback site, so for product improvement ideas, comments, and suggestions, go to www.getsatisfaction.com/quicken.

Quicken Support

Click Quicken Support on the Help menu to open the Quicken support site on the Internet. Here you can look through frequently asked questions as well as find links to other Quicken resources.

Submit Feedback on Quicken

This link opens a Quicken feedback page on the Internet. While you may think that your idea or concern is not "important," it is to Quicken. It is partly through this feedback that Intuit designs its products.

Join the Quicken Inner Circle

The Quicken Inner Circle is more than just a user feedback site. Intuit has created a collaborative "virtual" community online, one that works directly with product managers and others on the Quicken team. At some point, Quicken may merge this site with the Getting Satisfaction site described earlier.

Privacy Preferences

This command opens Quicken's Preferences dialog where you can set options about sending feature usage and connectivity success rates to Intuit. There is also a link to Intuit's privacy statement. Intuit takes the job of protecting your information very seriously. The policies and procedures taken by the company to protect all of your information is displayed in this message. The statement explains what information is collected by Quicken, how that information is used, and how you can find out more about Intuit's specific methods to ensure your information is safe at all times.

Log Files

This link contains other links to several files created in the "background" by Quicken. Should you ever need to contact Quicken Support, the helpful Quicken support person may ask you to refer to these files for troubleshooting.

There are several types of log files, and should you ever need to send them, Quicken will designate which one is required.

About Quicken

This tells you which version of Quicken you are using. Also in the About Quicken message are copyright information and credit to the many people who have made the program possible. Additional technical information about your Quicken file and system resources can be displayed by holding down CTRL and clicking Help | About Quicken. You may be asked for this information when troubleshooting with Quicken Support.

Upgrading Quicken

If you're wondering whether the version of Quicken installed on your computer is the best one for you, be sure to check out Help | Add Business Tools or Help | Add Rental Property Tools. With your Internet connection, these commands display a window that provides more information about features in Quicken Home & Business or Quicken Rental Properties. From this website, you can purchase either the Home & Business or Rental Property Manager version of Quicken.

Exiting Quicken

When you're finished using Quicken, choose File | Exit. This closes the Quicken application. You can also click the red *X* on the title bar to close the program.

Sometimes when you exit Quicken, you'll be asked whether you want to back up your Quicken data file. Learn how to back up data files in Appendix A.

Computing
with Quicken

chapter 2

In This Chapter:

- Reviewing basic terms
- Understanding computer processes
- Finding Quicken's online benefits
- Understanding the security features
- Getting connected
- Surfing the Web
- Understanding online financial services
- Applying for online financial services
- Resolving connectivity issues

As you learned in Chapter 1, Quicken Personal Finance Software is easy to install, and its various windows and features look much like the check registers with which most everyone is familiar. Many computer users are comfortable working with the program as soon as it is installed. However, some of the terms and processes described in Quicken may seem a bit foreign to some computer users. Terms like "right-click," "scroll," or "copy and paste" have been known to confound even the most seasoned web surfer.

Throughout this book, in the Quicken Help screens, and on the Quicken website, you'll see terms that may be unfamiliar. This chapter is designed to help you review some of the computer terms you may encounter and perform some more common computer tasks. It also explains how Quicken and the Internet connect, and how to set up your computer to take advantage of Quicken's online features to get up-to-date information, automate data entry, pay bills, and obtain Quicken maintenance updates automatically. You'll see a bit about surfing the Web and be introduced to Quicken.com, a source of information and services for Quicken users.

Computer Terminology

Most computer users know the mouse, whether it's tethered to your computer by a cord or operating independently with a wireless connection. Did you know that the mouse and the keyboard are called your *input* devices, while your monitor and printer are considered *output* devices? In this section, we review some of the common terminology associated with computer use.

Reviewing Basic Terms

These terms are in alphabetic order, not in order of their importance. This is by no means a complete list, just terms that you may encounter.

Bit

The smallest piece of information in a computer is a *bit*. It is displayed in computer code as a zero or a one. Think "off" or "on," like a light bulb being turned on and off. This is the way computers "talk," Eight bits equal one "byte," and 1,024 bytes equal one kilobyte, which is abbreviated KB. Today's computers talk in much bigger numbers, as shown here:

- **MB**   Megabyte, abbreviated as MB. One MB equals 1,024 KB.
- **GB**   Gigabyte, abbreviated as GB. One GB is approximately 1,000 MB.
- **TB**   Terabyte, abbreviated as TB. One TB is approximately 1,000 GB.
- **PB**   Petabyte, abbreviated as PB. One PB is approximately 1,000 TB.

What do all of these abbreviations really mean to you? They are a measure of space or capacity of the various pieces of digital equipment. For example, a CD has about a 700MB capacity. If your digital photos average 7MB, you'll see that you can store around 100 photos on that CD. The capacity of flash drives and hard disks are measured in gigabytes (GB). While file sizes vary, conceivably, you could save about 1,000,000 text pages on a 1GB flash drive.

Burn

This process has nothing to do with fire. It is the means by which you copy a file to a CD or DVD disk. It is called "burning" because these optical disks can only have files written to them using a laser process. The process is why you must have special hardware in order to "write" to one of these disks.

Click

A tap with your finger on the left mouse button. To click a mouse, you tap the button and then let go at once. Note that *clicking* a mouse button is different from dragging or holding a mouse button, which implies that you hold the button down without releasing it. *Click* or *click on* means to move your mouse pointer to an object or word somewhere on your screen and quickly tap the mouse button:

- **Double-click** Some procedures require a double-click, meaning that you must click the left mouse button twice in rapid succession.
- **Right-click** This means to tap the right mouse button. In most programs, this process will cause a context menu to appear.

CPU (Central Processing Unit)

The CPU is the brains of your computer. This performs all of the calculations working with those bits and bytes, and performs all of the tasks as instructed by you, the user, or by the instructions in the program you are using. The capability of a CPU is measured in "hertz." or cycles. Today, most CPUs process information in gigahertz, abbreviated GHz. One GHz processes information at the speed of one billion cycles per second:

- **Dual Core** processors have two units within one unit.
- **Quad Core** processors have four processing units within one piece of hardware.

Download and Upload

You see the term *download* used often when referring to the process of obtaining your financial data from your financial institution. It means to transfer information from one computer to another, usually over the Internet. In Quicken's case, we use the term to explain how the information is transferred from your bank's computer to your computer, using the Internet as the transfer agent. *Upload* means to transfer information from your computer to another computer, again, usually using the Internet.

Drop-Down List

You find drop-down lists throughout computer programs. In Quicken, they are usually a small rectangular box with a downward-pointing arrow on the right. Like menus, you have a variety of choices that you can click.

Folders

The information you create in a computer program is stored in a *folder*. You can create subfolders within each folder. Each item you create is called a *file*, and you store files within folders. For example, each Quicken data file is stored, by default, in a subfolder named Quicken within the My Documents folder on your computer.

Hard Drive/Disk

This is the main storage place on your computer. It is a round disk that looks a bit like a CD or DVD. It holds everything you save on your computer, including the operating system software, all of your programs (including Quicken), and all of the data you "save to the hard disk." Think of the hard disk as the filing cabinet for your computer. It is measured in GB, and the more GB available, the more information can be saved.

Hardware

Hardware is tangible, meaning you can touch it. Your monitor, computer tower or laptop, and your printer are all examples of hardware.

Icon

An icon is a small picture that is often a shortcut to a program or hardware device. For example, you open the Quicken program each day by clicking the Quicken icon on your desktop. You may tell the computer to print a document by clicking a printer icon.

Menu

A menu is a list of commands from which you can choose one of several options. The choices on the menu depend on what program you are currently using. You click the item you have chosen to select it.

Context menus appear when you right-click within a program. The choices will differ depending on which program you are using and what process you are currently using within that program.

Operating System

The operating system is the software program that runs all of your computer's primary functions. For example, the latest operating system sold by Microsoft is Windows 7. Earlier Windows operating systems were Windows Vista and Windows XP.

RAM

Random access memory (RAM) is the amount of room in which you can work at any one time. The more RAM you have, the more projects you can access at one time and the faster you will be able to finish those tasks. RAM is currently measured in gigabytes.

Software

This term refers to any program (also called an application) that uses computer language to instruct your CPU how to complete a task. Quicken is personal financial software.

Special Keyboard Keys

Several keys on your computer keyboard help you perform specific tasks as shown here:

- **ENTER key**   This key is your workhorse. You press the ENTER key to tell the computer to perform the action you just typed. For example, when I finish typing this paragraph, I'll press the ENTER key to go to the next line.
- **CTRL key**   This key, along with the ALT key, is often used in combination with another key to perform tasks quickly. See the section "Keyboard Shortcuts" later in this chapter for more information. There are two CTRL and two ALT keys on many keyboards, located at the bottom-left and bottom-right corners of the keys.

USB (Universal Serial Bus)

This is a special type of connection for items you attach to your computer, such as your mouse, keyboard, or a digital camera. It is a small rectangular connector. You may see a small icon by the connection on your computer that looks like the illustration shown here.

Understanding Computer Processes

There are a number of ways you can work with computers, some easier than others. Here are some common ways of making your relationship with the computer a better one.

Copy and Paste or Cut and Paste

Of all the day-to-day operations you perform on your computer, this may be the most common. By using the copy and paste procedure you can easily duplicate information from one location to another, even across programs or the Internet.

Using this procedure, you can move a file from your computer's internal hard disk to a flash drive attached to your computer, or copy that digital image of the garden's bounty onto an e-mail message. To copy a file in a Windows operating system:

1. Right-click the Start button at the bottom-left corner of your computer screen. Depending on your computer's operating system, you'll see an option with the word "explore" in it. In Windows 7, the option says Open Windows Explorer, as shown here. Click Explore or Open Windows Explorer, depending on your computer's operating system.

2. Locate the file you want to copy to another location. In our example, I've chosen the picture of the lighthouse. Note that the filename and its description are highlighted in a darkened box to indicate that the file has been selected.

3. Right-click the file to be copied. A context menu will appear, as shown here.

4. Click Copy from the context menu. Nothing changes, except the menu disappears and you are back at your original location with the file still selected.

5. In our example, we're going to copy this file to the desktop, so we close the open window by clicking the red X at the upper corner.

Recycle Bin

6. Since we want our copied file to appear on the desktop, we right-click a blank portion of the desktop and choose Paste from the context menu that appears.

7. Our copied file (in this case, a picture) now appears on the desktop, as seen here. Note that there are three icons on this desktop: the Recycle Bin, the shortcut to open the Quicken program (we can tell it is a shortcut because of the small arrow at the lower-left corner of the icon), and our copied image.

Quicken
Premier 2012

Lighthous...

Follow the same steps to cut and paste, but remember that the cut and paste process actually moves the object from one place to another and the file is no longer in its original location.

Correct an Error

There are several ways to correct an error when entering data into a computer program. Each has its uses, as described here:

- **BACKSPACE key**   On a standard keyboard, the BACKSPACE key is located on the right side of your keyboard, two rows above the enter key. Pressing this key deletes letters you have typed to the left of your mouse cursor's position. The placement of the BACKSPACE key may vary among laptop keyboards.
- **DELETE key**   On most standard computer keyboards, the DELETE key is located to the right and slightly above the ENTER key. Pressing DELETE eliminates what you have typed to the right of your mouse cursor's position.
- **Highlight and replace**   Using this method, you highlight what you want to correct and type your corrections directly over the highlighted text (see the "Highlighting" section next).

Highlighting

Another commonly used computer process is that of highlighting a selection. This tells the computer that you've selected just part of a document or file and want to do something with it. For example, if you want just part of an e-mail message to be capitalized, you can highlight just the words to be capitalized, as seen in the illustration on the next page. To highlight one or more words:

1. Position your mouse pointer to the left of the words or object you want to select (highlight).

2. Hold down your left mouse key, and drag your mouse over the words.
3. Let go of the mouse key. Your selection will appear, as shown next. You can then make the changes you choose, copy it to another location, or press the DELETE key to delete the selection.

Thinking about you and hope you have a great day! Happy Birthday!

Keyboard Shortcuts

Several keys on your keyboard, when used together, can help you accomplish tasks within Quicken. By default, Quicken uses the standard Windows shortcuts as shown in Table 2-1. Additional keyboard shortcuts available in Quicken are described in Appendix A.

To use a combination of keys to accomplish a task, select the item you want to use by highlighting it. Then, hold down the first key mentioned and press the second key. Release both keys to complete the task.

Table 2-1 • Common Keyboard Shortcuts

Keyboard Command	Action
CTRL-C	Copy a transaction
CTRL-X	Cut a transaction
CTRL-V	Paste a copied or cut transaction
CTRL-P	Opens the Print dialog

Save

Most computer programs have the capability of saving the data created within them. Quicken does this automatically, but other programs require that you save your work each time you are in the program. Remember, a file is a document, picture, graph, or other object you create with the help of a computer program. Files are stored in folders on your computer's internal hard disk or some type of external media, such as an external hard drive, a flash drive, or a DVD.

Scroll

If you have ever seen a webpage that does not display the entire page on the screen, you may have used the scroll function to move down the page in order to see all of the information being presented. This function allows you to move within a window to see all of the data that does not fit onto your screen. Your mouse may even have a scroll wheel in its center you can use to move up and down the screen.

A scroll bar only appears if there is information above, below, to the left, or to the right of where your mouse is positioned. There are several ways to scroll:

- Hold your left mouse button down while on the "scroll bar," as shown.
- Move your mouse up or down or side to side, depending on whether you are using a vertical or a horizontal scroll bar.
- Position your mouse key within the "elevator" on the scroll bar and, while holding down your left mouse button, drag the "elevator" up and down (or left and right) across the scroll bar.
- Position your mouse on one of the small arrows that appear on the scroll bar and hold down your left mouse button. The screen will move up and down or left and right.

Going Online

If you're already using your computer to access the features of the Internet, you probably know a lot about the Internet's capabilities. This section fills in any gaps in your knowledge by discussing some of Quicken's online benefits and addressing any security concerns you might have. Finally, for the folks who aren't already online, you will learn what you need to connect to the Internet to use Quicken's online features.

Finding Quicken's Online Benefits

Remember, you don't have to go online to use Quicken. Quicken is a good financial management software package, even without its online features. But Quicken's online features make it a great financial management software package. As you'll see in this section and throughout this book, Quicken uses the Internet to help you make better financial decisions. The best way to explain the benefits of going online is to list a few of the features that online users use.

Online Account Services

Two of the best reasons for using Quicken to manage your finances are the Transaction Download and Online Payment features.

If you have more than one checking or saving account, an investment account or two, and some credit card accounts, entering all of those transactions can be time-consuming. Many Quicken users depend on Quicken's online features to automate transaction entry and bill payments. As you'll see throughout this book, Quicken has all kinds of time-saving features. In the opinion of many users, the online features are the best of Quicken's many features.

If You Have a Bank Account, You Can Benefit

Throughout the month, you write checks and mail them to individuals and organizations. You enter these transactions in your checking account register. At month's end, you reconcile the account. You can do all this without going online; learn how in Chapters 4 and 7.

When you register for Transaction Download with your bank, you can download all bank account activity on a regular basis, so you know exactly when the transactions hit your account—even the ATM and debit card transactions you may forget to enter. If you register for Online Payment, you can pay your bills without licking another envelope or pasting on another stamp. Chapter 5 explains how all this works.

If You Have Credit Cards, You Can Benefit

Do you have credit cards? If so, you can take advantage of Quicken's credit card tracking features, which are covered in Chapter 4, to keep track of your charges, payments, and balances. You don't need to go online, but if you sign up for Transaction Download, all your credit card charges can be downloaded directly into Quicken, eliminating the need for time-consuming data entry, while giving you an up-to-date summary of your debt and how you spent your money. Learn more about this in Chapter 5.

If You Invest, You Can Benefit

Quicken can keep track of your investments, whether they are 401(k) accounts, mutual funds, or stocks. You can enter share, price, and transaction information into Quicken, and it will summarize portfolio value, gains, and losses. It'll even keep track of securities by lot. Chapter 9 explains how.

Again, you don't need to go online to track your investments, but with online investment tracking features, Quicken can automatically obtain quotes on all the securities in your portfolio and update your portfolio's market value. Depending on your brokerage firm, you may also be able to download transactions, account balances, and holdings. Quicken can also alert you about news stories that affect your investments and automatically download the headlines, so you can learn more with just a click. You can also get valuable up-to-date research information about securities that interest you, so you can make informed investment decisions.

If You Want to Save Money, You Can Benefit

If you're like most people, you spend money every day on the things you need or want to make your life better. Quicken can help you keep track of your spending by summarizing expenditures by category. It can also help you save money by enabling you to create a budget and keep your expenditures under control.

Understanding the Security Features

Perhaps you're already convinced that the online features can benefit you. Maybe you're worried about security, concerned that a stranger will be able to access your accounts or steal your credit card numbers.

Intuit and the participating banks, credit card companies, and brokerage firms have done all the worrying for you. They've come up with secure systems that protect your information and accounts.

PINs

A PIN, or personal identification number, is a secret password you must use to access your accounts online. If you have an ATM card or cash-advance capabilities through your credit card, you probably already have at least one PIN, so you may be familiar with the idea. The PIN simply prevents anyone from accessing the account for any reason without first entering the proper numbers.

An account's PIN is initially assigned by the bank, credit card company, or brokerage firm. Some companies require that your PIN consist of a mixture of letters and numbers for additional security. You can change your PINs to make them easier to remember—just don't use something obvious like your birthday or telephone number. And don't write any PIN or password on a sticky note attached to your computer's monitor!

If you think someone might have guessed your PIN, you can change it. In fact, it's a good idea to change all your PINs and passwords regularly—not just the ones you use in Quicken.

Encryption

Once you're online and you've correctly entered your PIN, the instructions that flow from your computer to the bank, credit card company, or brokerage firm are encrypted. This means they are encoded in such a way that anyone able to "tap in" to the transmission would "hear" only gibberish. Quicken uses Secure Sockets Layer (SSL), which is the industry-standard method for protecting and encrypting your data. Once the encrypted information reaches the computer at the bank, credit card company, or brokerage firm, it is unencrypted and then validated and processed.

Encryption makes it virtually impossible for any unauthorized party to "listen in" to your transmission. It also makes it impossible for someone to alter a transaction from the moment it leaves your computer to the moment it arrives at your bank, credit card company, or brokerage firm for processing.

Quicken also takes advantage of other security methods for online communications, such as digital signatures and digital certificates. Together, these security methods make online financial transactions secure—even more secure than telephone banking, which you may already use!

Getting Connected

To take advantage of Quicken's online features, you need a connection to the Internet. You get that through an Internet service provider (ISP) usually for a monthly fee. If you don't already have an account with an ISP, you must set one up before you can use Quicken's online features. Check your local phone book or newspaper to find an ISP near you, or check with your phone company or cable company—they probably offer Internet service. Once you find one, your ISP can explain everything you need to get connected and help you set up your computer to go online.

Testing Your Connection with a Visit to Quicken.com

A good way to test your Internet connection is to visit Quicken.com, the official Quicken website. This site offers information about Intuit products, as well as special features for registered Quicken users. You'll learn more about Quicken.com later in this chapter and throughout this book. For now, to make sure your Internet connection works, try connecting to Quicken.com.

1. From within Quicken, click the Tips & Tutorials tab.
2. Click the Quicken Services button.
3. If necessary, click Quicken.com Home Page to open   🐾 www.quicken.com
   the Quicken.com website.

What you see during the connection process will vary depending on your connection type. If you have a modem or use an online service, access software may start automatically to make the connection. You may be prompted to enter a user name or password. Other dialogs may appear.

When the connection is complete, Quicken requests the Quicken.com home page. It appears in a Quicken Internet window. Figure 2-1 is an example of the Quicken.com page; however, what you see may be different, as the page is updated regularly.

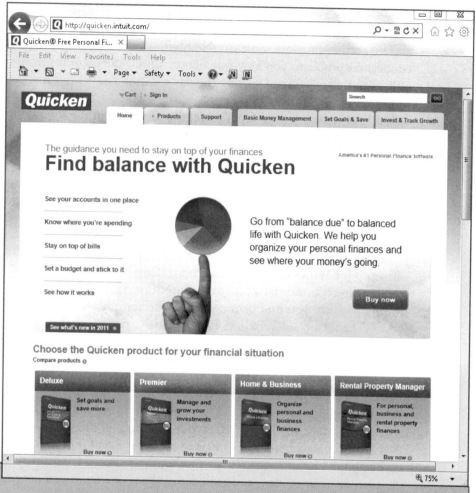

Figure 2-1 • The Quicken.com page provides articles and information about Quicken products and services, as well as useful money management information.

If you were already connected to the Internet when you accessed one of Quicken's online features, or if you have a direct connection to the Internet, you won't see the connection happening. Instead, the Quicken.com page simply appears in a Quicken Internet window (see Figure 2-1).

Troubleshooting Connection Problems

If you follow the instructions provided throughout this chapter, you shouldn't have any trouble connecting to the Internet with Quicken. But things aren't always as easy as they should be. Sometimes even the tiniest problems can prevent you from successfully connecting and exchanging data.

This section provides some troubleshooting advice to help you with any connection problems you may experience. Check this section before you start pulling out your hair and cursing the day computers were invented.

Setup Problems   If you have problems connecting to the Internet from within Quicken, exit Quicken and try connecting to the Internet from another program, such as your regular web browser or e-mail program:

- If you can connect to the Internet from another program but not from Quicken, the problem may be with Quicken's Internet connection setup. Try closing Quicken and reopening it. That may solve the problem.
- If you can't connect to the Internet from any other program or with dial-up networking (for dial-up connections), the problem is with your Internet setup for Windows, your modem (for dial-up connections), your network (for direct connections), or your router (for direct connections). You must fix any problem you find before you can successfully set up and connect with Quicken. Consult Windows Help for assistance.

Modem Problems   Problems with a dial-up connection may be related to your modem. Try each of the following, attempting a connection after each one:

- Check all cables between your computer and your modem (if you have an external modem), and between your modem and the telephone outlet.
- Check the telephone line to make sure it has a dial tone and that it is not being used by someone else or another program.
- Turn off your modem and then turn it back on. Or, if you have an internal modem, restart your computer. This resets the modem and may resolve the problem.

If you can connect but have trouble staying connected, try the following:

- Make sure no one is picking up an extension of the phone line while you are online.
- Make sure call-waiting is disabled by entering the appropriate codes for the dial-up connection.
- Have the phone company check the line for noise. If noise is detected, ask the phone company to fix the problem. (It shouldn't cost you anything if the line noise is the result of a problem outside your premises.)

Network or Router Problems   Problems with a direct (broadband) connection may be related to your network or router. Try these things, attempting a connection after each one:

- Check all cables between your computer and the network hub or router.
- Reset or turn your router off and then back on. This may clear the connection problems.
- Restart your computer. Sometimes resetting your computer's system software can clear network problems.
- Ask your system administrator to check your network setup.
- Consult your ISP for additional assistance.

Exploring Quicken's Web-Based Features

You access Quicken's web-based features from within Quicken software. In some cases, Quicken uses its built-in web browser to display information; in other cases, it opens the default browser on your computer. This section tells new Internet users a little more about using the Web and then explains how you can access Quicken's web-based features.

Surfing the Web

Let's take a moment to explain exactly what you're doing when you connect to Quicken.com and the other Quicken features on the Web. If you're brand new to web surfing—that is, exploring websites—be sure to read this section. But if you're a seasoned surfer, you probably already know all this information and can skip this section.

One more thing: This section is not designed to explain everything you'll ever need to know about browsing the World Wide Web. It provides the basic information you need to use the Web to get the information you need.

Going Online

When you access Quicken's online features, you do so by connecting to the Internet through your ISP. It doesn't matter whether you connect via a modem, a cable service, or a network, or whether your ISP is your local cable company, or Gabe's Internet Service. The main thing is having a connection or a conduit for information.

Think of an Internet connection as some PVC piping running from your computer to your ISP's computer, with a valve to control the flow of information. Once the valve is open (you're connected), any information can flow through the pipe in either direction. You can even exchange information through that pipe in both directions at the same time. This makes it possible to download (or retrieve) a webpage with your web browser while you upload (or send) e-mail with your e-mail program.

Quicken's online features use the pipe (or connection) in two ways:

- The integrated web browser enables you to request and receive the information you want. It's live and interactive—click a link, and a moment later your information starts to appear. Quicken can display webpages in its built-in Internet window or your default browser's window.
- Transaction Download, Online Payment, and several other features work in the background to communicate with financial institutions with which you have accounts. Quicken sends information you prepare in advance and retrieves the information the financial institution has waiting for you.

Navigating   The main thing to remember about the Web is that it's interactive. Every time a webpage appears on your screen, it'll offer a number of options for viewing other information. This is known as navigating the Web.

Hyperlinks and Forms   You can move from page to page on the Web in two ways:

- **Hyperlinks** (or links) are text or graphics that, when clicked, display another page. Hypertext links are usually underlined, colored text. Graphic links sometimes have a colored border around them. You can always identify a link by pointing to it—your mouse pointer will turn into a hand with a pointing finger, and a screen tip may appear to describe the link.
- **Forms** offer options for going to another page or searching for information. Options can appear in pop-up menus, text boxes that you fill in, check boxes that you turn on, or option buttons that you select. Multiple options often appear. You enter or select the options you want and click a button to send your request to the website. The information you requested appears a moment later.

Exploring Quicken.com
Quicken.com, the official Quicken site, supports Quicken users in several different ways. Click on any tab to open a menu:

- **Home tab**   This tab is the entry point to Quicken.com. It changes frequently, but Figure 2-1 is a good example. It provides links to articles, videos, and other money management information.

- **Products tab**   This tab provides links to the variety of Quicken products and services.
- **Support tab**   This tab displays answers to many frequently asked questions, has a direct link to Quicken support, and offers other resources for users of Intuit's personal financial products.
- **Basic Money Management tab**   When you click the Basic Money Management tab, you will see numerous links to articles and hints for good money management, as well as videos to help you with many financial matters.
- **Set Goals & Save tab**   The information found in this tab offers advice to help you save for that future goal, as seen in Figure 2-2.
- **Invest & Track Growth tab**   This tab features advice in the form of articles, videos, and other suggestions on investment issues for you.

Quicken.com is a dynamic website that changes frequently. The screen illustrations and features shown here may appear differently when you connect. In addition, brand-new features might be added after the publication of this book. The best way to learn about the features of Quicken.com is to check them out yourself.

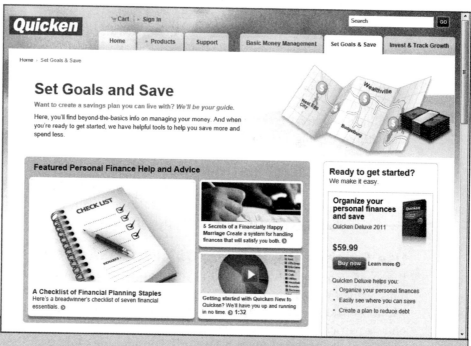

Figure 2-2 • Learn to set goals for savings on the Quicken.com website.

Financial Institution Services

If you're interested in keeping track of your finances with the least amount of data entry, you should be considering Quicken's online features Transaction Download and Online Payment. The beginning of this chapter explained the benefits of these features. Chapters 5 and 10 tell you how to use them. But you can't use them until you've set up an account with a participating financial institution and applied for the online account services you want to use.

When you create a bank, credit card, or investment account, Quicken prompts you to enter the name of your financial institution. Quicken determines whether your financial institution is one of the participating financial institutions, as many are. If you've already set up your accounts for online account services, you can skip this section. But you may find it useful if you're shopping around for another financial institution and want one that works with Quicken.

Understanding Online Financial Services

Participating financial institutions offer four types of online financial services:

- **Banking account access** enables you to download bank account transactions directly into your Quicken data file.
- **Credit/charge card access** enables you to download credit or charge card transactions directly into your Quicken data file.
- **Investment account access** enables you to download brokerage and other investment account transactions directly into your Quicken data file.
- **Online Payments** enable you to send payment instructions from within Quicken. This makes it possible to pay bills and send payments to anyone without writing a check.

Change Financial Institutions

If your bank or credit card company doesn't support online banking services with Quicken and you really want to use this feature, you can find a financial institution that does support them and open an account there.

Use Quicken Bill Pay and Quicken VISA Credit Card

If you're interested only in the bill-paying feature, you can use Quicken Bill Pay. This enables you to process payments from your existing bank accounts from within Quicken. There's no need to change banks or wait until your bank signs on as a participating financial institution.

If you'd like to earn Quicken Rewards, consider the Quicken VISA credit card. You can learn more about Quicken Bill Pay and the Quicken VISA credit card in the Quicken Services window; click the Tips & Tutorials tab to display the Quicken Services window.

Applying for Online Financial Services

Before you can take advantage of the online features in Quicken, you must apply for a user name and password from your financial institution. This gets the wheels turning to put you online. It may take a few days to get the necessary access information, so apply as soon as you're sure you want to take advantage of the online financial services features.

Online Topics

Once you've established your online services with your bank, you may encounter connection or other issues. This section discusses potential challenges with online connections. As each system and each ISP is unique, we cover only general subjects in this section.

Resolving Connectivity Issues

If you are unable to connect to the Internet from within Quicken, there may be some other program that is stopping the connection. After you've followed the steps in "Troubleshooting Connection Problems" earlier in this chapter, consider the possibility that another program on your machine is causing the disruption.

Antivirus and Firewall Settings

With the wide availability of antivirus and firewall programs, both free and fee-paid, some programs see Quicken trying to connect to the Internet as a threat and block the attempt. Check the program's settings and the documentation to alleviate this problem. Most programs of this type create a log, or list, of what programs they have blocked. Check that log to see if any references are made to Quicken. If so, change the settings to allow Quicken to access the Internet.

Bank Connection Fees

In our current economy, some banks are charging a fee for certain types of connections. These fees may say something like "Quicken Financial Connection Fee" or similar wording. These are not from Quicken, but from your bank. There are three types of connections available to Quicken users from financial institutions within the United States. The following sections explain the services provided with each type of connection and how it works.

Web Connect   This one-way connection allows you to go to your financial institution's website and download your transactions directly into Quicken. As with all online services, you must have received a user name and password and/or PIN to use this service. Your information is kept on the bank's website, and it is their service that transfers the information into your records. See Chapters 5 and 6 for the exact procedures. Each participating financial institution pays Quicken a fee to support this service.

Express Web Connect   With Express Web Connect you can download your transactions in the same way as Web Connect. The difference between Web Connect and Express Web Connect is that you connect from within Quicken rather than going to the institution's website, as you would with Web Connect. You will need to record your user name and PIN given to you by the bank in Quicken. The process is explained in Chapters 5 and 6.

With this type of service, your information is transferred from the institution to Quicken's safe-guarded server computers. Quicken performs the login information with your credentials and then obtains the information and sends it to your Quicken file. With this type of connection, the download may be performed once a day, usually after business hours. The information available to Quicken is determined by the bank. While financial institutions pay a fee to Quicken for inclusion in this program, most banks do not charge you, the end user, for this service.

Direct Connect   Direct Connect allows you to take advantage of all the online services offered by your financial institution. It is a two-way connection, meaning that not only can you download information from your institution into your Quicken records, but you can upload information as well. From within Quicken, you can transfer funds or pay bills, depending on what options are offered by your bank.

Your information is always in the control of your financial institution, rather than on a Quicken (Intuit) computer. Many institutions charge a fee for Direct Connect services, but this type of connection is the most complete and requires less of your time when downloading transactions. As with the other two types of connection, your bank pays a fee to Quicken for support of these services.

Working with Accounts, Categories, and Tags

Chapter 3

In This Chapter:

- *Understanding data files and accounts*
- *Reviewing account types*
- *Creating your first account*
- *Setting up other banking accounts*
- *Working with the Account List window*
- *Establishing categories and subcategories*
- *Working with the Category List window*
- *Displaying the Tag List window*
- *Creating a new tag*
- *Working with the Tag List window*
- *Getting started with monthly bills*
- *Tracking your spending goals to save money*

To use Quicken Personal Finance Software, you must set up your Quicken data file for your financial situation. This means creating accounts and entering starting balance information.

When you first set up your Quicken Personal Finance Software data file, it includes a number of default categories. Don't think you're stuck with just those categories. You can add and remove categories at any time. The same goes for accounts—you can add them as you see fit. Modifying the accounts and categories in your Quicken data file is a great way to customize Quicken to meet your needs.

This chapter explains how you can organize Quicken to fit *your* needs by modifying and working with accounts and categories. You'll also learn how to set up and use an additional optional categorization feature: tags.

Quicken opens to the Home tab's Main View, as seen in Figure 3-1, where you get started by entering your primary bank account.

Before You Begin

Before you start the setup process, it's a good idea to understand how Quicken's data files and accounts work. You'll also learn what documents to gather to help you set up your accounts properly.

Understanding Data Files and Accounts

All of the transactions you record with Quicken are stored in a data file on your hard disk. This file includes all the information that makes up your Quicken accounting system.

Data Files

Although it's possible to have more than one Quicken data file, it isn't usually necessary. One file can hold all of your transactions. In fact, it's difficult (if not downright impossible) to use more than one Quicken file to track a single

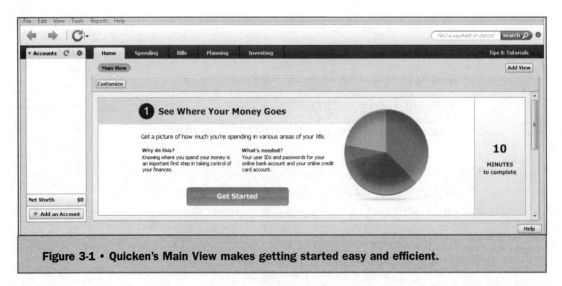

Figure 3-1 • Quicken's Main View makes getting started easy and efficient.

account, such as a checking or credit card account. And splitting your financial records among multiple data files makes it impossible to generate reports that consolidate all of the information.

When would you want more than one data file? For example, you may need two data files if you use Quicken to organize both your own finances as well as the finances of a relative who is in a long-term care facility. You might also create another data file for a community

> ### IN MY EXPERIENCE
>
> You'll notice throughout each chapter of this book that you are encouraged to create a backup copy of your files. *How* to do it is covered in Appendix A. *Why* to do it is even more important. If you have ever experienced a hard drive crash, you know the importance of backing up your data on a regular basis. Imagine losing several years of financial information in the blink of an eye. So, as you are reading through the techniques and how-tos in each chapter, remember that the information you are saving on your hard disk using Quicken should be copied or saved to another location as well. Any mechanism that is built can break, and usually at the most inopportune time. Back up, back up, back up your files!

group for which you are serving as treasurer. Each of these data files would have its own separate set of bank, credit, and asset accounts.

Appendix A covers a number of data file management tasks, including creating additional data files and backing up your data files.

Accounts

An *account* is a record of what you either own or owe. For example, your checking account is a record of cash on deposit in the bank that is available for writing checks. A credit card account is a record of money you owe to the credit card company or bank for the purchases on your credit card. All transactions either increase or decrease the balance in one or more accounts.

You create accounts within a Quicken data file so you can track the activity and balances in your bank, credit card, investment, and other accounts.

What You Need

To set up accounts properly, you should have balance information for the accounts that you want to monitor with Quicken. You can get this information from your most recent bank, investment, and credit card statements. It's a good idea to gather these documents before you start the setup process so they're on hand when you need them. If you use the online banking services from your financial institutions, make sure you have your passwords and personal identification numbers (PINs).

If you plan to use Quicken to replace an existing accounting system—whether it's paper-based or prepared with a different computer program—you may also find it helpful to have a list of account names you've used (called the "chart of accounts" by your accountant) or recent financial statements. This way, when you set up Quicken accounts, you can use familiar names.

Accounts

To track your finances with Quicken, you must create at least one account. While many of your expenditures may come from your checking account, you probably have more than one account that Quicken can track for you. By setting up all of your accounts in Quicken, you can keep track of balances and activity to get a complete picture of your financial situation. You don't have to add all of your accounts at once. You can start off tracking just the one or two accounts that you use most frequently and add accounts later.

Reviewing Account Types

This part of the chapter explains a bit more about Quicken's accounts and how you can create and modify your accounts. As discussed earlier, an account is a record of what you either own or owe. Quicken offers various kinds of accounts for different purposes. A link for each account you set up in Quicken appears in one of the three sections of the Account Bar. You can choose to hide accounts from the Account Bar, as discussed later in this chapter. Table 3-1 summarizes the accounts and how they are organized within Quicken.

What You Own

In accounting jargon, what you own are assets. In Quicken, an asset is one type of account; several other types exist as well.

Spending   Spending accounts, which are displayed in the Banking section of the Account Bar, are used primarily for expenditures. This section displays checking and cash accounts as well as your credit cards.

Savings   Savings accounts, which are also displayed in the Banking section of the Account Bar, are used to record the transactions in savings accounts.

Investment   Investment accounts, displayed in the Account Bar's Investing section, are for tracking the stocks, bonds, and mutual funds in your portfolio that are not in retirement accounts. Quicken distinguishes among two types of

Table 3-1 • Overview of Quicken Account Types

Account Type	Account Bar Section	Asset or Liability
Checking	Banking	Asset
Savings	Banking	Asset
Credit Card	Banking	Liability
Cash	Banking	Asset
Standard Brokerage	Investing	Asset
IRA or Keogh Plan	Investing	Asset
401(k) or 403(b)	Investing	Asset
529 Plan	Investing	Asset
House	Property & Debt	Asset
Vehicle	Property & Debt	Asset
Other Asset	Property & Debt	Asset
Debt	Property & Debt	Liability

investment accounts: Standard Brokerage (which may be used for one or more mutual funds) and 529 Plan.

Retirement   Retirement accounts, which are included in the Investing section, are for tracking investments in retirement accounts. Quicken distinguishes between two types of retirement accounts. One type includes individual retirement accounts (IRAs) or Keogh Plans, and the other combines 401(k) or 403(b) accounts. Retirement accounts should fall into one of these two broad categories.

Asset   Asset accounts, which are displayed in the Property & Debt section of the Account Bar, are used for tracking items that you own. Quicken distinguishes among three different types of asset accounts: House, Vehicle, and Other Asset.

What You Owe

The accounting term for what you owe, or your debts, is liabilities. Quicken offers two kinds of accounts for amounts you owe.

Credit Card   Credit cards, which you have designated as Liability accounts, are displayed in the Property & Debt section. See the section on "Account Intent" later in this chapter to see how to show your cards in this section of the Account Bar.

Debt   Debt (liability) accounts are displayed in the Property & Debt section. This section is for tracking loans, mortgages, and other liabilities. While it is possible to include credit cards in this section, most users opt to show their credit card accounts in the Banking section of the Account Bar.

If you are using either the Home and Business or Rental Property Manager editions of Quicken, you can also enter special business accounts such as Accounts Payable and Receivable.

Setting Up Quicken

After you have installed Quicken, its opening window offers easy access to features you can use to configure your Quicken data file. This Home tab's Main View includes several areas. This part of the chapter provides a tour of each area and explains how you can use it to set up a Quicken data file.

Creating Your First Account

To begin using Quicken, you must tell the program what bank and credit cards you wish to track. Click the Get Started button to begin. If you are connected to the Internet, a message box appears indicating that Quicken is updating its list of financial institutions. As Quicken often adds new financial institutions to their services, this update occurs regularly.

After the update is complete, the Add Your Primary Checking Account dialog box appears, as seen in Figure 3-2. Choose the name of your bank from the displayed list, or type its name in the Enter The Name Of Your Bank field. If your bank's name does not appear on this first group of names, when you type the first letters of your bank's name, a new list appears with a list of those institutions that begin with the letters you typed.

Note the Advanced Setup link at the bottom of the window. Use this if you do not want to download your information or if your bank offers more than one type of downloading service. See the section "Use Advanced Setup to Create a Manual-entry Account" later in this chapter for more information.

Click Next to continue. Depending on your financial institution, you may see a dialog displaying connection services are available for that financial institution. Make your choice and click Next. In the dialog that appears, as seen in Figure 3-3, you are prompted to enter your user name and password as provided by your bank. Should you want to save this password in the Quicken Password Vault, click Save This Password. See Chapter 6 for more information about the Password Vault.

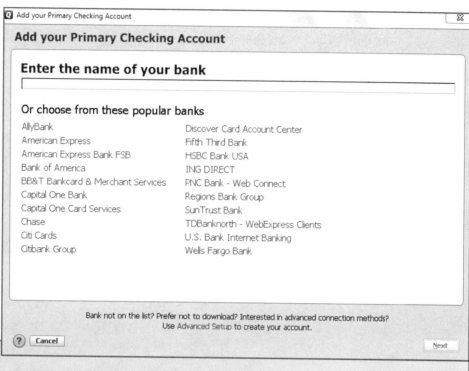

Figure 3-2 • Click the name of your bank or type it in to create your first checking account in Quicken.

Depending on your institution, you may be prompted for additional information about the branch, bank name, or account type. Enter any required information, and then click Connect to go online and download the information about your account. (If there are additional passwords or security phrases required by your bank, you are prompted to enter them. Do so and click OK or Next, depending on the prompt.) A message box appears indicating that Quicken is getting the information from your financial institution.

If you have more than one account that uses the user ID and password you entered, all of the accounts may be downloaded. If you have not yet set up any accounts, in Quicken each account will be called by the account name shown on your bank's records. If you have entered account information, you will be prompted to add, link, or ignore each of the downloaded accounts. See "Using Downloaded Accounts" later in this chapter.

After the download is complete, your account (or accounts if you have more than one at that bank) is shown on an Accounts Added list. Click Finish to

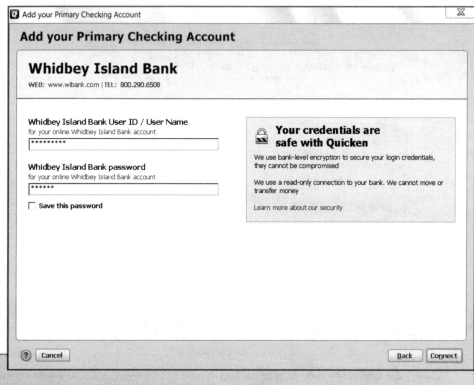

Figure 3-3 • Use the ID and password provided by your financial institution to add your primary checking account.

return to the Home tab's Main View. You will see each account that has been downloaded on the Account Bar as seen here. See "Setting Up Other Banking Accounts" next to add more accounts.

Setting Up Other Banking Accounts

After you have created your primary checking account, you can create additional new accounts with the Add An Account button that appears at the bottom of your Account Bar as shown here. No matter what type of account you create, Quicken steps you through the creation process, prompting you to enter information about the account, such as its name and balance. In this section, you'll learn how to use the Add Account dialog to set up new accounts.

Adding New Accounts

Quicken calls its default method of adding accounts "Simple Setup." This process begins by opening the Add Account dialog. You can open this dialog in several ways, as listed here:

> ### NEW IN QUICKEN 2012
>
> In earlier versions of Quicken, after the initial download completed, you had an option of changing, or "nicknaming," your downloaded accounts. In an effort to streamline the user's experience with Quicken, for new Quicken files with no previously added accounts, the downloaded accounts initially display with the name or number shown by the bank. Should you want to change the name to something more descriptive, you can do so in the Account Detail dialog, discussed later in this chapter. See "Using Downloaded Accounts" elsewhere in this chapter.

- Click Add An Account from the bottom of the Account Bar.
- Choose Tools | Add Account.
- Click CTRL-A to open the Account List. Click the Add An Account button at the bottom-right corner of the window.

You can also open the Account List by choosing Tools | Account List.

You can add a new asset account from the Property & Debt tab, from dialogs within the Lifetime Planner Plan Assumption dialog, and from the All Accounts view in the Home tab's Main View.

For example, to add an asset account from the Property & Debt tab:

1. Select the Property & Debt tab, and choose the new Property button.
2. Click Property Options | Add A House/Vehicle/Other Asset Account, or Add A New Loan to add a new account as shown here.

The Add Account dialog
that is displayed in the
Property section is more
asset-specific than the generic
Add Account dialog
described later and seen in
Figure 3-4.

> ### NEW IN QUICKEN 2012
>
> The Property button replaces the Account
> Overview button in the Property & Debt tab.
> This section has been revamped and has a
> much friendlier user interface. See Chapter 13
> for more information about the property and
> net worth section of Quicken 2012.

 The Property & Debt tab
may not appear when you first start working with a new Quicken file. To display
this tab, click View | Tabs To Show, and click Property & Debt.

The Add Account dialog seen in Figure 3-4 begins by asking what type of
account you want to create. From there its options change, depending on the
account type and whether you want to set it up for online account services, if
available.

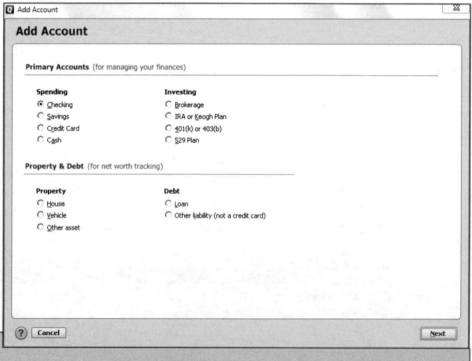

Figure 3-4 • The Add Account dialog makes adding new accounts quick and easy.

Using Downloaded Accounts

If your user name and password are connected to more than one account at a specific financial institution, all of the accounts may be downloaded when you connect. If you have already created accounts in Quicken, you will see a dialog from which you can perform an action for each of the downloaded accounts as shown here.

- **Add**   Use Add to create a new Quicken account with this information. You may rename the account to something more useful to you.
- **Link**   The Link option is used to identify a current Quicken account and combine the information in the download with that account. Make sure you have chosen the correct account.

If you do not link an account correctly, you can correct it later. See Chapter 5 for more information.

- **Ignore**   If you choose to ignore this downloadable account, the information will not be downloaded into Quicken.

Review each choice before you continue to ensure you have connected the correct Quicken account with each downloaded account. Figure 3-5 shows an example of the dialog.

Use Advanced Setup to Create a Manual-Entry Account

As mentioned earlier, the Advanced Setup option is used when you prefer to enter transactions manually, your institution does not offer download services, or you do not want to connect to the Internet at the time you are setting up the account. To use Advanced Setup:

1. Open the Add Account dialog as described in "Adding New Accounts" earlier in this chapter.
2. Choose the type of account you are entering (as seen in Figure 3-4), and click Next. If you are not connected to the Internet, you see a message

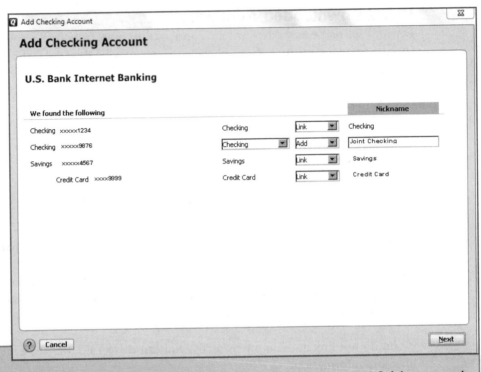

Figure 3-5 • Ensure you connect each downloaded account with the correct Quicken account.

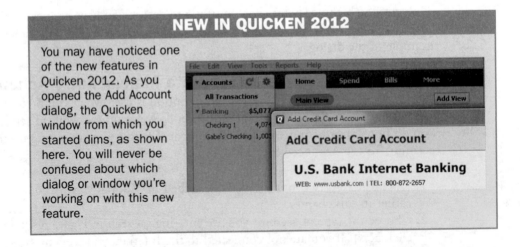

NEW IN QUICKEN 2012

You may have noticed one of the new features in Quicken 2012. As you opened the Add Account dialog, the Quicken window from which you started dims, as shown here. You will never be confused about which dialog or window you're working on with this new feature.

alerting you to this fact. You can choose to cancel the account creation or continue creating your manual account.

3. From the Add <type of account> dialog, click Advanced Setup at the bottom of the dialog, as shown here.

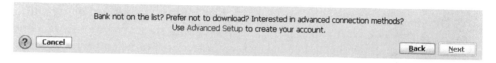

4. The Add <type of account> dialog appears, as seen in Figure 3-6. Choose one of the following:

   a. **I Want To Select The Connection Method Used To Download My Transactions**   This option is used when your bank has several methods of online services and requires you to choose the method, or you just want to tell Quicken how to download your information. Depending on your financial institution, you may be prompted to choose the type of service, enter your user ID and password, or answer additional questions.

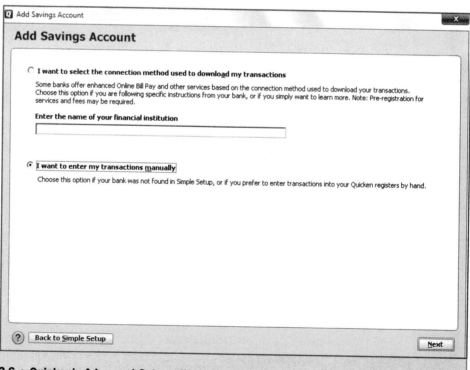

Figure 3-6 • Quicken's Advanced Setup offers choices when adding a new account.

b. **I Want To Enter My Transactions Manually**   Use this option if your bank has no relationship with Quicken, you cannot connect to the Internet, or you prefer to enter your information manually.

5. Since you are setting up a manual-entry account, the next screen prompts you for an account name or nickname. Consider giving each account a name that uniquely identifies it, such as Home Credit Card or Helene's Savings.

6. Click Next and you are asked to enter a statement ending date and balance as shown here. The balance you enter at this dialog becomes the opening balance of this account.

Add Credit Card Account

Add Credit Card Account

Enter the ending date and balance from your latest statement
Don't worry if you don't have your last statement- you can make changes to your account later.

Statement Ending Date   7/31/2011

Statement Ending Balance   126.09   This becomes the opening balance of your Quicken Account.

So that you can easily see balances, consider entering a line-of-credit account at your bank as a credit card rather than a liability account. This way, it will show in the Banking section rather than the Property & Debt section of the Account Bar.

Entering Account Information

Follow the prompts in the Add Account dialogs to enter required information for the account you are creating. Click the Next button to progress from one dialog to the next. You can click Back at any time to go back and change information. You know you're finished when the Next button is replaced with a Done or a Finish button; click it to save the account information.

Account information can include the financial institution in which the account is held (if applicable), an account name, the account balance, and the date of the account balance. Almost every type of Quicken account requires this information. If you don't know the balance of an account, you may set it to $0.00 and make adjustments later, either when you get a statement or when you reconcile the account. If the account is activated for online access, Quicken downloads most of this information as part of the account creation process.

You can find details for creating specific types of accounts throughout this book. Each type is displayed in its own section in the Account Bar at the left of your Quicken window:

- Banking section accounts are covered in Chapter 4.
- Investing section accounts are covered in Chapter 9.
- Property & Debt accounts are covered in Chapters 12 and 13.

Working with the Account List Window

You can view a list of all of your accounts at any time. Choose Tools | Account List or press CTRL-A. The Account List window appears (see Figure 3-7). This window displays a list of all accounts organized by type. If you want to see just

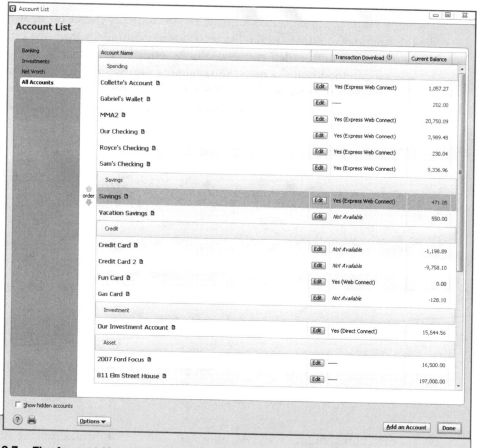

Figure 3-7 • The Account List displays information about all of your accounts.

one group of accounts—for example, your Banking accounts—click that group's name in the column to the left of the list. If you have entered only one type of account, such as banking accounts, there will be no choices displayed in the pane at the left side of the Account List window.

You can click the small gear icon to the right of the blue curly arrow at the top of the Account Bar to open the Account List.

Viewing Account Information

By default, Quicken displays each account in the Account List window (refer to Figure 3-7) by the account name (grouped by account type), transaction download settings, and the current balance. If you have told Quicken to hide any of your accounts, you can opt to display them in the list by clicking the Show Hidden Accounts check box at the bottom-left corner of the list. Add informational columns to the list by choosing commands from the Options button at the bottom-left corner of the Account List window, as shown next. Just select a command on the menu to toggle the display of information on or off. This makes it possible for you to fully customize the appearance of the list and the information shown. See "Working with Accounts" later in this chapter for more information.

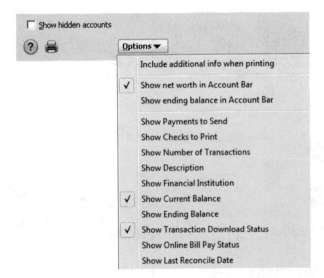

Select an account on the Account List, and click Edit to open the Account Details dialog seen in Figure 3-8. From this dialog you can change the name of

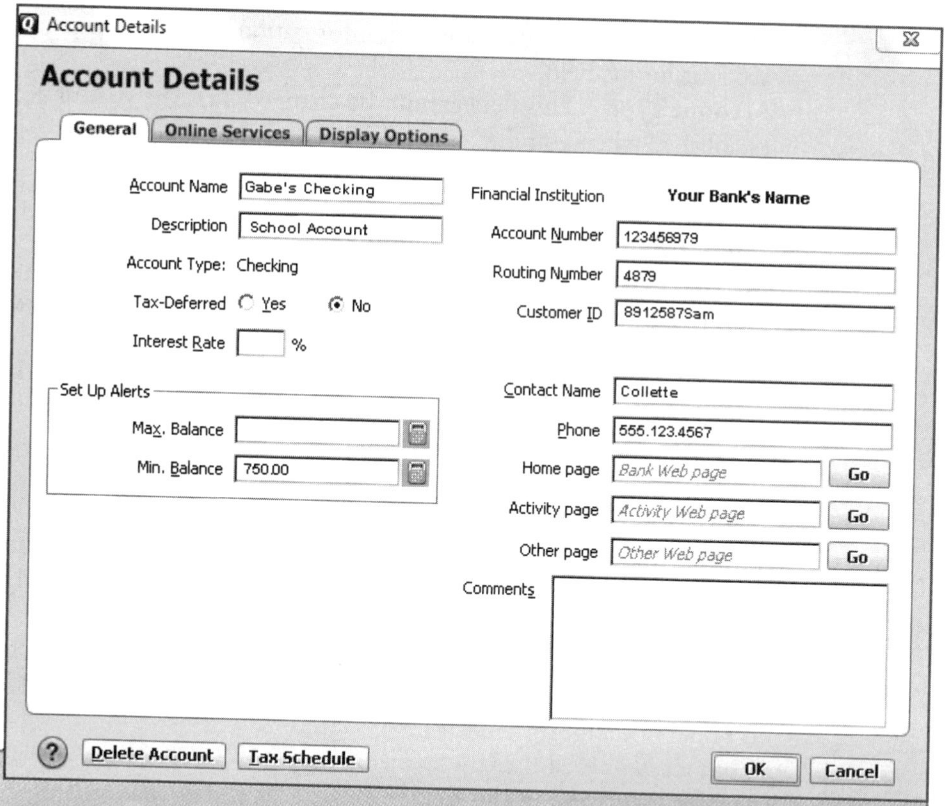

Figure 3-8 • Enter important information about each account in the Account Details dialog.

an account, enter additional account information, tell Quicken how to display the account, and modify the account's online services. Move between the tabs by clicking the tab with which you want to work.

General Tab

The General tab displays basic information about the account that you can view or edit, as shown in Figure 3-8. From this dialog you can enter information such as the interest rate you receive on this account, the account number, and create a link to the bank's home page. There are a number of options, of which only the account name is required. Not all of the options mentioned here will be available for all types of accounts:

- **Account Name**   By default, this is the name you (or the bank) entered when creating the account. You can change it here if you choose.

- **Description** Add any additional information to further identify this account in this field.
- **Account Type** This field cannot be changed. It is the type of account you established when you first created the account.
- **Tax Deferred** Click Yes to tell Quicken this is a tax-deferred account; click No if it is not.
- **Interest Rate** Enter the rate of interest, if any, for this account.
- **Set Up Alerts** Use this section to ask Quicken to alert you if this account reaches a maximum or minimum balance. See Chapter 6 for more information about setting alerts.
- **Financial Institution** If you have activated online services for this account, the name in this field cannot be changed. If you have set this account to enter transactions manually, you may enter the name of your financial institution in this field.
- **Account and Routing Numbers** If the account is activated for downloading, these fields appear filled in with the appropriate numbers. If this account is a manual account, only the Account Number field appears and is available for you to enter information.
- **Customer ID** This field appears for accounts that have been activated for download. If the account is set up for manual transaction entry, Customer ID does not appear.
- **Contact Name** Enter the name of the person with whom you normally work at your bank in this field.
- **Phone** Enter the local branch's phone number here so you won't have to look it up each time you call the bank.
- **Home/Activity/Other Page** Use these fields to enter the website(s) for your bank. Use the Go button to connect to these websites using your Internet connection.
- **Comments** Use this field for any additional information about this account.

On the bottom of the Account Details dialog are several other option buttons. From here you may access Quicken help by clicking the question mark, select an account to delete, or assign income tax information for a selected account.

When you first create an account, you tell Quicken what "type" it is—that is, Checking, Savings, Cash, and so on. See Figure 3-4 for a list of the types of accounts you can create. Once this type of account is set, you cannot change it. For example, if you create a Money Market Account as a "checking" type account, you cannot change it to a "savings" account.

Delete Account   The Delete Account button opens the Delete Account dialog. If you really want to delete an account, you must confirm the removal through this dialog. Purposely, Quicken does not make this process easy. You must type **yes** into the dialog and click OK to delete the account, as shown here. If you have scheduled bills or deposits for this account, they must be removed before you can delete it. See Chapter 6 for more information about scheduling transactions.

Remember that when you delete an account, you permanently remove all of its transactions from your Quicken data file. To get the account out of sight without actually deleting it and its data, consider hiding it instead, as described in "Hide This Account In Quicken" later in this chapter.

If you have only one account in Quicken, you still must use the Account Details dialog to delete that account.

Tax Schedule Information If the account has income tax implications, is tax-exempt, or tax-deferred, click the Tax Schedule button to use the optional Tax Schedule Information dialog shown here. As always, if you have any questions about the tax status of an account, check with your tax professional.

Online Services Tab

This tab allows you to modify the settings in each account for your institution's online services. If your financial institution offers the ability to use Quicken's One Step Update or Online Bill Payment, you can set those options here. You can also set up Quicken Bill Payment through this dialog. See Chapter 5 for more information about the online services offered by many financial institutions.

Display Options Tab

From this tab you tell Quicken how you want to display this account, as shown here. You may hide the account entirely in Quicken or only in the Account Bar. You may also tell Quicken to ignore the balance of this account in all of its net worth computations. In the Hide Or Show Accounts section, you see the options discussed in the following sections.

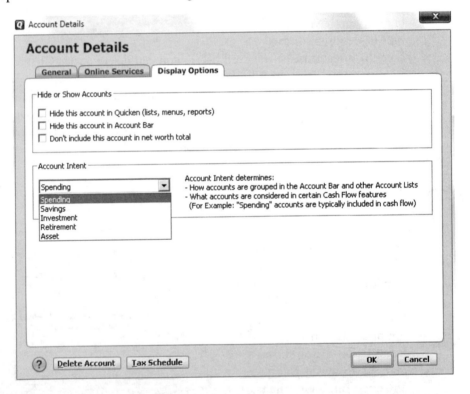

Hide This Account In Quicken   When this check box is selected, Quicken prevents the account from being displayed in lists, menus, and reports. Both of the two check boxes beneath it are disabled as well. This choice removes the account from view in any list in which it would appear, including the Account List window, unless you have opted to display hidden accounts. You may want to use this feature to remove accounts you no longer use or need to see—without removing the transactions they contain. Keep in mind that you cannot quickly use a hidden account in a transaction. If the account you want to hide is activated for online services, you see the message box shown next. If the account is no longer active, consider deactivating it. Otherwise, click Hide But Don't Deactivate. If you choose not to hide this account, click Cancel to return to the Account List.

To use a hidden account—for example, as one side of a transfer of funds—you must either unhide the account by turning off the Hide This Account in Quicken check box in the Account Details dialog or use the full name of the account enclosed in brackets in the Category field in the originating check register. The name in the Category field for this transaction would display as [ACCTNAME].

Hide This Account In Account Bar   To remove an account from the Account Bar, turn on this check box. Although the account remains visible in other lists and menus where it would normally appear, it no longer appears in the Account Bar. You may want to use this feature to keep the Account Bar short by excluding accounts you seldom access. Accounts set to be hidden only in the Account Bar are grouped in the Account Bar as "Other Accounts." To exclude an account's balance from subtotal and total calculations, as well as the net worth displayed in the Account Bar, turn on the Don't Include This Account In Net Worth Total check box. The account name will still show in the Account Bar, but no balance will display and the account total is not included in the Net

IN MY EXPERIENCE

Recently a student wanted to hide her 401(k) account in the Account Bar in Quicken. She opened the Account Details dialog and quickly checked the Hide This Account in Quicken button that hides the account from all lists, reports, and menus in Quicken. The next time she attempted to download her paycheck information, her 401(k) information had no place to go so Quicken created a new account for this information. She had to transfer the transactions from that new account to her real 401(k) account and reset her display options. The moral to this story is to be sure to select the option you really want—which, in her case, was the Hide This Account In Account Bar check box.

Worth computation at the bottom of the Account Bar as well as any net worth totals calculated in Quicken.

Account Intent   The Account Intent section lets you tell Quicken how you plan on using this account. For example, you might have a savings account that you actually are using as an additional retirement account. (However, you might want to check with your financial advisor to see if this is a wise use of your money.)

To let Quicken know how you intend this account to be used, choose a value from the drop-down lists. These choices determine how the account will display in both the Account Bar and other lists and reports.

Once you have made all of your modifications for this account, click OK to close the Account Details dialog and return to the Account List.

Working with Accounts

You can use options in the Account List window to reorganize accounts so they appear where you want them in the Account Bar.

Changing the Order of Accounts   By default, accounts are shown in alphabetical order in your Account List until you first move an account. As you first add accounts, they automatically sort themselves alphabetically. If you later decide to change the order and then add more accounts, the newly added accounts are inserted at the bottom of the section. To change the order in which accounts appear in the Account List window and Account Bar, select an account by clicking the line in which the name appears. Note that you must click somewhere on the account's line other than the name of the account or the Edit button. When you click the account name the account's register will open. Clicking the Edit button opens the Account Details dialog.

To move the account within its group, click the up or down Order button arrow to change the account's position. You can move an account to any position within its group. If you have only one account per account type, you will not see the Order button.

The order in which your accounts are shown in the Account List is how the accounts will display in the Account Bar as well.

Viewing Your Accounts   Each time you open the Account List, you can reset it to display only your Banking, Investments, or Net Worth (Property & Debt) accounts on the list. Click the group you choose to display on the left side of the Account List window.

IN MY EXPERIENCE

As you view your account balances in the Account List you may have noticed that the balances include the total with both dollars and cents displayed. However, by default, the Account Bar totals show the balances rounded to the nearest dollar. To avoid confusion, you may want to change how the balances are displayed in the Account Bar.

To show the cents column in the Account Bar, right-click in the Account Bar to open the context menu. Select Show Amounts if that choice is not checked. Choose Show Cents In Amounts to display both the dollar and cents balances for each account as seen here. Now the totals in the Account Bar match the totals in the Current Balance column in the Account List.

After you have made a selection, the Account Bar context menu closes automatically.

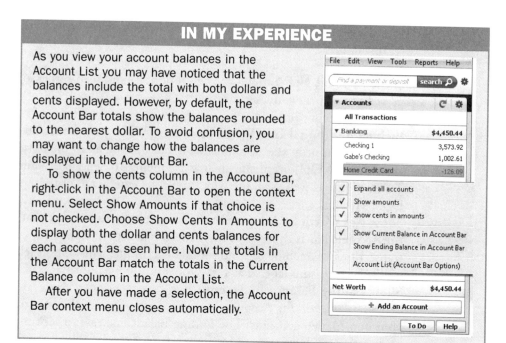

Show Hidden Accounts   Click the Show Hidden Accounts check box at the lower-left corner of your Account List window to display accounts you have marked as hidden. To hide them from the Account List, clear the check box.

Help Icon   Clicking the small question mark at the lower-left corner of the Account List opens Quicken Help to the section on managing your accounts.

Printing the Account List   Click the Printer icon at the bottom of the Account List window to print your list. The Print dialog appears as shown here. Click

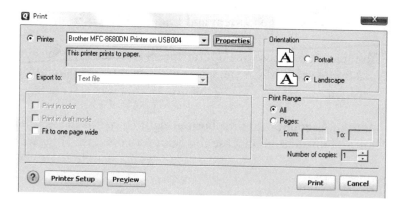

Preview to see how your list will appear. Click Close to close the preview window. Click Print to print the list.

Using the Account List Options   The Options menu, seen earlier, offers you several ways to display your Account List:

- **Include Additional Info When Printing**   When you choose this option, each time you print the Account List it will include all of the options you've chosen in the Options menu, such as Payments To Send and Number Of Transactions, as well as all the data from the General tab of the Account Details dialog.
- **Show Net Worth In Account Bar**   The Net Worth number that displays in the Account Bar is the sum of the current balances of all of your entered transactions on each of your non-hidden accounts. This option tells Quicken to display that sum labeled as Net Worth in the Account Bar.
- **Show Ending Balance In Account Bar**   As mentioned above, the Net Worth balance on the Account Bar is the sum of today's balance of each of your non-hidden accounts. The Ending Balance takes into account the bills or deposits you have entered for future dates. For example, if you have sent information to your bank to pay your phone bill next Tuesday, opting to show the ending balance would include that payment in your account's total on the Account Bar. The Ending Balance option displays the account's balance as of next Tuesday after the phone bill is sent, not what it is today.
- **Show Payments To Send/Checks To Print/Number Of Transactions/ Description/Financial Institution**   These options create new columns in the Account List that display the selected information. If you have chosen to include the additional information when printing, these columns will appear on your printed Account List report.
- **Show Current/Ending Balance**   This is similar to Show Net Worth/ Ending Balance In Account Bar, but it refers to the Account List. You may display both the Current and Ending Balances in the Account List.

You may only choose one option at a time in the Options menu. Each time you make a selection, the menu closes and you must reopen it to make another selection.

Add An Account   On the bottom-right corner of the Account List is the Add An Account button. Choose this button to open the Add Account dialog.

Done   When you have made all of your adjustments and are through with the Account List, click Done to close the dialog.

Categories

When you create a data file, Quicken automatically creates dozens of commonly used categories. Although these categories might completely meet your needs, at times you may want to add, remove, or modify a category to fine-tune Quicken for your use.

Establishing Categories and Subcategories

There are basically two types of categories:

- **Income** is incoming money. It includes receipts such as your salary, commissions, interest income, dividend income, child support, gifts received, and tips.
- **Expense** is outgoing money. It includes insurance, groceries, rent, interest expense, bank fees, finance charges, charitable donations, and clothing.

Subcategories

A subcategory is a subset or part of a category. It must be the same type of category as its parent category. For example, you may use the Auto category to track expenses to operate your car. Within that category, however, you might use one of the subcategories to record specific expenses, such as auto insurance, fuel, and repairs. Subcategories make it easy to keep income and expenses organized into manageable categories, while providing the transaction detail you might want or need.

Working with the Category List Window

You can view a list of all of your categories at any time. Choose Tools | Category List, or press CTRL-SHIFT-C. The Category List window appears (see Figure 3-9).

In this section, you'll learn how to use the Category List window to display, add, modify, delete, and perform other tasks with categories.

If you have added an Investment account, you may notice a group of categories with an underscore before their name as seen in Figure 3-10. These are special categories used by Quicken for such transactions as computing realized gains on investing accounts. These categories are hidden until you create an Investment-type account.

IN MY EXPERIENCE

Categories? Subcategories? Sounds confusing and like a lot of work? It is truly not much work, and using categories is well worth the time you spend doing it.

To use this wonderful feature, when you enter a transaction in Quicken, you'll classify it using one of your predefined categories. (Sometimes Quicken can even guess the right category the first time you enter a transaction for a payee!) The next time you enter a transaction for the same payee, Quicken automatically assumes the transaction will use the same category, so Quicken enters it for you. Much of the time, Quicken's assumption is right. And often you don't have to type the entire category and subcategory, usually just the first few letters. For example, type "Au" and the Auto category displays. Type a colon (:) and an "S" and your category and subcategory are entered as shown here.

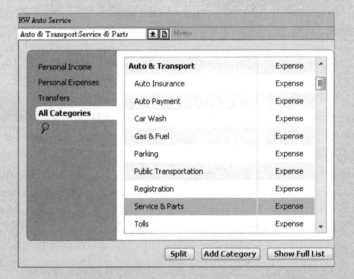

By properly categorizing transactions, you can get a true picture of where your money comes from and where it goes. You can create realistic budgets based on accurate spending patterns to help you save money. You can create tax reports that'll save you—or your tax preparer—time. You can even automate much of your tax preparation by exporting all those properly categorized transactions right into Intuit's TurboTax tax preparation software.

So don't leave the category field blank when entering your transactions. That extra step results in more complete reports and a clearer understanding of your finances.

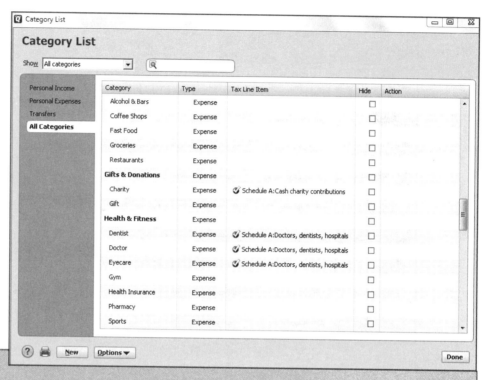

Figure 3-9 • The Category List shows the categories in your Quicken data file with which you can classify your transactions.

Changing the Category Display

The Category List window lists all categories and transfer accounts within three broad headings: Personal Income, Personal Expenses, and Transfers. You can click a heading on the left side of the Category List window to display just those categories within it. Or, click All Categories to display all categories in your data file. You can also use the Show drop-down list at the top of the window to display categories that meet certain criteria, such as tax-related categories or unused categories.

In the main part of the window, category names

NEW IN QUICKEN 2012

You may notice a search box to the right of the Show drop-down list. This is very useful if you have a great number of categories or can't remember exactly how you phrased a category. Taking a moment to search for an existing category can eliminate duplications!

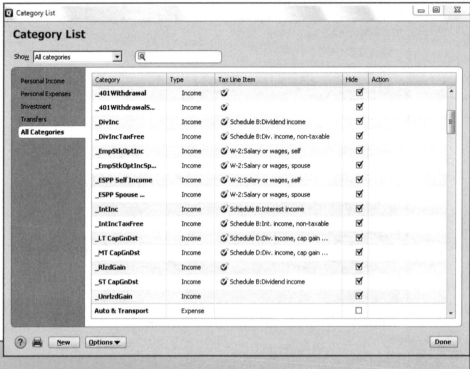

Figure 3-10 • Quicken creates special categories to perform calculations when working with your investments.

appear in an outline view, with subcategories indented beneath them. You can turn on the Hide check box for a category to remove it from lists and menus without actually deleting it from your Quicken data file.

You can also choose commands from the Options menu at the bottom of the window to determine what information appears with the category names in the Category List window. Figure 3-9 includes category names, Hide status, types, and tax-line item information. When you click a specific category, the Action buttons appear as shown here. (Chapter 17 explains more about assigning tax lines to categories.)

Gifts & Donations	Expense		☐	
Charity	Expense	✓ Schedule A:Cash charity contributions	☐	Edit Delete Merge
Gift	Expense		☐	

Creating a New Category

To create a new category, click the New button at the bottom of the Category List window (refer to Figure 3-9). The Set Up Category dialog appears. Enter information about the category, as seen in this example, and click OK.

If you have created groups of categories, there is an additional field in the Set Up Category dialog, called Groups. You can learn more about category groups in Chapter 16.

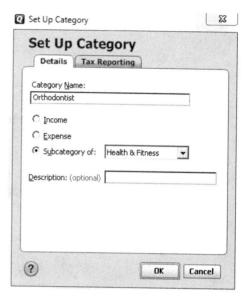

Here's a quick summary of the kind of information you should provide for each category.

Category Information   The basic category information, entered in the Details tab, includes the category name, which is required, and the description and the main category if this is a subcategory. You have the option of entering additional information in the Description field.

If you are familiar with charts of accounts used by many accounting folk, you can even use numbers in your Category name—for example, 61000-Auto Expense.

Tax Reporting   You can use the Tax Reporting options, seen here, to specify whether a category is tax-related and, if so, what tax form it appears on. This can be a real time-saver at tax time by enabling you to organize your income and expenditures as they appear on tax forms. You learn more about using Quicken at tax time in Chapter 17. You are not required to enter anything in this area.

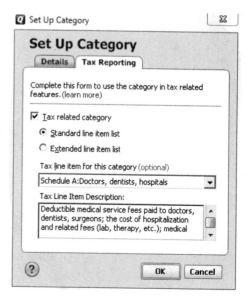

When you have set a tax line and tax form for your categories, you can display a small red circle with a check by each transaction by choosing Account Actions | Register Columns and checking Tax-related.

Click OK to close the Set Up Category dialog and return to the Category List.

Adding Multiple Categories at Once

Quicken makes it easy to add multiple related categories at the same time. For example, suppose you just started a small home business and want to add several categories for that endeavor to your Quicken data file. Click the Options button at the bottom of the Category List window (refer to Figure 3-9) and choose Manage Categories to open the Manage Categories dialog as shown here.

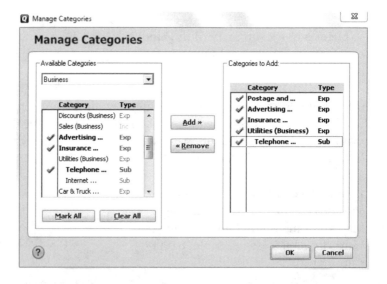

Select an option from the Available Categories drop-down list at the top of the dialog. In our example, we've used Business. In the Category list on the left, click to add a green check mark beside each category you want to add. When you click Add, the selected categories appear in the Categories To Add list. Click OK to add the categories and close the dialog.

Category Groups

The Assign Category Groups dialog, opened from the Options menu on the Category List, is very useful when grouping expense categories. You may also use groups when creating a budget. Category groups are explained in detail in Chapter 16.

IN MY EXPERIENCE

There are several caveats when working with categories:

- If you get an error message when entering a new category or subcategory, ensure there is not already a category with that name.
- You cannot use certain special characters in the name of a category or a subcategory, including : (colon) } { (brackets) / (slash) ^ (caret) | (pipe).
- If you have a payee from whom you purchase two or three categories of items, consider memorizing that payee. Then, each time you enter a transaction to that payee, you'll have two or three categories from which to choose. See Chapter 6 for more information on memorizing payees.
- You can quickly see how much you have spent on a specific category by clicking in the Category field on any register and choosing the mini-report icon. Another reason to use categories!
- Use the "Find and Replace" utility to recategorize all of the transactions for one payee. Chapter 4 explains how to use this utility.
- Use Renaming Rules to automatically categorize repeated downloaded transactions such as your cell phone or cable bills. Learn about Renaming Rules in Chapter 5.

Editing, Deleting, and Merging Categories

You use the Category List window (see Figure 3-9) to edit, delete, or merge categories. Select the name of the category with which you want to work. The Action buttons display in the Action column on the right side of the window, as shown earlier.

Before making any changes, back up your Quicken data file. That way, if you don't like the changes you've made, you can quickly go back to the file's state before you made the changes. See Appendix A for information on backing up Quicken data files.

Edit   Click a category to display the Action buttons. The Edit button displays the Set Up Category dialog (shown earlier) for the selected category. You can use this to make just about any change to a category. You can even "promote" a subcategory to a category by clearing the Subcategory Of: field.

Delete   When you choose to eliminate a category, first ensure you have a current backup. Then, select the category to display the Delete button in the Action column. Clicking the Delete button displays different dialogs, depending on the category that is selected. Quicken begins by warning you that the category and any subcategories beneath it will be deleted. Then

- If you selected a category without transactions, when you click OK, the category is deleted.
- If you selected a category or subcategory with transactions, a warning message appears that this category has been used in transactions. If you choose to delete the category, the Delete Category dialog, shown in the sidebar, appears. You can use this dialog to replace the category with another category throughout your data file. Choose another category from the drop-

Delete Category

You are about to permanently delete the category Natural Gas and all associated subcategories. Do you want to assign a new category to transactions that currently use this category?

Recategorize transactions to: | Gas & Electric

If you do not choose a replacement category, your affected transactions will be marked 'uncategorized'.

OK   Cancel

down list, and click OK. If you click OK without choosing a replacement category, any transactions that referenced the category you deleted will be marked as uncategorized. If the category you deleted has subcategories, this dialog appears for each subcategory that has transactions.

Merge   The Merge button lets you merge transactions using the currently selected category with transactions using another category. This, in effect, recategorizes all of the transactions for the selected category. Clicking Merge displays the Merge Category dialog as shown next. Choose the category to which you want to merge from the drop-down list. If you want to delete the category you selected, turn on the check box—this makes the dialog work the same way as the Delete Category dialog shown earlier. Click OK to perform the merge. One thing to keep in mind: if the category you selected is not used in any transactions, a dialog will tell you that there's nothing to merge and you can simply delete it.

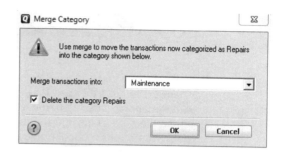

You can only delete or merge one category at a time. Deleting and merging categories does not work when more than one category is selected.

Tags

A tag is an optional identifier used to specify what a transaction applies to. For example, if you want to keep track of all the money you spent for your last vacation, no matter the category, you can create a tag named Vacation. Then each expense you incur, whether categorized as Clothing, Auto Maintenance, Dining Out, or whatever, can be "tagged" as part of that Vacation tag. Because Quicken can produce reports based on categories, tags, or both, tags offer an additional dimension for tracking and reporting information.

Using tags is completely optional. It's not necessary to set them up or use them at all. In fact, many Quicken users—including a few at Intuit—don't take advantage of this feature. It's your decision.

Displaying the Tag List Window

Quicken maintains a list of all the tags you create. You can display the Tag List window by choosing Tools | Tag List, or by pressing CTRL-L.

Creating a New Tag

Click the New button on the button bar in the Tag List window. The New Tag dialog, shown here, appears. Use it to enter information about the tag.

Only one piece of information is necessary: the tag name. You may want to make it short so it's easy to remember and enter. The description can be used to provide additional information on the tag's use. The copy number enables you to associate tags with different but similar activities. For example, if you have two

While not everyone uses tags, here are a couple of ways in which tags can prove very useful.

If you have children, you might create a separate tag for each child. Then, when you've got expenses for a specific family member, record the transaction with the appropriate tag name. (If you've got income related to that child, that's terrific; be sure to include the tag name with those transactions, too.) Then, when that partially grown bundle of joy asks for $457.49 to buy a new computerized tablet, you can show him a report of how much he's cost you so far when you suggest he save his allowance instead.

Another creative use of tags relates to tracking dues or membership fees for small groups in Quicken. Make each member's name a tag. Then, when you enter their dues for the current year—for example, using the category 2012 Dues—you can add each member's name in the Tag field as seen in Figure 3-11.

Since nearly all reports include the ability to customize and include tags, you can create some very useful information, whether it be for your family or that group for which you are acting as treasurer.

Figure 3-11 • Using tags creates an additional storehouse of information.

separate businesses for which you report activity on two Schedule Cs, you can assign Copy 1 to one business's tags and Copy 2 to the other business's tags.

When you click OK, the tag is added to the list. You can create as many tags as you like.

Working with the Tag List Window

You can use buttons that appear beside a selected tag in the Tag List window, as shown in Figure 3-12, to work with the tag list or a selected tag:

- **Edit** enables you to modify the currently selected tag name or other information.
- **Delete** enables you to delete the currently selected tag. When you delete a tag, the tag name is removed from all transactions in which it appeared, but the transaction remains properly categorized.

Displaying a Tag Field in an Account Register

By default, each account register displays a Tag field. You can easily toggle the display off and on.

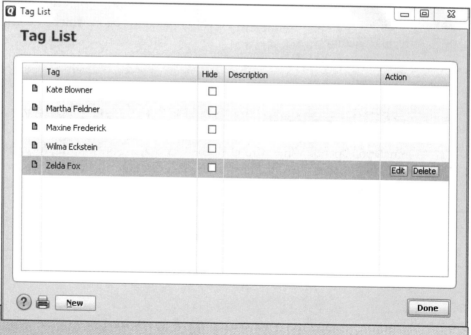

Figure 3-12 • The Tag List displays all of your current tags.

1. Open the account register. Click the small "gear" icon found at the top of the scroll bar below the Account Actions button. You can also click Account Actions | Register Columns to open the same list.
2. From the drop-down list, check or clear the Tag check box as shown here.

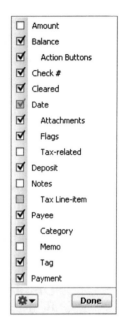

Other Setup Options

There are two additional sections in the Main View of the Home tab that you may use to help Quicken create your accurate financial picture. Both are discussed in detail in later chapters but are introduced here.

Getting Started with Monthly Bills

The second section of the Main View of the Home tab gets you started working with your regular bills, such as your mortgage or rent, phone bills, and so on. If you have downloaded and categorized transactions from your bank, selecting the Get Started button will open the Stay On Top Of Monthly Bills dialog. Click Add A Bill to add a new bill. Click Next to open a dialog in which you can add regular income.

For a complete description of working with your bills in Quicken, see Chapter 6.

Tracking Spending Goals to Save Money

This section helps you track specific expenditures so that you can watch how much you spend. When you click the Get Started button, the Monthly Spending/Saving Plan dialog appears. You can enter your goals for spending in each category. See Chapter 8 for an in-depth discussion about creating a spending plan.

Banking

This part of the book explains how to use Quicken Personal Finance Software to keep track of your bank and credit card accounts. It starts by explaining the basics of manually recording bank and credit card transactions, and then tells you how you can take advantage of online transaction entry and payment processing features such as Transaction Download and Online Bill Pay. It provides details about how you can tap into the power of Quicken to automate many entry tasks, thus saving you time. It also explains how to reconcile accounts and how to use Quicken's reporting features to learn more about what you have and how you're doing financially. This part has five chapters:

Part Two

Recording Bank and Credit Card Transactions

Chapter 4

In This Chapter:

- *Reviewing account and transaction types*
- *Working with bank accounts*
- *Using account registers*
- *Understanding splits*
- *Tracking credit cards with Quicken*
- *Writing checks*
- *Printing Quicken checks*
- *Transferring money*
- *Searching for transactions*
- *Sorting transactions*
- *Adding notes, flags, and alerts*
- *Attaching checks, receipts, or other images*

The heart of Quicken is its ability to manage your bank accounts. This is probably Quicken's most used feature. You enter the transactions, and Quicken Personal Finance Software keeps track of the source of your money, where you spent it, and your account balances. Quicken will even print your checks.

In much the same way, Quicken helps you track your credit card accounts. You may choose to enter transactions as you make them, download your transactions daily, or enter an entire month's charges and payments when you receive your credit card statement. Quicken keeps track of balances and offers you an easy way to monitor what you used your credit card to buy. It also enables you to know how much your credit cards cost you in terms of finance charges and other fees.

Getting Started

Quicken groups its account types into four general categories:

- **Spending** accounts, which include checking, savings, credit card, and cash accounts
- **Investing** accounts, which include brokerage, IRA or Keogh Plan, 401(k) or 403(b), and 529 Plan accounts
- **Property** accounts, which can include your house, vehicles, and other assets
- **Debt** accounts, which include loans and other non–credit card liability accounts

   This chapter focuses on what Quicken calls the "Spending" accounts, which are normally held at banks, credit unions, or similar financial institutions. Before you can use Quicken to track bank and credit card transactions, you should prepare by creating the necessary accounts and learning how recording transactions works. This section provides an overview of the spending account types, along with examples of transactions you might make. This chapter also reviews how to create these accounts.

Reviewing Account and Transaction Types

Many of the transactions you track with Quicken will involve one or more of its bank, credit card, and cash accounts. Here's a closer look at each account type, along with some transaction examples. As you read about these accounts, imagine how they might apply to your financial situation.

Bank Accounts

Quicken offers two types of accounts that you can use to track the money you have in a bank:

- **Checking** accounts are usually the first type of account you create in Quicken. These accounts are used to disburse funds, and include check writing privileges. These accounts generally have a lot of activity, with incoming deposits that increase the account balance and outgoing payments that decrease the account balance.

- **Savings** accounts are for your savings. These accounts normally don't have as much activity as checking accounts. You can use a Quicken savings account to track the balance in a certificate of deposit (CD), vacation savings plan, or similar savings account.

Some financial institutions consider CDs to be investment accounts, so you may not be able to download interest as you would with a regular savings account.

Generally speaking, banking account transactions can be broken down into three broad categories: payments, deposits, and transfers.

Payments   Payments are funds going out of your account. Here are some examples:

- You write a check to pay the teen who mows your lawn.
- You withdraw money from your savings account to put into a birthday card for your niece.
- You use your ATM card to withdraw cash for an auction.
- You use your debit card to buy groceries.
- You pay a monthly checking account fee.

Deposits   Deposits are funds put into your account. Here are some examples:

- Your employer deposits your paycheck directly into your checking account.
- You put the birthday check from your sister into your savings account.
- You put the cash from last weekend's garage sale into your checking account.
- Interest you've earned is posted to your money market account.

Transfers   A transfer is a movement of funds from one account to another. Here are some examples:

- You transfer money from an interest-bearing savings account to your checking account when you're ready to pay your bills.
- You transfer money from a money market account to your home equity line of credit account to reduce its balance.

Credit Card Accounts

Credit card accounts track money you owe, not money you own. Some credit cards, such as MasterCard, Visa, American Express, and Discover, can be used in most stores that accept them. Other credit cards, such as Macy's or Shell, can be used only in certain stores. But they all have one thing in common: if there's a balance, it's usually because you owe the credit card company money.

Credit card account transactions can also be broken down into two categories: charges and payments.

Charges   Charges result when you use your credit card to buy something or the credit card company charges a fee for services. Here are some examples:

- You use your MasterCard card to buy clothes for your growing soccer star.
- You use your Discover card to pay for a dinner with your co-workers.
- You use your Shell card to fill the gas tank on the way to work.
- A finance charge based on your account balance is added to your Macy's bill at month's end.
- A late fee is added to your Visa bill because they didn't receive the previous month's payment by the due date.
- Annual membership fees are added to your American Express bill.

The opposite of a charge is a *credit*. Think of it as a negative charge; don't confuse it with a payment. Here are some examples:

- You return the microwave to the store where you bought it and receive credit on your Visa card.
- You receive a rebate for purchases on your department store card.
- A special promotion earns you "cash back" on your Discover card.

Payments   Payments are amounts you send to a credit card company to reduce your balance, such as these examples:

- You pay the balance on your American Express card.
- You pay $150 of the $227 balance on your Visa card, as the rest of the balance is not yet due.

Cash Accounts

You can also use a cash account to track your cash expenditures. For example, you might create an account called My Wallet or Spending Money and use it to keep track of the cash you have on hand. Cash accounts are like bank accounts, but there's no bank. The money is in your wallet, your pocket, or the Mason jar on your dresser.

Cash accounts have two types of transactions: receive and spend.

Receive   When you receive cash, you increase the amount of cash you have on hand. Here are some examples:

- You withdraw cash from the bank for newspapers and lattes.
- You sell your *Mother Earth News* magazine collection for cash at a garage sale.
- You get a $20 bill in a birthday card from your aunt.

Spend   When you spend cash, you reduce your cash balance. Here are some examples:

- You pay a bridge toll on your way to work.
- You give your children their allowances.
- You put $20 in the collection plate at church.

Working with Bank Accounts

In Chapter 3, you learned how to add new accounts. Here are a few additional things to keep in mind when creating Quicken accounts:

- Ensure that each account has a name that clearly identifies it. For example, if you have two checking accounts, don't name them "Checking 1" and "Checking 2." Instead, include the bank name (such as "USA Bank Checking") or account purpose (such as "Joint Checking") in the account name. This prevents you from accidentally entering a transaction in the wrong account register. Remember, the name of the account register displays on the title bar of the Quicken window and at the top of each register, as seen here.

  Quicken 2012 Premier - myfamily - [Main Checking]

- If you create an account for which you manually enter transactions and include the balance date and amount from a bank statement—the recommended way—be careful not to enter transactions that already appear on the current statement or in previous statements.
- Entering your credit limit for a credit card account enables Quicken to alert you when you get close to (or exceed) your limit. If a credit card account doesn't have a credit limit—for example, a store charge card—you may want to enter your own personal spending limit. This makes it possible to take advantage of Quicken's alerts feature to prevent overspending in that account.
- Using a cash account to track every penny you spend, from the cup of coffee you buy at work in the morning to the quart of milk you pick up on your

way home that evening, isn't for everyone. You may prefer to track only large cash inflows or outflows and record the rest as miscellaneous expenses.

Adding Other Account Information

As you work with your accounts, there may be other information you want to include. For example, your credit card limit may be raised or your interest rate lowered on a savings account. To enter the new information:

1. From the Account Bar, right-click the account name you want to edit to open a context menu. Select Edit/Delete Account to open the Account Details dialog.
2. Enter or change the account information on the left side of the General tab. The dialog has different fields depending on the type of account. All account types allow you to change their account name and description. In addition
   - Checking and savings accounts let you change the following:
     - Whether the account is tax deferred
     - Interest rate
     - Maximum and minimum balances for which you can be alerted
   - For credit card accounts, you can change the following:
     - Interest rate
     - Credit limit
   - Investing accounts let you change the following:
     - Whether the account is tax deferred
     - An option to show the cash in the investment account in a checking account

 See more information about investing accounts in Chapter 9.

   - For all account types, the information on the right side of the dialog is similar, depending on the account type. You can modify the information only if the account is not set up for online services. Once the account is set up for online services, you may not change the financial institution name, account and routing numbers, or customer ID. You see the following:
     - The financial institution
     - The account and bank routing numbers
     - Your customer ID, if applicable to this type of account
   - You can always change:
     - The name of a contact at the financial institution
     - The phone number of the institution

- The financial institution's webpages, including the banking activity pages
- Any other comments you have about the account

From all of the tabs, you can access the Delete Account dialog and change the tax schedule information.

3. Use the Online Services tab to activate or deactivate online services, including online payment services, if they are available through your financial institution. See Chapter 5 for more information.
4. Use the Display Options tab to tell Quicken how to display this account. More information about hiding accounts in Quicken is covered in Chapter 3.
5. Use the Delete Account button to delete the account with which you are working. See Chapter 3 for more information about deleting accounts.
6. Click the Tax Schedule button to enter any tax information about this account. This option is discussed in more detail in Chapter 3.

When you have made all of your changes, click OK to close the Account Details dialog.

Quicken's Registers

To make the most of Quicken, you must enter transactions for the accounts you want to track. You can do this manually, as discussed in this chapter, or, if the account is enabled for online account services, you can track your account activity automatically via download, as discussed in Chapter 5. Either way, you'll need to know how to work with register transactions for your accounts.

You can enter transactions in several ways, based on the type of transaction:

- Use registers to record virtually any type of transaction, including manual checks, bank account payments and deposits, credit card charges and payments, and cash receipts and spending.
- Use the Write Checks window to record checks to be printed by Quicken.
- Enter transfers to transfer money from one account to another.

Using Account Registers

Quicken's account registers offer a standard way to enter all kinds of transactions. As the name suggests, these *electronic account registers* are similar to the paper checking account registers that come with your checks. To open an account's register, from the Account Bar, click the name of the account you want to open. The register opens to the right of the Account Bar as seen in Figure 4-1.

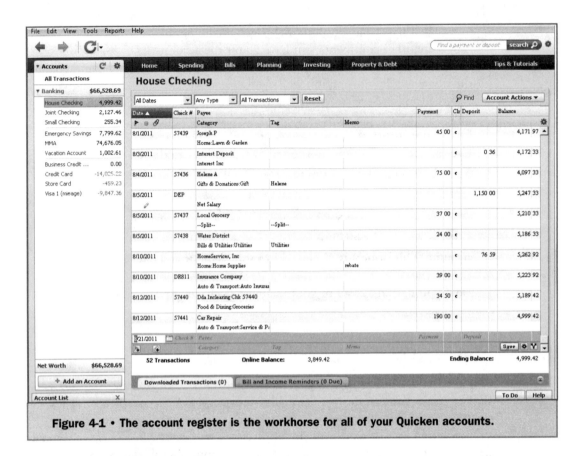

Figure 4-1 • The account register is the workhorse for all of your Quicken accounts.

The Account Bar

The Account Bar displays a list of the accounts you've chosen to display, including the total balance if you choose to display it. As seen here, the Account Bar displays your accounts in several sections: Banking, Investing, and Property & Debt. For the most part, you can designate the section in which you want your account to appear:

- The small downward arrow to the left of the word Accounts allows you to minimize the Account Bar to save room when working with other Quicken processes. When you click this arrow to minimize the Account Bar, it turns into an arrow pointing to the right. Click that right-pointing arrow to open the Account Bar once again.

- The blue curly arrow to the right of the word Accounts is a shortcut for updating your online accounts. See more about online accounts in Chapter 5.
- The small gear icon at the far right of the word Accounts is a shortcut to the Account List.
- **Net Worth** is the total of all of the amounts displayed in the Account Bar.
- **Add An Account** is a shortcut to the Add Account dialog.

You have several options for displaying information in the Account Bar. While most of the display options can be set in the Account List as described in Chapter 3, you can also open a context menu in the Account Bar with a right-click. The following menu options are available, as seen here.

- **Expand All Accounts** tells Quicken to display all of the individual accounts in each separate section of the Account Bar.
- **Show Amounts** tells Quicken to display the balance of each account. If you choose not to display the balance amount, you do not see the Net Worth total in the Account Bar.
- **Show Cents In Amounts** tells Quicken to include the cents rather than just the dollar amount of each account's balance.
- **Show Current/Ending Balance In Account Bar** tells Quicken whether to display the balance as of today or include transactions you've entered for future dates in the balance.
- **Account List (Account Bar Options)** opens the Account List when chosen from this context menu.

If you happen to right-click an account name in the Account Bar, the context menu contains Edit/Delete Account as well as the other options.

Overview of the Account Register

Before we discuss entry techniques, let's take a closer look at the account register window.

Range Selection Options   At the top of most account registers are options to customize the information displayed in your register. As seen next, drop-down lists enable you to filter the transactions that appear in the current register:

- The Dates drop-down list lets you filter the register to include all dates, specific time periods, or create a customized date range to display.
- The next drop-down list in bank account registers gives the ability to filter for Any (transaction) Type, Payments, or Deposits. In credit card account registers, your choices are Any (transaction) Type, Charge, or Payment.
- The next drop-down list allows you to filter the register by several criteria: Uncategorized, Unreconciled, Cleared, Uncleared, Flagged, and the default All Transactions.
- Reset sets the transactions register back to the default settings of All Dates, Any Type, and All Transactions.
- The Find icon displays the Quicken Find dialog, which you can use to search for transactions based on a variety of criteria. Learn how to search for transactions later in this chapter, in the section titled "Searching for Transactions."

See "Account Actions Menu" later in this chapter for information about the Account Actions button.

Downloaded Transactions   At the bottom of the account register are two tabs of information (see Figure 4-1). If these tabs are not visible, you have told Quicken to automatically add downloaded transactions to the banking registers. While this is covered in Chapter 5, you can quickly check your settings.

1. From the menu bar, click Edit | Preferences | Register | Downloaded Transactions | Downloaded Transactions Preferences | After Downloading Transactions.
2. Clear the Automatically Add To Banking Registers check box.
3. If you do not want your investment accounts added automatically, clear the Automatically Add To Investment Transactions Lists check box. See Chapter 10 for more information about downloaded investment transactions.
4. Click OK to save your settings and close the Preferences dialog.

Download Transactions or Downloaded Transactions displays a setup form for enabling transaction download or a list of transactions that have already been downloaded but not yet accepted into the account, respectively. Learn how to set up and work with the Transaction Download and Online Payment features in Chapter 5.

Bill and Income Reminders   The Bill And Income Reminders tab displays a list of upcoming, due, and overdue scheduled transactions, as seen here. See Chapter 6 for more information about scheduled transactions.

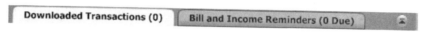

You can show or hide this information in the bottom half of the register window by clicking the small arrow button on the right end of the bar on which the tabs appear.

Account Actions Menu

This window's Account Actions menu, as seen here, includes a number of options you can use while in the register. There are three sections: Transactions, Reporting, and Register Views And Preferences. Note that many of the sections include keyboard shortcut commands. Learn more about keyboard shortcuts in Appendix A.

Transactions Section   In the Transactions section you can

1. Click Update Now to open the One Step Update Settings dialog for accounts that have online services. Enter the password given by your financial institution, and click Update Now.

NOTE

If the account is set up for Web Connect, when you click Update Now, your Internet connection will open your browser at the login page for that financial institution's website.

–Or–

Click Set Up Online to open the Add Account dialog for accounts that have not yet been activated for download.

2. Click Edit Account Details to open the Account Details dialog as described in Chapter 3.

3. Click Write Checks to open the Write Checks dialog. See "Writing Checks" later in this chapter.

4. Click Reconcile to open the Reconcile Details dialog. See Chapter 7 for complete instructions on reconciling your accounts.

5. Click Transfer Money to open the Transfer Between Quicken Accounts dialog. See "Transferring Money" later in this chapter for directions.

Reporting Section   The Reporting section allows you to

1. Click Account Attachments to open the Account Attachments dialog. See more information in the section "Working with Attachments" later in this chapter.

2. Click Account Overview to display a graphical recap of the selected account as well as the account's current status, as shown here.

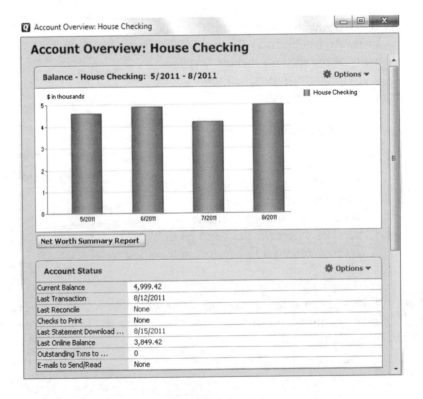

3. Click More Reports to see the information about this account in various report formats. Read more about creating reports in Chapter 8.

4. Click Print Transactions to open the Print dialog where you can print the register for this account. See Chapter 8 for more information about printing reports and graphs.

5. Click Export To Excel Compatible File to export this file in a .txt format. See more information about exporting files in Chapter 8.

Since the export utility prints your transactions to a text file, if your account has many years of transactions, the process may take a few minutes to complete.

Register Views and Preferences   The Register Views And Preferences section lets you set how this register displays.

1. Click Two-line Display to show your register information on two lines, as seen in Figure 4-1. If you clear that check box, you'll see the payee, the category, and the amount on just one line. One-line display is the default for Quicken 2012 as shown here.

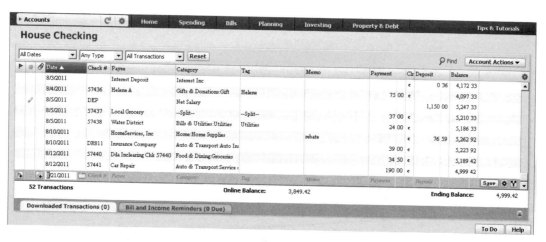

2. Click Sorting Options to tell Quicken how to organize your transactions in this register menu. See "Sorting Transactions" later in this chapter for more information.

3. Click Register Columns to open the Register Columns list as seen here. You can also click the small gear icon at the top of the register's vertical scroll bar to see this list. Learn more about this topic later in this chapter in the "Using Register Columns" section.

The example shown here has the register display set to the default one-line display. If you have set your register display to show two lines, your Register Columns list may look different from what is displayed here.

4. Click Register Preferences to open the Preferences dialog at the Register section as shown below. See Appendix B for more information on Quicken Preferences.

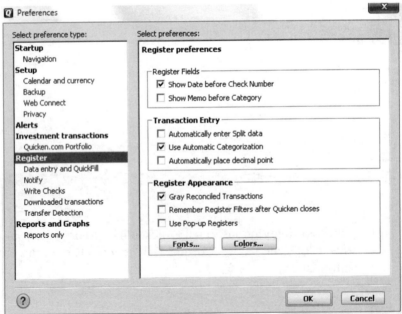

Basic Entry Techniques

To enter a transaction, first, open a register by clicking the account in the Account Bar. Begin by clicking in the first empty line at the end of the account register window (refer to Figure 4-1). This activates a new, blank transaction. You can then enter transaction information into each field and press ENTER to complete the transaction.

Although the entry process is pretty straightforward, here are a few things to keep in mind when entering transactions.

Advancing from Field to Field   To move from one text box, or field, to another when entering transactions, you can either click in the next field's text box or press the TAB key. Pressing TAB is usually quicker.

Many users feel more comfortable using the ENTER key to move between fields. To set this option, go to Edit | Preferences | Register | Data Entry And QuickFill | Data Entry. Click the Use Enter Key To Move Between Fields check box.

Using Icons   Icons appear when certain fields are active:

- When the Date field is active, a calendar icon appears, as seen here. You can click it to display a calendar, and then click calendar buttons to view and enter a date.
- When either the Payment or Deposit Amount field is active, a calculator icon appears as shown. You can click it to use a calculator and enter calculated results.
- When the Payee or Category field is active, a Report button appears. Click the Report button to display a pop-up report of transactions in that category or for that payee, like the one shown here. Click the *X* to close the report.

If you do not see the calendar, calculator, or report icons, you can turn them on by going to Edit | Preferences | Register | Data Entry And QuickFill and ensuring that the Show Buttons On QuickFill Fields check box is selected.

close X

Utilities

Last 6 months ▼ (All accounts)

Date	Amount
8/1/2011	-123.52
7/18/2011	-188.48
7/5/2011	-136.96
5/25/2011	-138.40
5/9/2011	-172.34
3/25/2011	-241.32
3/8/2011	-217.04
Total:	**-1,218.06**
Monthly Average:	**-203.01**

Show Report

Menu buttons, which look like triangles pointing down to a horizontal line, display drop-down lists of items applicable to the active field. You can enter an item by choosing it from the list's options or by simply typing the information.

Using the Number Field   The Check # (or Reference # in non-banking accounts) field is where you enter a transaction number or type. You can enter any number you like, or use the drop-down list (shown here) to display a list of standard entries; click an option to enter it for the transaction. You can also press the + or − key on the keyboard to increment or decrement the check number, respectively, while the field is active.

- **Next Check Num** automatically increments the most recently entered check number and enters the resulting number in the Check Number field.
- **ATM** is for ATM transactions. You may also want to use it for debit or check card transactions.
- **Deposit** is for deposits.
- **Print Check** is for transactions for which you want Quicken to print a check. Quicken automatically enters the check number when the check is printed.
- **Send Online Payment** is for accounts for which you have enabled Online Bill Pay.
- **Online Transfer** is for accounts that have been activated to transfer funds from one online account to another online account.
- **Transfer** is for a transfer of funds from one account to another.
- **EFT**, which stands for electronic funds transfer, is for direct deposits and similar transactions.

The Payee Drop-Down List and QuickFill   When you begin to enter information in the Payee field, a drop-down list of existing payees or payers appears. As you type, Quicken narrows down the list to display only those names that match what you have typed. You can enter an existing name from the list by selecting it. Quicken will fill in details from the most recent transaction for that name for you. This is Quicken's QuickFill feature, which you will learn more about in Chapter 6.

Automatic Categorization   After entering a payee for the first time, Quicken may fill in the category for you. This is Quicken's automatic categorization feature, which enters categories based on thousands of payee names programmed into it. You'll find that in most cases, Quicken assigns an appropriate category. But you can change the category if you like and, from that point on, Quicken's QuickFill feature uses your newly assigned category for future transactions to that payee. Chapter 6 provides more information about QuickFill.

Using the Category Drop-down List   The Category drop-down list organizes category and transfer accounts in the Category List window (which is discussed in Chapter 3). This drop-down list may appear automatically when you begin to enter a category in the Category field of the transaction area; if it does not, you can click the menu button on the right side of the field to display it. You can narrow down the display of categories by clicking a heading on the left side of the drop-down list. Then click the category name to enter it into the field.

Entering New Categories   If you type in a category that does not exist in the Category List and press ENTER, Quicken displays a message asking if you want to create a new category with that name. Click Yes to use the Set Up Category dialog to create a new category, or click No to return to the register and enter a different category.

If you turn off the Prompt Before Creating New Categories check box, Quicken automatically displays the Set Up Category dialog every time you enter a category that does not exist in the Category List. See more about categories in Chapter 3.

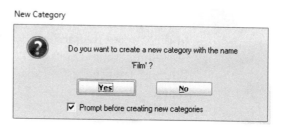

Entering Subcategories   When you choose a subcategory from the Category field's drop-down list, Quicken automatically enters the subcategory's parent category name, followed by a colon (:) and the subcategory name. To type a subcategory, use the first letter or two of the category, the colon, and then the first letter or two of the subcategory. QuickFill will match the category:subcategory.

Entering Multiple Categories   To enter more than one category for a transaction, click the Split button (a small, two-headed arrow pointing upward, as shown here) on the right side of the transaction entry area. See how to enter transactions with splits a little later in this chapter, in the section titled "Understanding Splits."

Using Register Columns   The small gear icon at the top of the balance column is used to tell Quicken which columns to display in your register and which ones to hide. Click the gear icon or choose Register Columns from the Account Actions menu to open the list seen in Figure 4-2. Each item toggles the selected column in your register off and on. While many of the items seem self-explanatory, there are several that might cause some confusion, so we explain the options here. You may see a slightly different list, depending on your register and its configuration.

- **Amount**   Selecting this option adds an amount column before the balance column. It displays deposits in black and payments in red.
- **Action Buttons**   When this is selected, the Save/More Actions/Split Transaction Into Multiple Categories buttons display in the selected transaction. See "Using Transaction Buttons" later in this chapter for more information.
- **Attachments, Status, and Tax-Related**   If any or all of these are selected, the Sort By Attachment, Sort By Status, and/or Sort By Tax-Related buttons appear at the top of the Date column, as shown here. See "Sorting Transactions" later in this chapter for more information. The small flag and attachment icons also appear before or underneath the date when

Figure 4-2 • You can customize the look of your check register by selecting the columns to display.

entering a new transaction.
- **Date**   This cannot be omitted.
- **Downloaded xxxxx**   These items are covered in Chapter 5.

After you have made your selections, click Done to close the Register Columns list.

If you don't like the way your register columns appear, open the Register Columns list and click the small gear icon at the bottom-left corner. From here you can choose to make all of your similar registers' displays the same as your current register or reset the columns to their default settings.

Using Tags   As discussed in Chapter 3, a tag is an optional identifier for specifying what a transaction applies to. Quicken displays a Tag field in the register. To include a tag in a transaction, simply enter the tag in that field. Quicken may display a drop-down list of valid tags for you to choose from. If you type a tag name that is not on the Tag List, Quicken displays the Set Up Tag window so you can create the tag on the fly. Review how to create tags in Chapter 3. You can use the Register Columns menu to turn off the Tag field display as seen in Figure 4-2.

Entering Memos   You can enter a brief memo (up to 64 characters) about the transaction in the Memo field to the right of the Category (or Tag) field. This memo can help you recall why you made the transaction.

Using Transaction Buttons   As shown here, three buttons appear in the second line of a two-line display register and inline with the active transaction in a one-line display register. You can use these buttons to work with the transaction:

- **Save** enters the transaction into the account register. If Quicken's sound option is turned on, you should hear a cash register ch-ching sound when you click it. (You can turn Quicken sounds on or off in the Preferences dialog, which is covered in Appendix B.)
- **More Actions**, a small black gear icon, displays a menu you can use to edit this transaction. See some of the More Action menu commands later in this chapter, in the section titled "Changing Transactions."
- **Split Transaction Into Multiple Categories**, a small two-headed arrow pointing upward, opens the Split Transaction window. The next section explains how to enter a transaction with splits.

Understanding Splits

A *split* is a transaction with more than one category. For example, suppose you pay one utility bill for two categories of utilities—electricity and water. If you want to track each of these two expenses separately, you can use a split to record each category's portion of the payment you make. This enables you to keep good records without writing multiple checks to the same payee.

To record a transaction with a split, click the Split icon in the account register or the Split button in the Write Checks window when entering the transaction. The Split Transaction window, which is shown next, appears. Click in the first blank line and select a category. If desired, enter a memo for the category in the Memo field. Then enter the amount for that category in the Amount field. Repeat this process for each category you want to include in the transaction. Here's what the Split Transaction window might look like with three categories entered.

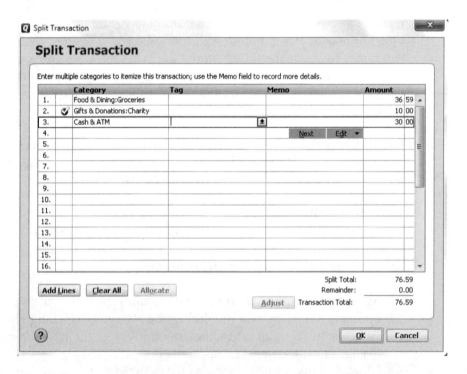

If you entered a transaction amount before clicking the Split button, you can monitor the Remainder and Transaction Total values in the Split Transaction window to make sure you've accounted for the entire transaction amount. If you entered an incorrect amount, you can click the Adjust button to adjust the transaction amount to match the split total. You may also allocate how the split distributes a remainder amount. See "Allocate a Split Transaction" later in this chapter.

If you need more lines to record all of the split amounts, click Add Lines. To clear all of your entries and start over, click Clear All.

When you're finished entering transaction categories, click OK or press ENTER. If you left the transaction amount empty before clicking the Split button, a dialog appears, asking if you want to record the transaction as a payment or deposit. Select the appropriate option and click OK.

As shown here, the word "Split" appears in the Category field for the transaction in the account register window.

Three buttons appear beside the Category field when you activate a transaction with a split:

- The green check mark displays the Split Transaction window so you can review and edit the transaction.
- The red X opens a message that allows you to clear all lines from the split. Use this option with care—it permanently removes all category information from the transaction.
- The Report icon prints a report about this transaction for a time period you can set.

Allocate a Split Transaction

As you are entering categories in a split transaction, you may notice that the Allocate button at the bottom of the Split Transaction dialog is activated. If you have entered several amounts and have just one remaining amount, you have two options for that remainder.

1. Click Allocate to open the Allocate Empty Split Line dialog as shown here.
2. Choose Distribute Proportionally Between All Other Split Lines to apportion the remaining amount in the same ratio as the other lines.

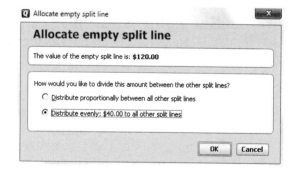

3. Choose Distribute Evenly: $nn.nn To All Other Split Lines.

As you saw in the previous illustration, we've chosen to distribute the remaining amount evenly between the other split lines.

Tracking Credit Cards with Quicken

Tracking bank account transactions and balances is just one part of using Quicken. It's also a great tool for tracking credit cards. Knowing how much you owe on your credit cards helps you maintain a clear picture of your financial situation.

How you use Quicken to track your credit cards depends on how accurate you want your financial records to be and how much effort you're willing to spend to keep Quicken up-to-date.

Credit Card Tracking Techniques

You can use either of two techniques for paying credit card bills and monitoring credit card balances with Quicken:

- Use your checking account register or the Write Checks window to record amounts paid to each credit card company for your credit card bill. Although this does track the amounts you pay, it doesn't track how much you owe or the individual charges.
- Use a credit card account register to record credit card expenditures and payments. This takes a bit more effort on your part, but it tracks how much you owe and categorizes what you bought.

Many Quicken users feel it's worth the extra effort to track your credit card expenditures and balances in individual credit card accounts. And if you utilize Quicken's Transaction Download feature for your credit card accounts, as discussed in Chapter 5, it won't take much time or effort to get the job done.

Recording Strategies

You can also use two strategies for recording transactions in credit card accounts. Choosing the strategy that's right for you makes the job easier to handle.

Enter as You Spend   One strategy is to enter transactions as you spend. To do this, you must collect your credit card receipts—which might be something you already do. Don't forget to jot down the totals for any telephone and online shopping you do. Then, every day or every few days, sit down with Quicken and enter the transactions.

While this strategy requires you to stay on top of things, it offers two main benefits:

- Your Quicken credit card registers always indicate what you owe to credit card companies. This prevents unpleasant surprises at month-end or at the checkout counter when you're told you've reached your limit. It also enables you to use the alerts feature to track credit card balances. Learn more about those features in Chapter 8.
- At month-end, you don't have to spend a lot of time entering big batches of transactions. All (or at least most) of them should already be entered.

Many just don't like holding on to all those pieces of paper. (Of course, once you have signed up for Transaction Download, all of the information is entered automatically. You can learn more about Transaction Download in Chapter 5.)

Enter When You Pay   The other strategy, which you may find better for you, is to enter transactions when you get your monthly statement. With this strategy, when you open your credit card statement, you'll spend some time sitting in front of your computer with Quicken to enter each transaction. If there aren't many, this isn't a big deal. But it could take some time if there are many transactions to enter.

Of course, the main benefit of this strategy is that you don't have to collect credit card receipts and spend time throughout the month entering your transactions. But you still have to enter them!

Entering Credit Card Transactions

Entering credit card transactions isn't very different from entering checking account or savings account transactions, as seen in Figure 4-3.

Entering Individual Charges   Open the account register for the credit card account. Then enter the charge transaction, using the name of the merchant that accepted the charge as the payee name. If you don't want to include a transaction number or receipt number, you can leave the Reference Number field empty if you have chosen not to hide that column as we have hidden it in Figure 4-3. Press TAB to move between the fields.

Entering Credits   Enter the transaction just as if it were a charge, but put the amount of the credit in the Payment box. This subtracts it from your account balance.

Figure 4-3 • You can set your credit card as well as your bank registers to a two-line display.

Entering Finance Charges   In the credit card account register, enter the name of the credit card company as the payee and the amount of the finance charge as a charge. You can use the Interest Exp category for the transaction.

Entering Payments   In the account register for your checking account or in the Write Checks window, enter a payment transaction with the credit card company name in the Payee box. Enter the credit card account name in the Category text box; you should find it as a transfer account in the Category drop-down list that appears when you activate the field. The checking account register transaction should look like the one shown here.

| CC#2 Bank | | | 139 | 55 |
| [Credit Card 2] | | | | |

Recording Credit Card Rebates   Some credit card companies offer rebates for purchases. How you record a rebate depends on how the rebate is received:

- To record a rebate received as a check, deposit the check as usual and enter the amount of the rebate as a deposit in that account.
- To record a rebate received as a reduction in the credit card account balance, enter the amount of the rebate in the credit card account as a payment. (Just remember that a rebate is not a payment that counts toward your monthly obligation to the credit card company.)

What you use as a category for this transaction is completely up to you. You may want to use the Interest Exp account, thus recording the rebate as a reduction in your interest expense. Or, perhaps, if the rebate applies to a certain purchase only, use the category you originally used for that purchase. For example, if you have a credit card that gives you a 5 percent rebate on fuel purchases, you might record the rebate using the Fuel category you created to track fuel expenses. If you have a lot of credit cards that offer rebates, you may want to create a Rebate income account and use that as the category for all rebate transactions. These are just suggestions. There is no right or wrong way to do it.

Entering Cash Transactions

Although Quicken enables you to keep track of cash transactions through the use of a cash account, not everyone does this. The reason: Most people make many small cash transactions every day. Is it worth tracking every penny you spend? That's something you need to decide.

Many people track only expenditures that are large or tax-deductible—for example, the $50 you gave to the Cancer Fund. You may want to do the same. If so, you still need to set up a cash account, but you don't need to record every transaction.

Cash Receipts   Cash receipts may come from using your ATM card, cashing a check, or getting cash from some other source. If the cash comes from one of your other accounts through an ATM or check transaction, when you record that transaction, use your cash account as the transfer in the Category field. That increases your cash balance.

Important Cash Expenditures   In your cash account, record large, tax-deductible, or other important cash expenditures like any other transaction. Be sure to assign the correct category.

Other Cash Expenditures   Throughout the week, you may spend $1 for a newspaper, $3 for a cup of coffee, and about $12 for lunch at your favorite hamburger joint. Recording transactions like these can be tedious, so don't bother if you don't want to. Instead, at the end of the week, compare your cash on hand to the balance in your cash account register. Then, enter a transaction to record the difference as an expenditure. You can use the Misc category and enter anything you like in the Payee field.

Writing Checks

Quicken's Write Checks window uses a basic check-like interface to record checks. You enter the same information that you would write on an actual check. You then tell Quicken to print the check based on the information you entered. (See how to print checks later in this chapter, in the section titled "Printing Checks.")

To open the Write Checks window, from your account register, click Account Actions | Write Checks or press CTRL-W. The Write Checks window, which is shown in Figure 4-4, appears. The name of the account from which you are writing this check appears in the drop-down list near the top of the window. If you need to choose another account, click the down arrow. Enter the necessary information for a check, and record the transaction.

Overview of the Write Checks Window

The Write Checks window is streamlined and user-friendly for 2012. The top of the dialog looks much like the checks you write by hand, including a space for a memo. The other options are discussed here.

Edit Address   If the address that appears in the Bill Pay Address field is incorrect, click Edit Address to open the Edit Address Book Record dialog. The Address Book is discussed at length in Chapter 6.

Category   Use the Category field to enter the category for this check. Click the Split icon should you need to use more than one category.

Record Check   The Record Check button records your check in the appropriate check register. You do not have to enter it twice!

Check Data   Quicken uses the space below Category and Record Check to show a list of the checks that are ready to print. In that way you can enter a number of checks and print them all at once. The information displayed is

- **Date**   This is the date you entered in the Date field in your check body.

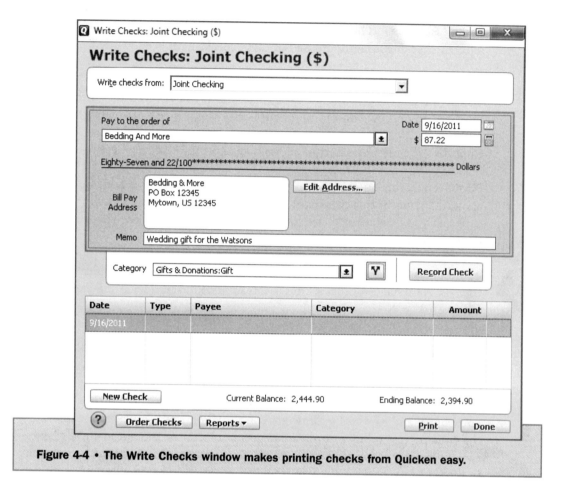

Figure 4-4 • The Write Checks window makes printing checks from Quicken easy.

- **Type** Normally, Print will appear in this field as the check is to be printed using Quicken.
- **Payee/Category/Amount** These are all entered directly from the check body above.

 You can use the Write Checks window to enter your online payments for accounts that are enabled for Online Payment. These show up as Send transactions when entered.

New Check Select the New Check button to add the next check in sequence for this batch of checks.

Current Balance The amount displayed in this field is the balance in the selected account before the checks are created.

Ending Balance The amount that displays in this field is the balance in your selected checking account after all of these checks have been printed.

Order Checks The Order Checks button uses your Internet connection to display the Checks & Supplies page of the Intuit Market window, with information on how you can order check stock that is compatible with Quicken.

Reports The Reports button allows you to print a Register Report.

Print Click this button when you are ready to print your checks. Learn more about that later in this chapter, in the section titled "Printing Checks."

When you have made all of your choices and entered all the checks for this work session, click Done to close the dialog.

To delete a check from the list of checks to be printed, select the check and press CTRL-D. A message appears asking if you want to delete the current transaction. Choose Yes or No.

Entering Transactions in the Write Checks Window

The Write Checks window (refer to Figure 4-4) is like a cross between a paper check and Quicken's account register window. You fill in the check form like you would fill in the blanks on a paper check. Quicken's QuickFill feature makes data entry quick and easy by recalling entry information from similar transactions to the same payee, and its automatic categorization feature can automatically "guess" the category for many new transactions. You must enter a valid Quicken category in the Category field, just as you would when entering a transaction in the account register. Clicking the Record Check button completes the transaction and adds it to the checks to print list as well as the account register.

Consult the section "Using Account Registers," earlier, for details about the information that should be entered into most fields. Here are a few additional things to consider when entering transactions in the Write Checks window.

Addresses on Checks If you enter an address on the check, you can mail the check using a window envelope. The address is automatically added to the Quicken Address Book. You can click the Address button in the Write Checks window to display the Edit Address Book Record dialog, which you can use to modify an address in the Address Book.

Check Memos Be careful when using the memo field if you are using window envelopes. Some envelopes display part of the memo field. If you have included account numbers or other personal information in the memo, that information may be visible to others.

Printing Checks

Quicken's ability to print checks enables you to create accurate, legible, professional-looking checks without picking up a pen (or a typewriter). In this section, you'll learn how to print the checks you enter in the Write Checks window, discussed earlier.

Before you can print checks from Quicken, you must obtain compatible check stock. Quicken supports checks in a number of different styles:

- Standard checks print just checks. There's no voucher or stub.
- Voucher checks pair each check with a similarly sized voucher form. When you print a voucher check, the transaction category information, including splits and tags, can be printed on the voucher portion.
- Wallet checks pair each check with a stub. When you print a wallet check, the transaction information is printed on the stub.

 Wallet checks are being phased out and will be replaced by Check 21 Compliant Wallet checks.

- Wallet checks (Check 21 Image Compatible).

In addition to these styles, you can get the checks in two different formats for your printer:

- Page-oriented checks are for laser and inkjet printers.
- Continuous checks are for pin-feed printers.

A catalog and order form for checks may have been included with your copy of Quicken. If so, you can use it to order checks. If you have an Internet connection, you can order checks online from within Quicken by clicking the Order Checks button in the Write Checks window (see Figure 4-4), or by clicking the Order [check type] checks link below the check style field in the Select Checks To Print dialog.

Quicken must also be set up to print the kind of checks you purchased. You do this once, and Quicken remembers the settings.

Choose File | Printer Setup | For Printing Checks to display the Check Printer Setup dialog, shown next. Use the drop-down lists and option buttons to specify

settings for your printer and check stock. The following are a few things to keep in mind when making settings in this dialog.

Partial Page Printing Options

If you select the Page-Oriented option and either Standard or Wallet checks in the Check Printer Setup dialog, you can also set options for Partial Page Printing Style. This enables you to set up the printer for situations when you're not printing an entire page of checks.

- **Edge** is for inserting the page against one side of the feeder. The left or right edge of the checks enters the feeder first.
- **Centered** is for centering the page in the feeder. The left or right edge of the checks enters the feeder first.
- **Portrait** is also for centering the page in the feeder, but in this case, the top edge of each check enters the feeder first.

If your printer supports multiple feed trays, you can also set the source tray for partial and full pages by choosing options from the Partial Page Printing and Full Page Printing drop-down lists.

Continuous Printing Options

If you select the Continuous option and either Standard or Wallet checks in the Check Printer Setup dialog, the dialog changes to offer two Continuous options:

- **Bypass The Driver** should be turned on for a continuous printer that skips checks or prints nothing.
- **Use Low Starting Position** should be turned on for a continuous printer that cuts the date or logo off your checks.

Checking the Settings for Page-Oriented Checks

If you're using page-oriented checks, you can check your settings by printing a sample page on plain paper. Here's how:

1. Click the Alignment button in the Check Printer Setup dialog.
2. In the Align Checks dialog, choose the Full Page, Two Checks, or One Check button. The Fine Alignment dialog appears.
3. Click Print Sample.
4. When the sample emerges from your printer, hold it up to the light with a sheet of check stock behind it. The sample should line up with the check.
5. If the sample does not line up properly with the check stock, set Vertical and/or Horizontal adjustment values in the Fine Alignment dialog. Then repeat steps 2 through 4 until the alignment is correct.
6. Click OK in each dialog to accept your settings and close it.

Printing Quicken Checks

Once setup is complete, you're ready to print checks.

Open the account register for the account you want to print checks for. Then insert the check stock in your printer and choose File | Print Checks, or click the Print button in the Write Checks window. The Select Checks To Print dialog, which is shown on the next page, appears. Enter the number of the first check that will be printed in the First Check Number box. Then set other options as desired. If you select the Selected Checks option, you can click the Choose button to display a list of checks and mark off the ones you want to print. Click Done in that window to return to the Select Checks To Print dialog.

When you click Print First Check or OK, Quicken sends the print job to your printer. It then displays a dialog asking if the checks printed correctly. You have the following two options:

- If all checks printed fine, just click OK.

- If a problem occurred while printing the checks, enter the number of the first check that was misprinted, and then click OK. You can then go back to the Select Checks To Print dialog and try again.

Transferring Money

You can easily record the transfer of funds from one account to another. You might find this feature especially useful for recording telephone or ATM transfers.

Using the Transfer Dialog

One way to record a transfer is with the Transfer dialog. Open the account register window for one of the accounts involved in the transfer transaction, and choose Account Actions | Transfer Money. The Transfer Money Within Quicken dialog, which is illustrated next, appears. Choose the source and destination accounts from the drop-down lists, enter a transaction date and amount, and any description, and click OK.

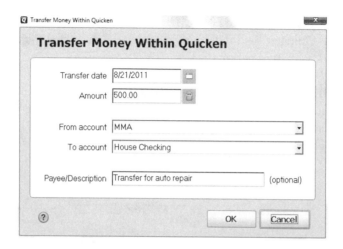

Recording a Transfer in the Account Register Window

The Transfer dialog isn't the only way to record a transfer. You can also record a transfer in the account register window of either the source or destination account. When you choose Transfer (TXFR) from the Check Number drop-down list, the Category drop-down list displays only transfer accounts. Choose the other transfer account from the list and complete the transaction.

The following illustrations show a transfer from a savings account to a money market account. Here's what the source (MMA) account transaction looks like. In this example the register for the MMA account is shown on one line.

TXFR	Transfer for auto repair	[House Checking]		500 00

And here's what the corresponding destination (House Checking) account transaction looks like. In our example, the House checking account's register displays two lines.

TXFR		Transfer for auto repair		500 00
		[MMA]		

Working with Existing Transactions

So far, this chapter has concentrated on entering transactions. What do you do when you need to modify a transaction you already recorded? That's what this section is all about.

Searching for Transactions

The Quicken Find dialog includes several drop-down lists to help you locate and work with transactions.

Using the Find Command

To use the Find command, begin by opening an account register. Click the Find icon, as seen here, or press CTRL-F.

The Quicken Find dialog appears, shown next.

Start by choosing an option from the Find drop-down list, which includes all register fields for a transaction. Then choose the matching option from the next field to indicate how the search criteria should be matched (this field is not labeled, but the first choice on the list is "Contains"). Enter the search criteria in the next field. To search backward (relative to the currently selected transaction), turn on the Search Backwards check box.

After setting up the search, if you click the Find button, Quicken selects the first match found in the account register. If you click the Find All button, Quicken displays the Search Results window, which lists all the matches it found. You can double-click a match to view it in the account register window. See an example here.

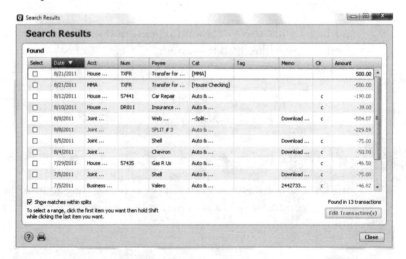

Using the Edit Transaction Command

To edit transactions, first find them and then in the Search Results window, select the transaction(s) by clicking the check box(es) in the Select column. Then click the Edit Transaction(s) button in the Search Results window. The Find And Replace dialog appears with the items you selected, as shown here.

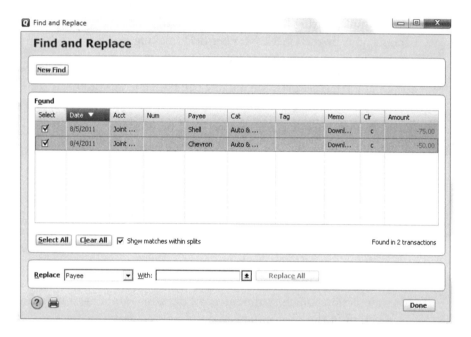

The items you selected in the Find and Replace dialog appear in the Found section of the dialog. You can click the New Find button to make the top part of the dialog look and work much like the Quicken Find dialog. You can turn on the Show Matches Within Splits check box at the bottom of the dialog if you want Quicken to find all matches, including those that appear in splits. Once you set up the search and click the Find button, a list of matches appears in the Found section of the dialog. Click beside each found item you want to change to place a check mark there. Then set options in the Replace and With boxes. Click Replace All to replace all selected items with the replacement option you specified.

You can also access the Find And Replace dialog by pressing CTRL-H or choosing Edit | Find/Replace.

Sorting Transactions

You can click a register's column heading or use the sort options to change how your transactions are displayed. Click Account Actions | Sorting Options in an account's register to open the menu from which you can change the sort order of transactions, as seen here. For example, sorting by check number groups the transactions by the Check Number field, making it easy to find a specific check. You can quickly move up and down your register to a specific date or transaction number by dragging the scroll box on the scroll bar.

○	by Attachments
○	by Category
○	by Check #
○	by Cleared
●	by Date
○	by Deposit
○	by Flags
○	by Payee
○	by Payment
○	by Status
○	by Order Entered
○	by Date / Order Entered

You can even sort by the flags. See "Adding Notes, Flags, and Alerts" later in this chapter.

Changing Transactions

Quicken enables you to change a transaction at any time—even after it has been cleared. This is especially useful when you find that a check has been categorized as groceries when it should have been categorized as a charitable donation.

Making Simple Changes   If all you want to do is change one of the fields in the transaction—such as the category, date, or number—simply find the transaction in the appropriate account register, make changes as desired, and click the Save button to record them.

Using the More Actions Menu   When you need to make more elaborate changes, use the More Actions menu. The More Actions menu appears when you click the small gear icon between the Save and Split icons as shown here. These icons appear when you have selected a specific transaction in your register.

The More Actions menu, as shown in Figure 4-5, offers a number of options for working with your transactions. Each is explained here:

- **Save** enters the transaction in the register. Choosing this command is the same as clicking the Save button or pressing ENTER.
- **Restore Transaction** enables you to change a transaction back to the way it was before you started changing it. This option is available only if you have made changes to the selected transaction.

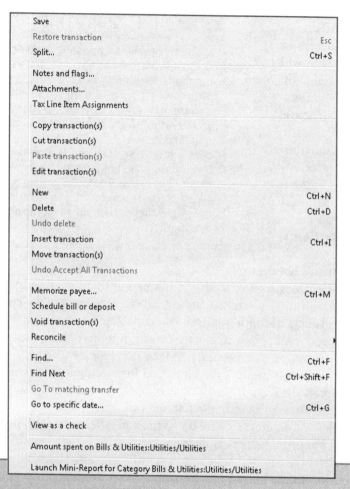

Save	
Restore transaction	Esc
Split...	Ctrl+S
Notes and flags...	
Attachments...	
Tax Line Item Assignments	
Copy transaction(s)	
Cut transaction(s)	
Paste transaction(s)	
Edit transaction(s)	
New	Ctrl+N
Delete	Ctrl+D
Undo delete	
Insert transaction	Ctrl+I
Move transaction(s)	
Undo Accept All Transactions	
Memorize payee...	Ctrl+M
Schedule bill or deposit	
Void transaction(s)	
Reconcile	
Find...	Ctrl+F
Find Next	Ctrl+Shift+F
Go To matching transfer	
Go to specific date...	Ctrl+G
View as a check	
Amount spent on Bills & Utilities:Utilities/Utilities	
Launch Mini-Report for Category Bills & Utilities:Utilities/Utilities	

Figure 4-5 • Quicken offers a number of options for working with your register transactions.

- **Split** opens the Split window for the transaction. Choosing this command is the same as clicking the Split button. You learned how to use the Split feature earlier in this chapter, in the section titled "Understanding Splits."
- **Notes And Flags** displays the Transaction Notes And Flags dialog (which is shown later in this chapter, in the section titled "Adding Notes, Flags, and Alerts") so you can add transaction notes, flag the transaction in a specific color, or create an alert for follow-up.
- **Attachments** displays the Transaction Attachments dialog (shown later in this chapter, in the section titled "Attaching Checks, Receipts, or Other Images") so you can attach checks, receipts, and other images to the transaction.

- **Tax Line Item Assignments** displays the dialog with which you can assign a line item to the transaction's category as discussed in Chapter 17.
- **Copy Transaction(s)** copies the selected transaction without removing it from the account register.
- **Cut Transaction(s)** selects the selected transaction and removes it from the account register so that it can be put in another register.

> ### IN MY EXPERIENCE
>
> Cutting, copying, and pasting are basic computer processes that are used in many programs. One thing to remember is that it is often better to copy a transaction, and paste it into the new register. While that does require you to return to the first register to delete the transaction from its original location, using copy protects against loss of the transaction. If you have children, pets, or power issues that might impact your computer during a cut-and-paste process, you might want to consider using copy instead of cut when moving information.

- **Paste Transaction(s)** pastes the last-copied transaction into the current account register. This option is available only after a transaction has been cut or copied. You might want to cut a transaction to paste it into another register if you realize that you entered it in the wrong register.
- **Edit Transaction(s)** displays the Find And Replace dialog (shown earlier in this chapter, in the section titled "Searching for Transactions") so you can use the Replace feature to modify the selected transaction(s).
- **New** enables you to create a new transaction for the account. This does not affect the currently selected transaction.
- **Delete** deletes the selected transaction. This is the same as clicking the Delete button in the button bar. Remember that deleting a transaction removes the transaction from the Quicken data file, thus changing the account balance and category activity.
- **Undo Delete** restores the transaction you just deleted. You must use this command immediately after deleting a transaction to restore it.
- **Insert Transaction** enables you to insert a transaction before the selected transaction in the account register. This does not affect the currently selected transaction.
- **Move Transaction(s)** displays the Move Transactions(s) dialog, which you can use to move a transaction from the current account register to a different account register. Simply choose an account name from the drop-down list and click OK to complete the move. This is sometimes a better option than the cut-and-paste option.

- **Undo Accept All Transactions** restores accepted transactions to unaccepted status. This command is available only if the last thing you did was accept transactions. Learn more about accepting transactions in Chapter 5.
- **Memorize Payee** tells Quicken to add the selected transaction to its list of memorized payees.
- **Schedule Bill Or Deposit** enables you to schedule the transaction for a future date or to set up the transaction as a recurring transaction. Learn more about scheduling transactions in Chapter 6.
- **Void Transaction(s)** marks the selected transaction as void. This reverses the effect of the transaction on the account balance and category activity without actually deleting the transaction.
- **Reconcile** enables you to indicate whether the transaction should be marked as Not Reconciled, Cleared, or Reconciled. Learn how to reconcile accounts in Chapter 7.
- **Revert To Downloaded Payee Name** (not shown) enables you to revert to the transaction payee downloaded from your financial institution's server. This option only appears if the transaction has been downloaded and its payee name has changed.
- **Find** displays the Find dialog, which is discussed earlier in this chapter, in the section titled "Searching for Transactions."
- **Find Next** searches for transactions matching the previously entered Find criteria.
- **Go To Matching Transfer** displays the selected transaction in the account register for the other part of a transfer. For example, if the selected transaction involves the checking and savings accounts and you are viewing it in the checking account register, choosing the Go To Transfer command displays the same transaction in the savings account register. This command is available only if the selected transaction includes a transfer.
- **Go To Specific Date** enables you to move to a different date within the register. This does not affect the currently selected transaction.
- **Cancel Payment** (not shown) sends a cancel payment instruction to your bank to stop an online payment. This option is available only for online payments that have not yet been made.
- **View As A Check** displays the selected transaction as a check in the Write Checks dialog. You can then easily print the transaction or make any other changes.
- **Amount Spent On <category>** will display a Category Report for this category if your cursor is in the category field in the selected transaction. If your cursor is in the payee field, the report will be Payments Made To <payee name>.

- **Utilities:Gas & Electric Budget** displays budget information about the selected category, if your cursor is in the category field.
- **Launch Mini-Report For** displays a small report window of the current payee's or category's transactions. The option that appears depends on the field that is selected when you display the menu.
- **Use Calculator** (not shown) opens the Quicken calculator. This option is available if your cursor is in a field other than the category or payee fields.

Selecting More Than One Transaction   You may need to work with more than one transaction at a time. To do this, you need to select multiple transactions. Here's how:

- To select several individual transactions in an account register, hold down CTRL and click each transaction you want to include. The transactions change color to indicate they are selected.
- To select a range of transactions, click to select the first transaction in the range. Then hold down SHIFT and click the last transaction in the range. All transactions between the first and the last transaction change color to indicate they have been selected.

It may be helpful to sort the register first to get the transactions you wish to select grouped together.

Quicken's Other Account Features

If you have ever spent several hours (or even days) looking for an invoice that contained a guarantee, Quicken's attachment feature is for you. You can add notes, flags, reminders, and image files to any transaction in your account. This makes it possible to store all kinds of digital information in your Quicken data file, including cancelled checks, receipts, or photographs.

If there's such a thing as a "Paperwork Reduction Act," then why do we seem to keep accumulating more and more paper? Bank statements, canceled checks, receipts…it never seems to end. But somehow, the moment we throw away an important tax-related document, that's the day we'll get a letter from the county, asking to see it.

That's where Quicken's electronic image attachment feature can help. If you have a scanner, you can digitize important papers and attach their image files to the transactions or accounts they relate to. Then, when you need to consult the document, you can quickly and easily find it in Quicken and view it on-screen. You can even print a copy with the click of a button! Sure beats dealing with file boxes.

Adding Notes, Flags, and Alerts

You can add a note, color-coded flag, or follow-up alert—or all three—to any Quicken transaction. First, select the transaction you want to add the item to. Then click the More Actions button, and from the menu, click Notes And Flags to open the Transaction Notes And Flags dialog seen here. You can also use the small flag or paper clip icons beneath or to the left of the date on a register line.

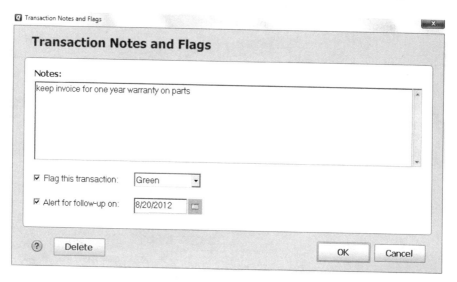

- To add a note, type the text of the note into the Notes box. This adds a flag icon to the transaction beneath the date. Pointing to the icon displays the note in a screen tip box.
- To flag the transaction, click the Flag This Transaction check box. Then choose a color from the drop-down list. This colors the flag icon placed above.
- To create a follow-up alert, turn on the Alert For Follow-Up On check box and enter a date in the box beside it. (You can add a follow-up alert only if the transaction is already flagged.) This adds an alert to the Alerts Center window, which is discussed in Chapter 6.

Click OK to save your settings.

Attaching Checks, Receipts, or Other Images

Quicken also enables you to attach image files from a file on disk, a scanner, or the clipboard to transactions or accounts. You can use this feature to file digital copies of important documents with the transactions or accounts they relate to.

Attaching Images to Transactions

You attach an image to a transaction in the account register window. Begin by selecting the transaction you want to attach the item to. Then click the More Actions button and select Attachments.

In the Transaction Attachments dialog that appears (see Figure 4-6), use the Attach New or Attach Another drop-down list to choose the type of attachment you want to add: Check, Receipt/Bill, Invoice, Warranty, or Other. Then click one of the Image From buttons:

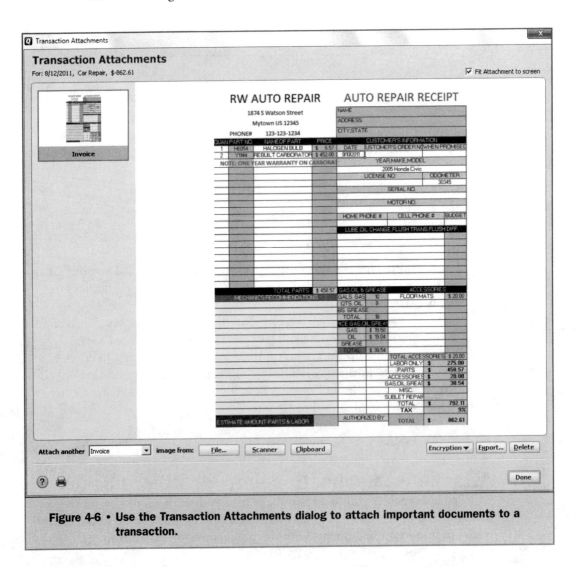

Figure 4-6 • Use the Transaction Attachments dialog to attach important documents to a transaction.

- **File** displays the Select Attachment File dialog, which you can use to locate, select, and open a file on disk. The file must be in a format readable by Internet Explorer, such as JPG, GIF, TXT, HTML, PDF, or PNG. When you click Open, the file's content appears in the Transaction Attachments dialog.
- **Scanner** may display the Select Source dialog, which you can use to select your scanner. It then displays your scanner's standard scanning interface, which you can use to scan an image. When the scan is complete, the image appears in the Transaction Attachments dialog.
- **Clipboard** pastes the contents of the clipboard into the Transaction Attachments dialog. (To use this option, you should select and copy an image before opening the Transaction Attachments dialog.)

Quicken allows you to add as many attachments as you like to a transaction. To add other attachments, just repeat the process. When you're finished, click Done to close the Transaction Attachments dialog. An Attachment icon appears beneath the transaction date to indicate that items are attached.

Working with Attachments

Once a file has been attached to a transaction, you can view, remove, replace, or print it at any time.

To work with a transaction attachment, click the More Actions icon for the transaction and select Attachments. The Transaction Attachments dialog (refer to Figure 4-6) opens. Click the thumbnail image or icon for the attached item to work with it.

You can use buttons in the Transaction Attachments dialog to work with attachments:

- **Help** (which appears as a question mark) displays the Quicken Personal Finances Help window, with links to topics about attaching digital images to transactions and accounts. Click a link to view the help information.
- **Print** (which appears as a small printer icon) prints the attachment.
- **Encryption** opens an option from which you can encrypt your attachment.
- **Export** saves the attachment as a file on your disk.
- **Delete** removes the attachment.
- **Done** closes the dialog.

Using Online Banking Features

Chapter 5

In This Chapter:

- *Understanding Transaction Download*
- *Introducing Online Payment and Quicken Bill Pay*
- *Reviewing security*
- *Setting up Online Account Services*
- *Using the Online Center window*
- *Downloading transactions*
- *Making online payments*
- *Transferring money between accounts*
- *Exchanging e-mail with your financial institution*

Life can be pretty hectic sometimes—too hectic to keep track of your bank accounts, pay bills before they're overdue, and buy stamps to mail those bills. Quicken Personal Finance Software's Online Account Services enable you to do most (if not all) of your banking from the comfort of your own home so banking can be a lot less of a chore. Several features can be used separately or together:

- **Transaction Download** enables you to download bank and credit card account activity, and transfer money online between accounts.
- **Online Payment** enables you to pay bills online without manually writing or mailing a check. (Quicken Bill Pay offers the features of Online Payment, even if your bank does not support it.)

This chapter explains how these features work and how you can use them to save time while keeping track of your finances.

The instructions in this chapter assume that you have already configured Quicken for an Internet connection. If you have not done so, do it now. This chapter also assumes that you understand the topics and procedures discussed in Chapters 3 and 4. This chapter builds on many of the basic concepts discussed in those chapters.

Just a reminder: Quicken does not handle the characters &, <, or > as part of a password.

Online Account Services

Here's a closer look at Quicken's Online Account Services, including what the services are, how they work, and how you can expect to benefit from them.

Understanding Transaction Download

Quicken's Transaction Download feature can perform several tasks, depending on your financial institution. Generally speaking, financial institutions can support Transaction Download three ways. You can quickly determine which method is used for a specific account. Press CTRL-A to open your Account List. The type of connection for each account is listed in the Transaction Download column of the list. If you do not see the Transaction Download column in your Account List, click Options | Show Transaction Download Status.

Direct Connect

Many financial institutions support direct communication between Quicken and the financial institution's server. This so-called Direct Connect method is the most powerful way to use the Transaction Download feature. To download transactions, you simply click a button in Quicken's Online Center window, provide brief instructions and a personal identification number (PIN), and wait while Quicken gets the information you want. At the same time, Quicken can send information such as payment or transfer instructions to your bank for processing. In this two-way communication, Quicken does all the work. Some institutions charge additional fees for using Direct Connect.

Since all of your financial information is stored on servers controlled by your financial institution, consider using the Quicken Password Vault to safely store your passwords. See Chapter 6 for more information about the Password Vault.

Express Web Connect

If a financial institution does not support Direct Connect but does support the download of transactions from its website, it may support a download method called Express Web Connect. This one-way communication downloads transactions directly into Quicken without requiring you to manually visit the financial institution's website.

Using this type of connection, your data is downloaded by Quicken and stored on one of their servers. (Usually, Quicken logs in and retrieves your information outside of business hours.) All of your login information as well as your data is stored on the Quicken server until you retrieve it via downloading of your transactions. At the time of this writing, no banks are charging you, the customer, for this type of connection.

If you're already using Quicken with Web Connect and your financial institution supports Express Web Connect, Quicken may prompt you to convert the download method to Express Web Connect. While Express Web Connect may simplify the downloading of transactions from your financial institution to your Quicken data file, some users have reported a delay in transaction dates, depending on when the transactions are downloaded by your financial institution.

Web Connect

Many financial institutions that don't support Direct Connect or Express Web Connect enable you to manually download specially formatted Web Connect files. To do this, you must log in to your financial institution's website using the information your financial institution supplies, navigate to a download page, and indicate what data you want to download. Once the Web Connect file has been downloaded, you may have to use File | File Import | Web Connect File to load your transactions into your register. If you have more than one account that uses Web Connect, consider downloading one account at a time the first time you download, if your financial institution allows it. This way you won't inadvertently import the wrong account's information into your register.

One important feature of Web Connect is you may be able to download a greater range of transactions by date than you can with Direct Connect and Express Web Connect. This may be helpful when you are first setting up your accounts so you can get the longest transaction history possible.

Downloaded Transactions

Bank account transaction downloads include all deposits, checks, interest payments, bank fees, transfers, ATM transactions, and debit card transactions that have been recorded by the bank. Credit card transaction downloads include all charges, credits (for returns or adjustments), payments, fees, and finance charges that have been recorded to your account. Quicken displays all of the transactions, including those you have not yet entered in your account register, as well as the current balance of the account. A few clicks and keystrokes is all it takes to enter the transactions you missed. This feature makes it virtually impossible to omit entries, while telling you exactly how much money is available in a bank account or how much money you owe on your credit card account—no more surprises in that monthly statement.

Additional Direct Connect Features

If your financial institution supports Direct Connect, you may also be able to take advantage of the following two features.

Transfer Money Between Accounts   If you have more than one bank account at the same financial institution, you can use Direct Connect to transfer money between accounts. Although many banks offer this feature by phone or on their websites, initiating the transaction from within Quicken is quicker and easier, and has the added benefit of entering it into your Quicken data file. Just enter a transfer transaction and let Quicken do the rest.

Send E-mail Messages to Your Financial Institution   Ever call the customer service center at your bank or credit card company to ask a question? If you're lucky, real people are waiting to answer the phone. But if you're like most people, your financial institution uses a call routing system that requires you to listen to voice prompts and press telephone keypad keys to communicate with a machine. Either way, when a real person gets on the line, you have to provide all kinds of information about yourself just to prove that you are who you say you are. Then you can ask your question. Some financial institutions offer an e-mail feature that's part of Direct Connect that enables you to exchange e-mail messages with your bank or credit card company's customer service department. You normally get a response within one business day.

Introducing Online Payment and Quicken Bill Pay

Online Payment enables you to send a check to anyone without physically writing, printing, or mailing a check. You enter and store information about the payee within Quicken. You then create a transaction for the payee that includes the payment date and amount. You can enter the transaction weeks or months in advance if desired—the payee receives payment on the date you specify.

Online Payment is one of the least understood Quicken features. Many folks think it can be used to pay only big companies like the phone company or credit card companies. That just isn't true. You can use Online Payment to pay any bill, contribute to your retirement account, donate money to a charity, or send your brother a birthday gift.

Explaining the Process

Suppose you use Quicken to send online payment instructions to pay your monthly bill at Jim's Hardware Store. You've already set up Jim's as a payee by entering the name, address, and phone number of his store, as well as your account number there. Quicken sends your payment instructions to your bank, which stores it in its computer with a bunch of other online payment instructions. When the payment date nears, the bank's computer looks through its big database of payees that it can pay by wire transfer. It sees phone companies and credit card companies and other banks. But because Jim's store is small, it's probably not one of the wire transfer payees. So the bank's computer prepares a check using all the information you provided. It mails the check along with thousands of others due to be paid that day.

Jim's wife, who does the accounting for the store (with Quicken Home & Business, in case you're wondering), gets the check a few days later. She deposits it with the other checks she gets that day. The amount of the check is deducted from your bank account and your account balance at Jim's. If you use Transaction Download, the check appears as a transaction. It also appears on your bank statement. If your bank returns canceled checks to you, you may get the check along with all your others.

The date the money is actually withdrawn from your account to cover the payment varies depending on your bank. There are four possibilities:

- One to four days before the payment is processed for delivery
- The day the payment is processed for delivery
- The day the payment is delivered
- The day the paper check or electronic funds transfer clears your bank

To find out when funds are withdrawn from your account for online payments, ask your bank. You might also want to search the Quicken Live Community to see the experiences other Quicken users have had with that financial institution.

Not all personnel at a given financial institution may know the answers to your questions. Try to talk to an online banking specialist if at all possible.

The Benefits of Online Payment

Online Payment can benefit you in several ways. You can pay your bills as they arrive, without paying them early—the payee normally doesn't receive payment before the payment date you specify. You don't have to buy stamps, and the bank never forgets to mail the checks.

Quicken Bill Pay

If your bank does not support Online Payment, you can still take advantage of this feature by signing up for Quicken Bill Pay. This fee-based service works with your checking account like Online Payment does.

Costs

The cost of Quicken's Online Account Services varies from bank to bank. Check with your bank to determine the exact fees. Here's what you can expect:

- **Transaction Download** is often free to all customers or to customers who maintain a certain minimum account balance. Otherwise, you could pay a fee for this service. The fee varies, reportedly around $3 per month, and is set by the financial institution.
- **Online Payment** is sometimes free, but more often it costs from $5 to $10 per month for 20 to 25 payments per month. Each additional payment usually costs 40¢ to 60¢. Again, some banks waive this fee if you maintain a certain minimum balance.
- **Quicken Bill Pay** is $9.95 for up to 20 payments and $2.49 for each set of five payments after that. (These prices are subject to change.) To learn more about and apply for Quicken Bill Pay, choose the Tips & Tutorials tab, and click Quicken Services. After reading the information about Quicken Bill Pay that appears in your browser window, click the 1 Month Free, Start Now! button to begin the process. Otherwise, click Close to return to Quicken.

Reviewing Security

If you're worried about security, you must have skipped over the security information in Chapter 2. Go back and read that now. It explains how Quicken and your financial institution's security policies work to make Online Account Services safe.

Setting Up Online Account Services

To use the Online Account Services supported by Quicken, you must configure the appropriate Quicken accounts. This requires that you enter information about your financial institution and the account with which you want to use these features.

Applying for Online Account Services

Before you can use one of the Online Account Services, you must apply for it—learn how at the end of Chapter 2. Normally, all it takes is a phone call, although some banks and credit card companies allow you to apply online.

The application process for these services usually takes a week, but may take less. You'll know that you're ready to go online when you get a letter with setup information. The setup information usually consists of the following.

PIN (Personal Identification Number) You'll have to enter this code into Quicken when you access your account online. This is a security feature, so don't write down your PIN on a sticky note and attach it to your computer monitor. Many financial institutions send this information separately for additional security.

Customer ID Number This is often your Social Security number or taxpayer identification number.

Bank Routing Number Although your bank might send routing number information, Quicken won't need it. It knows what financial institution you're using based on the information you provide when you create the account. That's why it's so important to choose the correct financial institution when you create an account. You may see the routing information received by Quicken in the Routing Number field in the General tab of the Account Details dialog.

Account Number for Each Online Access–Enabled Account This tells your financial institution which account you want to work with. In many instances, Quicken may not need this information either. However, depending on your financial institution, the account number may appear in the Account Number field of the General tab of the Account Details dialog.

Getting Started with Online Account Services

With customer ID and PIN in hand, you're ready to set up your account (or accounts) for Online Account Services. You can set up the account in a number of ways; rather than cover them all, this section covers the most straightforward method.

Keep in mind that if you set up an account using the online method, as discussed in Chapter 3, and you already have Online Account Access enabled at your bank, your account is set up for online access. You can verify this by following the instructions in the "Checking Online Account Service Status" section, later in this chapter.

Some companies, such as department stores, that offer online access on their webpages may not have the capability of downloading your transactions into Quicken.

Setting Up for Direct Connect, Express Web Connect, and Quicken Bill Pay

If you entered the account manually, in the Account Bar, click the account you want to set up to open its register. Click Account Actions | Set Up Online, as shown here. If the account is already set up for online access, the Account Action menu will show Update Now instead of Set Up Online.

Follow the directions in Chapter 3 to set up this account with online services.

When logging in to your financial institution, you may have to physically place the cursor each time so that it is in the password/security question field if there are multiple security questions.

Checking Online Account Service Status

You can confirm that an account has been set up for Online Account Services and determine what kind of connection it uses.

Open the Account List by pressing CTRL-A or by clicking the small gear icon on the Account Bar. Each account will display the type of connection, as shown next.

Account Name		Transaction Download ⑦	Online Bill Pay ⑦	Last Reconcile
Spending				
House Checking 🖹	Edit	Yes (Express Web Connect)	No (Activate Bill Pay)	8/3/2011
Main Checking 🖹	Edit	Yes (Direct Connect)	Yes Direct Connect Bill Pay)	6/30/2011
Fun Checking 🖹	Edit	Yes (Express Web Connect)	No (Activate Bill Pay)	8/2/2011

If the Activate Download link appears for an account, you can click the link to set up online services with the Add Account dialog. You can also select the account and click Edit to open the Account Details dialog. Click the Online Services tab. As explained in Chapter 4, you can use this dialog to activate or remove this account from online services.

Some banks use different passwords for Direct Connect services than for Web Connect or Express Web Connect.

More About Transaction Download

Quicken makes a distinction between two types of downloaded transactions:

- **Online transaction instructions** are those transactions that have been sent to your financial institution but have not yet cleared your account. For example, suppose you used your bank's website to pay one of your bills. This transaction is in your bank's computer server, but it hasn't been completed or cleared. After the bill has been paid, when you download transactions for that account, Quicken downloads the payment.
- **Cleared transactions** are those transactions that have cleared your account and are included in your current account balance. For example, suppose you made a deposit at the bank. As soon as the bank accepts the deposit, the deposit is said to have "cleared" and is included in your current bank account balance. Cleared transactions can include deposits, checks, online payments, ATM transactions, debit card transactions, bank or interest fees, and interest earnings.

If you have recently installed a new antivirus program and are experiencing trouble downloading your data, check the settings on the antivirus program to ensure that the program allows such activity.

By default, your downloaded transactions are listed so that you can review and accept them before they have been entered into your register. If you want all downloaded transactions to be loaded into your register automatically, click Edit | Preferences | Downloaded Transactions | Downloaded Transaction Preferences | After Downloading Transactions, and select the Automatically Add To Banking Registers check box.

The Online Center

While you can access online services from several of the various tabs, you can also use the Online Center to work with Quicken's online features. This window gives you access to all the lists and commands you need to download transactions, and, if you have Direct Connect, to create payments, transfer money, and exchange e-mail with your financial institution.

Using the Online Center Window

To open the Online Center window, choose Tools | Online Center. Figure 5-1 shows what the Payments tab of this window looks like with one financial institution selected.

A number of buttons and menus enable you to work with the window's contents:

- **Delete** removes the selected item. This button is not available in all tabs of the Online Center window.
- **Payees** (if you have set up online payments) displays the Online Payee List window, which is discussed later in this chapter in the section titled "Entering Online Payee Information."
- **Repeating** (if you have set up online payments) displays the Repeating Online tab of the Bill and Income Reminders list window. Learn more about using this feature later in this chapter, in the section titled "Scheduling Repeating Online Payments."
- **Contact Info** displays the Contact Information dialog for the currently selected financial institution, if it is offered. You can use the information in the dialog to contact the bank or credit card company by phone, website, or e-mail. Not all financial institutions have these options.
- **Password Vault** gives you access to Quicken's Password Vault feature, which is discussed in Chapter 6. (This option may appear only if you have online banking features enabled for accounts at more than one financial institution.)

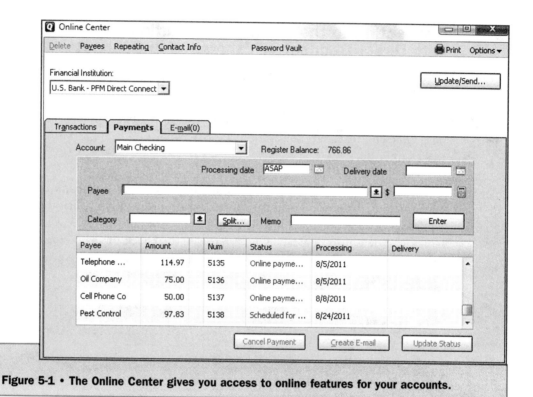

Figure 5-1 • The Online Center gives you access to online features for your accounts.

- **Print** prints the transactions that appear in the Payments tab window.
- **Options** displays a menu of commands for working with the current account or window.

Downloading Transactions

One of the main features of Online Account Services is the ability to download transactions from your financial institution into Quicken. There are several ways to start downloading your transactions after you have set up your online accounts:

- Use the Update/Send button of the Online Center window (refer to Figure 5-1).
- Click the blue right-curling arrow, as seen here, at the top of the Account Bar.
- Click the One Step Update arrow on the Quicken Toolbar.
- From an account's register, click Account Actions and choose Update Now.

Connecting to the Financial Institution with Direct Connect or Express Web Connect

If your financial institution supports Direct Connect or Express Web Connect, you can download all transactions from within Quicken.

If you ever have to restore a Quicken account from a backup, you may have to deactivate and reactivate the account. See "Deactivating Online Services" later in this chapter.

Using the Online Center window, choose the name of your bank or credit card company from the Financial Institution drop-down list. Click the Update/Send button. The One Step Update Settings dialog for that institution, which is shown next, appears. Click to toggle the check marks beside any instructions that appear, enter your password, and click Update Now.

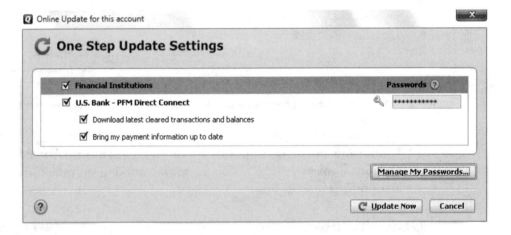

Quicken may display a dialog offering to save your passwords. If you click Yes, follow the instructions in Chapter 6 to set up the Password Vault feature. You may then need to reinitiate the download procedure.

Wait while Quicken connects to your bank. A status dialog appears while it works. When Quicken has finished exchanging information, the status dialog disappears and the One Step Update Summary window takes its place. Continue following the instructions later in the chapter, in the section titled "Comparing Downloaded Transactions to Register Transactions." Depending on your preference settings, you may only see the One Step Update Summary window if there is an error in the online session.

If you have chosen One Step Update by using the blue right-curling arrow, you will see a list of all of your accounts that have been activated for online services. You may choose to download transactions from one or all of them by entering your password(s).

Downloading a Web Connect File

If your financial institution supports Web Connect but not Express Web Connect, you'll have to log in to your financial institution's website and manually download the statement information, just as you did when you first set up the account for Online Account Services.

In the Online Center window, choose the name of your bank or credit card company from the Financial Institution drop-down list. If necessary, click the Update/Send button. Quicken connects to the Internet and displays your financial institution's login page. Log in, navigate to the page where you can download statements, and download the statement or transactions you want. If necessary, switch back to Quicken. It should automatically import the transactions you downloaded into the correct account. If you have chosen to automatically accept your downloaded transactions, you will see a small blue ball icon at the left of each of the downloaded transactions in your account register. Transactions that have been matched to scheduled transactions have a calendar icon in the same location.

If Express Web Connect or Direct Connect is available for an account, you may see a dialog offering to upgrade your connection.

IN MY EXPERIENCE

As explained in Chapter 3, it is not uncommon to set up accounts in Quicken and decide later to activate online services for these accounts. The first time transactions are downloaded into a Quicken file in which accounts have been set up, the user is prompted to either add the downloaded transactions into a new account or link to an existing account. An example of this is seen in Figure 5-2.

If the user links to an incorrect account, transactions may be downloaded into the wrong account. If you have not accepted the transactions into the incorrect account, simply delete the downloaded transactions. Then, download the information into the correct account. If you have accepted the transactions and they are in the register of the wrong account, you can move them into the correct account.

The best way to solve this issue is by deactivating online services for both accounts, moving any transactions that are in the wrong account into the correct account, and then reactivating the online service for both accounts. See "Deactivating Online Services" and "Moving Transactions" later in this chapter. However, before making any changes, back up your Quicken data, "just in case."

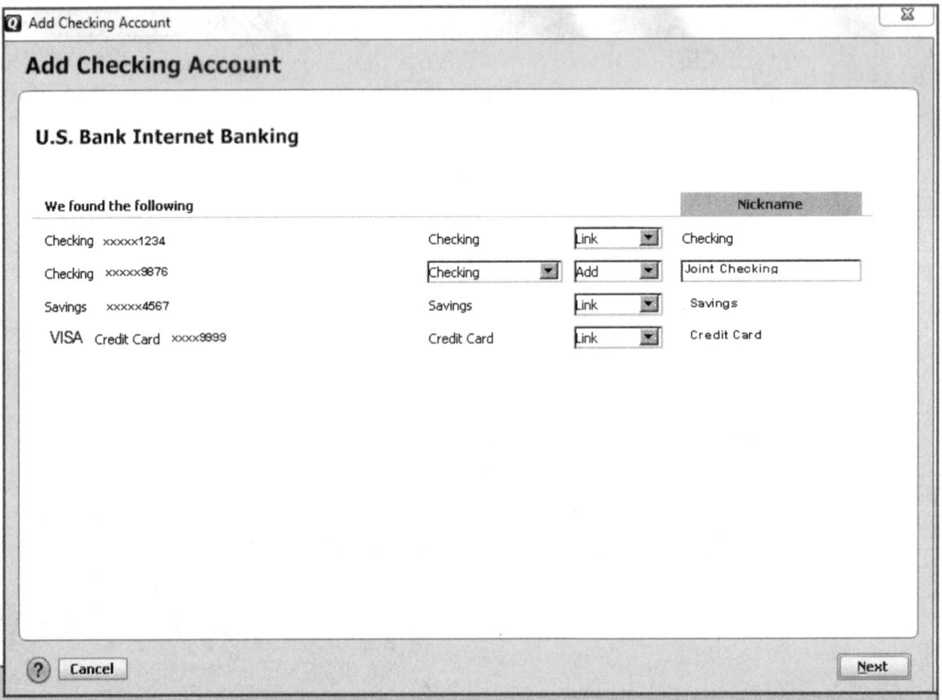

Figure 5-2 • Ensure you link to the proper account when downloading for the first time.

Click the Close button in the One Step Update Summary window to dismiss it. Then, click that account's name in the Account Bar to open the register for that account.

Unless you have chosen to turn on the Automatically Add To Banking Register preference, your downloaded transactions will appear in the Downloaded Transactions tab at the bottom of the register window. From there, you can use the directions in "Comparing Downloaded Transactions to Register Transactions."

Keep in mind that the first time you connect via Direct Connect, the bank normally sends all transactions from the past 60 or more days. (Some banks send a full year of transactions!) After that, only new transactions (items that have not been downloaded) will be downloaded. For Web Connect downloads, you can often specify the transaction period when you set up the download.

Deactivating Online Services

To deactivate (or disable) an account from online services:

1. From the Account Bar, right-click the account's name to display the context menu.
2. Choose Edit/Delete Account to open the Account Details dialog.
3. Click the Online Services tab.
4. Click Deactivate. (If you currently have unaccepted transactions, you must either accept the transactions or delete them before you can deactivate online services.) A message appears asking if you would like to deactivate the service. Click Yes to complete the deactivation.
5. A connection message box briefly appears while the service is deactivated.
6. Depending on the type of connection your financial institution offers, you may see a Remove Connection button. If so, click it.
7. Click OK to close the Account Details window and complete the deactivation.

Comparing Downloaded Transactions to Register Transactions

Your job is to compare the downloaded transactions to the transactions already entered in your account register. This enables you to identify transactions that you neglected to enter or that you entered incorrectly. In addition, because Quicken will automatically enter a date, transaction number, and amount—and in the case of some transactions, the payee and category (based on previously memorized transactions)—using this method to enter a transaction can be much faster than entering it manually in the account register window.

> **IN MY EXPERIENCE**
>
> If you have trouble downloading your transactions from a specific financial institution using either One Step Update or the Update Now command from the Account Actions menu in your account's register, there are two methods for resolving the issue. First, try deactivating that account and setting it up for online services again. If there is still a problem, go online to your bank's site and download the transactions manually. At the least, you'll discover if the problem is with your machine or originating at the bank.
>
> If the account is set up for Direct Connect or Express Web Connect, being able to successfully download from the financial institution's website does not necessarily eliminate that institution as the cause of the issue. Often Direct Connect and Express Web Connect use entirely different servers. Because the servers are different, it may be that the problem is with one of the server computers.

If you do not see the Downloaded Transactions tab at the bottom of your register as shown here, you may have told Quicken to automatically add downloaded transactions to the banking registers. To allow the tab to display, click Edit | Preferences | Downloaded Transactions | Downloaded Transaction Preferences | After Downloading Transactions, and clear the Automatically Add To Banking Registers check box.

The Status column in the bottom half of the account register window (refer to Figure 5-3) identifies three types of transactions:

- **Match** identifies transactions that match those in the register. This will happen if the transaction has already been entered in the Quicken register and has sufficiently close values, such as a slightly different date.
- **New** identifies transactions that are not in the register, or that are in the register but are different from the downloaded transactions. Maybe you transposed a number or the date is different. You would need to manually match these transactions so you do not get duplicates.
- **Accepted** identifies matched transactions that you have accepted. When a downloaded transaction has been accepted, a small "c" appears in the Clr column of the account register to indicate that the item has cleared the bank but has not yet been reconciled.

When you select a transaction in the bottom half of the window, the transactions below it shift down to make room for a blank line with an Accept button and an Edit menu. You can use these to work with the selected transaction.

Status	Date ▲	Num	Payee	Payment	Deposit
New	6/3/2011		Dda Inclearing Chk 57415	125.00	
New	6/5/2011		Interest Deposit		0.42
New	6/6/2011		Dda Inclearing Chk 57414	32.72	
New	6/6/2011		Dda Inclearing Chk 57413	75.00	
New	6/6/2011		Dda Regular Check 57417	1,338.88	
New	6/6/2011		Regular Deposit		1,500.00

Accept cleared transactions into register

Renaming Rules   Hide Accepted   Accept All   Accept   Finish Later

To Do   Help

Figure 5-3 • Match and accept your downloaded transactions in the bottom half of the register window.

Accepting a Matched Transaction   If a transaction matches one in the register, you can accept it by selecting it in the list at the bottom of the window and clicking the Accept button.

Entering and Accepting a New Transaction   To enter and accept a new transaction, select the transaction in the bottom half of the window. If the information on the transaction is complete and correct, click Accept. If you have entered the transaction in the register (the top half of the window), fill in any missing details, including the payee, category, and memo. Then click Save in the top half of the window or Accept in the bottom half. Quicken enters the transaction, if necessary, and marks it as Accepted.

Unmatching a Matched Transaction   If a matched transaction really shouldn't be matched, select it in the bottom half of the window and choose Unmatch from the Edit pop-up menu.

- **Unmatch** tells Quicken that it got the match wrong, but this command lets Quicken attempt to match it to another transaction. As a result, it may come up with another match. It's your job to determine whether the new match is correct. If it can't find a match, the status changes to New.
- **Make New** tells Quicken that the transaction shouldn't match any existing transaction. The status changes to New, and Quicken can then treat it as a new transaction.
- **Make All New** tells Quicken to make all of the downloaded but not yet accepted transactions new so you can manually match them.

Manually Matching a Transaction   If a downloaded transaction identified as New should match one in the register, or if a single transaction corresponds to multiple transactions in your account register, you can manually match them up. In the bottom half of the window, select the transaction that you want to match manually, and click the Edit button. Click Match Manually to open the Manually Match Transactions dialog. Turn on the check box(es) for the transaction(s) you want to include in the match. When you click Accept, Quicken creates an entry for the transaction.

If the transaction included multiple register transactions, the entry Quicken creates includes each of the register transactions on a separate split line. You can click the Split button for the transaction to edit it as desired. See Chapter 4 to review working with split transactions.

If you see a transaction that displays as "New" but you're sure you've entered it, check for small discrepancies, perhaps in the amount. You can force a manual match, or simply correct the item you've entered into your register and the item status will change to Match.

If you choose to have Quicken add your downloaded transactions into your banking register, you can still manually match a transaction. Register transactions that have not been matched with a downloaded transaction have a small icon, perhaps a pencil or a calendar near them. In a two-line register the icon appears beneath the transaction. If you use a one-line register, this icon appears to the left of the date. Click the icon and choose Match To A Downloaded Transaction.

You can also use the matching process on a transaction that Quicken fails to match correctly, or just use the manual matching process before the unmatching process. If there is a small error between you and the bank, you are prompted to accept one or the other, as seen in Figure 5-4, or correct your register.

Deleting a New Transaction   To delete any transaction, select it in the bottom half of the account register window, click Edit, and choose Delete from the Edit pop-up menu. A confirmation dialog appears; click Yes to remove the transaction from the list.

Sometimes the matching issue can be resolved, especially when reconciling an account, by choosing to display the Downloaded Posting Date column in your register, as seen here. Display this field in your register by choosing Account Actions | Register Columns | Downloaded Posting Date. Since reconciliations are date-driven, the posting date may be after the cutoff date of the reconciliation.

Date ▲	Posting Date
▶ ▣ 🖉	
5/31/2011	
6/6/2011	6/9/2011

Moving Transactions   If you have several accounts at the same bank and inadvertently accept transactions into the incorrect account, you can move either a single or multiple transactions.

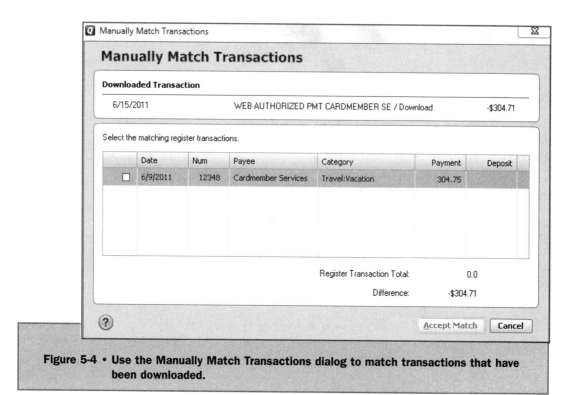

Figure 5-4 • Use the Manually Match Transactions dialog to match transactions that have been downloaded.

1. To move a single transaction, right-click the transaction. Choose Move Transaction(s) from the context menu.
2. The Move Transaction(s) dialog box appears. Choose the account into which you want to move the transaction from the drop-down list, as shown next.
3. Click OK.

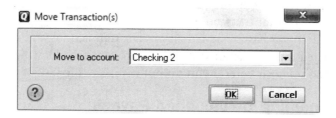

To move multiple transactions in a group in your register:

1. Click the first transaction to highlight it.

2. Hold down your SHIFT key and, while still holding it, click the last transaction in the group. All of the transactions will be selected. Release the SHIFT key.
3. Right-click in the highlighted area, and from the context menu, choose Move Transaction(s).
4. The Move Transaction(s) dialog box appears. Choose the account into which you want to move the transaction from the drop-down list.
5. Click OK.

To select multiple transactions that are scattered throughout your register:

1. Click the first transaction to highlight it.
2. Hold down your CTRL key and, while still holding it, click each transaction you want to move. All of the selected transactions will be highlighted. Release the CTRL key.
3. Right-click in the highlighted area, and from the context menu, choose Move Transaction(s).
4. The Move Transaction(s) dialog box appears. Choose the account into which you want to move the transaction from the drop-down list.
5. Click OK.

In each case, the transactions will be moved to the account you designated.

Accepting All Downloaded Transactions   The Accept All button accepts all transactions into your account register without reviewing them one by one. Keep in mind that some transactions may not be properly categorized, and some transactions may be matched to the wrong transaction, making it appear as if the downloaded transaction disappeared. Most Quicken users don't use Accept All without first examining each downloaded transaction to ensure it matched to the proper register transaction.

After you have reviewed all of your transactions and accepted, matched, and deleted the transactions, click Done to close the Downloaded Transactions tab. Choose Finish Later if you cannot complete the task at one sitting.

Renaming Downloaded Payees

One of the potentially annoying things about entering transactions by accepting downloaded activity information is the way your bank identifies payees. For example, one bank identifies the payee for a cable television company as "NationalCableofAmerica{026-144710}" instead of plain old "CableAmerica."

Fortunately, Quicken's Renaming Rules feature can automatically rename bank-assigned payee names with names you prefer.

You can also create and apply your own renaming rules. You do this with the Renaming Rules dialog, which is shown here.

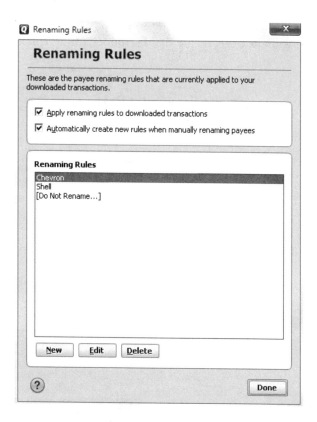

To open this dialog, click the Renaming Rules button at the bottom of the Downloaded Transactions tab of the register window, or choose Tools | Renaming Rules. The dialog lists all the renaming rules that have already been created. At the top of the dialog are options enabling the Renaming Rules feature and letting Quicken automatically create renaming rules for you. These are turned on by default, and most Quicken users opt to leave them turned on.

You can use buttons at the bottom of the list to add, modify, or remove renaming rules.

New   Clicking the New button displays the Create Renaming Rule dialog. Enter the name you want to see as the payee name in the Change Payee box.

Then choose an option from the first drop-down list to determine which field Quicken should match, choose a match option from the middle drop-down list, and enter match text in the text box. For example, if we wanted to change every downloaded item containing the text QuickFuel to Quick Stop Fuel, we'd set the dialog as shown here. You can click the Add New Item button to add another line of matching criteria; doing so tells Quicken to match any criteria you enter. When you click OK in the dialog, the renaming rule is added to the list.

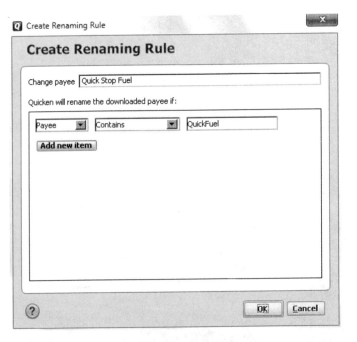

Edit   Clicking the Edit button displays the Edit Renaming Rule dialog, which looks and works just like the Create Renaming Rule dialog just shown. This dialog enables you to modify settings for the selected renaming rule.

Delete   Clicking the Delete button removes the selected renaming rule from the list.

IN MY EXPERIENCE

One of the reasons to download your transactions is to eliminate the need to enter all of your checks into your register. However, some banks do not include check numbers or payees in their downloaded transactions, as seen next. For these accounts you might consider entering your checks so that you only need to match them to the downloaded item. Otherwise, if you have a lot of transactions, it may take a bit of time to enter the information for each downloaded item. You can cut down on your data entry time by using scheduled reminders and memorized payees.

You'll have to click OK in the confirmation dialog that appears to remove the rule.

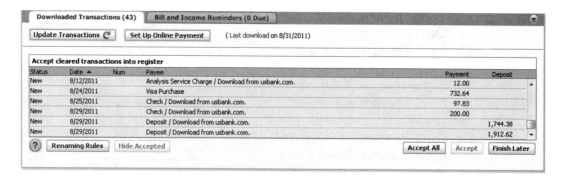

Making Online Payments

Paying your bills from within Quicken is one of the ways that Quicken can save you time. If your bank supports Online Bill Pay, this may be the best choice for you. This section explains how to set up online payees, enter payment information for one-time and repeating payments, and work with payment instructions.

Entering Online Payee Information

To send payments from your account, your bank must know who and where each payee is. To ensure that your account with the payee is properly credited, you must also provide account information. You do this by setting up online payees:

- From the Tools menu, click Online Center to open the Online Center dialog. Click Payees to open the Online Payee List. You can also choose Online Payee List from the Tools menu to open the list.
- Financial Institution offers a drop-down list of all the institutions for which you have enabled Online Bill Pay. Choose the institution that has the account from which you will be paying this payee. The payees you have added for the displayed institution are listed, showing the payee name, the lead time for this payee, and the account number. Some financial institutions do not provide the lead time for online bill payments.
- New opens the Set Up Online Payee dialog, shown on the next page.

- Enter the name of the online payee in the Name field and any description that might be needed in the optional Description field. 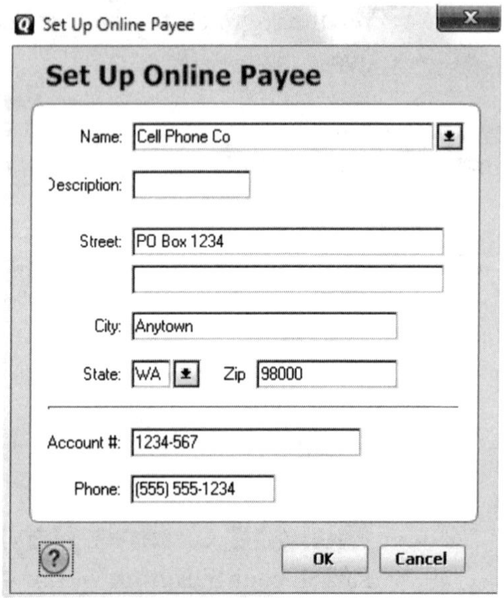
- Enter a mailing address, city, state, and ZIP code. If you skip over one of these required fields, Quicken will prompt you for the information.
- Enter an account number and phone number. Again, if you do not enter this information, you are prompted for it.
- Click OK when you have completed entering the information. The Confirm Online Payee Information

message appears displaying the information you just entered, as shown next. Check the information in this box carefully. If there is an error, your payment might not reach the payee, or it might not be properly credited to your account. Remember, your bank will not be sending a billing stub with the payment—just

the payment. When you're satisfied that the information is correct, click Accept. The new payee is added to Online Payee List. If the information is not correct, click Cancel and you are returned to the Online Payee dialog.

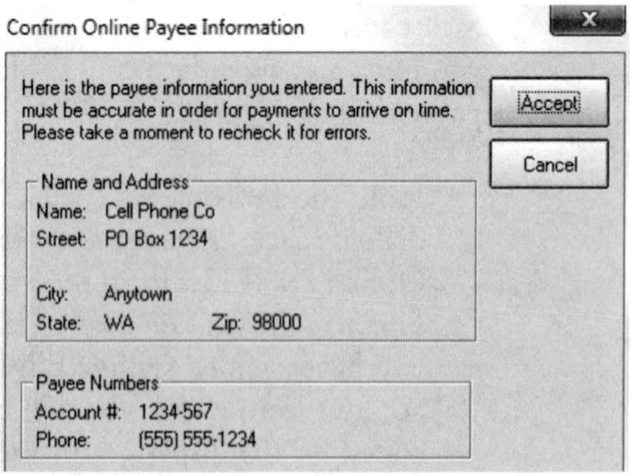

- Help (the small question mark in the yellow circle) opens the paying bills online section of Quicken Help.
- Print (the printer icon) prints a list of online payees.

When printing your list, you may see some of your information *truncated*, or cut off, if it is too long for the column. However, if you print to a tab-delimited text file, there is no truncation.

- Edit enables you to modify the information for the selected online payee. However, note that you cannot change the account number without deleting the payee and setting up a new payee.
- Use switches you back to the Payments tab of the Online Center window and inserts the selected payee into the payment form.
- Report displays a report of all payments made to the selected online payee.
- Delete removes the selected online payee. Deleting a payee simply deletes the payee's information from the Online Payee List window. It does not change any transactions for a payee. You cannot delete a payee for which unsent payment instructions exist.
- Done closes the Online Payee List.

Entering Payment Instructions

To enter additional online payment instructions, click Tools | Online Center | Payments, as seen in Figure 5-5. Ensure you are using the correct financial institution if you have more than one set up for online payments. Fill in the fields in the middle of the window with the following payment information:

- **Processing Date** is the date the bank should begin processing the payment. For some banks, this date is fixed based on the Delivery Date field and can't be changed.
- **Delivery Date** is the date you want the payee to receive payment. This should be before the date the bank will either create and mail the check or make the electronic funds transfer. The check may be received before the delivery date, depending on the mail (if the check is mailed). The date you enter, however, must be at least the same number of business days in advance as the lead time for the payee—usually four days. That means if you want to pay a bill on Wednesday, June 29, you must enter and send instructions to your bank on or before Friday, June 24. To process the payment as soon as possible, just enter today's date and Quicken will adjust the date for you. For some banks, the delivery date cannot be changed; instead, specify a processing date that allows enough time for the payment to be made on a timely basis.
- **Payee** is the online payee to receive payment. Quicken's QuickFill feature fills in the payee's name as you type it. If desired, you can choose it from the drop-down list of online payees. If you enter a payee that is not in the

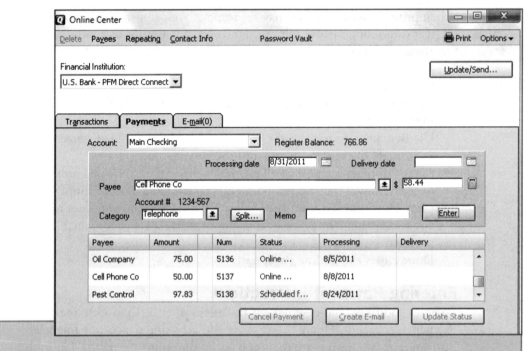

Figure 5-5 • Use the Payments tab in the Online Center window to enter information about online payments.

Online Payee List window, Quicken displays the Set Up Online Payee dialog so you can add the new payee's information. This enables you to create online payees as you enter payment instructions.

- **$** is the amount of the payment.

If you have set your Quicken Preferences to use the ENTER key when moving between fields, this process ignores your Preference setting and uses ENTER to ENTER the online payment.

- **Category** is the category for the transaction. You can enter a category, choose one from the drop-down list, or click the Split button to enter multiple categories.
- **Memo**, which is optional, is for entering a note about the transaction.

When you've finished entering information for the transaction, click ENTER. Depending on your financial institution, a message box may appear reminding you that you need to allow enough time for the payment to be processed by your financial institution. Click OK to continue or Cancel to return to the payment. Click the Don't Show This Message Again check box to keep the message from appearing.

The transaction appears in the list in the bottom half of the window with the words "Payment request ready to send" in the Status column beside it. You can repeat this process for as many payments as you want to make.

Entering Online Payments in the Account Register

Another way to enter an online payment instruction is to simply enter the transaction in the appropriate account register. Click the Bills tab, click Manage Reminders, and double-click the transaction on the list or click ENTER. The Enter Transaction dialog appears with SEND in the Method/Check Number field. Make any changes or additions in the dialog, and click Enter Transaction to enter it into the register. You may find this method quicker.

Payment and Delivery Dates

Don't let the Processing Date and Delivery Date options confuse you. The Delivery Date is the important date. It determines whether your payment will make it to the payee on time. Whenever possible, give the bank an extra few days. So, for example, if a bill is due on June 29, instruct the bank to pay on June 25. This isn't because of a lack of confidence in Quicken or the bank. It's because the Postal Service must still deliver the check.

If the Delivery Date field on your form can't be changed, don't panic. Just enter a processing date at least four days (or more) before the date you want the payment to arrive. That should give your bank enough time to get the payment to the payee without getting you in trouble.

Many banks do not accept online payment instructions on the day you want to send the payment. Call your bank to find out how much time they require for processing your online payment.

Scheduling Repeating Online Payments

Some payments are exactly the same every month, such as your rent, a car loan, or your monthly cable television bill. You can set these payments up as repeating online payments.

The process begins when you schedule the online payment once, indicating the payee, amount, and frequency. Quicken sends the instructions to your bank. Thirty days before the payment is due, your bank creates a new post-dated payment based on your instructions and notifies you that it has created the payment. Quicken automatically enters the payment information in your account register with the appropriate payment date. The payment is delivered on the payment date. This happens regularly, at the interval you specify, until you tell it to stop. Because you don't have to do a thing to continue paying regularly, the more payments you make with this feature, the more time you save.

(Using this feature to pay an amortized loan such as a mortgage works a little differently. Learn about it later in this chapter, in the section titled "Linking a Repeating Online Payment to an Amortized Loan.")

Set a Repeating Online Payment

Bill reminders are explained in depth in Chapter 6, so this section will cover only repeating online payments.

1. From the Bills tab, choose Add Reminders | Bill Reminder.
2. Enter the name of your payee in the Pay To field. Click Next.
3. In the Add Bill Reminder dialog, set the date, the amount, and the account from which you will be paying this bill, as shown next.

Be sure to choose an account in which you have activated Online Bill Pay in Step 3.

4. Enter a category, tag, or memo if necessary.
5. Click the Use Online Bill Pay check box.
6. Click Optional Settings if necessary to display your options. Click the Make This A Repeating Online Payment check box.

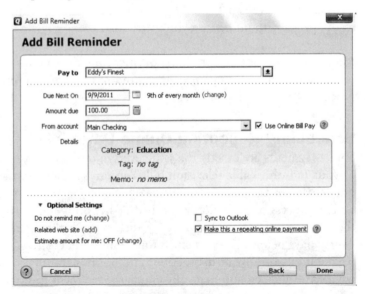

7. Click Done.

If this is a new online payee, you will be prompted to enter address and account number information so that your payment can be processed by your bank.

There are two very important things to remember when using the Add A Reminder dialog to create a repeating online payment:

- Click the Use Online Bill Pay check box to tell Quicken that the payment will be made online.
- Click the Make This A Repeating Online Payment check box. This tells Quicken to send one instruction for multiple repeating payments.

When you click Done to save the payment instruction, it appears in the Repeating Online tab of the Bill And Income Reminders list window, as seen next.

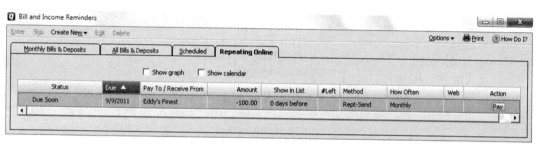

You can use the buttons at the top of the Bill And Income Reminders dialog to work with items listed in the Repeating Online list window:

- **Enter** records the selected repeating online payment in the register. Even if there is only one repeating online transaction in the Repeating Online list window and that transaction appears to be highlighted, if you have not clicked the transaction, Enter is grayed out.
- **Skip** skips payment of the selected repeating online payment. Even if there is only one repeating online transaction in the Repeating Online list window and that transaction appears to be highlighted, if you have not clicked the transaction, Skip is grayed out.
- **Create New** enables you to create a new scheduled transaction or paycheck. Learn more about this menu in Chapter 6.
- **Edit** displays the Edit Repeating Online dialog so you can modify the details of the repeating online payment. Even if there is only one repeating online transaction in the Repeating Online list window and that transaction appears

to be highlighted, if you have not clicked the transaction, Edit is grayed out. If you right-click the repeating online transaction, you can select Edit from the context menu.

- **Delete** removes the repeating online payment from the list, thus canceling future payments. You must click Delete in the confirmation dialog that appears to remove the transaction. Even if there is only one repeating online transaction in the Repeating Online list window and that transaction appears to be highlighted, if you have not clicked the transaction, Delete is grayed out. You can right-click the repeating online transaction and select Delete from the context menu.

- **Options** offers commands for changing the sort order of payments in the list; however, you may have to click the header of the column by which you want to sort to make it sort properly.

- **Print** prints a list of repeating online payments.

- **How Do I?** displays the Quicken Personal Finances Help window with instructions for managing your spending and completing tasks with the Bill And Income Reminders list.

Linking a Repeating Online Payment to an Amortized Loan

Repeating online payments are perfect for paying off loans. After all, loan payments are the same every month and must be paid by a certain date. You can set up a repeating online payment instruction, send it to your financial institution, and let Quicken and your bank make the payments automatically every month for you.

Set up the repeating online payment instruction for the loan payment as instructed in the earlier section "Scheduling Repeating Online Payments." Don't worry about all the categories that are part of a loan payment transaction. Just choose the loan account as the category. You don't even have to get the date or amount right. When you link the transaction to the loan, Quicken will make the necessary adjustments. Click Done to complete the instruction.

Press CTRL-SHIFT-H to display the Loans window. If necessary, choose the loan account's name from the Choose Loan menu in the button bar to display the information for the loan for which you want to use the payment instruction.

Click the Edit Payment button to display the Edit Loan Payment dialog. Then click the Payment Method button. In the Select Payment Method dialog, select Repeating Online Payment. Then choose the repeating online payment instruction you created from the Repeating Payment drop-down list.

Click OK in each dialog to dismiss it. Click Done at the View Loans dialog. Quicken links the loan payment to the repeating online payment instruction. It makes changes to the payment instruction, if necessary, to match the payment categories and split information. The next time you connect to your financial institution, the instruction will be sent and payments will begin.

Repeating Online Loan Payments

Setting up a loan payment as a repeating online payment has got to be one of the best time-saving features available in Quicken. It does all kinds of neat things for you.

First, it ensures that your loan payment is made regularly, on a timely basis, with no monthly effort on your part. Second, it automatically adjusts the balance of your loan principal account (a debt account) by accurately calculating interest and principal paid for every entry. (You know these amounts change every month, right? Can you imagine doing the entries manually? Egads!) And since the loan account balance is updated with every payment, your net worth is always up to date.

Just set it and forget it. That should be this feature's slogan. And if you're confused about how to set up a loan in Quicken, you'll see how in Chapter 12.

Sending Payment Instructions

Once your payment instructions have been completed, you must connect to your bank to send the instructions. In the Online Center window, click the Update/Send button. Quicken displays the One Step Update Settings dialog, which lists all of the payment instructions, including any repeating payment instructions. Enter your password and click the Update Now button.

Wait while Quicken connects to your bank's server and sends your payment (or payment cancellation) instructions. When it has finished, it displays the Online Update Summary window. Click Close.

In the Payments tab of the Online Center window, the words "Scheduled for delivery on" followed by the payment date appear in the Status column beside the payment instructions that have been sent to your bank.

Canceling a Payment

Occasionally, you may change your mind about making a payment. Perhaps you found out that your spouse already sent a check or that you set up the payment for the wrong amount. For whatever reason, you can cancel an online payment that you have sent to your bank—as long as there's enough time to cancel it.

When you send a payment instruction to your bank, it waits in the bank's computer. When the processing date (determined by the number of days in the payee's lead time and the payment date) arrives, the bank makes the payment. Before the processing date, however, the payment instructions can be canceled. If you send a cancel payment instruction to the bank before the processing date, the bank removes the instruction from its computer without sending payment to the payee. Quicken won't let you cancel a payment if the processing date has already passed. If you wait too long, the only way to cancel the payment is to call the bank directly and stop the check.

Keep in mind that canceling a payment instruction isn't the same as stopping a check. If you send the cancel payment instruction in time, the bank should not charge a fee for stopping the payment.

Canceling a Regular Online Payment   In the Online Center window, click the Payments tab, select the payment that you want to cancel, and click the Cancel Payment button. Click Yes in the confirmation dialog that appears. Use the Update/Send button to send the cancel payment instruction.

Stopping a Single Repeating Online Payment   In the Online Center window's Payments tab, select the payment you want to stop, and click the Cancel Payment button. Click Yes in the confirmation dialog that appears. Use the Update/Send button to send the cancel payment instruction. Note that the payment may not appear in the Online Center window unless you have reviewed and approved all downloaded payment transactions, as instructed earlier in this chapter.

Stopping All Future Payments for a Repeating Online Payment   In the Repeating Online tab of the Bill And Income Reminders window, select the payment you want to stop, and click Delete. Click Delete in the confirmation dialog that appears. The transaction is removed from the list. Then use the Update/Send button in the Online Center window to send the cancel payment instruction.

IN MY EXPERIENCE

In our area, several banks have changed hands. Several clients were concerned about how this would affect their online services. Usually, it is a simply matter of deactivating online services for the accounts with the original bank and then reactivating with the new bank. Some transitions have even allowed the customers to use their original bank passwords and PINs, but most require that you obtain a new user name, password, and PIN from the new bank.

Online payments must be changed as well. One client found they still could not deactivate the original account even after deleting all the recurring online payments he had set. After looking through his check register, he found a check from several months prior that he had marked to send. Once he located and changed the status of that payment, he was able to deactivate the accounts from the original bank and reset them for the new bank.

Transferring Money Between Accounts

Quicken makes it easy to record your transfers between accounts. If you have more than one account enabled for Online Bill Pay via Direct Connect at the same financial institution, you can even transfer money from one account to the other directly from Quicken.

To record a transfer of funds that you make with a phone call or on the financial institution's website:

1. From the Account Bar, select the account you from which you want to transfer the funds.
2. Click Account Actions | Transfer Money or press CTRL-SHIFT-T.
3. The Transfer Money Within Quicken dialog appears, as seen here.

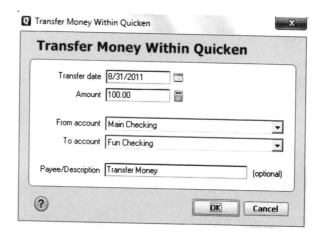

4. Enter the transfer information—source account, destination account, and amount—in the fields in the middle of the window.
5. Click OK. The information is added to the list of transfers at the bottom of the window. The transaction will appear in both check registers.
6. Be sure to call the bank or go to the website to actually give them the instructions to transfer funds.

To create an online transfer, both accounts must be activated with Direct Connect and be at the same bank under the same customer identification number. Some financial institutions allow you to pay a credit card that is associated with the same identification number in this manner as well.

To create the online transfer:

1. In a new transaction line, click the Date field and enter today's date. You may not schedule an online transfer in the future. Financial institutions process transfer instructions on the same day they are received.
2. In the Check # field, click the downward arrow, and select Online Transfer from the list. It will appear in your Check # field as Oxfr.
3. Enter a description, if you choose, in what is normally the Payee field.
4. In the Payment column, enter the amount of the transfer. Press TAB to move to the Category field. Choose the account to which you want to transfer the money from the drop-down list that appears.
5. Click Save to enter the transaction.

Use the One Step Update dialog to send the instructions to your financial institution. You may also use the Online Center to send an online transfer.

1. Click Tools | Online Center.
2. Select the appropriate account from the Financial Institution drop-down list.
3. Click the Transfers tab.
4. In the Transfer Money From field, choose the account from which you want to transfer the funds from the drop-down list.
5. In the To field, choose the account where the money is going from the drop-down list.
6. Enter the amount in the Amount field.
7. Press ENTER.
8. Click Update/Send to send the instructions to the bank.

Whether you use the Online Center method or the account register method, you must send the transfer instructions to the bank in order for the transaction to take place.

Transfer Detection

A Quicken feature scans your transactions as they are being downloaded to detect transfers between your accounts. When Quicken finds what looks like a matched pair of transfer transactions, it can automatically create the transfer in Quicken for you or ask you for confirmation first.

Exchanging E-mail with Your Financial Institution

You can use the E-mail tab of the Online Center window to exchange e-mail messages with financial institutions for which you have enabled Online Account Services via Direct Connect. Keep in mind that not all financial institutions support this feature. Also, remember that this communication is between you and your financial institution, not Intuit (the makers of Quicken). It is intended primarily for exchanging information about your account, not technical support for using Quicken.

Creating an E-mail Message

In the E-mail tab of the Online Center window, click Create. If a Create dialog like the one shown here appears, use it to set general options for your e-mail message. If your message is about an online payment, choose the account from the Account drop-down list, and select the payment from the Payments list. Even if there is only one payment in the list, you must select it or the OK button remains disabled.

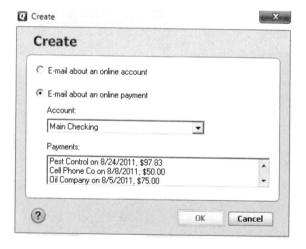

When you click OK, a Message window appears. Use it to compose your e-mail message. When you click OK again, the message is saved. It appears in the bottom half of the E-mail tab of the Online Center window, ready to be sent to your financial institution.

Exchanging E-mail Messages

Using e-mail is a lot like having a box at the post office. When you write a letter, you have to get it to the post office to send it to the recipient. When you receive a letter, you have to go to the post office and check your box to retrieve it. E-mail works the same way. Connecting is a lot like going to the post office to send and retrieve messages.

In the Online Center window, click the Update/Send button. Quicken displays the Online Update window, which includes any e-mail messages you may have created that need to be sent. Enter your password and click the Update Now button. Then wait while Quicken establishes an Internet connection with your bank and exchanges e-mail.

Reading an E-mail Message

When your bank sends you an e-mail message, it appears in the E-mail tab of the Online Center window. To read the message, select it and click Read. The message appears in a message window. If desired, you can click the Print button to print the message for future reference. You can also click Delete to delete the e-mail once you no longer need it.

Automating Transactions and Tasks

In This Chapter:

- *Setting up alerts*
- *Working with alerts*

Quicken Personal Finance Software includes a number of features to automate the entry of transactions. This chapter tells you about QuickFill, Billminder, and the other features you can use to automate transaction entries or remind yourself when a transaction is due. It also explains how you can use Quicken's One Step Update feature to handle all of your online tasks at once. These features can make data entry and other Quicken tasks quicker and easier.

Before you read this chapter, make sure you have a good understanding of the data entry techniques covered in Chapter 4. This chapter builds upon many of the basic concepts discussed there.

Bills and Income Reminders

A favorite Quicken feature is the ability to tell Quicken about the bills, deposits, and other transactions that need to be made in the future—especially the ones that happen on a regular basis. This feature, when fully utilized, doesn't just prevent you from forgetting to pay bills; it can completely automate the transaction entry process. Starting from the time you first create your Quicken file, you can create reminders to help you stay on top of your monthly bills.

This part of the chapter tells you more about bill and income reminders, including how to set up and use them.

Being Reminded

Generally speaking, you can be "reminded" about two types of transactions:

- One-time transactions are future transactions that you expect to record only once. For example, suppose you are arranging to purchase some furniture. You have already paid a deposit for the furniture and you know that the balance will be due at month-end, when the furniture is delivered. You can schedule that month-end payment in advance.

 Some Quicken users prefer to enter this future transaction in their check register with the date it will be paid.

- Recurring transactions are transactions that occur periodically on a regular basis. Many of your monthly bills are good examples: rent or mortgage payments, car payments, utility bills—unfortunately, there are too many to list!

Reminders aren't only for payments. You could create a reminder for incoming funds, too, such as an expected bonus or a monthly child-support check you receive. You can even schedule your paycheck—but it's better to use Quicken's Paycheck Setup feature, which is discussed later in this chapter, to do that.

Making the Most of Bill and Income Reminders

Quicken's Reminders feature is one of the best time-saving features Quicken offers. By taking full advantage of this feature, you can minimize the time you spend entering transactions into Quicken.

Throughout this chapter and this book, bill reminders, scheduled transactions, and scheduled reminders all are used and mean the same process—saving information about a payee or a transaction so that you can pay or enter the information at a future time.

Here are a few suggestions from seasoned Quicken users about how you can make the most of the feature. See how many you can use—and how much time they can save you.

- Schedule all recurring transactions, such as rent, utilities, and other regular bills. Include recurring deposits, such as your paycheck, or other income.
- Use Paycheck Setup to track gross pay and deductions. While it takes some time to set up (see "Using the Paycheck Setup Wizard" later in this chapter), doing so can help you utilize Quicken's tax planning and reporting features, which are discussed in Chapter 17.
- Let Quicken automatically enter transactions whenever possible. While this option works best with items that are the same amount each time they are made, letting Quicken do the work saves you time.
- Use the Online Payment or check printing features.
- Record transactions several days in advance so your account register reflects both the current and future balance. Just be sure to enter the transaction due dates rather than entry dates when entering them into Quicken.

Remember that creating a reminder is not the same as recording a transaction. You must record a transaction to have it appear in the appropriate register, print a check for it, or send an online payment instruction for it. Creating the reminder is only part of the job. You still have to make sure each transaction is entered in a timely manner.

Creating Reminders from Downloaded Transactions

You can create a scheduled transaction in Quicken in several ways. When you first install Quicken, in the Home tab's Main View, click the Get Started button. If you have downloaded your bank account transactions, you may already see outgoing transactions that appear to be recurring transactions, as seen next. The Review Bills dialog lists these transactions.

You may remove the transactions or edit them, as seen next. If you do not want to enter a transaction as a recurring transaction into Quicken, select that transaction and click Remove in the Action column.

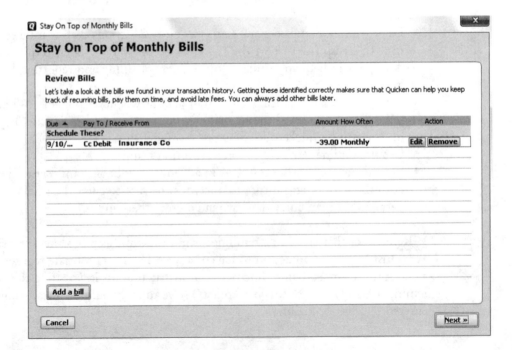

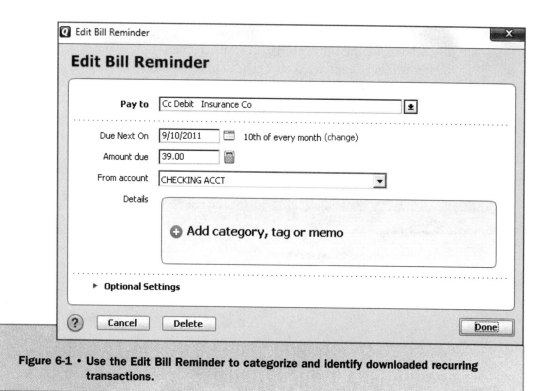

Figure 6-1 • Use the Edit Bill Reminder to categorize and identify downloaded recurring transactions.

To edit a transaction:

1. Select the transaction and click Edit. The Edit Bill Reminder dialog appears as seen in Figure 6-1.
2. Click in the Pay To field to change or correct the payee of this transaction.
3. Click in the Due Next On field to change the date if necessary. You may either type the information or use the calendar on the right of the field.
4. Click Change to the right of the Due Next On field to change how often the item recurs. For further information about the Change dialog, see "Setting Up Reminders in the Bills Tab" later in this chapter.
5. Click the Amount Due field to change the amount, if necessary. You may either type the new amount or use the small calculator to the right of the field.
6. If necessary, change the spending account that appears in the From Account field with the drop-down arrow.
7. Click anywhere within the Details section to add a category, tag, or memo. See "Setting Up Reminders in the Bills Tab" for additional information. Click OK to close the dialog and return to the Edit Bill Reminder dialog.

8. The Optional Settings section is covered in the section "Setting Up Reminders in the Bills Tab" later in this chapter.

9. After you have completed changing or entering the information, click Done/Next. If you have recurring income items, you will see Next; if not, you see Done.

10. If you have recurring income items, follow Steps 1 through 9 for each income item. When you have completed the income items, click Done. You are returned to the Home tab's Main View in the Stay On Top Of Monthly Bills section, as seen next. Note that the Bill And Income Reminders section now includes the recurring items.

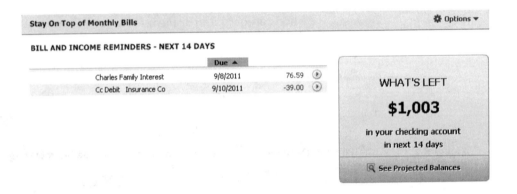

Work in the Home Tab's Main View

After you have set up recurring bills from downloaded transactions, you can continue to work in the Stay On Top Of Monthly Bills section in the Home Tab's Main view. Click the Options menu, from which you can do the following:

- Choose to display the reminders for the next 7, 14, 30, or 90 days, or 12 months.
- Open the Add Reminder dialog.
- Go directly to the Bills tab, from which you can work with reminders, see what bills and income are due in the near future, and see your projected balances for the next 12 months or even longer, if you choose. See "Setting Up Reminders in the Bills Tab" next in this chapter.

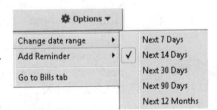

Each reminder displayed on the list is a link. Click the amount to open the Edit Reminder dialog. Click the arrow to the right of the amount to see a menu, shown here, from which you can do the following:

- Enter the reminder into the appropriate register, which opens the Enter Expense Transaction dialog. This means the transaction will be entered into the register immediately rather than waiting for the update bill date you set earlier. The transaction will be dated the date you specified, showing in the register with that date in the future.
- Skip this one entry.
- Click Edit to open a submenu from which you can
  - Edit this one reminder—and open the Edit Reminder dialog.
  - Edit this and all future reminders, which opens the Edit Bill Reminder dialog. If the reminder is an income or transfer reminder, the Edit Income Reminder or Edit Transfer Reminder dialog will open.
  - Delete this and all future reminders, which opens a message that you are about to delete a scheduled bill or deposit. You must click OK to delete the reminder or click Cancel to close the message without deleting the reminder.

See What's Left

The What's Left section at the right of the Stay On Top Of Monthly Bills section shows how much is available until your next income comes in.

If any of your accounts are overdrawn you will see "Risk of Overdraft" displayed at the bottom of the What's Left section. Click the link to display the Projected Balances dialog. You can also look at the balance of your accounts in the Account Bar to see which of your accounts are currently overdrawn.

If your accounts are all positive (not overdrawn), you will see a See Projected Balances link instead of the Risk Of Overdraft link. Click See Projected Balances to display the balances in each of your spending accounts. This is the same information you see in the Bills tab's Projected Balances view. Click Close to dismiss the Projected Balances dialog.

Setting Up Reminders in the Bills Tab

The Bills tab is the place to work with your reminders. If you did not download any recurring transactions, when you first click the Bills tab, you will see a Get Started button, as seen in Figure 6-2.

To begin, click the Get Started button. The Stay On Top Of Monthly Bills dialog appears as seen next.

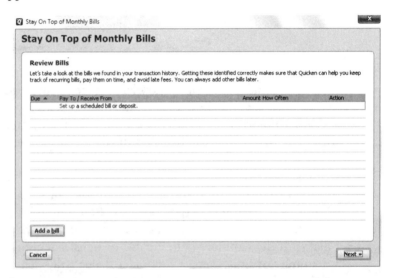

1. Click Set Up A Scheduled Bill Or Deposit to open the Add Reminder dialog seen next. When you are first working with your Quicken file you may only see the choice to open bill and income reminders. As you add more accounts, you may see another option: Transfer Reminder.

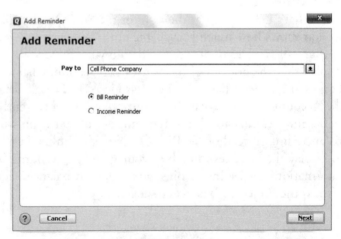

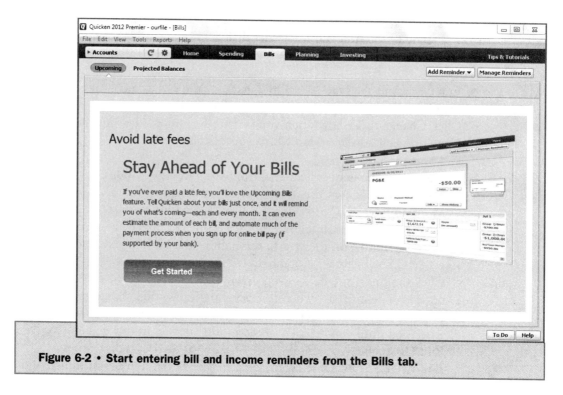

Figure 6-2 • Start entering bill and income reminders from the Bills tab.

2. In the Pay To field, type the name of the payee or choose a payee from the drop-down list. If you are setting up bills in a new Quicken file, you will probably not have any payees on your list yet.

3. Choose the type of reminder you are adding: Bill or Income, and click Next. The Add Bill Reminder dialog appears, as seen here, with the Pay To field prefilled with the information you entered in Step 2.

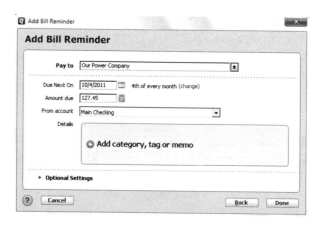

To go directly to the Add Bill Reminder dialog, click the Add A Bill button.

4. Enter a date in the Due Next On date field. You can also choose a date from the Calendar to the right of the field.

5. Click Change to set how often you need to be reminded about the bill. The Change dialog appears, from which you can change
   a. The start date
   b. How often the item is deducted from your account. Choose an option from the drop-down list. Your options are Weekly, Monthly, Twice A Month, Quarterly, Yearly, Twice A Year, Only Once, and To Pay Estimated Tax (which follows the IRS estimated tax payment schedule). Then set options in the area to the right of the How Often field; the options change based on the frequency you select.
   c. Click the End Date field's drop-down arrow to display the End Date options. These specify when the recurring transaction should end.
   d. **No End Date**, which is the default option, keeps the transaction scheduled until you delete it or set another option in this dialog.
   e. **End On** enables you to set a specific date for the last transaction.
   f. **End After** or **End Date** enables you to specify the number of transactions before they automatically end or the date on which the payments end. What you see will depend on what you enter in the How Often field.
   g. If all of the information on the Change dialog is correct, click OK to close the dialog and return to the Add Bill Reminder dialog.

6. Enter an amount in the Amount Due field, or use the Calculator to the right of the Amount Due field. You can also leave this field blank if the amount of the transaction varies from month to month.

7. Enter the account from which this bill is to be paid in the From Account field. You may also choose from the drop-down list, which will display all of your non-hidden accounts.

The drop-down list displays all of your non-hidden accounts, including credit card, savings, and investing accounts.

8. Click anywhere within the Details section to add a category, tag, or memo. (It is best to enter at least the category; that way, each time this transaction is downloaded, it will be categorized correctly.) The Category dialog appears:

a. Type a category or choose one from the drop-down list. You can even split the category—see the split icon to the right of the Category field? (Review categories and splits in Chapters 3 and 4.)

b. Enter a tag if you choose. Review how tags work in Chapter 3.

c. Type a memo.

d. Click OK to return to the Edit Bill Reminder dialog.

9. Click the Optional Settings link to set additional information for this bill, as seen here.

10. Click the Change link by the Remind Me 3 Days In Advance option to be reminded at a different time schedule, as seen here. From this dialog

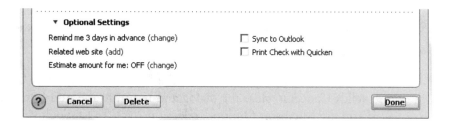

a. You can use the up or down arrows to increase or decrease the number of days before the bill is due to be reminded. You can also type in the number.

b. You can tell Quicken to enter the bill for you automatically and specify the number of days before the bill is due that you want the bill to be entered.

c. You can tell Quicken to count only business days when calculating the reminder days.

d. Click OK when you've made your changes to return to the Add Bill Reminder dialog.

11. Click the Add link next to the Related Web Site option to add the payee's website. Click OK after you have typed the website address to return to the Add Bill Reminder dialog.

12. Click the Change link next to the Estimate Amount For Me option to open the Estimate dialog:

    a. The Fixed Amount option displays a text box you can use to enter a dollar amount that the transaction will always use. You can change the amount when the transaction is entered, if necessary.

    b. Click the drop-down list to choose Previous Payments. This option tells Quicken to create an estimate based the payments you have made previously. You set the number of payments, as seen here.

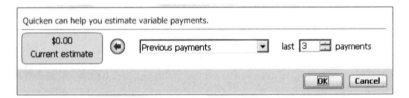

    c. The other option on the drop-down list is Time Of Year. This is used when you make recurring payments at a specific time of year.

If your Quicken file does not have enough data to estimate either Previous Payments or Time of Year information, you will see a pop-up message telling you this.

    d. If you have set any estimates in the Estimate dialog, click OK. Otherwise, click Cancel to close the dialog and return to the Add Reminder dialog.

13. If you use Microsoft Outlook, select the Sync To Outlook check box to synchronize your due date reminder with the Outlook calendar.

14. Select the Print Check With Quicken check box to tell Quicken to print the check for this bill when it is due. Print Check With Quicken records the transaction as a payment using a check to be printed. Entering the transaction, of course, decreases the balance in a banking account. The Check Number field in the account register is set to PRINT, which signals Quicken to include the transaction with other checks to be printed. Use this option for scheduling transactions using Quicken's check printing feature, which Chapter 4 discusses in greater detail.

15. Click Done to close the Add Bill Reminder dialog.

Working with the Bills Tab

Quicken displays reminders in several places:

- From the Bills tab, click the Manage Reminders button.
- From the Quicken menu bar, click Tools | Manage Bill & Income Reminders.
- From the Main View of the Home tab, in the Stay On Top Of Monthly Bills section, as discussed in the section "Work in the Home Tab's Main View."

Use the Bills tab, shown in Figure 6-3, to view upcoming bills and other scheduled transactions in a number of different ways.

Figure 6-3 • The Upcoming view in the Bills tab lets you display your upcoming bills in several ways.

- Add Reminder enables you to add a bill, income, paycheck, or transfer reminder, as discussed earlier in this chapter.
- Manage Reminders displays the Bill And Income Reminders window (refer to Figure 6-5).

Upcoming Button

The Upcoming button's view (shown in Stack view in Figure 6-3) shows each upcoming scheduled transaction with a note-like interface. Click one of the transactions, and its details appear in the middle of the window. Use the horizontal scroll bar at the bottom of the window to display upcoming transactions. You can use a transaction's buttons to enter, skip, or edit the transaction. Clicking a Show History button displays a payment history for that payee.

You may change the way the information is displayed by clicking the View As drop-down list, as seen here:

- **Stack** displays each item in a "stack" as if they were papers on top of each other. You can use the Due Within Next drop-down list to choose the time period. Your options are 7, 14, and 30 days. You can choose to not include items that have been paid by clearing the Include Paid check box.
- **List** displays information about the status, due date, pay to or receive from information, and amount of each transaction. From this view you can enter, edit, or skip the transaction. The Due and Include Paid options are the same as in the Stack view.
- **Calendar** shows all transactions in a calendar view that includes transactions and their amounts, as well as the ending total banking account balance. You can use the arrows by the current month area to scroll through months. Learn more about how the Calendar works later in this chapter in the section "Using the Financial Calendar."

The Calendar view does not show cash or bills paid from any Brokerage accounts, nor can you indicate which accounts to include on the Bills tab's Calendar view, even if you have designated those accounts in the full Calendar view. See "Using the Financial Calendar" later in this chapter.

- **Monthly List** shows all scheduled transaction reminders for the current month. You can choose another month by using the arrows to the left and right of the current month.

Projected Balances

This button's view (see Figure 6-4) shows projected balances and your upcoming transactions in a list view. While the default is to display all spending accounts, you can select a single account to view from the Select Accounts drop-down list

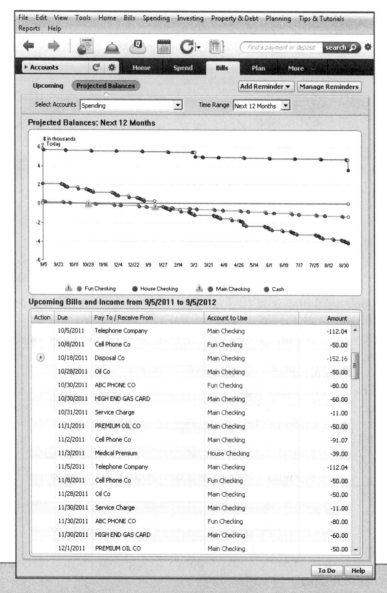

Figure 6-4 • The Projected Balances graph shows your future bank balances and upcoming bills for the time period you select.

or choose Multiple Accounts to open the Projected Balance selection dialog as
shown here. This dialog allows you to choose two or more spending or credit
card accounts to display. Click the Show (Hidden Accounts) check box to
include them in the cash flow view.

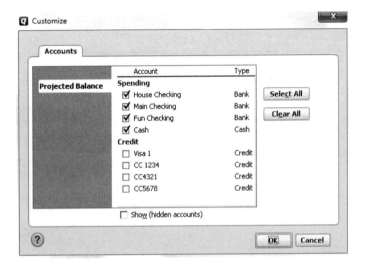

Click Select All to choose all displayed accounts or Clear All to start over with
your selection. Click OK to close the dialog.

You may choose a time period to display by clicking the Time Range drop-
down list. You may choose the next 7, 14, 30, or 90 days; the next 12 months;
or create a customized time period.

The Projected Balances snapshot of the graph includes all of the accounts you
have selected for the time period selected. A legend showing the account or
accounts represented in the line graph appears at the bottom of the section, as
seen in Figure 6-4.

In the Upcoming Bills And Income From *nn/nn/nnnn* to *nn/nn/nnnn*
section, as shown in Figure 6-4, you can work with your transaction reminders
as follows:

- Click the right-pointing arrow in the circle icon in the Action column to
  enter, skip, or edit the selected transaction.
- Click the account name in the Account To Use column to be taken to that
  account's register.
- Click the transaction's amount in the Amount column to open the Edit
  Reminder dialog.

If a pencil icon appears in the Action column, that indicates the item has been entered (or paid) and you cannot edit the amount from the Upcoming Bills And Income list. In other words, you can only edit amounts for unpaid reminders from this list.

Working with Reminders

Scheduling a transaction was the hard part. (Not very hard, though, was it?) Entering, editing, and skipping a scheduled transaction is easy. Here's one way— some say the quickest and easiest—to work with reminders.

Click the Bills tab, and then click the Upcoming button to display that view (refer to Figure 6-3). Select a reminder. The options described here may be on the selected item's transaction list, as in the List or Monthly List views, the Calendar date in the Calendar view, or the reminder itself in the Stack view.

> ### IN MY EXPERIENCE
>
> Many Quicken users don't use the Bills tab or the Bill And Income Reminders screen. Instead, they have a Bill And Income Reminders snapshot on a customized view in the Home tab that segregates the bills and the income into separate sections. If they include income reminders for dividend reinvestments, for example, having the bills separate makes it much easier to find and pay them. See Appendix B to learn how to customize the views in the Home tab.

Enter In all views except the Calendar view, if the transaction has not already been entered, the Enter button displays the Enter Transaction dialog. Use this dialog to finalize settings for a transaction. When you click Enter Transaction, the transaction is entered into the account register. The dialog will be labeled Enter *X* Transaction, where *X* is Expense or Income.

Skip In all views except the Calendar view, the Skip button skips the transaction if it has not already been entered into the account register. The transaction moves down in the list, and its due date changes to the next due date.

Edit In all views except the Calendar view, the Edit button displays the Edit Transaction Reminder dialog when the transaction has not yet been entered into the account register. This dialog looks and works very much like the Add Transaction Reminder dialog shown earlier in Figure 6-3. Use this dialog to modify settings for the transaction's future entries. If the transaction is an instance of a recurring transaction, the Edit button appears as a menu with the following two options:

- **Only This Instance** displays the Edit Reminder dialog that enables you to change the date and amount of the transaction.
- **This And All Future Reminders** displays the Edit Transaction Reminder dialog, as discussed earlier. The dialog will be labeled Edit *X* Reminder, where *X* is Income or Expense.

Managing Reminders

In the Bills tab, click Manage Reminders or press CTRL-J to open the Bill And Income Reminders window (refer to Figure 6-5), which displays current and future transactions. If you have previously scheduled transactions or repeating

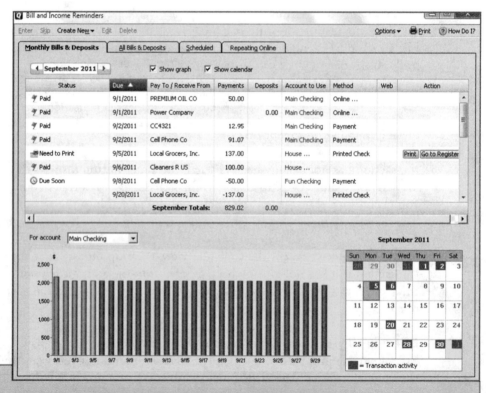

Figure 6-5 • The Bill And Income Reminders window presents information about current and upcoming financial transactions.

online transactions, the Bill And Income Reminders window has four tabs. Until you have created either one or both, there are only two tabs visible.

Bills and Income Reminder Button Options

You can use button options in both the Monthly Bills & Deposits and the All Bills & Deposits tabs to enter, skip, create, edit, or delete scheduled transactions. You must select a transaction to activate all but the Create New option.

- **Enter** opens the Enter [type of] Transaction dialog shown next. Enter the appropriate information, and click Enter Transaction. If the reminder is for investment income, you may see a dialog titled Edit Income – Income (Div, Int, etc.).

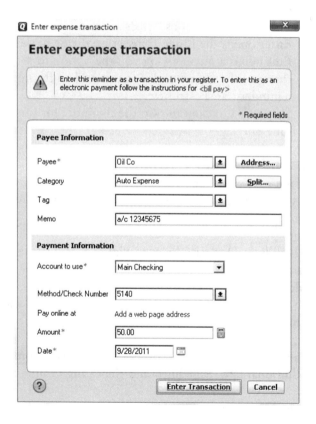

- **Skip** enables you to skip the payment (or next payment) of that transaction.
- **Create New** enables you to create a new scheduled transaction. See "Setting Up Reminders in the Bills Tab" earlier in this chapter.

- **Edit** opens the Edit Bill (or Income) Reminder dialog in which you can modify each area of the reminder as shown in Figure 6-1.
- **Delete** removes the scheduled transaction. It does not remove any transactions that have already been entered in a register.
- **Options** offers commands for changing the way the Bill And Income Reminders window is sorted. You can also change the sort order by clicking the Due, Pay To/Receive From, Payments, or Deposits column header. Depending on the tab in which you are working, you may also be able to sort by amount.
- **Print** prints a list of scheduled transactions.
- **How Do I?** displays the Quicken Personal Finances Help window with instructions for completing tasks with the Bill And Income Reminders window.
- **Action buttons** on individual transaction reminders can also be used. To access the action buttons, select a reminder and choose from the following:
    - **Enter** opens the Enter Transaction dialog discussed earlier in the chapter.
    - **Edit** opens a menu giving you the option to change only this reminder or this and all future reminders, as shown here.

    > Only this instance
    > This and all future reminders

    - **Skip** tells Quicken to skip the reminder for this time only.

Bills and Income Reminders Tabs

There are up to four tabs available in the Bill And Income Reminders window. Until you have scheduled some transactions and set up online payments, you will only see the first two tabs described here:

- **All Bills & Deposits** (refer to Figure 6-5) displays all types of scheduled reminders.
- **Monthly Bills & Deposits** displays all reminders for the month. You can click the arrows beside the name of the month to view reminders for other months.

When you have scheduled transactions or set up online payments, you will see two additional tabs: Scheduled and Repeating Online.

- **Scheduled** displays the deposits and payments that you have scheduled for this month. Remember, until you have set up an account with Online Payment capabilities, you will not see the Scheduled tab.
- **Repeating Online** lists repeating payments you have scheduled to be paid online.

Display Check Boxes

Two check boxes enable you to display additional information in the window, as shown in Figure 6-5:

- **Show Graph** displays a column chart showing cash flow for selected accounts for the month.
- **Show Calendar** displays one or two calendars that indicate dates on which transactions will be made.

Schedule These?

The Schedule These? list at the bottom of a Bill And Income Reminders window, when present, displays transactions that Quicken "thinks" you might want to schedule for the future. See the next illustration for an example. It builds this list based on categories used in the transactions or transactions you have entered more than once. Here are a few things you can do to work with this list:

- To schedule a transaction in the list, click the Yes button beside it. Quicken displays the Edit Bill (or Income) Reminder dialog so you can turn the transaction into a scheduled transaction.
- To remove a transaction from the list, click the No button beside it.

QuickFill and Memorized Payees

As you enter transactions, Quicken is quietly working in the background, memorizing transaction information for each payee. It creates a database of memorized payees. It then uses the memorized payees for its QuickFill feature.

Understanding QuickFill

QuickFill works in two ways:

- When you enter the first few characters of a payee name in the Write Checks or account register window, Quicken immediately fills in the rest of the name. When you advance to the next text box or field of the entry form, Quicken fills in the rest of the transaction information based on the last transaction for that payee.
- You can select a memorized payee from the drop-down list in the Payee field of the Write Checks or account register window. Quicken then fills in the

rest of the transaction information based on the last transaction for that payee.

QuickFill entries include amounts, categories, and memos. They can also include splits and tags. For example, you might pay the cable or satellite company for television service monthly. The bill is usually the same amount each month. The second time you create an entry with the company's name, Quicken fills in the rest of the transaction automatically. You can make adjustments to the amount or other information as desired and save the transaction. It may have taken a minute or so to enter the transaction the first time, but it'll take only seconds to enter it every time after that.

By default, the QuickFill feature is set up to work as discussed here. If it does not, check the QuickFill options to make sure they are set properly. To check these options:

1. Click Edit | Preferences | Register | Data Entry And QuickFill.
2. Ensure all of the check boxes are selected, as shown here.

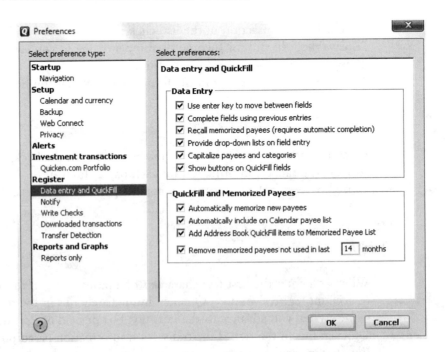

3. Click OK to close Quicken Preferences.

IN MY EXPERIENCE

If you use memorized transactions and the QuickFill feature is completing more information than you want it to, edit the transaction in the Memorized Payee List. For example, if you pay activity fees for each of your children to the local young people's club, you may want to use a different memo for each child's dues. After you have memorized the transaction, open the Memorized Payee List and clear out the Memo field or Tag fields. Then, click the Lock check box.

NOTE You could also memorize the payee with a different memo for each child or create a tag for each one. Learn more about tags in Chapter 3.

To show the Lock column in the Memorized Payee List, click Options and click Show Locked Status Column In The List. Each time the transaction is entered, just change or enter the information that is different from the transaction that has been memorized.

Utilizing the Memorized Payee List

If desired, you can view a list of your memorized payees, as shown in Figure 6-6. Just choose Tools | Memorized Payee List or press CTRL-T. The list displays the last transaction you entered for each payee.

Depending on the type or category for a payee, you may see more than just the last transaction in the Memorized Payee List.

If a payee does not appear on the Memorized Payee List and you believe it should, check your Preferences. Click Edit | Preferences | Data Entry And QuickFill. Select the Remove Memorized Payees Not Used In Last *nn* Months check box or change the amount of in the Months field.

Select a memorized payee to display the Edit and Delete action buttons. Edit displays the Edit Memorized Payee dialog for the currently selected transaction, as seen on page 185:

- The **Payee Name** field displays the payee name as it is currently entered. You may change the name or any of the other fields as required.
- You may also leave the **Category**, **Tag**, **Memo**, or **Amount** fields blank so that data can be changed each time you use this payee. If the amount paid to this payee changes each time, leave the amount blank.

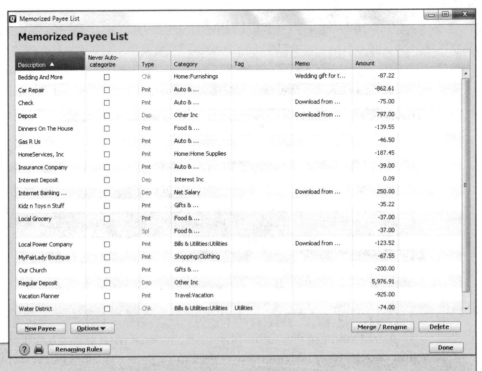

Figure 6-6 • Each line in the Memorized Payee List represents the last transaction recorded for a payee.

- The **Never Auto-categorize This Payee During QuickFill Or Downloads** tells Quicken to let you enter the proper category for this payee.
- Click **Lock And Leave This Payee Unchanged When It Is Edited In A Register** to ensure the transaction stays blank in the Memorized Payee List.
- **Show This Payee In The Calendar Memorized Payee List**, which is selected by default, determines how this item is displayed in the Calendar (see image at the top of the next page). See "Using the Financial Calendar" later in this chapter.
- **Delete** displays a dialog asking you to confirm that you really do want to delete the selected item. If you delete the transaction, it is removed from the Memorized Payee List only—not from any register in the Quicken data file.
- The **Memorized Payee Report** icon is hard to see. It is located to the right of the Delete button. Click this icon to open a Payee Report about this payee.

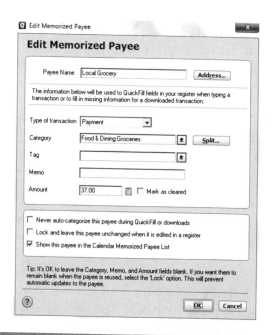

IN MY EXPERIENCE

If you enter your register transactions manually, the Memorized Payee List helps you in two different ways. To use either of the following methods, the QuickFill and Data Fill preferences must all be checked, as discussed in "Understanding QuickFill" earlier in this chapter.

1. With QuickFill activated, you can simply start typing the name of the payee in the Payee field.
2. Type the first few letters, and the previous transaction for this payee will be replicated in the register.
3. Use the ALT-A keyboard shortcut to save the transaction if the information is correct for the current entry.

You can also use the Memorized Payee List as follows:

1. Open the register from which the item will be paid, and click the next available line. Use the CTRL-T keyboard shortcut to open the Memorized Payee List.
2. Right-click the memorized payee transaction you want to use.
3. From the context menu that appears, click Use to paste the item into your register.
4. Click Save or use the ALT-A keyboard shortcut to save the transaction.

You may want to build a Memorized Payee List from all of your existing cash flow accounts. To do so:

1. From the menu bar, click Tools.
2. Hold down CTRL-SHIFT and click Memorized Payee List.
3. Your new Memorized Payee List displays.

Memorized Payee List Activities

You can use buttons at the bottom of the Memorized Payee window to change what displays in the list, add, merge, rename, or delete memorized payees on the Memorized Payee List:

- **New Payee** displays the Create Memorized Payee dialog, which is similar to the Edit Memorized Payee dialog. You use the Create dialog to create brand-new transactions without actually entering them into any register of your Quicken data file. Just fill in the fields to enter transaction information, and click OK. The new transaction appears in the Memorized Payee List window.
- **Options** opens a menu that allows you to choose to display the "Lock" and the "Show On Calendar" columns in the Memorized Payee List.

 The financial calendar is covered in more detail later in this chapter. You can also choose to lock the transaction. This means that on the Memorized Payee List, the transaction is the same each time. However, a locked transaction can be changed in the register when the payment is actually made.

- **Merge/Rename** displays the Merge And Rename Payees dialog, shown here, which you can use to enter a new name for the selected payee.
- Use the **Delete** button to delete one or more payees from the list.
- The question mark icon opens the **Quicken Personal Finances Help** window with additional information for completing tasks with the Memorized Payee List window.
- The printer icon opens the **Print** dialog with which you can print the Memorized Payee List.
- **Renaming Rules** opens the Renaming Rules dialog as explained in Chapter 5.

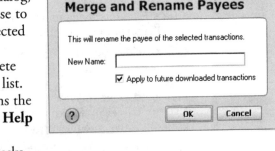

 Use the CTRL-M keyboard shortcut after you have entered a transaction to memorize the payee and the category.

Creating Scheduled Transaction Groups

If you regularly enter several transactions into the same investment account, consider creating a Transaction Group.

1. From your investing account, memorize the transaction you want to schedule. To memorize a transaction, right-click the transaction and choose Memorize Investment Transaction. You can also use the keyboard shortcut CTRL-M to memorize your transaction. A dialog will appear letting you know this payee is about to be memorized. Click OK.

If you memorize more than one transaction for the same security, you will see a warning that transaction is already memorized. However, you can choose to Replace, Add, or Cancel the transaction. One Quicken user used the Add option to create three memorized investment transactions for the same security with different memos for her employee 401(k) contribution, the employer match, and the catch-up contribution.

2. Press CTRL-J to open the Manage Bill & Income Reminder dialog. From that menu, click Create New | Scheduled Transaction Group. The Create Transaction Group dialog appears.
3. Enter a name for your group, the account you want to use, the next due date, and the frequency. Choose Investment and check the items you want to remember.
4. Click OK to close the dialog.

Using the Financial Calendar

Quicken's Calendar, shown in Figure 6-7, keeps track of all your transactions—past and future—by date. You may open the Calendar by choosing Tools | Calendar or by pressing CTRL-K.

Calendar Buttons

You can use buttons to work with the window's contents:

- **Go To Date** enables you to go to a specific calendar date. Click the Calendar icon, and use the tiny calendar that appears to locate and select the date you want. Or enter the date in the edit box and click the Go button.
- **Arrow buttons** on either side of the month's name enable you to move from one month to another.

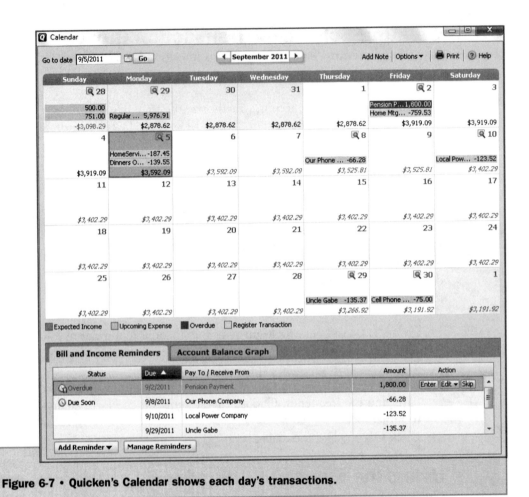

Figure 6-7 • Quicken's Calendar shows each day's transactions.

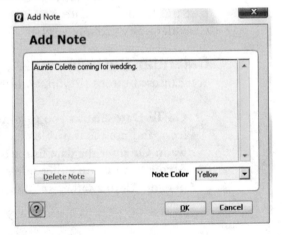

- **Add Note** enables you to enter a note for a selected date, as seen here. You can even change the color of your note. The Note icon then appears on the Calendar on that date. Depending on your monitor settings, the icon may be hard to see!

- **Options** offers commands for viewing and working with the contents of the Calendar window, as seen here.
- **Print** prints the Calendar.
- **Help** displays the Quicken Personal Finances Help window with information about using the Calendar.

The Transactions Window

When you double-click a calendar date (or single-click an already selected date), the Transactions window, which lists all the transactions for that date, appears, as shown next.

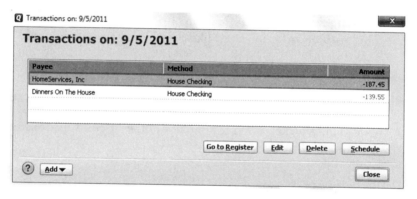

You can use buttons in the window to work with transactions.

- **Add** enables you to enter a new transaction. From this menu you can
  - Add an expense transaction
  - Add an income transaction
  - Add a new reminder
- **Enter** opens the Enter Expense Transaction dialog from which you can enter the selection into the register. If the transaction has already been entered into the account register, this button changes to Go To Register and opens the appropriate register at that transaction.
- **Edit** enables you to modify the currently selected transaction. If this transaction has not been entered into the register, the Edit <type> Reminder dialog displays. If it has been entered into the register, the Edit Register Transaction dialog appears.
- **Delete** removes the selected transaction. This option is only available for transactions that have already been entered into the register.

- **Skip** lets you skip the transaction for this date. This option is only available for transactions that have not been entered.
- **Schedule** enables you to create a new scheduled transaction based on the selected transaction. This option is only available if the currently selected transaction is not a scheduled transaction.
- The **Help** icon opens Quicken Help at the section explaining how to work with the Calendar.
- **Close** closes the window.

Account Balances

The dollar amounts that appear in the bottom of each calendar date box show the total account balances for the accounts displayed in the window, taking all payments into consideration. (You can specify which accounts to include by choosing Select Calendar Accounts from the Options menu in the button bar.) This feature works, in effect, like a simplified forecasting tool.

Useful Quicken Features

In addition to the Bill and Income Reminders, Memorized Payees, and QuickFill, Quicken offers a number of other useful functions to help you with your financial recordkeeping.

Minding Your Bills

Quicken's Billminder feature makes it possible for you to monitor upcoming bills and scheduled transactions without starting Quicken. This application displays a window that summarizes upcoming transactions. It also includes a convenient button to run Quicken, should you decide to take action on a listed item.

To open Billminder, choose Start | All Programs | Quicken 2012 | Billminder. But to make the most of Billminder, you may want to configure it so it automatically starts each time you start your computer. To do this, click the

Options button in the Billminder button bar to display Billminder options as shown here. Select the Enable Billminder On Windows Startup check box. You can set other configuration options as desired to determine when Billminder should appear. Then click OK.

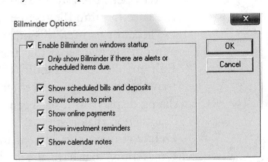

Using the Paycheck Setup Wizard

Quicken's Paycheck Setup Wizard feature offers yet another way to automate transactions. You use it to enter information about your regular payroll check and its deductions. Then, when payday comes along, Quicken automatically enters the payroll deposit information based on the Paycheck Setup transaction.

Although you can use Paycheck Setup to record payroll checks with varying amounts and deductions—such as a check with varying hourly wages or overtime pay—it can be a real time-saver if your paycheck is the same (or almost the same) every payday. If your paycheck does vary, be sure to include all possible deductions, even if their values are often zero. Then it'll be easy to just plug in different values when you need to.

One of the most complex split transactions is tracking your paycheck deductions. Quicken allows you to set up your recurring paycheck so that all the deductions can be fed into separate categories. This is done through Quicken's Bill and Income Reminders.

1. Click the Tools menu, click Bill & Income Reminders, click Create New in the menu bar at the top, and click Income Reminder. The Add Reminder dialog box will open.
2. Click Paycheck Setup Wizard at the bottom of dialog box. The Paycheck Setup dialog box will open. To track all deductions, click Gross Amount, and click Next.

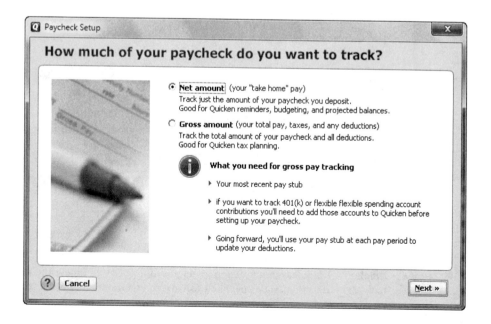

Many experienced Quicken users prefer to use the Classic menus instead of Standard menus. In this case, Classic menus offer easy access to the Paycheck Setup Wizard. Click View | Classic Menus | Bills | Add Reminder | Paycheck Reminder.

3. Click whether it is your paycheck or your spouse's, and type the name of the company from whom you are earning the paycheck. Press TAB to move to the Memo field. Type any additional information in this optional field, for example, if you receive two checks, one for base pay and one for commissions. Click Next to open the Track Paycheck dialog box shown in Figure 6-8.

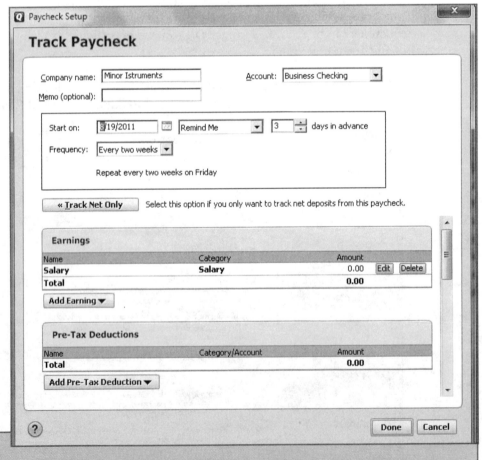

Figure 6-8 • Quicken's Track Paycheck dialog gives you the ability to follow the amounts you have deducted from your paycheck for taxes, insurance, and other items.

4. Click the Account field down arrow, and select the bank account into which this income is deposited. Press TAB, enter or select the date, indicate whether you want it automatically entered or just a reminder, and finally select the frequency on which you get paid.

5. If you change your mind and want to track your net pay only, click Track Net Only.

6. Otherwise, click Edit or Amount opposite Salary to open the Amount field. Enter the gross amount of income you receive. If you do not receive the same amount each time, enter an average.

7. If you have other components of your income, such as a regular bonus or commissions, click Add Earning, select the category of other earnings, enter the amount, and click OK.

8. If you have pre-tax deductions, such as 401(k) contributions, click Add Pre-Tax Deduction, select the category, select the account, enter both the contribution and employer-matching amounts, if applicable, and click OK.

Depending on your company's insurance plan, some health insurance premiums are deducted *after* taxes, not before.

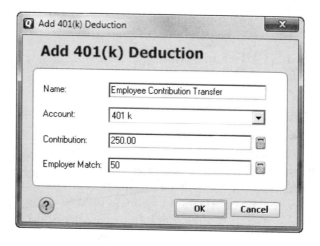

By entering deduction information from your regular paycheck, Quicken can create tax reports, help you plan for taxes, and export information to TurboTax for year-end tax reporting.

9. Click in the amount field next to each of the tax items that are on your pay stub and enter the amount. If you want to make any changes to the name and category, click Edit, make the changes, and click OK. However, it is best to stay with the standard tax categories, as Quicken has already linked those categories with the proper tax-line items.

10. Click After-Tax Deduction, which includes health insurance and stock purchases, correct the name if needed, select the category you want to use to collect this deduction, enter the amount, and click OK. Repeat this for multiple deductions.

11. If you want to split your paycheck deposit over two or more accounts, click Add Deposit Account, select the additional account, type any memo information you want, enter the amount of your paycheck that will go into that account, and click OK.

12. When you have entered all of the paycheck information you want to track, click Done to close the Track Paycheck dialog box.

13. You will be asked if you want to enter year-to-date information. If you choose the default to enter that data, click OK, click in each of the Year To Date amount fields, type the desired amount, and, after entering all you want, click Enter to close the dialog box. Otherwise, click I Do Not Want To Enter This Information, and click OK.

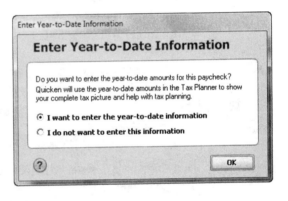

Creating the Address Book

Quicken's Address Book feature automatically stores the address information you enter when using the Write Checks window. You can also use this feature to modify or delete existing information or add new records. Keeping track of addresses with the Address Book makes it easy to insert addresses when writing checks and to look up contact information when you need to follow up on transactions.

Choose Tools | Address Book to display the Address Book window (see Figure 6-9). It lists all the records in the Address Book.

You can use buttons and menus to work with Address Book window contents:

- The **Group** drop-down list lets you choose between All Groups and any of the other groups you have established within Quicken.

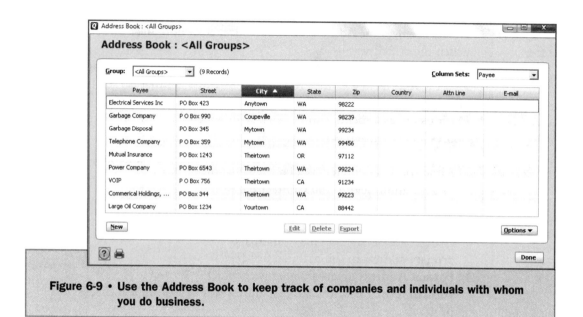

Figure 6-9 • Use the Address Book to keep track of companies and individuals with whom you do business.

- **Column Sets** drop-down list lets you view each of the various Address Book tabs in a columnar display. There are different columns in each column set. Each column set allows you to display different Address Book record data.
- **New** enables you to create a new Address Book record.
- **Edit** enables you to edit a selected record, as shown next.

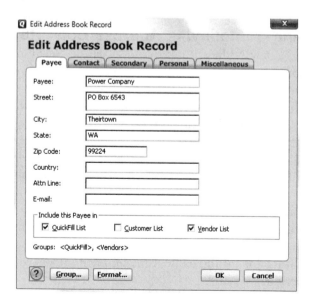

- **Delete** removes the Address Book record. It does not affect transactions in which the record was used.
- **Export** opens the Export Address Records dialog. From this dialog you can send the records in a format you choose to a text file that can be used in other programs.
- **Options** opens a menu, shown next, with which you can work with your Address Book entries:
  - **Switch Names And Organization** swaps the name you have entered as a contact into the Organization field in the Contact tab of the Address Book record.
  - **Switch Payee & Secondary Addresses** changes an address you have entered as the primary address to the main address.
  - **Format Address** opens a dialog with which you can format how the payee's address will appear on the checks you print.
  - **Assign To Groups** opens a dialog with which you can assign this payee to a group within Quicken.
  - **Select All/Select None** selects all or none of the payees in the Address Book.
- **Print** offers commands for printing Address Book record information.
- **How Do I?** displays the Quicken Personal Finances Help window with instructions for working with the Address Book.

Adding or Modifying Address Book Records

To add a new Address Book record, click the New button in the Address Book window. The Edit Address Book Record dialog, shown earlier, appears.

You also use the Edit Address Book Record dialog to edit an existing record. Simply select the record in the Address Book window, and click the Edit button in the button bar. You can also double-click the entry to open it if you choose.

The Edit Address Book Record dialog has five tabs for recording information. Click a tab to display its options, and then enter the information you want to store. Here's what you can enter in each of the five tabs:

- **Payee** is for the information that would normally appear in a Write Check window, as well as some additional contact information. From this tab, you can also tell Quicken to include this payee in other lists.
- **Contact** is for the name, title, phone numbers, and website of a specific person.

- **Secondary** is for a secondary mailing address and e-mail address.
- **Personal** is for personal information, such as spouse and children's names, birthday and anniversary, an ID number if you need one, and still more phone numbers.
- **Miscellaneous** is for additional information, such as user-defined fields and notes.
- Click OK to save your entry.

Printing Entry Information

You can print the information in the list in three formats: list, labels, and envelopes.

Start by selecting a group from the Group drop-down list at the top of the Address Book window. From the group of records that displays, select a payee or several payees whose information you want to print.

If you want to change the format of a specific record, choose that record and click Options | Format Address to open the Format Print Check Address dialog seen here. Set the options and click OK.

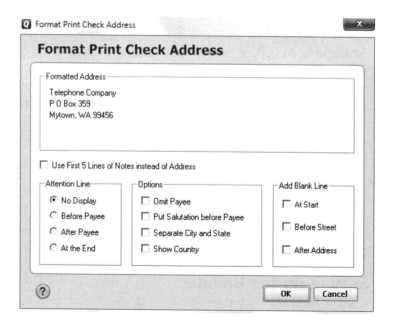

From the Address Book window, click the Print icon to open a drop-down list of printing options. These options are List, Labels, and Envelopes.

List Choosing List displays a Print dialog just like the one that appears when printing Quicken reports. Use it to enter printing options, and then click OK to print the list. See Chapter 8 for more information about printing lists and reports.

Labels Choosing Labels displays the Print Labels dialog. It includes a list of commonly used Avery label products; be sure to select the right one before you click the Print button. To print a sheet of return address labels, choose an address from the drop-down list in the Return Address area, and select the Return Address (Whole Sheet) option in the Print Selection area. Click Print to print your labels.

Envelopes Choosing Envelopes displays the Print Envelope dialog. Use it to print #10 envelopes for Address Book records. Just set options in the dialog, put envelope stock into your printer, and click the Print button. Click Done to close the Address Book window.

One Step Update and the Password Vault

As discussed in Chapters 5 and 9, many of Quicken's online features use One Step Update to update information and download transactions entered on the Web. But that's not all One Step Update can do. This feature makes it possible to handle many of your connection chores at once. When used in conjunction with the Password Vault feature, you can click a few buttons, enter a single password, and take a break while Quicken updates portfolio and account information for you. You can even schedule updates to occur automatically when Quicken isn't running.

Using One Step Update

The idea behind One Step Update is to use one command to handle multiple online activities. This eliminates the need to use update commands in a variety of locations throughout Quicken. One command does it all.

Setting Up the Update

Choose Tools | One Step Update or click the Update button (the blue right-curling arrow) in the Account Bar. If a dialog appears asking if you want to set up the Password Vault, click No for now. You'll see how to use this feature later in this chapter, in the section titled "Entering the Password Vault." The One Step Update dialog, which is shown in Figure 6-10, appears. It lists all of the items that can be updated. Check marks appear for each item that will be

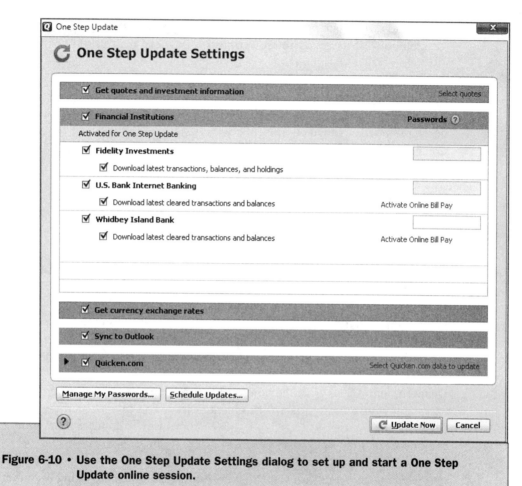

Figure 6-10 • Use the One Step Update Settings dialog to set up and start a One Step Update online session.

updated when you connect. You can click the check boxes to toggle the check marks there.

Get Quotes And Investment Information   This area offers one option to download security quotes, asset classes, financial headlines, and security-related alerts. You can select which quotes should be downloaded by clicking the Select Quotes link. Learn more about downloading quotes in Chapter 12.

Financial Institutions   The Financial Institutions area lists all of the financial institutions for which Online Account Services have been enabled. Your list will differ from the one shown here—unless we have the same financial institutions! You can enter your password in a box to the right of each institution name when you're ready to update your data. Note that this part of the dialog scrolls; be sure to scroll down if necessary to set options for financial institutions at the bottom of the list.

Get Currency Exchange Rates   If you have enabled multiple currency transactions in Quicken Preferences, you will see this option. Otherwise, it does not appear. (To enable multiple currency support, click Edit | Preferences | Calendar And Currency, and select the Multicurrency Support check box. Click OK to close the Preferences dialog.)

Sync To Outlook   If you use Microsoft Outlook, you can synchronize your reminders with your Outlook calendar. These reminders will appear in your Outlook calendar as "All Day Events."

If you use your Outlook calendar to "remind" you, make sure to run a One Step Update each time you make changes in the Bills And Reminders dialog. Otherwise, the changes you made in Quicken will not be updated in Outlook. Conversely, if you make changes in Outlook, remember to make the same change in Quicken. One Step Update works from Quicken to Outlook, not from Outlook to Quicken.

Quicken.com   The Quicken.com area lists preferences for uploading or exporting your Quicken data with Quicken.com. You can access these Quicken Preferences by clicking the Select Quicken.com Data To Update link. Your options are as follows:

- Selecting accounts you want to view online. All of the investing accounts you have entered into Quicken are displayed. You can choose which, if any, you want to view.
- Click Send My Shares to track the value of your current holdings.
- Click Send Only My Symbols if you want general information about your stock holdings.
- By default, your Watch List (see Part Three for more information about Watch Lists) is tracked in Quicken.com. Clear this check box if you don't want it tracked.
- Change My Quicken.com Credentials At Next One Step Update will open the Quicken Preferences dialog at the Quicken.com Portfolio dialog. If you select the Change My Quicken.com Credentials At Next One Step Update check box and click OK, a warning appears reminding you that you may not

be able to sync your Quicken.com account if you change your name and password. From this warning message select Yes or No.

• Click OK to close Preferences and return to the One Step Update dialog.

Updating Information

Make sure check marks appear beside the items you want to update in the One Step Update dialog. If necessary, enter passwords in the text boxes beside financial institutions for which you want to update data. Then click Update Now. If Quicken offers to save your passwords, click No for now. Learn how to use the Password Vault feature later in this chapter. Quicken establishes a connection to the Internet and begins transferring data.

When the update is complete, the One Step Update Summary dialog appears. As shown in Figure 6-11, it summarizes the activity for the update. Click the disclosure triangles to the left of financial institution names to reveal a list of

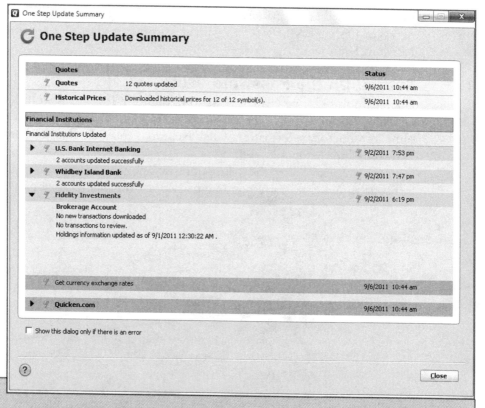

Figure 6-11 • The One Step Update Summary displays the results of your One Step Update.

accounts and activity. You can click the name of an account in the window to go to that account's register, or click the Close button at the bottom of the window to dismiss it.

The One Step Update Summary dialog does not appear if you have previously told Quicken to display the summary only when there is an error.

Entering the Password Vault

You might find it a nuisance to have to type in each password when you use the One Step Update feature—especially if you connect to more than one or two financial institutions. This is when the Password Vault can help.

Quicken's Password Vault feature enables you to store all your financial institution passwords in one central location. The passwords are then protected with a single password. When you use One Step Update, you enter just one password to access all financial institutions. You must have Online Account Access or Online Payment set up with at least one institution to use the Password Vault feature.

Setting Up the Password Vault

Choose Tools | Online Center | Password Vault Or Tools | Password Vault | Set Up New Password Vault. The Password Vault Setup dialog appears. It provides some introductory information. Click Next to display the first window of the Password Vault Setup.

As shown next, follow the instructions in each tab to choose financial institutions and enter corresponding passwords. You'll enter each password twice

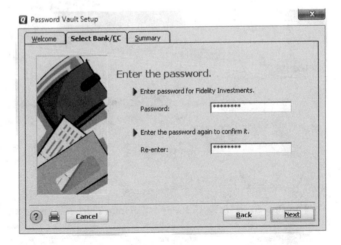

because the characters you type do not appear on screen; this is a secure way of making sure you enter the same thing both times. You can do this for any combination of financial institutions for which you have set up online access.

When you've finished, select the No option if you have no other passwords to enter. Select Yes if you have other accounts you wish to include in the Password Vault. Enter as many as you choose, and when all have been entered, click No when asked whether you want to enter additional passwords. Click Next to continue.

You are prompted to enter a password, and re-enter it, to protect the Password Vault. Enter it in each box and click Next.

When you click Next, the Summary tab of the Password Vault Setup window appears. It displays a list of your financial institutions and indicates whether a password has been stored for each one.

You can use buttons in this dialog to change or delete a selected password, print all passwords, or change the Vault password. When you've finished working with the window's contents, click Done. Quicken creates the Password Vault.

If you choose to print your passwords, do not leave the printed list in plain sight or affix it to your monitor.

Using the Password Vault

Using the Password Vault is easy. Simply choose Tools | One Step Update or click the Update Accounts button in the Account Bar. You will no longer be prompted for any passwords. Simply continue using One Step Update in the usual way, but with one difference: You don't have to enter passwords for any of the financial institutions for which a password has been entered in the Password Vault.

IN MY EXPERIENCE

When you create a password in Quicken (or anywhere else), use a password that has at least one letter, one digit, and uppercase as well as lowercase letters. Do not use a password that is a family member's (or your own) birthday, anniversary, or street address. A strong password has the following characteristics:

- Contains at least eight characters.
- Combines letters, numbers, and symbols. (However, some symbols cannot be used by some financial institutions. Generally speaking, an exclamation point [!] or a question mark [?] are okay.)
- Cannot be found in an English (or other language's) dictionary.
- Is not a name.
- Is not scribbled on a sticky note on your monitor.
- Is not shared with others.

In addition, consider changing your password at least once every three to six months and making each new password substantially different from the last password you used.

You can also use the Password Vault in conjunction with the Update/Send button in the Online Center window, which is discussed in Chapters 5 and 10. Clicking that button automatically displays the Password Vault dialog. Enter your password and click OK; Quicken performs the update.

Editing the Password Vault

Once you've created a Password Vault, you can modify it to change passwords or add passwords for other financial institutions. Choose Tools | Password Vault | Add Or Edit Passwords. In the Edit Password Vault dialog that appears, click the Change Vault Password button to change the password to your Password Vault. Click Change Password to change the passwords for any account. Click Delete Password to delete an account's password. When you've finished, click Done.

Deleting the Password Vault

You can delete the Password Vault if you decide you no longer want to use it. Choose Tools | Password Vault | Delete Vault And All Saved Passwords. Then click Yes in response to the confirmation dialog that appears. Quicken deletes the Password Vault. From then on, you'll have to enter passwords for each financial institution when you use One Step Update.

The user name for your accounts is shown in the Password Vault in conjunction with the name of your financial institution. Should the bank issue you a new user name, you can change it in the General tab of the Account Details dialog for that account. It cannot be changed in the Password Vault.

Scheduling Updates

You can schedule updates to occur when you're not using Quicken. Then, when you start Quicken, your data file is already updated with information from your financial institutions, and, if you've disabled automatic transaction download, ready to review and accept into your account registers. Your Quicken.com information can also be automatically updated based on information in your Quicken data file.

Setting Up the Schedule

To set up a schedule, begin by choosing Tools | Schedule Updates. The Schedule Updates dialog, which is shown next, appears. Set options in each area of the dialog and click OK.

The following sections look at each of the options.

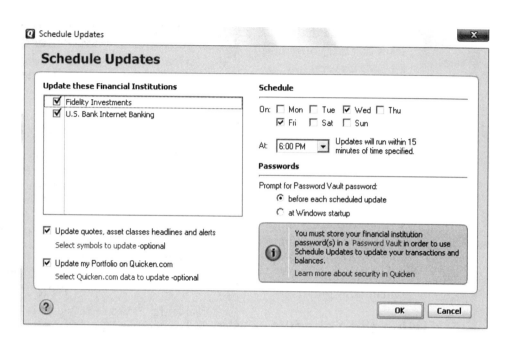

Items To Schedule   The update area lists all of the items in the One Step Update dialog discussed earlier in this chapter. Click to toggle check marks beside each item you want to include in the schedule.

Schedule   The Schedule area determines when the updates will occur. Select the check boxes for each day of the week you want the updates to occur, and then choose a time from the At drop-down list. Since your computer must be running for the updates to take place, set options for when you know your computer will be turned on. Updates will not occur, however, if Quicken is running; this ensures that the automated feature does not interrupt your work with Quicken.

Passwords   Security options enable you to indicate when your computer should prompt you for the Password Vault password. (The Password Vault feature must be set up and used in conjunction with scheduled updates.) You have two options:

- **Before Each Scheduled Update**   This option displays the Password Vault Password dialog just before each update. You may want to select this option if the update is scheduled for a time when you expect to be at work on your computer. This is a more secure option, since it requires you to be present just before the update takes place. If you're not around, however, the update will not take place as scheduled.

- **At Windows Startup** Choosing this option displays the Password Vault Password dialog when you start Windows. This option can make scheduled updates more convenient, since you can step away from your computer while the update is in progress.

Using the Schedule
Using the schedule is easy.

1. Exit Quicken, since a scheduled update will not occur when Quicken is running.

> ### IN MY EXPERIENCE
>
> Sometimes it's hard to remember what passwords are for what purpose. Just to review them:
>
> - **Data File Password** This is the password, if any, you have created using File | Set Password For This Data File.
> - **Vault Password** You set and use this password when working with the Password Vault. All of your financial institutions' login information is stored safely within the Password Vault.
> - **Login Information** These are the user names, passwords, and PINs given to you by your financial institution so that you can access and/or download the information from their server into Quicken.
>
> In order for Scheduled Updates to function, you must have your login information stored in the Password Vault for each of the financial institutions you want to update. Also, both your computer and your Internet access must be on; however, the Quicken must be closed to run the Scheduled Update.

2. When you are prompted for the Password Vault password (which happens just before the update), enter the password. (If you have told Quicken to prompt for the Password Vault password at Windows Startup, your Password Vault Password will already have been entered.)
3. Click Update. Quicken does the rest.

Changing the Schedule
To change the schedule, choose Tools | Schedule Updates to display the Schedule Updates dialog. Make changes in the dialog as desired to modify settings. To cancel scheduled updates, clear the check boxes beside each day of the week. When you're finished making changes, click OK.

About Alerts

If you're juggling multiple bank, credit card, and investment accounts along with taxes, reminders, and several insurance policy renewal dates, Quicken's Alerts feature can really help you keep your sanity. After all, who can keep track of all those balances and keep them where they should be? Quicken can! Financial superhero!

For example, suppose you have a checking account and a money market account. The checking account may be free, but only if the balance is at least $1,000. The money market account earns interest, but you're allowed to make only a limited number of monthly expenditures, so it can't replace the checking account. This kind of situation is perfect for Quicken's Alerts feature. Set it up so Quicken tells you when your checking account balance is getting too low—so you can transfer money from your money market account and avoid paying fees—or too high—so you can transfer money to your money market account and earn a little bit of interest on it.

The Alerts feature can also prevent embarrassment at a checkout counter by warning you when a credit card balance is getting dangerously close to its limit. Likewise, it can remind you to pay your credit card bill so even if your balance is relatively low, you won't forget to make that monthly payment on time.

This section discusses the kinds of alerts Quicken offers and explains how to set them up.

Viewing Available Alerts Groups

Quicken offers four different groups of items for which you can set alerts. To enable them, open the Tools menu, choose Alerts Center, click the Setup tab, and then open the group with which you want to work. Here's an explanation of the alerts you can set in each group.

Banking Alerts

- **Account Min. Balances** enables you to set minimum balances for your checking and savings accounts. You can set a minimum amount and a reminder amount for each account, as shown in Figure 6-12. Quicken will alert you when the account balance falls below the reminder amount you specify.
- **Account Max. Balances** enables you to set maximum balances for your checking and savings accounts. Quicken alerts you when the account balance climbs above the amount you specify.
- **Credit Card Limits** enables you to set limits for your credit card accounts. You can set a limit amount and a reminder amount. Quicken alerts you if the balance exceeds the reminder amount.
- **Check Reorder Notice** tells Quicken to alert you when you reach a certain check number. You can set this option for checking and savings accounts. This feature can be used whether you use checks provided by your bank or another printer, or checks you purchase exclusively for use with Quicken.

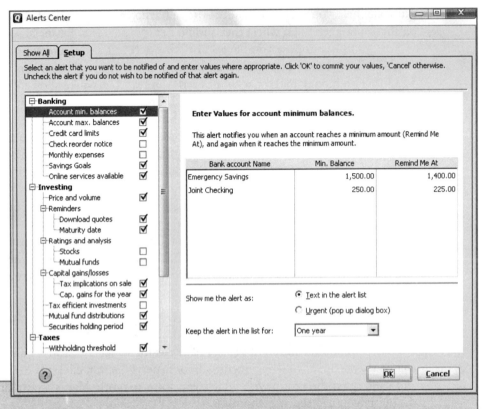

Figure 6-12 • Quicken Alerts can help you remember important financial deadlines.

- **Monthly Expenses** enables you to specify maximum monthly spending amounts for any Quicken expense category. If you exceed the limit you specified, Quicken alerts you to this fact.
- **Savings Goals** tells Quicken to alert you when you fall behind on a savings goal. This option works directly with Quicken's Savings Goals feature, which you learn about in Chapter 16.
- **Online Services Available** tells Quicken to alert you when one of your financial institutions supports Online Account Services. Quicken can learn about new financial partners when you connect to the Internet to utilize other features. Online Account Services is discussed at length in Chapter 5.

In addition, Quicken offers three other General group reminder alerts that fall in the banking group:

- **Online Transactions** tells Quicken to remind you to download transactions from your financial institution if you haven't done so for 30 days or more.

- **Scheduled Bills Or Deposits Due Soon** tells Quicken to remind you in advance of any scheduled transactions that are due.
- **Send To Quicken.com** tells Quicken to remind you to export your portfolio to Quicken.com when holdings change.

Investing Alerts

Chapter 11 discusses setting the Investing group alerts.

Tax Alerts

See Chapter 17 for a discussion on the three Taxes group alerts that are available for your use.

General Alerts

In addition to the three alerts discussed earlier in this section in "Banking Alerts," you can set alerts for the following:

- **Insurance Reappraisal**   Use this alert to remind you of insurance policy renewal dates and to ensure that your current coverage amounts are up to date.
- **Mortgage Reappraisal**   This is a particularly useful alert if your mortgage has a variable interest rate, requires a balloon payment, or requires other, periodic attention.

Setting Up Alerts

You set up alerts from the Setup tab of the Alerts Center window, as seen in Figure 6-12. Click the name of one of the alerts to view and set it.

Setting Basic Options

To set an alert, begin by selecting the name of the alert on the left side of the window. If necessary, click the check box to select it. Then click the value you want to change on the right side of the window and enter a new value. Not all alerts have values you can change; for example, the Online Services Available alert is a simple on or off setting made with the check mark.

Setting Display Options   You can tell Quicken how to notify you with the two options in the bottom half of the Setup window:

- **Text In The Alert List** displays the alert as an item in an Alerts snapshot only, which you can see in the Alerts Center Show All tab and when you add alerts to another view.

- **Urgent (Pop Up Dialog Box)** displays the alert in a dialog when you start Quicken. You must dismiss this in-your-face alert by clicking the OK button in the dialog before continuing to work with Quicken.

Keep the Alert in the List For   You can set the amount of time the alert should remain in the Alerts snapshot. The default setting is One Month, but you can use the drop-down list to choose One Day, One Week, One Month, One Quarter, or One Year.

Finishing Up

When you're completely finished setting alerts, click OK to close the Alerts Center window. The alerts will work quietly in the background, watching your financial dealings. When it's time to go to work, they appear as you specified.

Working with Alerts

Once you've set up alerts, you can view, modify, or delete them as desired. Here's how.

Viewing Alerts

You can view alerts in the Show All tab of the Alerts Center window. Click Tools | Alerts Center | Show All to display them.

Modifying Alerts

You can change the way an alert works at any time. Open the Tools menu, and choose Alerts Center | Setup (refer to Figure 6-12). Then follow the instructions in the earlier section titled "Setting Up Alerts" to change alert settings.

Deleting Alerts

To delete an alert, display the Show All tab of the Alerts Center. Click the Delete button beside each alert you want to delete. A confirmation dialog appears. Click OK to delete the alert.

To prevent a deleted alert from getting reestablished and appearing again in the future, use the Setup tab of the Alerts Center window to clear the check box for the alert in the list on the left side of the window.

You can select multiple alerts and click one of the selected Delete buttons to delete all of the selected alerts. To select multiple alerts, click the first alert, then hold down SHIFT and click the last alert you want to delete. Click any of the Delete buttons within the highlighted selection.

Reconciling Your Accounts

Chapter 7

In This Chapter:

- Starting a reconciliation
- Comparing transactions to a paper statement
- Identifying reconciled items
- Finishing up
- Reconciling for the first time
- Reconciling credit card accounts
- Printing a reconciliation report
- Undoing reconciled transactions

Often, the task of manually balancing, or reconciling, your bank account each month is not your favorite chore. However, you may open your bank statement each month and, using the paper form and a hand calculator, total all the checks and deposits. There's a lot of adding when it comes to totaling the outstanding checks and deposits, and the longer you wait to do the job, the more adding you'll need to do. And for some reason, it hardly ever comes out right the first time you try. Maybe you've even failed so many times that you've given up.

In this chapter, you will learn why it is important to reconcile your bank statements and how you can do it—quickly and easily—with Quicken Personal Finance Software.

Reconciling Bank Accounts

Reconciling an account refers to the process of comparing transactions in your account register to transactions on the account statement sent to you by your bank. Transactions that match are simply checked off. You'll need to account for transactions that appear only in one place such as in your account register or the bank's account statement.

In this section, you'll review the basics of reconciling a bank account with Quicken: comparing transactions, making adjustments, and finishing up.

Starting a Reconciliation

You may reconcile your bank statement with the traditional paper statement sent by your bank or reconcile your account online. We'll begin with a paper statement.

Open the account register for the account you want to reconcile. Click the Account Actions button, and choose Reconcile. What happens next depends on whether the account is enabled for online access.

Quicken does not supply a reconciliation form for cash accounts.

Accounts without Online Account Access

If the account is *not* enabled for online access, the Reconcile Details dialog, which is shown next, appears. It gathers basic statement information prior to reconciling the account. Enter information from your bank statement in the appropriate boxes. (Enter service charge and interest earned information *only* if you have not already entered it in the account register.) Then click OK to continue.

Reconcile Details

Reconcile Details

*Required

The last statement ending date: 6/30/2011

Enter the following from your bank statement

Opening Balance: *	1,988.23
Ending Balance: *	1,998.12
New Statement Ending Date: *	6/30/2011

Categorize your interest and bank charges, if any

Service Charge:	8.00	Date:	6/30/2011
Category:	Fees & Charges:Bank Fee		
Interest Earned:	0.11	Date:	6/30/2011
Category:	Interest Inc		

OK   Cancel

Reconciling Accounts

If you have been reconciling your bank statements for a long time, you may be tempted to skip this chapter. But, please reconsider. This information can save you time, money, and frustration, so please rethink your decision and take the few minutes to read through the chapter.

Reconciling your checking account is important. It helps you locate differences between what you think you have in the account and what the bank says you have. It can help you track down bank errors (which do happen once in a while) or personal errors (which, unfortunately, seem to happen more frequently). Completely balancing your checking account and making adjustments as necessary can prevent you from accidentally bouncing checks when you think you have more money than you really do. That can save you the cost of bank fees and a lot of embarrassment.

If you keep track of all bank account activity with Quicken, reconciling your bank accounts is easy. You won't need to use the form on the back of the bank statement. You won't even need a calculator. Just use Quicken's reconciliation feature to enter beginning and ending balances, check off cleared transactions, and enter the transactions you missed. You'll find you're successful a lot more often with Quicken helping you out.

IN MY EXPERIENCE

Recently a client reported that during a reconciliation the screen images seemed to flicker and disappear. We fixed the problem by clicking Edit | Preferences | Setup | Setup Preferences and clearing the Turn On Animation check box. We then selected Register | Register Appearance and cleared the Use Pop-up Registers check box.

You can use Quicken's reconciliation feature to balance any Quicken banking account—including credit card accounts. Although this chapter concentrates on checking accounts, you'll find information for reconciling other accounts, including credit cards, as well. You can also reconcile checking accounts linked to investment accounts. This is useful if you write checks or pay bills with the linked account.

Reconciling Accounts with Online Account Access

If the account is enabled for Online Account Access, Quicken may begin by displaying a suggestion that you download transactions to update your check register, as seen here.

If your account is not up to date, take a moment to go online and update your account. Unless you manually enter each of your transactions, downloading is the only way you can be sure that all transactions recorded by the bank are included in your account register. Choose Download Transactions For This Account, and click OK to go online and download this account's latest transactions. The One Step Update Settings dialog appears, as shown next. Enter your password for this account, and click Update Now. After your update is complete and you have accepted the downloaded transactions, the One Step Update Summary dialog box displays. Click Close to close it and return to the account's register. Press CTRL-R to open the reconciliation dialog.

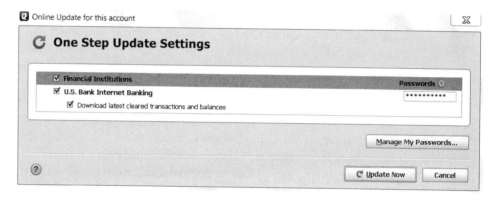

 Depending on your Preferences settings, you may not see the One Step Update Summary unless there are errors during your download. Also, unless you have told Quicken to automatically enter your downloaded transactions into your banking account register, you will have to accept and match your downloaded transactions. See Appendix B for additional information on setting your Preferences in Quicken.

Click Reconcile Without Downloading to continue with the reconciliation, and click OK. Click Cancel if you want to stop the reconciliation process entirely.

 If you have not yet registered your copy of Quicken, you may be prompted to go online and do so before you can download transactions. This requires Internet access.

After you are up to date, or if you have chosen not to update at this time, Quicken displays the Reconcile <account name> dialog.

As you can see, this dialog offers two options for reconciling the account:

- **Use Paper Statement** helps you reconcile the information in your Quicken account register to your bank statement. It is a traditional account reconciliation, and it works just like the account reconciliation you perform for an account without Online Account Access. If you select this option, enter the bank statement ending date and ending balance in the appropriate boxes. The opening balance is the sum of all of the transactions in the register with "R" in the Clr column.
- **Use Online Balance** enables you to reconcile the account to the balance that was last downloaded for the account. When you select this option, you don't have to enter anything in the boxes. Selecting the Auto Reconcile Downloaded Transactions check box tells Quicken to reconcile the account to your financial institution's online balance automatically each time you download and accept transactions. With this Auto Reconcile feature enabled, you never have to reconcile the account again. However, you trust the bank to make no mistakes.

After setting options in this dialog, click OK to continue.

Comparing Transactions to a Paper Statement

The next step in reconciling the account is to compare transactions that have cleared on the statement with transactions in your account register. For this, Quicken displays the Reconcile window (shown in Figure 7-1), which displays all payments, checks, and deposits for the account you are reconciling.

You can use button bar buttons within this window to work with its contents:

- Click New to switch to the account register window for the account you are reconciling so you can enter a new transaction. To return to your reconciliation, click either the Reconcile:<name of account> button at the bottom-left corner of the check register. You may also use the Return To

NEW IN QUICKEN 2012

Quicken 2012 displays all of your button bar choices at the bottom of the Reconcile window. While by default the entries are sorted in descending order with the most recent date at the top, you can sort the entries in either ascending or descending order by clicking the heading in each section. For example, to sort by date in the Deposits section, click Date. To reverse the order in which the column is sorted, click the heading name a second time.

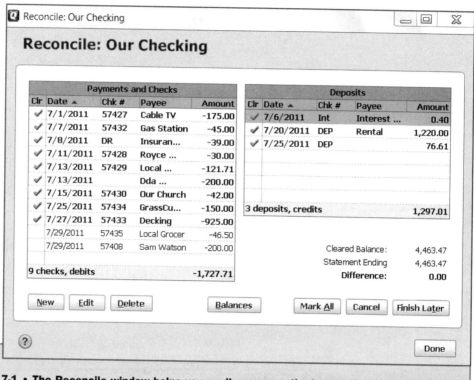

Figure 7-1 • The Reconcile window helps you easily compare the transactions in your register to the items on your paper bank statement.

Reconcile button that displays at the top of your register to the left of the Account Actions button. Both buttons are shown here.

- Select a transaction and click Edit to switch to the account register window so you can modify that selected transaction.
- Click Delete to remove a selected transaction. A prompt appears asking if you want to delete the transaction. Click Yes to remove the transaction from the account register.
- The Balances button displays the Statement Summary dialog shown earlier or the Reconcile Paper Statement dialog (which is similar to the top half of the Reconcile Online Account dialog shown earlier) so you can check or change entries there.

In previous versions of Quicken, the Balances button was called "Back To Reconcile Details."

- The Mark All button is a toggle between Clear All and Mark All that either eliminates the green check mark beside a marked item or marks all of the items in the Reconcile window as being cleared by the bank.
- Click Cancel to leave the reconciliation. You will see a message asking if you want to save your work, as seen here.

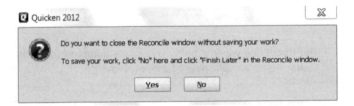

- The Finish Later button saves your work, closes the Reconcile window, and returns you to the account register.
- Click the question mark at the bottom-left corner of the Reconcile window to display the Quicken Personal Finances Help window in the account reconciliation section.

Reconciling to a Bank Statement

Your job is to check off the items in the window that also appear on your bank statement. While you're checking off items in your Quicken register, be sure to check off the same items with a pen or pencil on your bank statement.

If the account is enabled for Online Account Access and you have been downloading and comparing transactions regularly to accept them into your account register, many of the transactions in the Reconcile Bank Statement window may already be checked off. This speeds up the reconciliation process.

IN MY EXPERIENCE

If you have set up Savings Goals (see Chapter 16), you may see "Contributions To Goals" or "Withdrawals From Goals" as items on your account register. These are only for your information and do not affect your bank account. To hide them while you are reconciling your account, click Account Actions, and in the Register View And Preferences section, click Hide Savings Goals as shown here.

IN MY EXPERIENCE

A hidden field—Downloaded Posting Date—controls which transactions are presented in the Reconcile window for accounts with downloaded transactions. You can have this field display in your register by selecting Account Actions | Register Columns. In the menu that appears, check Downloaded Posting Date, and a new column appears on your register next to the Date column. This is handy information if transactions you expect to appear in the current reconcile do not appear—the date the bank posted the transaction may be outside the date range of your reconciliation.

While you're checking off transactions in Quicken and on your bank statement, look for differences between them. Here are some of the differences you might encounter:

- An item that appears on the bank statement but not in your account register is an item that you did not enter. You may have omitted the transaction for a number of reasons. Perhaps it was a bank adjustment that you were not informed about. Or maybe you simply forgot to enter a check. To enter an omitted transaction, click New on the button bar to switch to the register window. Enter the transaction in the register, click Enter, and click either the Reconcile:<account name> button at the bottom-left corner of the register or the Return To Reconcile button at the upper-right corner of your register to continue the reconciliation. Then click to place a check mark in the Clr column beside the item to mark it as cleared.

- An item that has a different date or amount in your register than that shown on the bank statement is usually due to an error—yours or the bank's. If the error is yours, you can edit the transaction by double-clicking it in the Reconcile window. This displays the account register window with the transaction selected. Edit the transaction and click the Save button. Then click the Reconcile:<account name> button at the bottom-left corner of the register or the Return To Reconcile button at the upper-right corner of the register to continue the reconciliation.

- Items that appear in your account register but not on the bank statement are items that have not yet cleared the bank. These are usually transactions prepared just before the bank's closing date, but they can be older. Do not check them off. Chances are you'll check them off the next time you reconcile. If, during a bank reconciliation, you discover any uncleared items that are older than two or three months, you should investigate why they have not cleared the bank. You may discover that a check (or worse yet, a deposit) was lost in transit.

Reconciling to an Online Balance

If you've recently downloaded and accepted transactions for the account, reconciling to an online balance shouldn't take much time. Items you've already reviewed and accepted will be checked off. Some more recent transactions may not be checked off because they haven't cleared your bank yet. Your job is to look for older transactions that appear in your Quicken account register that aren't checked off. These could represent stale payments that may have been lost in transit to the payee or errors (or duplications) you made when manually entering information into your Quicken account register. Follow up on all transactions more than 60 days old to see why they haven't been included with your downloaded transactions.

Remember that each bank downloads slightly differently. Some banks may download only the check number and not the name of the payee. Others may include both the payee and the check number. For some banks, the type of download you choose makes a difference. For example, one bank may charge a fee for Direct Connect that downloads both the payee and the check number, but for Web Connect the downloaded information includes only the check number. Other banks may download transactions only from one statement date to the next statement date, so some transactions you expect to appear will not appear until the next bank statement cycle. See Chapter 5 for more information on the types of downloads available from financial institutions.

Identifying Reconciled Items

When you download your transactions during the month, Quicken marks the Clr column with a "c" because the transaction has been posted at the bank. This does not mean it has been formally reconciled. Once you have finished the reconciliation, whether reconciling to a paper statement or using the online balance as your accepted balance, Quicken will mark each of the transactions in the Clr column with a capital "R," meaning the transaction has been reconciled.

You can change a "c" to an "R" or clear the Clr column entirely. Click in the column to bring up the menu, as shown here. Be careful about changing a reconciled item unless you are making corrections.

As shown in Figure 7-2, Quicken uses the Clr column in an account register to identify items that either have cleared the bank or have been reconciled:

- **c** indicates that the item has cleared the bank. You'll see a c in the Clr column beside items that you have checked off during a reconciliation if you have not completed the reconciliation. You'll also see a c beside items downloaded and accepted using Quicken's Online Account Access feature, as discussed in Chapter 6.
- **R** indicates that the item has been reconciled.

If you want to change a transaction's cleared status, click in the Clr column to see several choices, as shown here. Choose from among the following:

- **Uncleared** indicates that the transaction has not yet been cleared by the bank.

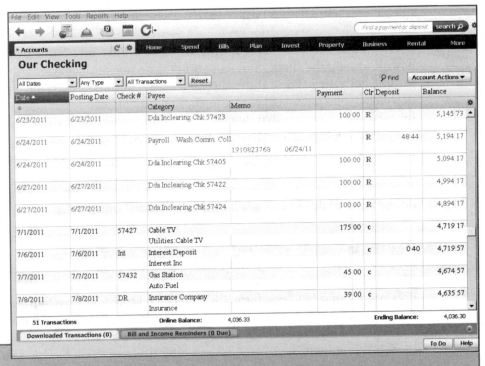

Figure 7-2 • Outstanding transactions in your check register are in black, while items that have been reconciled are in gray.

- **Cleared** indicates that the bank has cleared the item, but the item has not yet been reconciled.
- **Reconciled** shows that the item has been reconciled. To make it even more obvious that a transaction either has cleared your financial institution or has been reconciled, reconciled transactions appear in gray print rather than black as seen in Figure 7-2.
- **Reconcile This Account** begins the reconcile process as discussed earlier in this chapter.

You can toggle the gray color of reconciled transactions to black by clicking Quicken Preferences | Register | Register Appearance | Gray Reconciled Transactions. Gray Reconciled Transactions is chosen by default.

Finishing Up

When you reconcile a bank account with Quicken, your goal is to make the difference between the cleared balance and the statement ending balance zero.

You can monitor this progress at the bottom of the
Reconcile window, as shown here.

Cleared Balance:	4,263.47
Statement Ending	4,263.47
Difference:	**0.00**

Mark **A**ll | Cancel | **F**inish La**t**er

When the Difference Is Zero

If you correctly checked off all bank statement
items and the difference is zero, you've successfully
reconciled the account and you can click the Done button.

If You Can't Get the Difference to Zero

Sometimes, try as you might, you just can't get the difference to zero. Here are a
few last things to check before you give up:

- Make sure all the amounts you checked off in your account register are the
  same as the amounts on the bank statement. Keep in mind that if you made
  a transposition error—for example, 87.91 instead of 87.19—the difference
  between the two amounts will be evenly divisible by 9. In this case, 87.91
  minus 87.19 is .72—a number evenly divisible by 9.
- Make sure you included any bank charges or earned interest.
- Make sure the ending date and balance you entered are the same as those on
  the bank statement.
- Check to see if any of the deposits were entered as checks or checks as deposits.
- Verify that none of the transactions were entered twice.
- Watch for penny differences. Occasionally the bank will see an 8 as a 3 or a
  4 as a 1.

If you checked and rechecked all these things and still can't get the difference
to zero, click Done. Quicken displays a dialog like the one shown here that

indicates the amount of the difference and offers to make an adjustment to your account register for the amount. Click Adjust to accept the adjustment. The amount of the adjustment will be recorded without a category. If you want to continue trying to find the difference, click Cancel to return to the Reconcile window.

If you have entered a transaction and marked it as having been reconciled (marked with an "R" in the Clr column) and it then is downloaded from the bank via Web Connect, depending on your financial institution, that transaction may show in your downloaded transactions list as "New." Verify that the recently downloaded transaction is, indeed, a duplicate and delete the transaction.

IN MY EXPERIENCE

From time to time a deposit shows on the bank statement that does not seem to match anything in your register. It is possible you've deposited two or more checks together at the bank yet entered the deposits separately in your register. If you often have several checks to deposit at the same time, create a split deposit as explained in Chapter 4. This way, the total deposit will match the bank statement.

If any of the checks in a group is a "form," such as a payroll check, consider using two deposit slips so that each deposit shows separately on the bank statement. Some folks even use an undeposited checks account in Quicken where they enter the individual checks, then enter a transfer from the undeposited checks account to their checking account in the amount of the group of checks deposited. This allows you to track greater detail about each check than grouping the deposits in a split transaction.

Reconciling for the First Time

Suppose you have a checking account that you've been using for several years. Recently, you purchased and installed Quicken. You set up your checking account in Quicken, using the ending balance on your most recent bank statement—say it was dated 4/30/11—as the beginning balance in the account. After setting up the account, you entered all transactions dated after 4/30/11 into the account register.

May arrived, and you received your 5/31/11 bank statement. Following the instructions in this chapter, you reconciled the account for the first time. But you discovered that the 5/31/11 bank statement included checks you wrote before 4/30/11 that were outstanding (had not cleared the bank) as of the 4/30/11 bank statement. If you didn't consider these transactions in your reconciliation, there is a difference between the cleared balance and the statement ending balance. What do you do about these transactions?

This is the question asked by some new Quicken users. They think they need to make some kind of adjusting entry in Quicken before starting the reconciliation. Instead, Quicken provides two options:

- If you want to record the transactions in your Quicken register—perhaps to make charges to categories more complete—record them. You can do this during the reconciliation by clicking the New button on the Reconcile window's button bar (refer to Figure 7-1) as explained earlier in this chapter. Once the transactions have been entered, be sure to check them off in the Reconcile window. The difference should go away.
- If you don't want to record the transactions—perhaps you don't care how the categories are affected—let Quicken make an adjusting entry for you at the end of the reconciliation. That adjustment is the sum of any deposits or checks that had not cleared the bank by the 4/30/11 statement.

Once that first reconciliation is complete, you should have no further problems—unless, of course, the 6/30/11 bank statement includes one or more very old checks from before 4/30/11. Then the same situation results, with the same options and resolution.

A note here: be careful of old checks you have written that may suddenly clear. A good example of this is a check you wrote as a donation to a local children's sport activity. It may sit in someone's desk for several months before that person notices it and puts it into the bank. Each bank has their own policy on "stale-dated" checks, meaning that only checks within a certain period are honored. However, checks can slip through with dates as old as last year!

Other Reconciliation Tasks and Features

Quicken offers a number of other reconciliation features that you might find useful. Here's a quick look at them.

Reconciling Credit Card Accounts

You can reconcile a credit card account the same way you reconcile a bank account. If you try to enter all credit card transactions as you make them throughout the month, it's a good idea to use the reconciliation feature to compare your entries to the credit card statement, just to make sure you didn't miss any. If you simply enter all credit card transactions when you get your statement, reconciling to the statement really isn't necessary.

Many Quicken users go online frequently to view both their bank account and credit card balances to ensure there are no fraudulent or unidentified charges.

Reconcile a Credit Card without Online Access

Choose the account you want to reconcile from the Account Bar to open that account's register. Press CTRL-R to begin the reconciliation. When you reconcile an account for which you have not enabled Online Access, Quicken displays the Reconcile: Credit Card dialog as shown here.

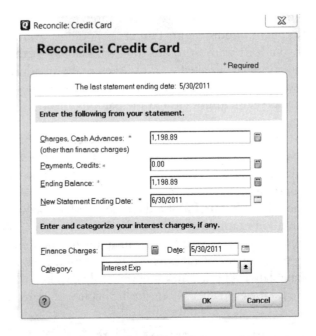

As you can see, you are prompted to enter the total charges, including cash advances, you made during the billing period as well as any payments or credits that have been made on the account. You can find this information on your paper credit card statement. Enter the new statement ending date, any finance charges, and the date they were assessed. Note the red asterisks by the required fields. You must enter a number or date in these fields, even if the number is zero. Click OK to move to the Reconcile window, which looks and works almost exactly like the Reconcile window that was shown in Figure 7-1.

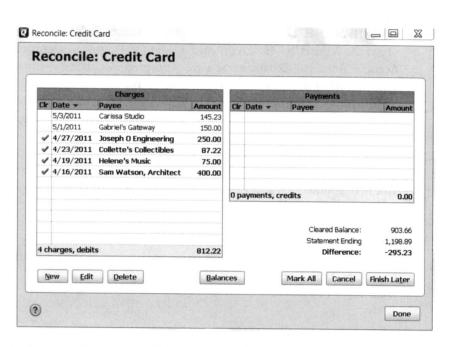

As shown earlier, as you click each cleared transaction, a small green check mark appears. Click Mark All to clear every transaction shown in the Reconcile window. Click Done when the Difference field shows zero. You return to the account register, where you will notice each transaction displays an "R" in the Clr column, as shown here.

Date ▲	Reference #	Payee		Charge	Clr
▶ 🖉		Category	Memo		
4/16/2011		Sam Watson, Architect		400 00	R
		Home Improven			
4/19/2011		Helene's Music		75 00	R
		Entertainment			
4/23/2011		Collette's Collectibles		87 22	R
		Gifts Given	Mom's birthday		
4/27/2011		Joseph O Engineering		250 00	R
		Home Repair/L₁			
5/1/2011		Gabriel's Gateway		150 00	R
		Charitable Dona			
5/3/2011		Carissa Studio		145 23	R
		Home Improven			
5/6/2011		Royce's Repair		91 44	R
		Auto:Maintenan			

Reconcile a Credit Card with Online Access Enabled

Open the register for the credit card account you want to reconcile. Click Account Actions | Reconcile. You are prompted to either download any current transactions or proceed to the reconciliation process without downloading. See "Reconciling Accounts with Online Account Access" earlier in this chapter for more information. For this example, we are choosing to reconcile without downloading.

Click Reconcile Without Downloading, and click OK to proceed. The Reconcile Online Account window for the current account appears, as seen next. You may choose to reconcile to a paper statement, in which case you must enter a value (which can be zero) in each of the fields. If you accept the online balance method, note the Balance As Of date and recognize that the balance displayed is what the bank has cleared as of that date.

If you have chosen to reconcile the account to your online balance, click Auto Reconcile After Compare To Register to change the "c" in the Clr column of your register to an "R."

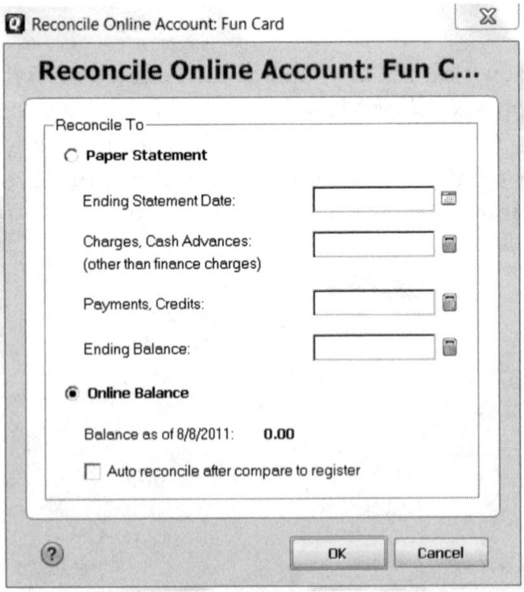

After you have completed the reconciliation, if there is a balance on the account, Quicken asks if you want to make a payment, as shown next. If you choose to make a payment, select the bank account from the drop-down list and tell Quicken if you are going to print a check through Quicken or write the check. If your choice is to print a Quicken check, the Write Check window displays. If you choose not to make a payment at this time, click No.

If you have enabled online payments for this account, either through your financial institution or Quicken Bill Pay, you may see an additional option to pay online.

When your credit card balance is zero, a message box appears stating that there is no payment required, as you have an outstanding balance of zero. Click OK to close the message box.

Adjusting Your Register

If you can't successfully get the credit card reconciliation to work, Quicken offers to make adjustments. The following illustration shows the Adjust Balance dialog for a hopelessly messed-up account that needs adjustments. Choose a date for the adjustment, and click Adjust to make the entry, which will show as a balance adjustment in your register as of the date you enter in this dialog.

Be careful about clicking any Don't Show Me This Screen Again check boxes. You only get one chance to do this, and at some point, you may want to see the dialog. To do so, you will need to reset the Quicken Warnings preference. Click Edit | Preferences | Alerts | Warnings | Reset Quicken Warnings.

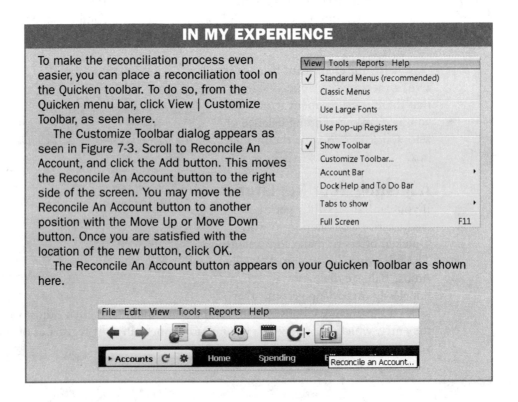

Printing a Reconciliation Report

At the end of a bank account reconciliation, Quicken displays a dialog that offers to create a reconciliation report. If you click Yes, the Reconciliation Report Setup dialog, shown here, appears. Give the report a title if you

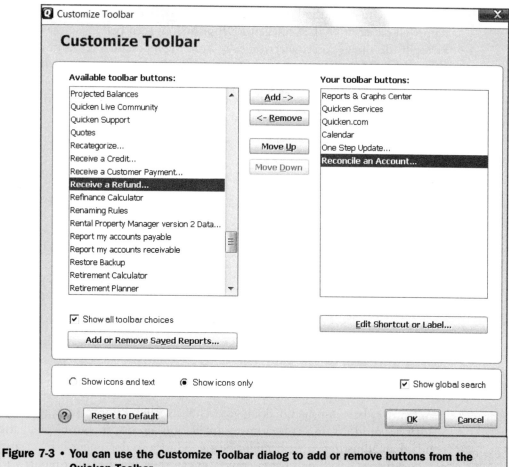

Figure 7-3 • You can use the Customize Toolbar dialog to add or remove buttons from the Quicken Toolbar.

wish, set the date at which the balance is to be shown, and tell Quicken to show either all of the transactions as of the bank balance date or just a summary of all the transactions and each transaction that has not yet cleared the bank.

The reconciliation report is only available for bank accounts, not credit card reconciliations!

You can also tell Quicken to show the transactions that affect any Saving Goals you have set. See Chapter 16 for more information about Savings Goals.

Click OK to open the Print dialog shown next. You may choose to print the report on paper or to the Quicken PDF printer, as seen here. Saving your report as a .pdf file allows you to electronically store the report in a location you choose on your hard drive. If your report is a long one, you can choose to print just one or two pages. In the Print Range section of the Print dialog, click Pages and enter the page number from which you wish to start in the From field and the page number with which you want to end in the To field.

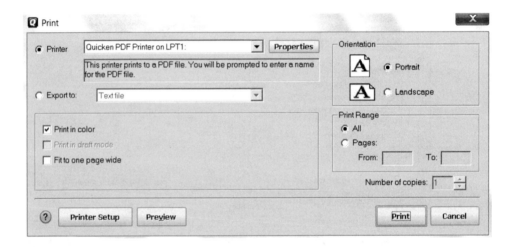

When you have finished making your choices, click Print to print the report.

Even if you don't normally print reconciliation reports, if your reconciliation required an adjusting entry, it might be a good idea to document it by creating a report, either as a .pdf or a paper copy. You can then file the paper report with your bank statement and canceled checks, or store the .pdf with an electronic copy of your statement and pictures of your processed checks. Quicken does not save copies of your reconciliations from previous months. To ensure you have a copy, either print a hard copy or save your report as a .pdf through the Quicken PDF Printer. Some Quicken users take advantage of the Transaction Notes And Flags feature to save specific transaction information. Chapter 4 discusses this feature in more detail.

You can print a current reconciliation report at any time. Open the register for which you want the report, and from the Reports menu, click Banking | Reconciliation to open the Reconciliation Report Setup dialog.

Undoing Reconciled Transactions

From time to time you may have to clear previously reconciled transactions or even undo an entire reconciliation. Be aware—this is *not* recommended! However, computers are not always consistent, banks occasionally merge and their records get skewed, a user will sometimes make a mistake and so on. *Before* you make any changes to any reconciled transaction, do a backup of your data. See Appendix A for instructions on creating a backup.

To unclear a transaction you have inadvertently marked as reconciled:

1. Select the transaction and click in the Clr column.
2. Change the notation to Uncleared if it has not been downloaded or to Cleared if the transaction has cleared the bank.

If you need to clear several transactions in a row:

1. Click the first of the transactions, hold down your SHIFT key, and click the last transaction in the group, as seen here.

Date ▲	Posting ...	Check #	Payee		Payment	Clr	Deposit	B
▶ ● ℓ			Category	Memo				
6/7/2011	6/7/2011		Check		152 01	R		
			Healthcare:Phys	Download from				
6/8/2011	6/8/2011		Monthly Maintenance Fee Waive			R	8 95	
				Download from				
6/8/2011	6/8/2011		Cancelled Ck Return Fee		5 00	R		
				Download from				
6/8/2011	6/8/2011		Monthly Maintenance Fee		8 95	R		
				Download from				
6/14/2011	6/14/2011		Check		29 86	R		
			Healthcare:Phys	Download from				
7/11/2011	7/11/2011		Cancelled Ck Return Fee		5 00	R		
				Download from				
7/19/2011	7/19/2011	Check #	Check		54 66	R	*Deposit*	
			Healthcare:Phys	Download from				

2. Note that each selected transaction is highlighted. Right-click someplace within the highlighted area, and from the context menu that appears, click Reconcile and choose either Not Reconciled or Cleared. In our example, shown here, we are changing each of the reconciled transactions to Not Reconciled.

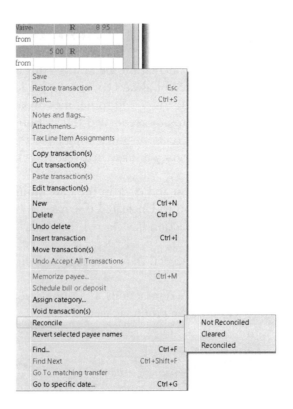

3. Each transaction in the group now shows that it has not
   been cleared, as seen here.

If the transactions you want to change are not in a row (listed
one after the other), follow the procedure shown in Step 1, but
hold down your CTRL key and click each transaction you want
to change. These transactions will now be highlighted and you
can continue with Steps 2 and 3.

Payment	Clr	Deposit
152 01		
		8 95
5 00		
8 95		
29 86		
5 00		
54 66		

Examining Your Banking Activity

In This Chapter:

- *Exploring the Spending graph*
- *Using the Spending register*
- *Reviewing report and graph types*
- *Creating reports and graphs*
- *Working with a report window*
- *Customizing reports and graphs*
- *Working with subreports*
- *Saving reports and graphs*
- *Exporting your reports*
- *Printing reports and graphs*

By now you may agree that entering financial information into Quicken Personal Finance Software is a great way to organize it. But sometimes organizing information isn't enough. Sometimes you need to see concise summaries of the information you entered in the form of balances, activity reports, and graphs.

Quicken provides the kind of information you're looking for in the form of snapshots, reports, and graphs. This chapter discusses Quicken's Spending tab by telling you about the snapshots of information it offers and how you can take advantage of its alerts. It also explains how you can create, modify, and save standard and custom reports and graphs for all Quicken tabs.

A Closer Look at the Spending Tab

Previous chapters in this part of the book have explored many aspects of Quicken's banking area, including accounts, transaction entry, Online Account Services, automation features, and reconciliations. But the Spending tab offers a place for examining the results of your work with your banking accounts.

In this part of the chapter you will go on a guided tour of the Spending tab's reporting and graphing features so you can take advantage of all of the elements found in that section of Quicken.

Exploring the Spending Graph

When you click the Spending tab, a graph appears that displays the total amount (see Figure 8-1) you have spent from all of your banking accounts for the last 30 days. The top of the window shows the total in all categories. Next is a colorful

Figure 8-1 • From the Spending tab you can generate a number of graphs and reports.

pie chart with a legend to the right explaining the category associated with each of the "pie slices." The lower part of the window displays the transactions in register format.

Accounts

The Accounts drop-down list, seen here, lets you decide which accounts to display in the Spending graph. You can choose from the following:

- **All Accounts**, which includes all of the accounts that appear in the Banking section of the Account Bar.

If you pay from a brokerage account, you must use the Custom account setting from the drop-down list and select the account from that list.

- **All Checking/Savings/Cash/Credit Cards** includes the accounts you have so named in Quicken.
- At the bottom of the drop-down list, all of your banking accounts are listed so that you can choose to use just one in your Spending graph.
- Choose Custom to open the Customize dialog, which allows you to choose more than one account to display in your graph. In the example shown here,

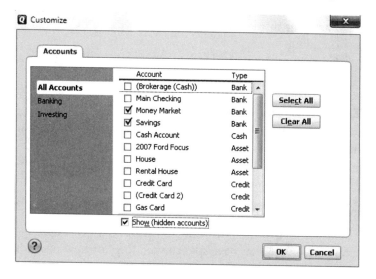

we've chosen to display both the Money Market and the Savings accounts. In our example, we've also told Quicken to show all the hidden accounts. If you clear that check box, only the accounts you've opted to display will show.

When you open the Customize dialog, you will see all of your accounts listed, not just your banking accounts.

Time Period

While the default for your Spending graph is the last 30 days, you can use this drop-down list to choose any time period you wish. Your options are

- **All Dates**, which includes every date for which you have entered a transaction into Quicken.
- **This Month**, which displays just the spending you've done since the first of the current month.
- **Last Month** includes your expenditures in the last calendar month.
- **Last 30/60/90 Days** options are self-explanatory.
- **Last 12 Months** includes all of your expenditures for the last 365 days (or 366 days in leap years).
- **This Quarter** includes the information from the first day of this calendar quarter through today.
- **Last Quarter** presents your spending for the most recent calendar quarter before this quarter.
- **This Year** presents all of your spending since the first of January through today.
- **Last Year** displays all of last year's spending.
- **Custom** lets you set the date range for your graph, as seen here.

This Month, This Quarter, and This Year display all of the spending for those respective time periods, even future dated transactions. For example, if today is 8/21/2011 and you have a transaction entered for 8/24/2011, the 8/24/2011 transaction will show in the spending for This Month, This Quarter, and This Year.

Transaction Types

The Income/Spending drop-down list has only two options. You can choose to show how much you have spent (Spending) or how much has been added to your accounts (Income).

Reset and Find Buttons

The Reset button, located next to the Spending/Income drop-down list, resets your graph to the default of All Accounts, Last 30 Days, and Spending.

The Find button opens the Quicken Find dialog seen here. Learn more about the Quicken Find dialog in Chapter 4.

Using the Spending Register

The register shown at the bottom of the Spending tab's Transaction view displays all of the transactions from the accounts you have chosen in the Accounts drop-down list at the top of the Spending graph. It includes an Account column, in which Quicken displays the account into which the transaction was entered.

By default, this register is sorted by date, with the earliest date first. You can tell Quicken which columns to display and which columns to hide, as seen in Figure 8-2. To access the list of Register Columns, click the small gear icon at the upper-right corner of the register. When you move your mouse over the icon, the Register Columns label will appear as shown next. Click the check box for each column you want the

Figure 8-2 • You can select the columns that appear in the Spending tab's Transactions register.

register to display. Clear each check box for columns you don't want to use. When you have finished your selections, click Done.

Your register list may not look the same as the one in the illustration. Listed items and order vary by the type of account and the services you have activated on each account.

If you want to return to the default register column settings, click the gear drop-down arrow at the bottom-left corner of the register columns list.

You can adjust the width of each of these columns by placing your cursor on the line between two columns and dragging to the left or right as shown here. The two-line display shows the Category, Tag (if you've chosen to show the Tag column), and Memo columns on the second line instead of the first. If you choose to show two lines, you cannot adjust the column width of the items on the second line.

Date ▲	Account	Check #
8/8/2011	Small Checking	27458
8/8/2011	Main Checking	12051

The Reports Button

The Reports button in the Spending tab makes it easy for you to quickly print a variety of reports. See "Creating Reports and Graphs" later in this chapter for an overview of the reports that Quicken can produce for you.

The Account Actions Button

When you click the Account Actions button in the Spending tab, the menu gives you several choices. As shown here, it allows you to print both reports and the transactions in the displayed register.

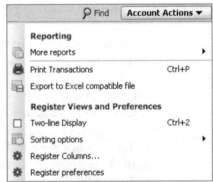

Account Actions Menu Reporting Section This provides links to even more useful reports available in Quicken:

- **More Reports** lets you create a variety of reports such as a Banking Summary Report and a Cash Flow Comparison. See "Quicken Reporting Overview" later in this chapter for complete information about the reports Quicken can create.

- **Print Transactions** opens a Print Register message, as shown here. Type a title for your report. If you want split transactions to be printed, click the Print Split Transactions check box and click Print. The Print dialog appears from which you can select the printer, number of

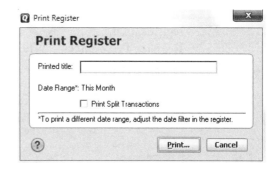

copies, and the orientation of your report. The register will print with the information for the dates you have indicated in the date field at the top of the Spending tab.

You may not see your split transactions in the report you print from the Spending tab. To see the report with splits properly displayed, run the same report from a banking account register. Click Account Actions | Print Transactions or press CTRL-P from the register.

- **Export To Excel Compatible File** sends the information on the currently selected register to an Excel file, formatted as a .txt file.

Account Actions Menu Register Views And Preferences Section

This section is where you tell Quicken how to display your register in the Spending tab:

- **Two-Line Display**   This choice shows each transaction on two lines. Its keyboard shortcut is CTRL-2, which toggles between a two-line and one-line display.
- **Sorting Options**   By default, registers are sorted by date. This option allows you to choose another column by which to sort your register, as seen here.
- **Register Columns**   This option opens a list from which you can tell Quicken what register columns to display in the Spending tab's register. It is the same

list you see when choosing the gear icon located above the scroll bar in the register itself.

- **Register Preferences**   When you select this option, the Preferences dialog opens to Register Preferences from which you can tell Quicken how you want your register to appear. As seen in the illustration, there are several choices that affect the register's display. You can learn more about Quicken Preferences, what they are, and how to set them in Appendix B.

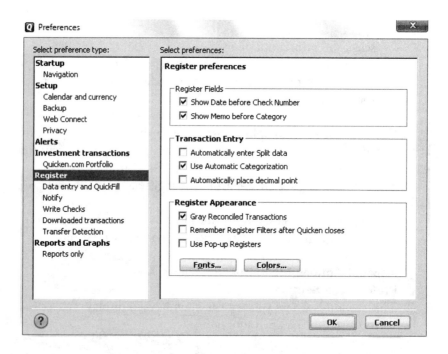

Quicken Reporting Overview

Quicken offers a variety of reports and graphs, each of which can be customized to meet your needs. When you spend time entering data into Quicken, Quicken crunches the numbers for you and provides reports and graphs to analyze your spending habits, help you find ways to save money, and format your data to submit information to financial institutions when you apply for loans or credit cards.

In this section, you'll learn about the types of reports and graphs Quicken offers. Then you'll see how you can use a variety of techniques to quickly create reports and graphs based on the information in your Quicken data file. The techniques in this part of the chapter apply to the reports and graphs you create for any Quicken data, regardless of where it appears.

Reviewing Report and Graph Types

Within Quicken are two kinds of reports and graphs: standard reports created by Quicken and reports you have customized, created, and saved. Here's an overview of each one.

Standard Quicken Reports

When you click Reports on the menu bar, Quicken displays a number of

standard reports and graphs, organized by topic: Banking, Comparison, Investing, Net Worth & Balances, Spending, Tax, EasyAnswer, and Graphs. If you do not see the Net Worth & Balances reports section, turn on the Property & Debt tab by clicking View | Tabs To Show | Property & Debt.

This section discusses standard reports found in the Deluxe edition of Quicken 2012. If you are using the Premier, Home & Business, or Rental Property Manager versions of Quicken, you have additional reports available.

For example, the Banking topic includes Banking Summary, Cash Flow, Cash Flow By Tag, Missing Checks, Reconciliation, and Transaction reports. These reports and graphs clearly show banking-related information. EasyAnswer reports and graphs answer specific, predefined questions, such as, "Where did I spend my money during the period…?" and "How much did I spend on…?" You select a question and then provide optional information, such as a date range, payee, or account. Quicken gathers the information and generates the report or graph.

Customized and Saved Reports

You can create custom reports and graphs based on standard reports and graphs. This multiplies your reporting capabilities, enabling you to create reports or graphs that show exactly what you need to show. When you save your custom reports and graphs, they can be re-created quickly, with just a few mouse clicks, to display current information.

Creating Reports and Graphs

With Quicken, creating a report or graph is as simple as clicking a few buttons. You can use several techniques: choosing a report or graph from the Reports menu, setting options in the Reports & Graphs Center window, using the Reports button, and choosing commands from contextual menus. In this section, you'll learn to use all of these techniques.

Reports & Graphs Center

The Reports & Graphs Center window (see Figure 8-3) offers one way to create reports and graphs. Open the Spending, Planning, or Investing tab, and from the Reports button, choose All Reports | Reports & Graphs Center to display it. You can also access the Reports & Graphs Center from the Quicken menu bar by clicking Reports | Reports & Graphs Center.

Click one of the topics in any of the Quicken Standard Reports sections to display a list of the available reports and graphs. The icon that appears to the left of the report name indicates whether you are choosing a report or a graph. Those items that have both the graph and the report symbol to their left let you choose between the two when you create the report.

To create a report or graph, click its name. Set the Date Range option in the settings field. Click the Customize button to further customize the report or graph, as explained in the section titled "Customizing Reports and Graphs." Then click Show Report or Show Graph to display the report or graph. Figure 8-4 shows an example of a report.

The All Reports Menu

The All Reports menu can be opened from the Reports button in the Spending, Planning, and Investing tabs. It includes a number of submenus, each of which corresponds to a report topic. To create a report or graph from the All Reports

> **IN MY EXPERIENCE**
>
> Recently a client asked how he could find the beginning and ending balance on his transaction report from last month. When he looked at the report again, he saw that the beginning balance for the account (or accounts if you've included more than one bank account) is shown at the top of the report and the ending balance shows on the bottom line entitled "Balance." You may find as well that most of the Quicken reports do have the information you need—you just have to look a bit at the report you've created.
>
> Another person asked why one of her checks showed up in the Income category of her report. When she double-clicked that transaction, she found she had entered that check into the register with an income category rather than an expense category. Once she found the error, it was easily corrected—she just had to change the category.

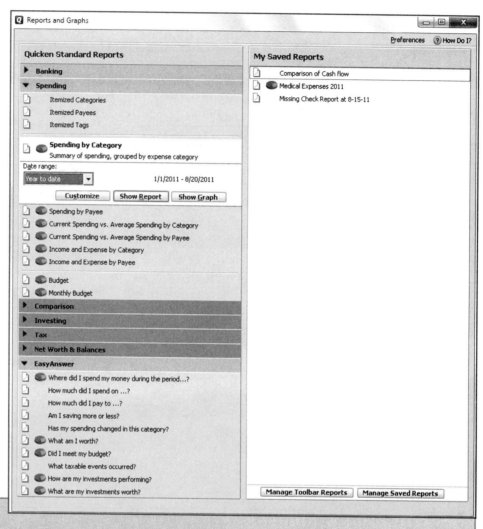

Figure 8-3 • You can access the Reports & Graphs Center from several locations in Quicken.

menu, click a topic submenu, and then click a report name. Quicken creates the report with default date settings, usually the current year to date.

If you have chosen to customize all of your reports and graphs before creating them in Quicken Preferences, a Customize dialog appears before the report is displayed.

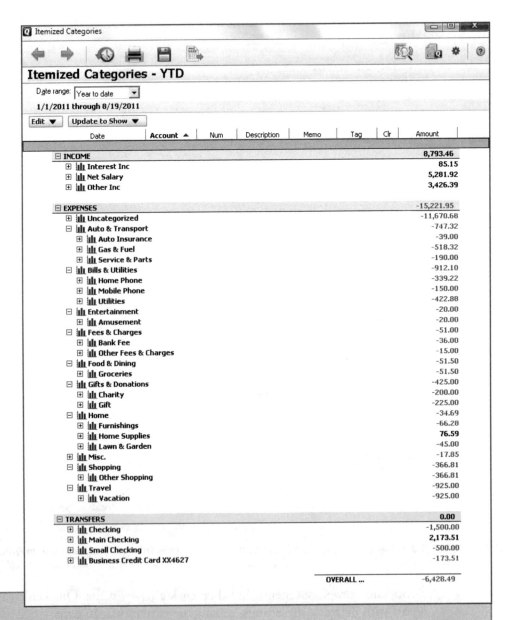

Figure 8-4 • You can create reports that show both your income and expenses by category.

If you start creating reports and find that you often want to change settings or adapt the report in some way, you can tell Quicken to open the customization dialog at the time you select a report to create. To set this preference, click Edit | Preferences | Reports & Graphs; then, from the Customizing Reports And Graphs section, click Customize Report/Graph Before Creating, as shown here.

IN MY EXPERIENCE

One of the really great things about reports in Quicken is the ability to sort from within the report. For example, select a Transaction report from the Banking section of the Reports & Graphs Center. Set your date range and click Show Report. Once the report is displayed, click any of the headings to sort by that heading. For example, sorting by category or tag can produce some very useful reports.

Close OK to close the Preferences dialog. Then, the next time you want to create a report, the Customize dialog will open. Learn more about customization in the "Customizing Reports and Graphs" section later in this chapter.

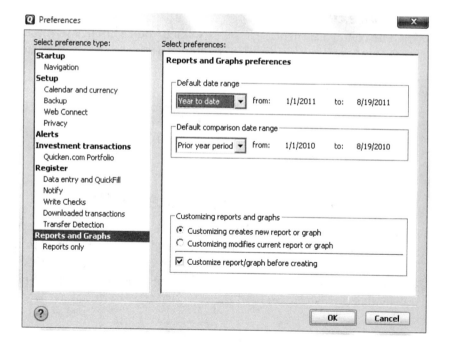

Reports from Other Menus

You can also create a report by using the menus in some windows. This normally creates a report based on information selected within the window.

For example, you could create a Register report for a specific account. From the register for that account, click the Account Actions button, and choose More Reports | Register Report.

A Mini-Report button also appears in an account register window when you activate the Payee or Category field. Clicking this button displays a pop-up mini-report of recent activity for the payee or category, as shown here. Clicking the Show Report button in the mini-report opens a report window with the information.

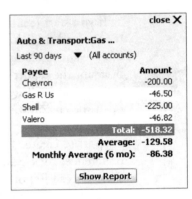

 If you hover your mouse key over the word "Split" in a transaction, the mini-report icon is available from each separate category.

Contextual Menus

The contextual menu that appears when you right-click (click the right mouse button) while pointing to an item sometimes includes a command that will create a report for the item. For example, right-clicking the name of a payee in the account register window displays a context menu that includes the Payments Made To and Launch Mini-Report For Payee *nnnnn* at the bottom of that context menu. An example is shown here.

> Payments made to Shell
>
> Launch Mini-Report for Payee Shell

Working with Reports and Graphs

Although Quicken's standard reports and graphs can often provide just the information you need, you may want to do more with them. In this section, you will see how you can customize reports and graphs, save the reports and graphs you create so they're easy to re-create, and print reports and graphs so you have hard copies when you need them.

Working with a Report Window

When you create a report or graph, it appears in a report window, as seen in Figure 8-4. This window has a number of features and options you can use to work with reports.

Tool Bar Icons

The report window includes a number of tool bar icons, as seen in Figure 8-5, that work with report contents:

> **NEW IN QUICKEN 2012**
>
> Quicken has streamlined the reports and graphs area by offering icon tools on one toolbar.

- The **Back** arrow returns you to the Reports & Graphs Center when you have created your report from that center. The arrow does not appear if you have created your report from a Reports button within the Spending, Planning, or Investment tab. If you have created a subreport, you may see both forward and back arrows.
- The **History** icon displays a list of the parent report and all subreports you have created. Choose the name of a report to display it. If you choose the Show Report List command, a Report History navigation bar appears, listing all reports related to the window. Click the Hide Report List button to hide the list.
- The **Forward** arrow is available only if you have clicked the Back button, and it allows you to move through subreports.
- Click the **Print** icon to send the report or graph to the printer or a file.
- Click the **Export** icon to display a menu that includes commands for exporting the report's contents in three ways: Export Report To Excel Compatible Format, Copy Report To Clipboard, and Export To PDF Format. See more information about exporting in "Exporting Your Reports" later in this chapter.
- The **Save** icon saves the current report. Learn more about saving reports in the section titled "Saving Reports and Graphs," later in this chapter.
- Click the **Find** icon to open the Find And Replace dialog, which you can use to modify transactions that make up the report. Chapter 4 explains even more uses for the Find And Replace dialog.

Figure 8-5 • Use the icons on the Tool Bar displayed in each report to modify your report.

- The **Customize** icon, which looks like a small gear, displays the Customize dialog, which you can use to customize the currently displayed report. The Customize dialog is covered later in this chapter, in the section titled "Customizing Reports and Graphs."
- The **Delete** icon, as shown, deletes the report from the Report History List. This button is gray if the report has not been added to the report list. See more about the report list in the section titled "Saving Reports and Graphs," later in this chapter.
- The familiar **Help** icon is the last item on this Tool Bar. When you click the question mark from a report, Quicken Help opens to answer your questions about reports and graphs.

Hiding or Displaying Report Detail

You can show or hide the details for some reports by clicking a plus (+) or minus (–) button beside a report line. For example, clicking the minus button beside Auto & Transport in the following illustration collapses the subcategories beneath Auto & Transport to show just the main category totals. The button then turns into a plus button, which indicates there are hidden details.

Some reports include additional items that allow you to change what appears on the current report without using the Customization dialog. Appearing under the report title, these additional items include

- The Expand All and Collapse All buttons do the same thing as the plus and minus signs by individual categories, but for all groups in that report.
- The Edit drop-down list, which displays in transactions reports, allows you to
  - Delete a selected transaction (or a group of transactions)
  - Recategorize the selected transaction (or group)
  - Retag the selected transaction or group of transactions
  - Rename selected payees
  - Edit transaction memos

When you double-click a transaction shown on a report, you are taken to that transaction in the appropriate account register. You can return to the report by clicking the report's name at the bottom of the register. An illustration showing the Itemized Payees report is shown here.

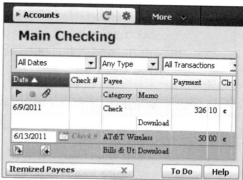

- Date Range and Subtotal By fields allow you to change the focus of the current report.

Spending Trends

One of the very useful tools you will see in Quicken Reports is the Spending Trend report. When you click the Spending Trend symbol to the left of a category or payee, as seen here, a small

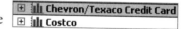

graph, shown next, appears that shows the trend for this category or payee over the last year.

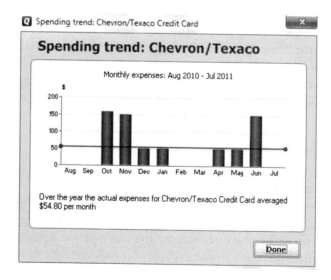

To choose only one bank for a report, use the Accounts tab in the Customization dialog and clear the checks from all the other accounts.

Customizing Reports and Graphs

You can customize just about any report or graph you create so it displays only the information you choose. When you can customize it, however, depends on how you create it:

- When you create a report or graph using the Reports & Graphs Center window (refer to Figure 8-3), you can customize it before or after you create it.
- When you create a report using other commands, you may be able to customize it only after you have created it, unless you have set your preferences to always display the Customization dialog.

EasyAnswer reports do not display a Customize button when you create them from the Reports & Graphs Center; however, once the report is displayed on your screen, the Customize icon is available.

- Once your report appears on your screen, you can always customize that report with the Customize icon.

Customization options vary from one type of report or graph to another. It's impossible to cover all variables in this chapter. Here are the most common options so you know what to expect. You will probably agree that Quicken's reporting feature is very flexible and can take you well beyond the basics.

You can adjust the columns on most reports by placing your mouse cursor on the line between the heading and dragging to the left or right as you require.

Using the Customize Dialog

To customize a report or graph, click the Customize button in the options area for the report or graph in the Reports & Graphs Center window (refer to Figure 8-3) or the Customize button at the top of the report window (refer to Figure 8-4). The Customize dialog, which is shown at the top of the next page, appears. The dialog's full name includes the name of the report or graph.

The Customize dialog includes up to seven tabs of options that you can set to customize the report:

- **Display** enables you to set display options for the report, such as the title, row and column headings, organization, number formatting, and columns.

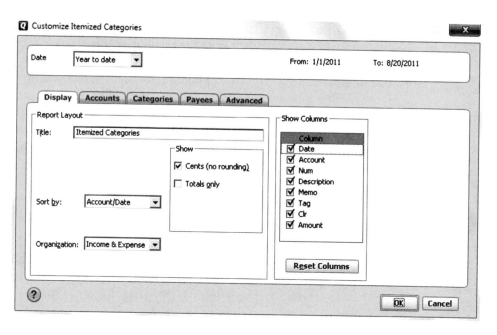

- **Accounts** lets you select the accounts that should be included in the report. Quicken will include transactions or balances in this report for only the accounts you specify.
- From **Categories** you can select the categories to include in the report. If desired, you can use this tab to include only transactions for which the payee, category, or memo contains certain text.
- The **Payees** tab shows options from which you can select the payees to include in the report. If desired, you can use this tab to include only transactions for which the category, payee, or memo contains certain text.
- The **Tags** tab lets you select the tags you want to show in your report.

When working with split transactions where some items have tags and others do not, ensure you have cleared the Not Tagged check box in the Tags tab in the Customize dialog so that the non-tagged items are not included in your report.

- The **Advanced** tab offers different options, depending on the report with which you are working. For example, you can set additional criteria for transactions to be included in the report, such as amount, status, and transaction type. It is also from this Advanced tab that you can tell Quicken to exclude all transfers you make between your accounts.

- The **Securities** tab, available on some reports, allows you to choose the securities you want included in the report. From this tab you can also instruct Quicken to include hidden securities.
- The **Actions** tab, shown in some investment reports, lets you opt to display only certain investment actions you have taken, such as purchases or sales.
- The **Security Types** tab, again only available in some investment reports, lets you determine which security type is displayed on the report.
- The **Investing Goals** tab allows you to create a report that displays the current status of your various investing goals.

If you have established category groups, you may also see a Category Group tab in Summary, Comparison, or Budget reports.

Once you have set options as desired, click the Show Report or Show Graph button as necessary.

There are additional investing and tax schedule reports available only in the Premier or higher editions of Quicken.

If the custom report or graph isn't exactly what you want, that's okay. Just click the Customize button in the report or graph window and change settings in the Customize dialog to fine-tune the report or graph. When you click OK, Quicken creates a new report. You can repeat this process until the report or graph is exactly the way you want it.

Using QuickZoom

The QuickZoom feature enables you to create a report or graph on the fly. Simply double-click a report line item, graph bar, or legend item. Quicken generates and displays a subreport for the item you double-clicked. Click the Back arrow to return to your original report.

Working with Subreports

Quicken creates a subreport each time you customize an existing report or graph, or create a QuickZoom report and save it. As you can imagine, it's easy to accumulate quite a few of these subreports when experimenting with Quicken's reporting features. This can be reduced somewhat by changing your preference settings. Select Edit | Preferences | Reports And Graphs | Customizing Reports And Graphs, and select Customizing Modified Current Report or Graph. Click OK to close the Preferences dialog.

To view a specific subreport, choose its name from the History menu in the report window's toolbar. The view changes to the report.

You can also choose Show Report List from the History menu in the toolbar to display the Report History List. Click the name of the report you want to view to display it.

You can click the Back or Forward button at the top of the navigation bar to move among subreports you have already viewed.

To delete a subreport, display it and then click the Delete icon in the Tool Bar. You can also delete any subreport (other than the first in the report list) by right-clicking the subreport name in the Report History List and selecting Delete This Report from the context menu.

Saving Reports and Graphs

You'll often create a predefined report and customize it to create a report you want to be able to see again and again. Rather than creating and customizing the report from scratch each time you want to see it, you can save the report's settings. Then, when you want to view the report again, just select it from a list and it appears. You can do the same for graphs.

Saving a Report or Graph

To save a report or graph, start by creating, customizing, and displaying it. When it looks just the way you want, click the Save icon in the report window's toolbar. The Save Report dialog, which is shown next, appears.

Enter a name and description for the report or graph in the appropriate boxes. To save the report or graph in a specific folder, choose the folder name from the Save In drop-down list. You can create a new folder by clicking the Create New Report Folder option, entering a name for the folder in the dialog that appears, and clicking OK. To save all versions of the report that you create, turn on the Save Report History check box. When you're finished setting options, click OK to save the report.

Viewing a Saved Report or Graph

When you save a report or graph, it appears in a number of places throughout Quicken, organized by folder if you have saved them into specific folders.

The Reports & Graphs Center Window   Saved reports and graphs appear in the My Saved Reports area of the Reports & Graphs Center window, as seen here. Click the name of the report or graph, change the date range if you choose, and click Show Report or Show Graph to display it.

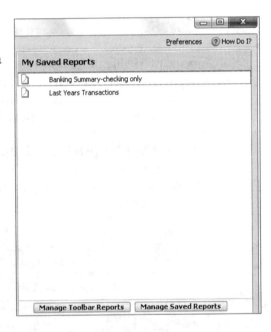

The My Saved Reports & Graphs Submenu   Saved reports and graphs also appear on the Reports menu as My Saved Reports & Graphs. (This submenu appears only if at least one report has been saved.) Choose a report name to display it. If you have a lot of saved reports, you will see an item, More Saved Reports & Graphs, which you can click to open the Reports And Graphs window.

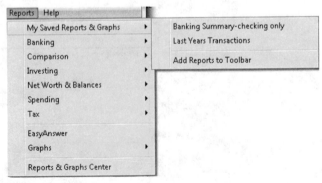

Managing Saved Reports

Quicken offers two tools for managing saved reports: the Manage Saved Reports and Manage Toolbar Reports dialogs. You can open both of these dialogs by clicking the appropriate button within the Reports And Graphs window as seen in Figure 8-3.

Manage Toolbar Reports   When you open the Reports & Graphs Center and look at the My Saved Reports pane, you may see one or two buttons at the bottom of the pane: Manage Toolbar Reports and Manage Saved Reports.

When you click the Manage Toolbar Reports button, you will see a dialog as shown next. This dialog allows you to add saved reports to the Quicken Tool Bar for easy access. (This option appears only when you have chosen to show the Quicken Tool Bar. Click View | Show Toolbar if you do not see this button on the My Saved Reports pane of the Reports And Graphs dialog.)

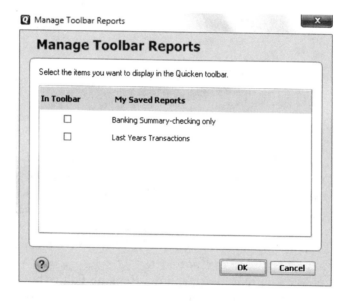

- In the dialog, click the check box of each report you want to show as an icon in the Quicken Tool Bar. Then, click OK to save your settings.
- If you have created your own folders, as described in "Managing Saved Reports" later in this chapter, for your saved reports, you can choose to have one or more of those folders display on the Quicken Tool Bar as well. When you click a saved report folder icon on the Tool Bar, it will appear as a pop-up menu button that lists the reports within it. You can learn more about customizing the Quicken Tool Bar in Appendix B.

Managing Saved Reports The Manage Saved Reports dialog, shown next, enables you to organize saved reports by folder, edit report settings, or delete reports. Select the item you want to work with in the report list, and click a button:

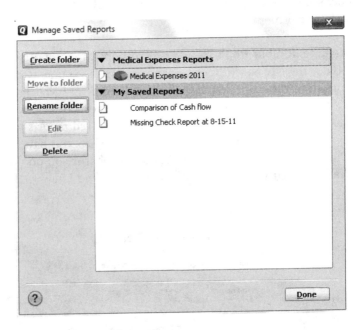

- **Create Folder** displays the Create New Report Folder dialog. Enter a name for the folder in the Name box, and click OK. The folder appears in the list.
- **Move To Folder** displays the Move To Report Folder dialog. When you select a report from the list, this button becomes available. Click the Move To Folder button to open the dialog, and select a different folder from the Name drop-down list. Click OK when you've made your choice, and the report is moved to that folder.
- Select a current folder, and the **Rename Folder** button becomes available. From the dialog that appears when you click this button, enter a new name for the folder in the Name box and click OK. The folder's name changes.
- When you have selected one of the saved reports, the **Edit** button is available for use. This button allows you to enter a new name and description for the report. Click OK to save your changes.
- **Delete** removes any selected item. When you click this button, a confirmation dialog appears. You must click OK to permanently delete the item.
- **Done** closes the Manage Saved Reports dialog and returns you to the Reports And Graphs screen.

Exporting Your Reports

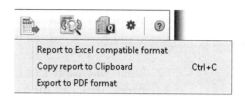

Another method of working with your reports is to export them into other formats or programs. From your report's toolbar, choose the Export icon to see this menu.

As you can see, there are three choices, each of which is explained in the sections that follow.

Report To Excel Compatible Format

This option saves your report into a .txt file that can be used with the Microsoft Office Excel program. The file is saved as a tab-delimited file with the file extension .txt. To save your file in this format:

1. From the Export menu, choose Report To Excel Compatible Format to open the Create Excel Compatible File dialog, as seen next.

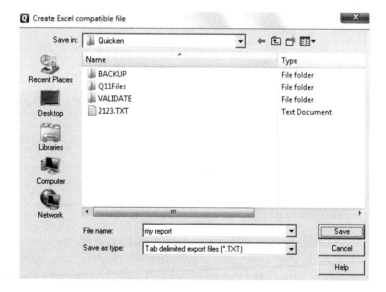

2. Browse to find the folder into which you want to save this file, and click that folder.
3. Enter a name for your file, and click Save. The file will have a .txt extension. The new file is saved into the folder you designated and you are returned to your report window. See "Work with Your Saved Excel File" next to see how to open the file in Excel.

Work with Your Saved Excel File

Once you have saved the file, you can work with it in Microsoft Excel. To do so:

1. Open Microsoft Excel. (The illustrations in this section refer to Microsoft Excel 2010, but the application works in similar ways with earlier versions of Excel.)
2. Click File | Open. Choose All Files instead of All Excel Files as the type of file for which you want Excel to look. (See the next illustration.) Locate the folder into which you saved your file. When the folder opens, select the file you saved and click Open.

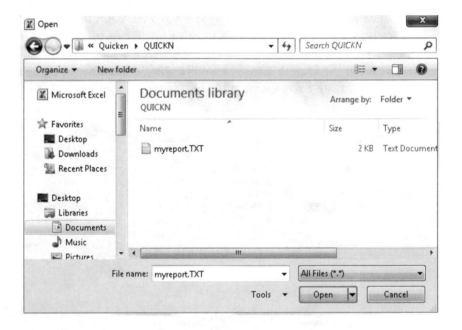

3. The Text Import Wizard appears as shown on the top of the next page.
4. Ensure that Delimited is selected, which it may be by default. Click Next.
5. Make sure that Tab is selected from the Delimiters column. Click Next to continue.

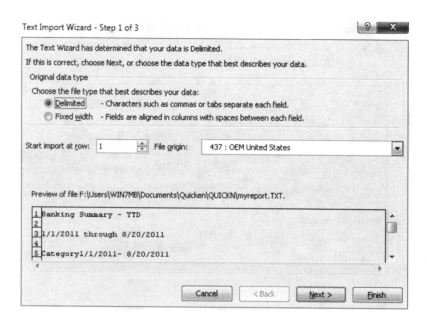

6. At the last step (shown next), choose General and then click Finish to complete the import.

7. Your Excel worksheet appears, as shown in Figure 8-6. You may have to make the columns wider to see the information on the report. If so, place your cursor on the line between the column letters and drag to the right.

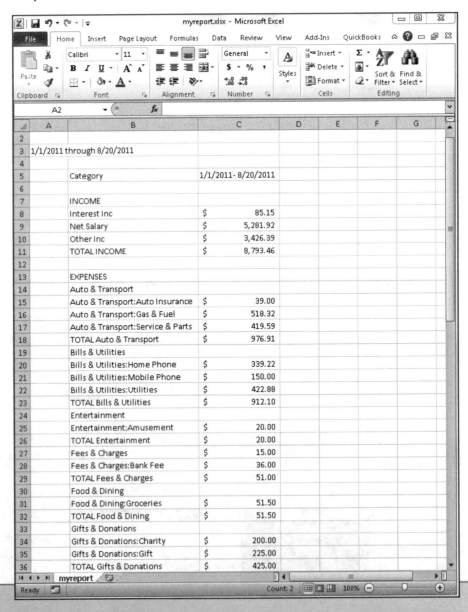

Figure 8-6 • Quicken's ability to export report data to Microsoft Excel is handy for many Quicken users.

8. You may also have to format the numbers to be shown as dollars and cents. To do this, highlight the cells with numbers in them and click the $ tool on the ribbon.

9. Save the file in an Excel format. To do so:
   a. Click File.
   b. Click Save As. From the Save As dialog, choose an Excel Workbook format and click Save.

> ### IN MY EXPERIENCE
>
> One of the best things about exporting report data into Microsoft Excel is how easy it is. But, you may have a number of changes to make to the data once it's in Excel. There are often a number of changes that need to be made to use the report in a meaningful way. Note that both the subcategory amounts and the total of those amounts are data that has been transferred. So, we would have to create another column for the totals so that any grand totals are not doubled. Depending on the report you export, be aware that you may have to make a few changes to make the data usable in Excel.

Copy the Report to the Clipboard

Use this option to copy the report into another Windows program. You can also use the keyboard shortcut CTRL-C. To "paste" this report into another program, use the keyboard shortcut CTRL-V. You can even use this method to copy the report into Microsoft Excel—a much easier process than the one described earlier.

Export to PDF Format

PDF stands for Portable Document Format. This format, patented by Adobe Systems, allows the reader to view and/or print a document from nearly any computer or word processor. This option is particularly useful if you are saving the report to e-mail it or sharing the file with someone who does not have either Quicken or Microsoft Office. To save as a .pdf file:

1. From the Export Data menu, click Export To PDF Format.
2. The Print dialog appears. In the Printer field you will see "Quicken PDF Printer on *nnnn*" rather than your regular printer.
3. Click Print. The Save To PDF File dialog appears. Locate the folder into which you want to save your file, type a name, and click Save. Your file is now saved with a .pdf extension.

Printing Reports and Graphs

One of the best things about reports and graphs is the ability to print them and share them with others. You can create hard copies for your paper files, print a copy to take to your tax professional (and make that person *very* happy), or you can include professional reports with a loan application.

To print a report, subreport, or graph, begin by displaying it in the report window. Then click the Print icon on the window's toolbar. The Print dialog appears, as seen in Figure 8-7. Set options as desired and click Print.

Here's a look at the available options.

Print To Print To options determine the destination of the printed report or graph. You have two choices:

- **Printer** prints to the printer you choose from the drop-down list, which includes all printers, faxes, and related devices you have set up in Windows. This is the option you'll probably select most often. Clicking the Properties button displays the Properties dialog for the currently selected printer.
- **Export To** makes it possible to export the report information in one of three formats you choose from the drop-down list: Text File, Tab-Delimited (Excel-Compatible) Disk File, or PRN (123-Compatible) Disk File. This option is only available if you are printing a report.

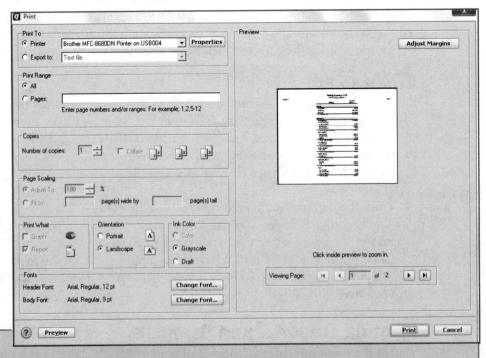

Figure 8-7 • **The Print dialog offers many options for your printed Quicken reports.**

Print Range   The print range determines which pages will print. You can use this if the printed report is more than one page. The default setting is All, which prints all pages of the report. To print a range of pages, select Pages and then enter the page numbers for the page range you want to print.

Copies   The Copies box determines how many copies of the report will print. If you enter a value greater than 1, you can select the Collate check box to collate the copies as they are printed.

Page Scaling   Page Scaling options enable you to resize a report or graph to a specific percentage or to fit on a certain number of pages. These options are only available for certain printers.

Print What   You can toggle two check boxes to determine whether Quicken should print a graph or report or both. The available options depend on what's in the report window.

Orientation   Orientation determines how the printed report will be viewed. The options are Portrait or Landscape. These are standard options offered by all programs. The icon beside each orientation option illustrates it.

Ink Color   Select one of three options to determine the ink color and quality of the printout: Color (available only if a color printer is selected from the Printer drop-down list), Grayscale, or Draft.

Fonts   Use the two Change Font buttons to change the header and body typefaces of the report or graph. Clicking the button displays the Font dialog, which you can use to set standard font options, such as font, size, and style.

Preview   The Preview area shows a thumbnail preview of the document. You can click the buttons in the Viewing Page area to scroll through all pages of the report. To change the margins for the document, click the Adjust Margins button. The Preview area changes to offer boxes for entering margin values. To view a full-size preview, click the thumbnail in this area or click the Preview button at the bottom of the dialog.

Managing Your Investment Accounts

This part of the book explains how you can use Quicken Personal Finance Software to track your investments. It begins by explaining the basics of tracking investments in Quicken and then goes on to explain how you can use Quicken's online investment tracking features to download investment information from your brokerage firm and exchange information with Quicken.com. Along the way, it provides a wealth of information you can use to invest wisely and maximize your investment returns. Finally, it explains how you can use Quicken's Investing tab and reporting features to keep an eye on your portfolio and investment returns.

By the way, throughout these three chapters, the Investment Transaction list, which serves as a register for your investment accounts, will be referred to both as the transaction list and as the register.

This part has three chapters:

Entering Your Investment Transactions

Chapter 9

In This Chapter:

- *Understanding your portfolio*
- *Managing your portfolio*
- *Creating investment accounts*
- *Working with placeholder entries*
- *Understanding the Investment Transaction list*
- *Using the Investment Transaction dialog*
- *Entering common transactions*
- *Entering transactions in the Transaction List*
- *Editing transactions*
- *Adjusting balances*
- *Viewing the Security List*

Investments offer individuals a way to make their money grow. Although more risky than deposits made to an FDIC-insured bank, stocks, bonds, mutual funds, and other types of investments have the potential to earn more. That's why many people build investment portfolios as a way to save for future goals or retirement.

In this chapter, you will be introduced to investments and portfolio management and then you will learn how to use Quicken Personal Finance Software to keep track of the money you invest.

Quicken Investment Basics

An *investment* is a security or asset that you expect to increase in value and/or generate income. There are many types of investments—Table 9-1 lists some of them. This chapter concentrates on the investments you can track with the features in Quicken's Investing tab.

Type of Investment	Type of Account
CD	Savings account or standard brokerage account
Money market fund	Savings account or standard brokerage account
Stocks in your possession	Standard brokerage account
Brokerage account with one or more securities	Standard brokerage account securities, with or without an associated cash, checking, or interest-earning account
Employee stock options	Standard brokerage account
Employee Stock Purchase Plan (ESPP)	Standard brokerage account
Dividend Reinvestment Program (DRIP)	Standard brokerage account
Bonds, including U.S. Savings Bonds	Standard brokerage account
Treasury bills	Standard brokerage account
Single mutual fund with no cash balance	Single mutual fund account or a standard brokerage account
Variable or fixed annuities	Standard brokerage account
401(k) or 403(b) plan	401(k) or 403(b) account
529 Educational Savings Plan	529 plan account or Educational IRA (529) account (this account is sometimes known as a Coverdell ESA [IRA])
Traditional IRA, Roth IRA, or Education IRA	IRA account
Keogh Plan, SEP-IRA, or SIMPLE-IRA	Keogh plan or SEP-IRA account
Real estate	Asset account
Real estate investment trusts (REITs) or partnerships	Standard brokerage account

Table 9-1 • Quicken Accounts for Various Investment Types

Before you learn how to use Quicken to track your investments, here's a review of Quicken's investment accounts and a more detailed explanation of why investment tracking is so important.

Understanding Your Portfolio

The term *portfolio* refers to the total of all of your investments. For example, if you have shares of one company's stock, shares in two mutual funds, and a 401(k) plan account, these are the items that make up your portfolio.

Types of Investment Accounts

Your Quicken portfolio can include four types of investment accounts. You can have as many investment accounts as you need to properly represent the investments that make up your portfolio.

Standard Brokerage   A standard brokerage account is for tracking a wide variety of investments handled through a brokerage firm, including stocks, bonds, mutual funds, and annuities. Like the account at your brokerage firm, it can track income, capital gains, performance, market values, shares, and cash balances for multiple securities.

IRA or Keogh Plan   An IRA or a Keogh account is for tracking a variety of retirement accounts, including standard IRA, Roth IRA, Coverdell Education Savings Account (formerly known as Education IRA), SEP-IRA, SIMPLE-IRA, and Keogh plans.

401(k) or 403(b)   A 401(k) or 403(b) account is for tracking 401(k), 403(b), or 457 plans, in which you make regularly scheduled, pretax contributions toward investments for your retirement. This type of account can track performance, market value, and distribution among investment choices. If you (and your spouse) have more than one plan, you should set up a separate account for each.

529 Plan   A 529 plan account is for tracking 529 Educational Savings Plans. These plans enable multiple family members to make pretax contributions to invest money for a family member's college education. This type of account enables you to track cash, money market, and securities activity and balances.

Choosing the Right Type of Account

Sometimes, it's not clear which kind of account is best for a specific type of investment. Table 9-1 offers some guidance.

Keep in mind that you can also track many types of investments in asset accounts. But Quicken's investment accounts enable you to better track and report on the income, capital gains, and performance of your investments.

This chapter concentrates on investment accounts tracked in standard brokerage, IRA or Keogh, 401(k) or 403(b), and 529 plan accounts. Consider what type of account your financial institution requires for downloading transactions as you decide between a single mutual fund account and a standard brokerage account.

If you want to track the maturity dates of your CDs, you may need to use the standard brokerage account, as Quicken considers CDs to be investment instruments.

Managing Your Portfolio

At this point, you may be wondering why you should bother including investment information in your Quicken data file. After all, you may already get quarterly (or even monthly) statements from your broker or investment firm. What you may not realize, however, is how you can benefit from keeping a close eye on your investments. Take a look at what portfolio management with Quicken can do for you.

Centralizing Your Investment Records

Unless you have only one brokerage account for all your investments, you probably get multiple statements for the stocks, bonds, mutual funds, and other investments in your portfolio. No single statement can provide a complete picture of your portfolio's worth—however, Quicken can. By entering the transactions and values on each statement within Quicken, you can see the details of your entire portfolio in one place.

Knowing the Value of Your Portfolio on Any Day

Brokerage statements can tell you the value of your investments on the statement's ending date, but not what they're worth today—or what they were worth on July 20, 1994. Quicken, however, can tell you what your portfolio is worth on any day for which you have entered—or, better yet, downloaded— security prices, and it can estimate values for dates without exact pricing information. If you like to keep your portfolio's value up-to-date with the latest security prices, you can retrieve prices online. Chapter 10 shows you how to take advantage of this feature.

Keeping Track of Performance History

Manually compiling a complete pricing and performance history for an investment is no small task, especially for periods spanning multiple statements. If you consistently enter investment information in your Quicken data file, however, preparing performance charts and reports is as easy as choosing a menu command or clicking a button.

Additional Enhancements in Quicken Premier

Those using Quicken Premier or higher can opt to update stock quotes every 15 minutes. Other features found in the Premier and higher versions are the ability to create snapshots of your portfolio value versus its cost basis, a "Growth of 10K" chart, and average annual return. In addition, these versions offer a buy/sell preview as well as a mutual fund ratings from Morningstar snapshot.

Calculating Capital Gains Quickly and Easily

Calculating the gain on the sale of an investment isn't always easy. Considerations include not only the purchase and selling prices, but also commissions, fees, stock splits, and purchase lots. Quicken can take all the work out of calculating capital gains, even if you're just considering the sale and want to know what its impact will be. This is extremely helpful at tax time, as Chapter 17 explains.

A couple of other helpful things about keeping track of your investments in Quicken:

- Brokerages only keep records for so long, so if you have had dividend-paying stocks where you have reinvested the dividends for many years, Quicken will handily keep track of every lot even if your brokerage's history does not go back that far.
- If you change brokerages or your brokerage is acquired by another brokerage, often your cost basis information is not retained by the financial institution. If you have your investments in Quicken, you can easily transfer the cost basis information to the new account.
- If any of your securities have gone through an acquisition or merger, the tax treatment and associated changes to your cost basis are not always tracked, or tracked correctly, by the brokerage. You can use Quicken to accurately track these events.
- If you are keeping custodial accounts for a minor, when that minor is old enough to take over handling of the account, you can give them a complete buy/sell/cost basis history.

Creating Investing Accounts

Before you can begin tracking your investments with Quicken, you must set up the investment accounts you'll need. Basic information about setting up accounts is contained in Chapter 3. This chapter provides the specifics for creating investing accounts. As you'll see on the following pages, when you create an investment account, Quicken not only prompts you for basic account information, but also gathers information about your security holdings. When you're finished creating an account, it's all ready to use for entering transactions and creating reports.

Choosing the Type of Investing Account

Begin by clicking Add An Account from the Account Bar. In the Add Account dialog indicate the type of account you want to create. You can refer to Table 9-1 if you need help deciding. The option you select will determine certain settings for the account. For example, if you choose an IRA or Keogh plan, Quicken will set tax-deferred options that would not be set if you selected a standard brokerage account. Then click Next. You may see a message that Quicken is updating.

Using Simple Start to Create an Account

Quicken's extensive online account access features make it possible to automate data entry for accounts held in participating financial institutions, including many brokerage firms. To take advantage of these features, Quicken starts the account creation process for standard brokerage, IRA or Keogh Plan, or 401(k) or 403(b) accounts by prompting you to enter the name of your brokerage firm or choosing one from the list provided.

  If you have chosen the default Simple Start method of creating your account, after you have clicked the name of your broker, with your Internet connection, Quicken verifies the connection to your broker and opens a window in which you are prompted to enter the user ID and password given to you by your broker. Quicken may display dialogs that prompt you for additional information about the account. The dialogs that appear and the order in which they appear vary, depending on the financial institution you indicated. Once you have entered your login information, click Connect to proceed with the account setup. After you have proceeded through any dialogs prompting for additional info, Quicken retrieves the account info and transactions, creates the account, and displays an Account Added screen.

As explained in Chapter 3, it is not uncommon to set up accounts in Quicken and decide later to activate online services for these accounts. The first time transactions are downloaded into a Quicken file in which accounts have been set up, the user is prompted to either add the downloaded transactions into a new account or link to an existing account. Be sure to link any existing account with the correct downloaded account.

Using Advanced Setup   If your institution's name is not on the Simple Setup list, has other connection methods, or you just prefer not to download, you can set up your account manually. After you have chosen the type of investing account you want to set up, at the dialog where you are prompted for your institution's name, click Advanced Setup at the bottom of the window. From this dialog, as explained in Chapter 3, you have two options:

- **I Want To Select The Connection Method Used To Download My Transactions**   Select this option if your institution offers more than one online service or if you have been given specific instructions how to connect to their website.
- **I Want To Enter My Transactions Manually**   Select this option if your account is held by an entity that does not offer online services, or you just prefer to enter your transactions by hand. Use this option as well if the account you are creating is not held at a financial institution—for example, an account to track the value of securities in your safe deposit box.

Account Name and Other Basic Information   Depending on your account, you'll be asked for other information. Quicken displays dialogs that prompt you to enter certain types of accounts and other basic information, including the account name, statement ending date, and cash and money market balances. Depending on the type of account, you may also be prompted for additional information as discussed next.

For IRAs
- Who owns the IRA.
- What type of an IRA it is.
- If you have not entered a cash value or more than one mutual fund, you may be asked whether this is a single mutual fund account.

For 401(k) or 403(b) Accounts   You will need to enter variations of this basic information for several types of accounts, most notably the 401(k)s:

- Statement ending date
- Employer name (either current or previous employer)
- Who owns the account
- Whether you have loans (and how many) against the account
- What securities you have in the account
- Whether you want to set up your paycheck information
- If the account tracks the number of shares, whether the statement lists the number of shares of each security

For 401(k) or 403(b) accounts, Quicken displays a dialog that asks whether you want to track loans against the account. If you have any loans against the account, be sure to indicate how many you have. Quicken will then display one or more dialogs prompting you for information about your loan(s).

Securities Held   A dialog like the one shown in Figure 9-1 prompts you to enter security ticker symbols and names. Enter one security per line, using the TAB key to move from one box to the next. If you don't know the ticker symbol for a security, you can click the Ticker Symbol Lookup button to look it up online. If you need to enter more than five securities in the dialog, click the Add More button to add more lines. Don't enter bonds in this dialog; you can add them later.

Current Holdings   After you have entered the ticker symbols for your securities, click Next. With your Internet connection Quicken updates and verifies the symbols and displays a dialog like the one shown on the following page. Enter the total number of shares for each security. For a 401(k) account, you may see a Total Market Value column. If the type of security—Stock, Mutual Fund, or Other—is incorrect, select the correct option.

Figure 9-1 • Use Advanced Setup and enter each security you hold for investment accounts that do not have download services available.

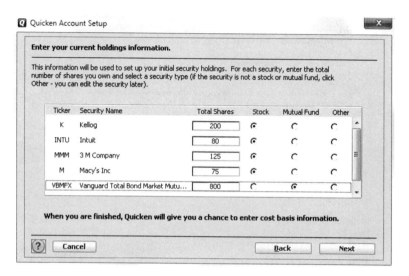

When you click Next, Quicken displays a summary dialog confirming your entries and encouraging you to enter the complete transaction history for each of your holdings, similar to the one shown here.

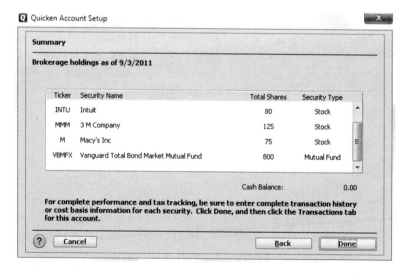

Click Done. You may see a message asking if this is a single mutual fund account if you have not entered a cash balance and have entered only one mutual fund security, as seen next. If you are creating this type of account, click Yes. Otherwise select No and click Next again. Quicken displays an Account Added window. Click Finish to close the window.

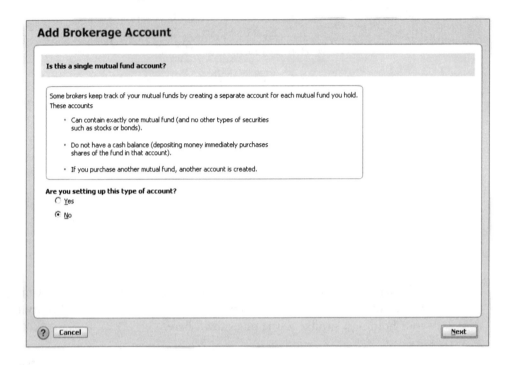

Paycheck Setup   When you create a 401(k) or 403(b) account, Quicken displays a dialog that asks whether you want to set up your paycheck. Quicken's Paycheck Setup feature is great for automatically entering 401(k) contributions and loan payments. Learn about setting up your paycheck in Quicken in Chapter 6.

Working with Placeholder Entries

Quicken automatically creates special transactions, called placeholder entries, in investment accounts when you enter—either manually or via Online Account Access—currently held securities as part of the account setup process. These transactions make it possible to get up and running quickly with Quicken's investment tracking features, but they lack the information Quicken needs to create accurate investment reports.

Here's how it works. When you create an investment account, you tell Quicken what securities are in the account and how many shares of each security you currently own. But Quicken doesn't know when you bought those shares or what you paid for them. Without this historical cost information, Quicken can't calculate your return on investment or your capital gains (or losses) when you sell the security.

Although you can work with a Quicken investment account as soon as it's created, to get the most out of Quicken's investment tracking features, you should replace the placeholder entries it creates with investment cost information. This section explains how.

The placeholder "locks" the number of shares and cash balance for the given date to the number specified in the placeholder. If you enter transactions before the placeholder date, the cash balance will not be affected. This can be a good thing, as you don't have to account for where the cash came from for securities purchased long before you started tracking in Quicken, but it can also be a bad thing if you don't understand how the placeholder works. Many Quicken users wonder why cash is not subtracted from the account when they enter a "buy" transaction. Thus, many users don't use placeholders to avoid these sorts of complications.

Viewing Placeholder Entries for an Account

You can find an account's placeholder entries with the rest of the transactions for that account. Choose the account from the Account Bar to open its Transaction List (register). You can also click the Portfolio button after clicking the Investing tab and click the name of the account you want. You will see the placeholder transactions on the Transaction List. Figure 9-2 shows an example of an investment account that includes several placeholder entries.

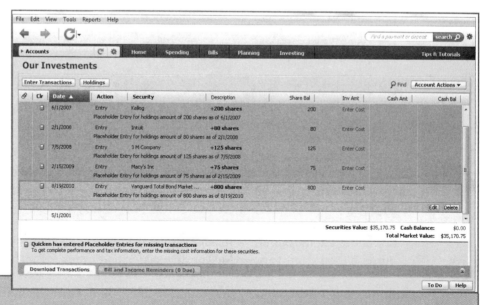

Figure 9-2 • Placeholder entries provide share balance information, but not investment cost.

If placeholder entries are not visible, you may need to set the preference for viewing hidden investment transactions. Select Edit | Preferences. Click Investment Transactions, and then select the Show Hidden Transactions check box. Click OK to save the preference and close the dialog.

Entering Cost Information for Placeholder Entries

To enter security cost information, begin by selecting the placeholder entry you want to work with. Click the Enter Cost link to display the Enter Missing Transactions dialog shown here.

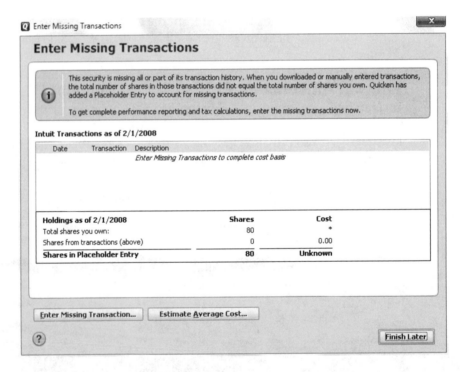

 Transactions entered in the investment account before the date of the placeholder entry will not affect the cash balance of the investment account. It is often better to delete the placeholder and then enter all the historical transactions.

Two buttons at the bottom of the dialog offer methods for entering historical cost information for a security: Enter Missing Transaction and Estimate Average Cost.

Enter Missing Transaction   This option enables you to enter the individual transactions that make up the total number of shares you hold. In many cases, these transactions include purchases, stock dividends, and stock splits. This option gives you the most accurate records, but if you have many transactions, entering them all could be time-consuming. When you click this button, Quicken displays the Shares Bought dialog, shown next, which enables you to enter transaction details for a security acquisition. If the account is a 401(k) account, you may see an extra button labeled Cash Source. You will find how to enter new transactions, such as purchases and stock dividends, later in this chapter, in the section titled "Investment Transactions."

1. Complete the transaction information by moving through the fields with your TAB key.
2. The transaction date should already be filled in. If you need to change the date, enter the correct date.

If you need to change a date for a placeholder transaction, it must be before the date you have entered for the placeholder when you set up the account.

3. The Account and Security Name fields are prefilled, and you cannot change the information.
4. Enter the number of shares you purchased on the date of the placeholder transaction. If this placeholder contains more than one lot, enter the oldest

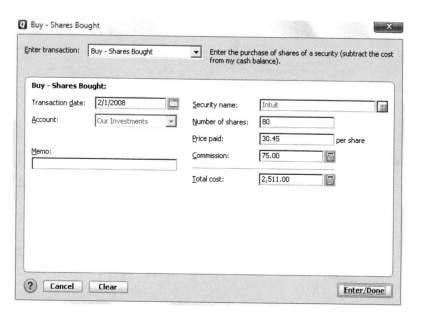

lot first. You will have to enter each lot separately to ensure your investment account is correct.

5. Enter the price you paid for each share in the Price Paid field.

6. Enter the amount of any commission you paid for this transaction. Quicken calculates your total cost.

7. If you have made any errors, click the Clear button. If you want to start over, click the Cancel button. Otherwise, click Enter/Done.

A warning message appears telling you that you are attempting to record a transaction on the same date as a placeholder transaction, that your share balance will not be affected, and are you sure you want to do this. Click Yes to close the message and return to the Enter Missing Transactions dialog. If you have entered all the transactions to account for all the shares in the placeholder, you will have the option to click Done to close the Enter Missing Transactions dialog. Otherwise, you will see a button labeled Finish Later.

Estimate Average Cost This option enables you to enter an average estimated cost for all of the shares you hold. Although this method is less accurate than entering individual transactions, it's a lot quicker and may be sufficient if you don't need detailed records of stock costs. You can always go back later and use the Enter Missing Transaction button to record more accurate acquisition details.

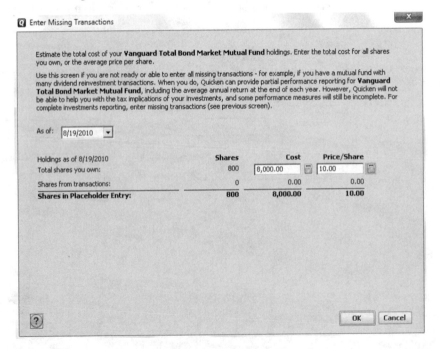

If needed, click the Enter Cost link in the placeholder transaction to open the Enter Missing Transactions dialog.

When you click the Estimate Average Cost button, a dialog like the one shown on the previous page appears. Enter either the total cost of the shares in the Cost box or the average price per share in the Price/Share box. Quicken makes any necessary calculations. Click OK to save the entry and return to the register. The item will be shown as an entry and still show that it is a placeholder entry, as seen in Figure 9-3.

Working with Investment Accounts

To view an account's information, select the account name from the Account Bar. This opens the register for this account, as seen in Figure 9-3. From this Transaction List you can enter transactions and perform other activities.

The most important part of properly tracking investments is recording all investment transactions. This includes purchases, sales, dividends, and other activity affecting your portfolio's value. This will make life much easier when you are ready to sell the security.

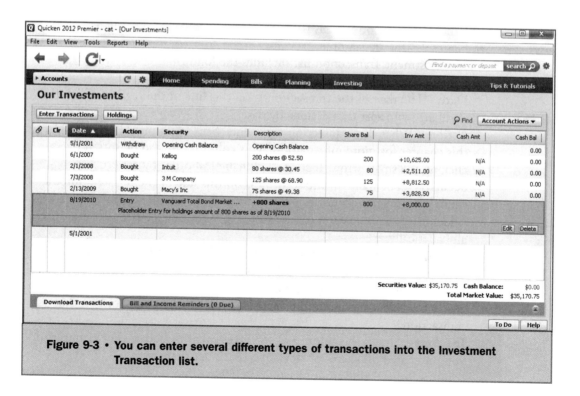

Figure 9-3 • You can enter several different types of transactions into the Investment Transaction list.

Before you enter a transaction, you must have all of its details. In most cases, you can find the information you need on a monthly statement, confirmation form, or receipt you receive from your broker or investment firm. The information varies, depending on the transaction, but it generally should include the security name, transaction date, number of shares, price per share, and any commissions or fees.

For income tax purposes, it is better to record total cost rather than price per share, as that is the value you enter on Schedule D of your federal income tax return.

This section provides some information and advice for understanding the Investment Transaction list and entering the most common transactions into investment accounts.

Understanding the Investment Transaction List

The Investment Transaction list looks very much like the check registers. However, instead of the familiar Date, Check Number, and Payee fields, the Investment Transaction list has fields that pertain to your investing activities. See Figure 9-3 for an example.

The Investment Transaction list includes the following:

- **Date** The date of the transaction is on this line of the register. Click the small arrow to sort transactions by date.
- **Action** What this transaction represents. See "Investment Actions" later in this chapter for more information. This column can also be sorted by clicking the small arrow. It sorts in alphabetical order by action.
- **Security** The name of the security is on this line of the register. Since a single investment account can contain a wide variety of securities, each one is identified. This column can be sorted using the small arrow. It is sorted alphabetically.
- **Description** What action is represented. For example, if the Action column says "Bought," the number of shares of the named security and the price paid are shown in this column.
- **Share Bal** Shows the number of shares you purchased or sold on that transaction.
- **Inv Amt** Shows the amount of the investment in dollars. For example, if you purchased 50 shares of stock at $18.22 per share with a $35.00 commission/fee, this amount would be $946.00.

- **Cash Amt**   This column displays cash transactions for this account.
- **Cash Bal**   This column displays any cash balance in the account after the transaction on this line of the register.

> ### NEW IN QUICKEN 2012
>
> Share Balance is the cumulative total of shares for that security on the date of the transaction. If you have three transactions for a security, each buying 10 shares, the Share Balance will show 10, 20, and 30 for the corresponding three "buy" transactions. You need to select the transaction to see how many shares were involved in that particular transaction.

If your account has a linked checking account, the Cash Amt and Cash Bal columns do not appear in the Investment Transaction list.

Working with the Buttons

In addition to the register lines, at the top of the Transaction List are three buttons, each with several options.

Enter Transactions   Clicking the Enter Transactions button opens the investment transaction dialog as described later in this chapter.

Holdings   Clicking the Holdings button opens an Account Overview window for this account. Similar to the Portfolio view in the Investing tab, you can see the current value, recent and historical performances, and the tax implications of the transactions in this account, as seen in Figure 9-4. See Chapter 10 for a complete review of the Account Overview window.

Account Actions   From the Account Actions button, a menu appears. The Account Actions menu (seen here) gives you access to several investment-related activities. The menu is divided into three sections: Transactions, Reporting, and Register Views And Preferences. Each is described next.

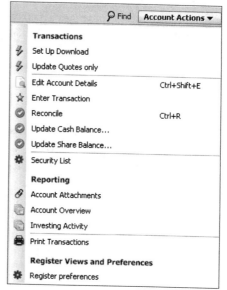

- **Set Up Download** will appear if you have not yet activated this investing

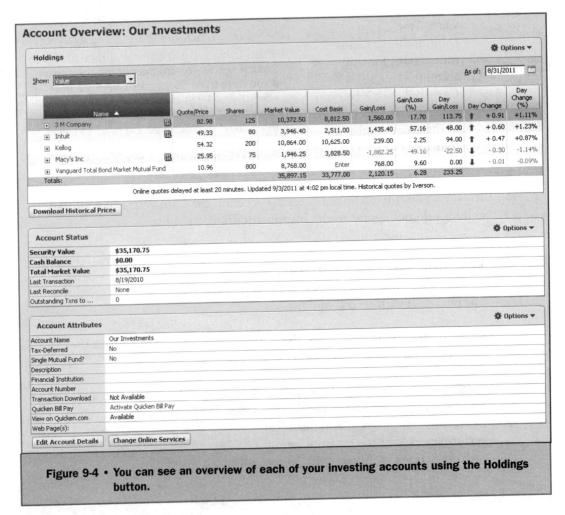

Figure 9-4 • You can see an overview of each of your investing accounts using the Holdings button.

account for online services. If your financial institution offers online services, click Set Up Download to start the process.

- **Update Transactions** (not shown) opens the One Step Update Settings dialog. Enter your password and click Update Now to update your accounts.
- **Update Quotes Only** prompts Quicken to use your Internet connection to download the latest quotes on your holdings and Watch List. Learn more about the Watch List in Chapter 10.
- **Edit Account Details** displays the General Information tab of the Account Details dialog, which you can use to enter or edit basic information about the account, including its name, tax-deferred status, account number, and contact information. From this dialog you can also enter information about

fees and commission charges for this account. Click Fees to open the Transaction Fees dialog. After you have entered the information, as either a dollar amount or a percentage, click OK to close the dialog.

- **Enter Transaction** opens the investment transaction dialog as described later in this chapter.
- **Reconcile** opens the Reconcile dialog. See Chapter 10 for information on reconciling investment accounts.
- **Update Cash/Share Balance** works as described in "Updating an Account's Cash Balance" and "Updating an Account's Share Balance" later in this chapter.
- **Security List** opens the Security List. See "Viewing the Security List" later in this chapter.

You will see a Checking Account entry here if the investment account has a linked checking account.

- **Account Attachments** opens the Account Attachment dialog. See Chapter 4 to learn how to work with attachments.
- **Account Overview** opens the Account Overview window. See "Using the Account Overview Window" later in this chapter and Chapter 10 for more detailed information.
- **Investing Activity** opens a report about your investing activity for time ranges you can set.
- **Print Transactions** gives you the opportunity to print your Transaction List.
- **Register Preferences** opens the Preferences dialog to the Investment Transactions section. See Appendix B for more information about preferences.

Using the Investment Transaction Dialog

You enter transactions into an investment account with the investment transaction dialog. This dialog, which is named for the type of transaction you are entering, is a fill-in form with all of the fields you need to enter transaction details.

To open the investment transaction dialog, click the Enter Transactions button in the register for the account in which you want to enter the transaction (refer to Figure 9-3). It looks like the dialog shown on the top of the next page when you first open it. If the account is a 401(k) account, you may see a Cash Source button in the dialog.

Investment Actions

To use the investment transaction dialog, you must begin by choosing a transaction type (or action) from the Enter Transaction drop-down list. There are dozens of action types organized into two categories: investment transactions and cash transactions.

Investment Transactions   Investment transactions directly affect your security or investment account balances, unless you have placeholders. See "Working with Placeholder Entries" earlier in this chapter.

- **Buy – Shares Bought** (shown earlier) enables you to add shares to an investment account. The cost of the shares (plus any commissions) is deducted from the account's cash balance (or another account's cash balance).
- **Sell – Shares Sold** enables you to remove shares from an investment account. The proceeds from the sale (net of any commissions) are added to the account's cash balance (or another account's cash balance).
- **Div – Stock Dividend (Non-Cash)** enables you to add shares of a security paid as a dividend.
- **Reinvest – Income Reinvested** enables you to account for investment income (such as dividends) that is reinvested in the security. This is common with dividend reinvestment plans and mutual funds.

- **Inc – Income (Div, Int, Etc.)** enables you to record income from interest, dividends, and capital gain distributions.
- **Add – Shares Added** enables you to add shares to an investment account without an exchange of cash. You might use this option to add shares received as a gift.
- **Remove – Shares Removed** enables you to remove shares from an investment account without an exchange of cash. You might use this option to remove shares you have given to someone else as a gift.
- **Adjust Share Balance** enables you to create a placeholder entry transaction to make your share balance agree with your brokerage statement. You can enter cost information later, as discussed earlier in this chapter, in the section titled "Working with Placeholder Entries."
- **Stock Split** enables you to record additional shares received as a result of a stock split.
- **Return Of Capital** enables you to record the return of part of your investment capital.
- **Miscellaneous Expense** enables you to record investment expenses other than commissions.
- **Margin Interest Expense** enables you to record the amount of interest paid as a result of purchasing securities on margin.
- **Bonds Bought** enables you to record the purchase of bonds.
- **Grant Employee Stock Option** enables you to record the receipt of an employee stock option.
- **Exercise Employee Stock Option** enables you to use an employee stock option to buy stock.
- **Reprice Employee Stock Option** enables you to change pricing information for stock options.
- **Bought ESPP Shares** enables you to buy shares in an Employee Stock Purchase Plan.
- **Sold ESPP Shares** enables you to sell shares purchased through an Employee Stock Purchase Plan.
- **Short Sale** enables you to record a short sale of a security.
- **Cover Short Sale** enables you to record the purchase of stock to cover a short sale.
- **Corporate Name Change** enables you to record the change of the name of a company for which you own stock. This preserves the old name information; simply editing the security name in the Edit Security dialog does not.
- **Corporate Securities Spin-Off** enables you to record securities obtained through a spin-off of a smaller company from one of the companies in which you own securities.

- **Corporate Acquisition (Stock For Stock)** enables you to record securities obtained in exchange for other securities you own, normally as a result of a corporate acquisition.
- **Mutual Fund Conversion** lets you record the information for a mutual fund that you currently hold that is being replaced by another fund. Here you record the price per share after the conversion is complete. This is new in Quicken 2012.
- **Cash Transferred Into Account** enables you to record the transfer of cash into the investment account.
- **Cash Transferred Out Of Account** enables you to record the transfer of cash out of the investment account.

If the investment account has a linked checking account, you will not see the Cash Transferred options.

- **Shares Transferred Between Accounts** enables you to move shares from one Quicken investment account to another.
- **Reminder Transaction** enables you to enter an investment reminder. You may find this option useful if you want to conduct a transaction at a future date and are worried that you may forget to do it. If the Reminder Transaction has a future date, the reminder will not appear in the alert list until that future date.

Cash Transactions   Cash transactions affect the cash balance in an investment account. These actions make it possible to track an investment account's cash balance without using a linked cash account.

- **Write Check** enables you to record a check written from an investment account.
- **Deposit** enables you to record a cash deposit to an investment account.
- **Withdraw** enables you to record the withdrawal of cash from an investment account.
- **Online Payment** enables you to record an online payment from the investment account's cash balance. To use this feature, the account must be enabled for Online Payment or Online Bill Pay. Chapter 5 discusses Online Payment.
- **Other Cash Transaction** enables you to record any type of transaction that affects the investment account's cash balance.

Completing the Transaction

Investment transaction dialogs and forms are generally self-explanatory and easy to use. Simply fill out the fields in the form, and click one of the Enter buttons:

- **Enter/New** enters the current transaction and redisplays the investment transaction dialog so you can enter another transaction.
- **Enter/Done** enters the current transaction and dismisses the investment transaction dialog.

Entering Common Transactions

Although page count limitations make it impossible to review every kind of investment transaction in this book, here's a look at a few common transactions. They should give you a solid understanding of how the investment transaction dialogs work so you can enter your transactions.

Buying Shares

A security purchase normally involves the exchange of cash for security shares. In some cases, you may already own shares of the security or have it listed on your Watch List. In other cases, the security may not already exist in your Quicken data file, so you'll need to set up the security when you make the purchase.

Start by selecting the investing account with which you want to work. Click Enter Transactions to display the Buy – Shares Bought dialog shown earlier. Enter information about the shares you have purchased:

- **Transaction Date** is the date of the transaction.
- **Account** is the name of the account you selected. You cannot change the option chosen from this drop-down list. If the account name is incorrect, click Cancel, open the correct investing account, and start over.
- **Security Name** is the name of the security. If you enter the name of a security that doesn't already exist in Quicken, the Add Security To Quicken dialog, which is discussed later in the section titled "Adding a New Security," appears so you can add the security to Quicken.
- **Number Of Shares** is the number of shares purchased.
- **Price Paid** is the per-share price.
- **Commission** is the amount of commissions you paid to your brokerage or investment firm.
- **Total Cost** is calculated by Quicken. Enter the total cost and number of shares, and let Quicken calculate the price paid. The total cost and number

of shares is what gets reported on IRS Schedule D when you sell the shares. The total cost and number of shares should match exactly what your brokerage reports, and the price per share can be off by a few pennies. Better to record the info so you can correctly report your buys and sells at tax time and be confident if you are audited.

- **Memo** lets you enter any comments about this transaction.
- **Use Cash For This Transaction** enables you to specify an account from which the total cost should be deducted. By default, this option is set to use cash from the same investment account. If the brokerage account has a linked checking account, the cash source will default to the linked checking account; this cannot be changed.

When you're finished entering information about the transaction, click one of the Enter buttons. The transaction appears in the Transactions list for the account.

If you want to add security shares to an account without an exchange of cash, use the Add – Shares Added action. Its form asks for most of the same information but does not affect any cash balances.

Selling Shares

A security sale also involves the exchange of cash for security shares. Normally, you dispose of shares you already own, but in some instances, you may sell shares you don't own. This is called selling short, and it is a risky investment technique sometimes used by experienced investors. (To record short sale transactions, use the Short Sale or Cover Short Sale action.)

IN MY EXPERIENCE

When working in your investing accounts, always ensure you are in the correct investment account and double-check the security name to be sure the security you wish to sell is in that account. Even experienced Quicken users report issues when they try to sell a security that is not in the account or the security name is similar. This is also where entering the correct number of shares, including all necessary decimal places for transactions, becomes critical. If you rounded the numbers or entered any incorrect numbers, you may not be able to sell the number of shares you wish. The new Share Balance column can be useful in troubleshooting this issue, as it shows the exact number of shares you have for each security.

To sell shares, choose Sell – Shares Sold in the investment transaction dialog to display the Sell – Shares Sold dialog, which is shown next. Enter information about the shares you have sold:

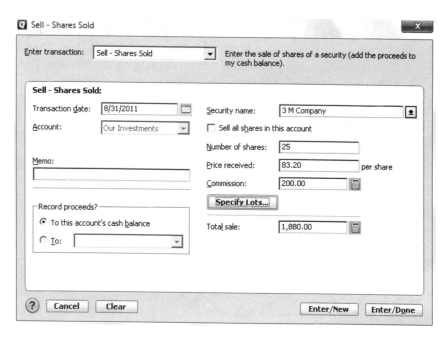

- **Transaction Date** is the date of the transaction.
- **Account** is the name of the account in which the transaction should be recorded. You cannot change the option chosen from this drop-down list if you are entering a transaction from within the account's Transaction window; if it's wrong, click Cancel, open the correct account register, and start over.
- **Security Name** is the name of the security. You can choose an option from the drop-down list.
- **Sell All Shares In This Account** tells Quicken to automatically enter the total number of shares you own in the Number Of Shares box.
- **Number Of Shares** is the number of shares sold.
- **Price Received** is the per-share price.
- **Commission** is the amount of commissions you paid to your brokerage or investment firm.

- **Specify Lots** enables you to specify which shares you are selling when you have multiple purchase lots, as seen next. You can use this option for additional control over capital gains. For example, if you want to take advantage of long-term capital gains tax breaks, you could sell shares that have been in your possession for more than 12 months. If you want to record a loss, you could sell shares that cost more than the selling price. Obviously, your options will vary, depending on the lots, their acquisition prices, and your selling price. If you select this option, click the Specify Lots button to display a dialog like the one shown next. (This dialog may include an Enter Missing Transactions button if placeholder entries exist for the security.) Use the dialog to enter shares in each lot you are selling, or select one of the Auto Select options and click OK. If you don't use the Specify Lots button to select lots, Quicken automatically sells the oldest shares (First In, First Out, or FIFO, method). Consult your tax professional if you want to select lots other than FIFO to determine what the IRS limitations might be.

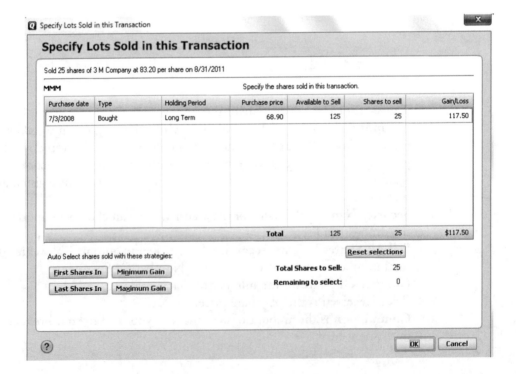

You need to be able to instruct your brokerage which lots you are selling. Not all brokerages allow tax lot–specific transactions. The Specify Lots button will be grayed out if you do not have any shares of the selected security in the account where you are entering the sell data. It will also be grayed out if the security uses average cost, like a mutual fund.

- **Total Sale** is calculated by Quicken dividing the total sale amount by the number of shares. Total Sale can also be determined by multiplying the per-share price by the number of shares and deducting the commission. These are the proceeds from the sale. The technique Quicken uses is determined by the data you enter. However, your broker reports the total sale amount on the 1099B Form he or she sends at the end of each year. This is the number you report on Schedule D of your annual income tax report. Therefore, total sale amount is more critical than the price per share.
- **Memo** lets you enter any comments about this transaction.
- **Record Proceeds?** enables you to specify an account to which the net proceeds should be added. If the investment account has a linked checking account, usually all proceeds go to the linked checking account.

When you click one of the Enter buttons, Quicken records the transaction.

Dividend Payments and Other Income

Many investments pay dividends, interest, or other income in cash. (That's why they're so attractive to an investor!) Recording this activity in the appropriate Transaction List enables Quicken to calculate performance accurately while keeping account balances up-to-date, as well as helping you at tax time.

Keep in mind that many mutual funds are set up to reinvest income rather than pay it in cash. Do not use the steps in this section to record a reinvestment of income. Instead, use the Reinvest Income action to enter transaction information.

To record dividend or interest income, choose Inc – Income (Div, Int, Etc.) from the drop-down list in the investment transaction dialog to display the Inc – Income dialog, shown on the top of the next page. Enter information about a cash payment on an investment:

- **Transaction Date** is the date of the transaction.
- **Account** is the name of the account in which the transaction should be recorded. You cannot change the option chosen from this drop-down list if you are entering a transaction from within the account's Transaction window; if it's wrong, click Cancel, open the correct Transaction List, and start over.

Inc - Income (Div, Int, etc.)

Enter transaction: Inc - Income (Div, Int, etc.) ▼   Enter the receipt of cash income (interest, dividends, or capital gains distributions) that you did NOT reinvest.

Inc - Income (Div, Int, etc.):

Transaction date:	9/16/2008	Security name:	Kellog
Account:	Our Investments	Dividend:	68.00
Transfer account:		Interest:	0.00
Memo:		Short-term cap gain dist:	
Annual Dividend		Mid-term cap gain dist:	
		Long-term cap gain dist:	
Category for Miscellaneous:		Miscellaneous:	
Requires 'Misc' Amt			
		Total proceeds:	68.00

? Cancel   Clear   Enter/New   Enter/Done

- **Transfer Account** enables you to specify an account into which the income is deposited. Leave this blank if the cash is deposited directly into the investment account. If the investment account has a linked checking account, the linked checking account will be designated as the transfer account and cannot be changed.
- **Memo** enables you to enter a brief note about the transaction.
- **Security Name** is the name of the security. You can choose an option from the drop-down list. If the transaction isn't related to a specific security—for example, interest paid on a cash balance in a brokerage account—you can leave this field blank.
- **Dividend, Interest, Short-Term Cap Gain Dist, Mid-Term Cap Gain Dist, Long-Term Cap Gain Dist**, and **Miscellaneous** are fields for entering various types of income. In most cases, you'll use only one or two of these boxes.
- **Total Proceeds** is the total of all income amounts calculated by Quicken.
- **Category For Miscellaneous** is the category you want to use to record miscellaneous income. This field is available only if you enter a value in the Miscellaneous field.

When you click one of the Enter buttons to record the transaction, it appears in the Transaction List.

Other Transactions

Other transactions are just as easy to enter as purchases, sales, and income. Simply choose the appropriate option from the drop-down list in the investment transaction dialog, and enter the transaction information in the form that appears. If you have the transaction confirmation or brokerage statement in front of you when you enter the transaction, you have all the information you need to record it.

If you need additional guidance while entering a transaction, click the Help button (question mark icon) in the Enter Transaction dialog to learn more about the options that must be entered.

> ### IN MY EXPERIENCE
>
> You may wonder what the BoughtX and XIn/XOut items in your register's Action column mean. The X simply indicates that the action had no impact on the cash balance of the account and the transaction was transferred between accounts.

To quickly recalculate transactions in an account, use the keyboard shortcut CTRL-Z.

Entering Transactions in the Transaction List

You can also enter investment transactions directly into the Transaction List window. This feature makes entering transactions quicker for experienced Quicken users.

To begin, scroll down to the blank line at the bottom of the register. Click the line to activate it, and enter the transaction date in the Date column. Then choose an action from the pop-up menu in the Action column and press TAB. The two lines for the transactions fill in with italicized reminders of the information you should enter into each field. Fill in the fields with transaction details, and click Enter.

Editing Transactions

You can quickly edit transactions from your account's register. In the register for the account (refer to Figure 9-3), select the transaction you want to edit. Click in the field you want to modify, and make the desired change. When you're finished, click Enter.

You can also select the transaction and select the Edit action button, as shown here. The Edit dialog appears. Change any of the fields and click Enter/Done.

You can also right-click the transaction to open the context menu. Choose Edit to open the Edit dialog.

A few transaction types cannot be edited: Exercise Employee Stock Option and Sold ESPP Shares. These transactions must be deleted and re-entered if a change is needed.

Adjusting Balances

Occasionally, you may need to adjust the cash balance or number of shares in an investment account or update the balance in a 401(k) account. Here's how.

Updating an Account's Cash Balance

You can adjust the balance in an investment account with a cash balance. In the Account Bar, click the name of the account you want to adjust. From the register that opens, choose Account Actions | Update Cash Balance. The Update Cash Balance dialog appears. (Note that this dialog will not display downloaded cash balance information if the account is not enabled for online access.) Enter the date and the correct balance in the text boxes, and click Done. Quicken creates an adjusting entry.

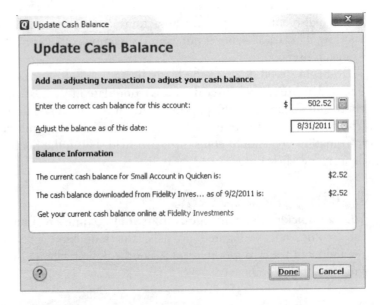

Updating an Account's Share Balance

You can adjust the number of shares in an investment account. In the Account Bar, click the name of the account you want to adjust. From the Transaction List, choose Account Actions | Update Share Balance to display the Adjust Share Balance dialog. (This is the same as choosing the Adjust Share Balance action in the investment transaction dialog.) Enter the adjustment date, security, and correct number of shares in the dialog. When you click Enter/Done, Quicken creates a placeholder entry that adjusts the share balance. Learn more about placeholder entries in the section titled "Working with Placeholder Entries," earlier in this chapter.

Updating 401(k) or 403(b) Balances

401(k) or 403(b) account balances change every time you make a contribution through your paycheck. To adjust the balance, click the name of the 401(k) or 403(b) account in the Account Bar to open its register. Click the Account Actions menu, and choose Update 401(k) Holdings. Then follow the prompts in the Update 401(k)/403(b) Account dialog that appears to update the information. Click Next to display the next page. When you're finished, click Enter/Done to record the adjustment.

You will only see the Update 401(k) Holdings item in the Account Actions menu if the 401(k) account is manual. You will not see the item if the 401(k) account is enabled for transaction download.

Remember, if you set up your paycheck as discussed in Chapter 6, Quicken will automatically record contributions to your 401(k) or 403(b) account every payday.

Working with Securities

This chapter talks a lot about securities. But exactly what are they?

In Quicken, a security is a single investment that has a share price. Examples of securities include stock shares for a specific company, bonds for a specific company, and mutual funds offered by investment firms. Normally, when you own a security, you own a certain number of shares. To calculate the total value of the security, you'd multiply the number of shares you own by the most recent per-share price.

This part of the chapter explains how you can use the Security List to add a new security, choose market indexes, download quotes, edit security details, and more.

Viewing the Security List

The Security List window (see Figure 9-5) simply lists the securities in Quicken's data file. You can use this window to add, edit, delete, or hide securities, including *Watch List securities*—securities you don't own but want to monitor. To open this window, press CTRL-Y. You can also access the list from the Account Actions menu in an Investment Transaction list or from the Investing tab's Tools menu.

Adding a New Security

To add a new security to your Quicken data file—either as a holding or a Watch List item—click the New Security button at the bottom of the Security List window (refer to Figure 9-5). The Add Security To Quicken dialog appears, displaying screens that prompt you for information about a security.

As shown on the top of the next page, Quicken starts by prompting you for the security's ticker symbol and name. Entering the correct ticker symbol when you have an Internet connection can automate much of the security setup process. If you don't know the ticker symbol and have an Internet connection, you can click the Look Up button to connect to the Internet and look up the symbol.

Security ▲	Symbol	Type	Asset Class	Download Quotes	Watch List	Hide	
3 M Company	MMM	Stock	Large Cap Stocks	☑	☐	☐	
ADOBE SYS INC	ADBE	Stock	Unclassified	☑	☐	☐	
Dow Jones Industrials	DJI	Market Index	Unclassified	☑	☐	☐	
GLW	GLW	Stock	Large Cap Stocks	☐	☑	☐	Edit Report Delete
HEINZ H J CO	HNZ	Stock	Unclassified	☑	☐	☐	
Intuit	INTU	Stock	Large Cap Stocks	☑	☐	☐	
Kellog	K	Stock	Large Cap Stocks	☐	☐	☐	
Macy's Inc	M	Stock	Large Cap Stocks	☑	☐	☐	
NASDAQ Composite	COMPX	Market Index	Unclassified	☑	☐	☐	
Russell 2000	IUX	Market Index	Unclassified	☑	☐	☐	
S&P 500 Index	INX	Market Index	Unclassified	☑	☐	☐	
STANDARD MICROSYS CP	SMSC	Stock	Unclassified	☑	☐	☐	
Vanguard Total Bond Market ...	VBMFX	Mutual Fund	Asset Mixture	☑	☐	☐	

New Security | Choose Market Indexes | ☐ Show hidden securities | Mark All

Done

Figure 9-5 • The Security List window offers many ways with which you can work with your investments.

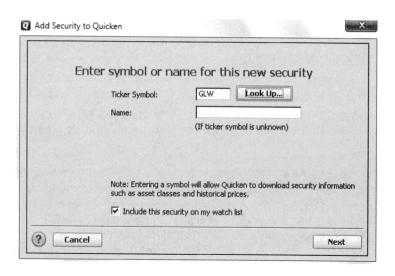

The first screen also offers a check box labeled Include This Security On My Watch List. Selecting this check box tells Quicken to track the security, even if you don't own any shares.

When you click Next, Quicken connects to the Internet to obtain information about the security based on its ticker symbol. If it finds the ticker symbol, it displays the information it has downloaded in the Add Security To Quicken dialog. Click Done to add the security to the Security List.

If Quicken can't find information about the security on the Internet, it displays a dialog enabling you to correct the ticker symbol or add the security

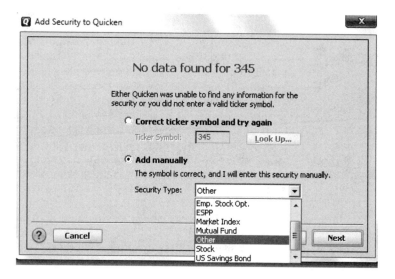

manually. If you made an error when entering the ticker symbol, you can enter the correct symbol in the Ticker Symbol text box and click Next to try looking it up on the Internet again.

If you select the Add Manually option, select a security type—Bond, CD, Emp. Stock Option, ESPP, Market Index, Mutual Fund, Other, Stock, or U.S. Savings Bond—and click Next. Another dialog appears, prompting you for additional information about the security, such as its asset class (for a stock),

IN MY EXPERIENCE

Several students have asked the definition of "asset class." Strictly speaking, an asset class is a group of similar securities, such as equity instruments or stocks, income instruments such as bonds, and cash equivalents such as money market accounts. Within each asset class are categories. Quicken uses the shorthand name of "asset classes" to define types or categories of securities. When you enter "asset class" information in Quicken, you are categorizing the asset as one of eight different security "types":

- **Domestic Bonds**   These bonds are issued and traded in the currency of the country in which they are traded. That means they are not subject to fluctuations in currency exchange rates.
- **Global Bonds**   These bonds are traded in any international market, either foreign or domestic. The same bond issue may be offered in several countries at the same time.
- **Large Cap Stocks**   These securities are offered by large, publicly traded companies with a "market capitalization" of at least $10 billion dollars. (Market capitalization is simply a generally accepted value of a company.)
- **Small Cap Stocks**   Securities offered by a publicly traded firm with a market capitalization of between $200 to 300 million and $2 to 3 billion.

 Quicken gets its asset information from Value Line. As shown in the Asset Allocation Guide, Value Line uses $4.0 billion as the market capitalization value to delineate between large-cap and small-cap domestic stocks. If you download the asset class for a mid-cap stock, it will be assigned Large Cap or Small Cap as its asset class, depending on whether its market cap is above or below $4.0 billion. To access the Asset Allocation Guide, click Investing | Asset Allocation Guide. To see the information about Value Line, click How Do I Update Asset Classes on the left of the Asset Allocation Guide. Select Common Questions About Downloading Asset Classes | What Asset Classes Are Assigned And Where Does the Information Come From.

- **International Stock**   These are securities sold by a company that is not in the United States.
- **Cash/Other/Unclassified**   Assets that do not fit one of the other classifications.

asset class mixture (for a mutual fund), and bond type and maturity and call dates (for a bond). Enter whatever information you have for the security, and click Done to add the security to the Security List.

If you select Employee Stock Option or ESPP, you start the wizards for those security types.

Choosing a Market Index

The Market Indexes option enables you to add common market indexes, such as the Dow Jones Industrial Average and the S&P 500 Index, to the Security List. This lets you download quotes for these indexes when you download security prices, as discussed in Chapter 10.

Working with Individual Securities

When you select a security on the list, three action buttons appear. It is with these buttons that you can edit or delete a security as well as run a report. You can also access these actions by right-clicking the security name.

Editing a Security   You can edit a security to correct or clarify information you previously entered for it. Select the security's name in the Security List window (refer to Figure 9-5), and click the Edit button that appears on the right of that row. The Edit Security Details dialog appears; the illustration seen here shows what it looks like for a stock. Enter or edit information in the dialog, and click OK to save your changes.

Deleting a Security   Delete removes the currently selected security from your Quicken data file. You cannot delete a security that has been used in a transaction.

Creating a Report   When you select a security and click the Report button at the right of the selected row, you will see a Security Report, which summarizes all activity for the security. From the report window, you can customize, save, or print this report. See more about working with reports in Chapter 8.

In addition to the actions and buttons already discussed, there are two more buttons on the Security List:

- The **Help** icon displays the Help window with the Manage Securities section displayed.
- **Print** opens the Print dialog from which you can print your Security List.

Security Type List Each security in the Security List must be assigned a security type. To see the Security Type List, open your Security List and select any security. Choose the Edit action button to open the Edit Security Details dialog. Click the Edit Types button to open the Security Type List, which is shown here, to display a list of security types.

You can use buttons to modify the list:

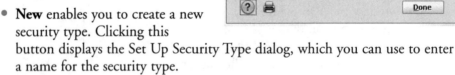

- **New** enables you to create a new security type. Clicking this button displays the Set Up Security Type dialog, which you can use to enter a name for the security type.
- **Edit** enables you to change the name of the currently selected security type.
- **Delete** enables you to remove the currently selected security type from the list.

Be cautious about editing or deleting security types. You can cause yourself some serious headaches by doing so.

- The **Help** icon displays the Quicken Personal Finances Help window with instructions for working with the Security Type List.
- **Print** prints the Security Type List.

Investing Goal List As illustrated next, the Investing Goal List window displays a list of all investment goals. You may find investment goals useful for organizing your investments based on what you expect them to do for you. You can assign a goal to a security by clicking the Other Info button in the Edit Security Details dialog for the security.

To see the Investing Goal List, open your Security List and select any security. Choose the Edit action button to open the Edit Security Details dialog. Click the Other Info button to open the Additional Security Information dialog. From this dialog, click Edit Goals to display the Investing Goal List dialog. Use the following buttons to work with the list:

- **New** enables you to create a new investment goal. Click this button to open the Set Up Investing Goal dialog in which you can enter a name for the goal.
- **Edit** enables you to change the name of the currently selected investment goal.
- **Delete** enables you to remove the currently selected investment goal from the list.
- **Print** prints the Investing Goal List.
- The **Help** icon displays the Quicken Personal Finances Help window with instructions for working with the Investing Goal List.

Using the Account Overview Window

The Account Overview window displays the holdings and status of an investment account. To access this window, select an account from the Account Bar, and from the Account Actions menu, choose Account Overview or the Holdings button. This window is organized into snapshots of information about the currently selected account. See Chapter 10 for more detailed information.

Using Transaction Download and Research Tools

In This Chapter:

- *Reviewing your investing accounts*
- *Setting up transaction downloads*
- *Using the Online Center window*
- *Exploring the Account Overview window*
- *Setting up the download*
- *Creating a Watch List*
- *Viewing downloaded quotes*
- *Exporting your portfolio*
- *Utilizing Quote Lookup*
- *Using Online Research*

Quicken offers three separate features for tracking investments online:

- **Downloading Transactions** enables you to download transactions and balances for your investment accounts. This helps automate the entry of investment transactions and keeps your Quicken records in sync with your brokerage firm's records.
- **Quotes Download** enables you to obtain current and historical quotes; asset allocation information; and news headlines about individual stocks, mutual funds, and other investments. This automates the tracking of market values

and provides valuable information you can use to make better investment decisions. This feature can also alert you to important information about securities you own or watch.

- **Quicken.com Update** enables you to put a copy of your investment portfolio on the Quicken.com website, where you can track its value from any computer connected to the Internet—without Quicken.

This chapter tells you about each of these features and explains how they can help you save time and stay informed about your investments. It also tells you about some of the features on Quicken.com that can help you research investments.

The instructions in this chapter assume that you have already configured your computer for an Internet connection. If you have not done so, do it now. This chapter also assumes that you understand the topics and procedures discussed in Chapters 2 and 6, and it builds on many of the basic concepts discussed in those chapters.

Transaction Download

You can download transactions, balance details, and holdings information directly from the financial institutions with which you maintain investment accounts. Each transaction can then be entered into your Quicken investment account with the click of a mouse button. You can also review downloaded account balance details and compare downloaded holdings information to the information recorded in your portfolio.

Reviewing Your Investing Accounts

When you click the Investing tab for the first time, you are taken to the Portfolio view of your investing accounts. This allows you to view information about an account. Learn more about the individual views of the Investing tab in Chapter 11.

Click an account name, either in the Portfolio view or from the Account Bar, to be taken to the account's Transaction List. See "Reviewing and Accepting Transactions" later in this chapter for more information about investing account transactions.

From the Portfolio View

When you are in the Investing tab's Portfolio view, you can see the securities held in an investing account by clicking the small right-facing arrow to the left of each account, as seen here. The arrow turns into a downward-facing arrow, and the name of each security within that account is displayed. Clicking the small plus sign to the left of a security shows you all the lots of that security you have entered in Quicken, listed from oldest purchase to newest purchase.

Click a security's name to open the Security Detail View. You may also sort by the Action and the Security columns.

From the Account Bar

Click an account's name to open the Transaction List. Each transaction is displayed on a separate line. Unlike banking and asset registers, the Account Actions menu does not have an option to change this view to a two-line display. To show your list as two lines:

1. Click Edit | Preferences | Investment Transactions | Investment Transaction List Preferences.
2. From the List Display drop-down list, choose Two Line, as seen next.
3. Click OK to close the Preferences dialog.

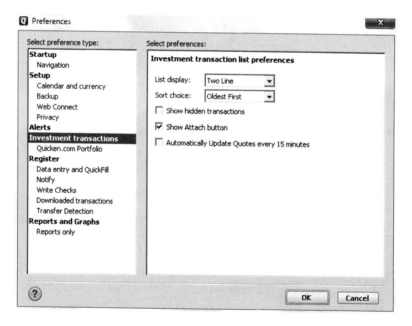

You may sort your transactions in an investment account's Transaction List by clicking the Date arrow, as seen here. See "Using the Security Detail View" later in this chapter for more information. If the arrow is pointing up, the transactions will be sorted with the oldest date on

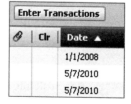

the first line of the Transaction List. If the arrow points down, the transactions are sorted with the most recent transaction listed first.

You may also change the default date display in the Investment Transaction List Preferences by choosing either Oldest First or Most Recent First.

Many brokerage and investment firms support the downloading of transactions. If you set up your investing account as a manual account using Advanced Setup as described in Chapter 9, consider changing to online services if your brokerage offers them. Downloading transactions saves time and effort, and ensures that your Quicken records match those of your broker. However, your broker's records, or at least the records your broker will download, may not be accurate or complete, especially in the case of corporate mergers, Employee Stock Purchase Plan (ESPP) buys and sells, and other complex investment transactions. You'll want to ensure that what gets downloaded makes sense.

Setting Up Transaction Downloads

To download transactions for an account, you must first configure the account for this. This requires that you enter additional information for the account(s) you want to track, including your user ID and a password, and in some cases, the account number.

Applying for Transaction Downloads

Before you can download transactions, you may need to apply for this. Learn how at the end of Chapter 2. Normally, all it takes is a phone call, although many brokerage and investment firms allow you to apply online through the company website.

Not all brokerage firms have an application process. Some brokers simply provide Quicken access information on their websites. To access your account with Quicken, you simply configure Quicken with the same user ID and password you use to access your account via the Web. There's no need to wait for an application to be processed and additional information to be sent. Check your brokerage firm's website to see if these instructions apply to you.

If you do need to apply for Quicken access to your account, it may take up to a week for the application to be processed. You'll know that you're ready to go online when you get a letter with setup information. The setup information may consist of the following.

Customer ID   This may be your Social Security number or some other ID the brokerage firm provides.

Account Number   This is the number for your account at the brokerage firm.

Password or PIN   You'll have to enter your password or PIN into Quicken when you download transactions. If your brokerage firm sends this information, they may send it separately for additional security.

Setting Up the Account and Downloading Transactions

Setting up to download your transactions is a simple process, once you have your identification numbers. When the information is correctly set up, the process happens quickly.

1. From the Account Bar, right-click the account name you want to set up, and from the context menu, click Edit/Delete Account. The Account Details dialog appears. Click the Online Services tab.
2. Click Set Up Now. The Add Brokerage Account dialog appears. Type the name of the financial institution, and click Next.
3. Enter the user name and password you received, and click Connect. Any accounts that Quicken finds at the institution are listed. You may be prompted to tell Quicken if you wish to add, link, or ignore accounts found at the financial institution, as seen next.

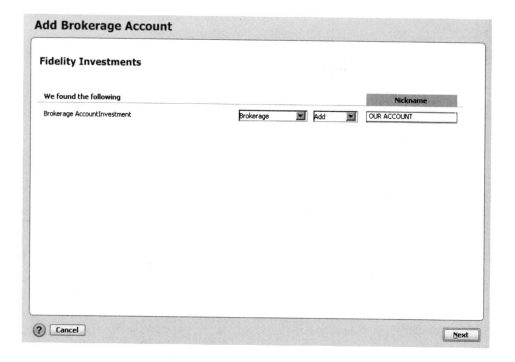

4. You also may be prompted to enter a nickname for each account. If so, type the name you want to use, and click Next. Quicken connects to the Internet to download transactions and balances for your account. When it's finished, you see the Account Added dialog with the name of your account, as well as the number of transactions that were downloaded. Click Finish to close the dialog.

If you have more than one account at a specific financial institution, you may see all the accounts listed and an Add, Link, or Ignore nickname list.

Activate Web Connect

If your institution does not offer Direct Connect services yet, you may be able to use Web Connect services. You may recall from Chapter 5 that Web Connect services enable you to download information from your institution's website. To do this, you must log in to your financial institution's website using the information your financial institution supplies, navigate to a download page, and indicate what data you want to download. Once the Web Connect file has been downloaded, Quicken reads it and knows exactly which Quicken account it applies to.

1. From the Online Services tab of the Account Details dialog, click Set Up Now.
2. Choose the name of your financial institution from the list, or type part of the name to bring up another list starting with the letters you typed.
3. Enter the name of your account, if necessary. If your financial institution does not have the ability to download information into Quicken, you must enter an account name. If your financial institution does have the ability to download information into your Quicken file, you will be prompted to enter your login credentials. Click Connect to download your account's information.
4. Complete each step of the dialog as explained in Chapter 9. At the last screen, you may see a link to your financial institution's website. Click that link to log onto that website.
5. While each institution is slightly different, at some point you will be prompted to enter your user ID and/or password, as shown next. Depending on your institution, you may be asked for additional information, such as your security question, before you have access to your account.

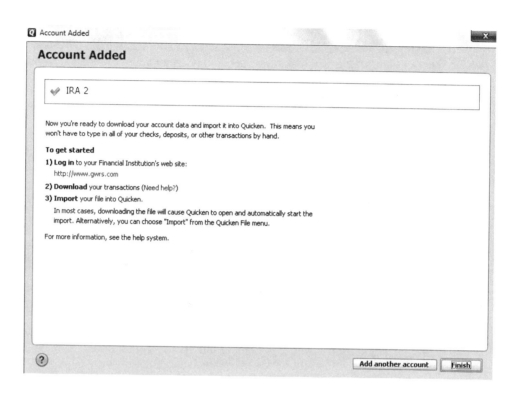

You may tell Quicken to save your Web Connect downloads to a specific file. To do so, click Edit | Preferences | Web Connect | Web Connect Preferences, and click the Give Me The Option Of Saving To A File Whenever I Download Web Connect Data check box. Click OK to close the Preferences dialog.

Reviewing and Accepting Transactions

After you download, the One Step Update Summary appears showing that the account has been updated successfully. A small red flag to the left of your account in the Account Bar indicates that there are transactions to review. See Figure 10-1 for an example of an account with downloaded transactions.

Depending on your preference settings, you may not see the One Step Update Summary unless there is an error.

NEW IN QUICKEN 2012

Quicken 2012 has the ability to accept and enter your downloaded transactions automatically. To enable this action, click Edit | Preferences | Downloaded Transactions | Downloaded Transaction Preferences | After Downloading Transactions, and click the Automatically Add To Investment Transaction Lists check box.

You can also tell Quicken which accounts to use for this automatic entry.

1. Right-click the account's name in the Account Bar, and choose Edit/Delete Account to open the Account Details dialog for that account.
2. Click the Online Services tab.
3. Click the Automatic Entry Is: Off link. The Automatic Transaction Entry dialog appears.
4. Choose one of the three choices:
   a. Click Use The General Account Preference That Applies To All Investing Accounts if you want to have the option you chose in Preferences apply to this account.
   b. Click Yes – Always Automatically Add Transactions For This Account if you want Quicken to enter all downloaded transactions without your acceptance.
   c. Click No – Never Automatically Add Transactions For This Account. [I Will Review And Accept Transactions Individually.] if you want to review each transaction before it is entered into the account's Transaction List.
5. Click OK to close the Automatic Transaction Entry dialog.

If you are in the account's Transaction List, click Downloaded Transactions to review and accept the items that have been downloaded. You may handle your downloaded transactions in two different ways:

- **Review Each Transaction** This method is best used if your account information is currently up to date. It allows you to look at each of the downloaded transactions before deciding to accept them into your "official" Transaction List. Consult Chapter 5 for details. In most cases, you'll simply select a new or matched transaction and click the Accept button to accept it. Once you have accepted the transaction, it appears in your Transaction List (register) with a small "c" in the Clr column, indicating that the transaction has been processed by your financial institution.

- **Accept All** This choice is best the first time you download transactions because it is the fastest. When you click this, all of the transactions are transferred to the Transaction List and the Cash Amt and Cash Bal fields are updated. The Downloaded Transactions pane will disappear. When you click Accept All, if there are sold or removed transactions in the download, you may need to follow prompts in a dialog so you can enter additional required

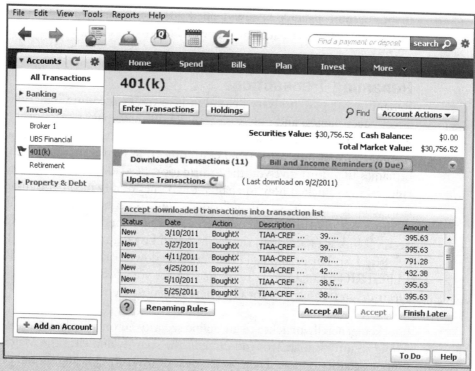

Figure 10-1 • Downloaded transactions for an investment account may be reviewed before they are entered into the account's Transaction List.

information. However, after the first time you download, be sure to back up before you accept all the transactions. If you have been entering transactions manually, the download may be slightly different, causing duplication and incorrect balances.

Remember that downloaded transactions that have not been accepted may not be entered in your Investment Transaction list. Thus, your Transaction List and portfolio balances may be misstated until you accept all downloaded transactions.

IN MY EXPERIENCE

Many Quicken users seldom, if ever, use Accept All for any type of downloaded transactions. If they do, they will often perform a backup first from which they can restore their original data.

At a minimum, users have recommended that after doing a backup, you take the time to review all of the downloaded transactions thoroughly before you click that Accept All button.

If your account balance as downloaded does not match your Quicken balance, an extra adjusting transaction will be added.

Renaming Transactions

Renaming rules are not very helpful in investment accounts. The rules only affect payee names, and only cash transactions have payees. However, you may want to rename some transactions in order to make them consistent with your naming conventions, or to avoid cluttering your Transaction List with a variety of names that don't give you the information needed. In this case, you can create rules telling Quicken how to change the names of downloaded transactions. You can "rename" securities in downloaded transactions by matching the downloaded security to a security in your Security List. Once the Matched With Online Security link is established, the security will be renamed to the name from the Security List. For example, TD Ameritrade downloads GE as GENERAL ELECTRIC CO COM, but you may prefer your Security List to use "General Electric," so transactions for GE are renamed to General Electric.

Quicken generally matches to an online security automatically, but if you find the wrong security is matched, you can edit the security and clear the Matched With Online Security option. Then, at the next download, Quicken should prompt you to match the security. Editing the security and changing the name changes the

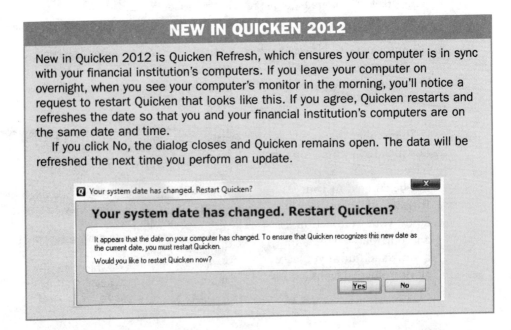

NEW IN QUICKEN 2012

New in Quicken 2012 is Quicken Refresh, which ensures your computer is in sync with your financial institution's computers. If you leave your computer on overnight, when you see your computer's monitor in the morning, you'll notice a request to restart Quicken that looks like this. If you agree, Quicken restarts and refreshes the date so that you and your financial institution's computers are on the same date and time.

If you click No, the dialog closes and Quicken remains open. The data will be refreshed the next time you perform an update.

security name displayed in the Transaction List. This process is useful after your first download to clean up the security names to the name you want displayed.

To rename transactions, click the Renaming Rules button in the Downloaded Transactions tab, or choose Tools | Renaming Rules. The Renaming Rules dialog is displayed. It shows the list of existing rules—by default, "Do Not Rename" is initially the only rule. Learn more about Renaming Rules in Chapter 5.

Using Multiple Currencies

As our world becomes smaller, some investors are finding they need to use multiple currencies with their transactions. Quicken supports this need in several ways.

To set up multicurrency usage, click Edit | Preferences | Calendar And Currency, and click the Multicurrency Support check box. The Portfolio view in the Investing tab will now include a field for the currency to be used, as seen here. While the default is the U.S. dollar, you have a number of other choices as well.

Click OK to save the Preferences change.

When you have enabled multicurrency usage, your One Step Update downloads will automatically include currency exchange rates. If you do not want to include the exchange rates, clear the Get Currency Exchange Rate check box in the One Step Update Settings dialog.

Using the Online Center Window

You can also use the Online Center to download account information and compare it to data in your Quicken file. From the menu bar, choose Tools | Online Center. If necessary, choose the name of your brokerage firm from the Financial Institution drop-down list near the top of the window.

If you have not set up any accounts for online downloads, you will not see the Online Center in the Tools menu.

The buttons offer a number of options you can use for working with the Online Center window:

- **Delete** deletes a selected item.
- **Contact Info** displays the Contact Information dialog for the currently selected financial institution. You can use the information in the dialog to

contact the bank or credit card company by phone, website, or e-mail if this service is offered by your financial institution.

- **Password Vault** gives you access to Quicken's Password Vault feature, as explained in Chapter 6. (This option only appears if you have enabled Online Account Services for accounts at more than one financial institution and have not yet set up the Password Vault feature.)
- **Trade**, if offered by your financial institution, connects to the Internet and displays your brokerage firm's home page in an Internet window. You can then log in to make online trades.
- **Print** prints the transactions listed in the Transactions List window.
- **Options** displays a menu of commands for working with the current window.

 Unusual in Quicken, there is no Help button or icon in the Online Center. However, you can always press the F1 key from within Quicken to open Quicken Help.

Downloading Transactions

To download transactions, make sure the brokerage firm is selected in the Online Center window, and then click the Update/Send button. Depending on the type of connection that is offered by your financial institution, you may see the One Step Update dialog or be connected directly to your financial institution's webpage.

Enter any user names and/or passwords as required. If you are using One Step Update, click Update Now. Wait while Quicken connects to your financial institution.

When Quicken is finished exchanging information, a One Step Update Summary window appears to summarize the activity that took place while you waited. Depending on your preference settings, you may not see the One Step Update Summary dialog unless there is an error. Click Close. If you have downloaded the information from a Web Connect website, sign off, if required, and close the connection to your institution's website.

If you display the Online Center window again, you'll see any transactions you downloaded in the bottom half of the window's Transactions subtab.

Adjusting the Cash Balance

If the cash balance in your Quicken account doesn't match the cash balance at your brokerage firm, you can adjust the cash balance with the Update Cash Balance dialog. From the Account Bar, click the account you want to adjust. The account's Transaction List appears. From the account's Transaction List, click

Account Actions | Update Cash Balance. Enter the correct cash balance and the date, and click Done. Quicken adjusts the account accordingly.

In the same way, use the Update Share Balance option to make any corrections to the number of shares in an account.

Reconciling Your Account

To keep your electronic investing accounts reconciled to your statement, you can perform a periodic reconciliation. If your account does not match your statement, you can adjust it with the Reconcile dialog. Select the account in the Account Bar to open the Transaction List. From the Account Actions menu, select Reconcile. The Reconcile dialog will appear as shown here. Enter the starting and ending cash balance amounts and the statement ending date, and click OK.

If the brokerage account has a linked checking account, you will see a warning message telling you the account can only be reconciled from the linked checking account. Click OK to dismiss the warning.

A list of the transactions is displayed. On the left are those transactions that decrease the cash balance, and on the right are those that increase it. As you click each transaction, the difference in the lower-right area of the dialog reflects the increase or decrease. Your account is successfully reconciled when the difference is equal to zero. If you want to start by marking all of the transactions, click Mark All. This is particularly helpful when you have a lot of transactions. When you have marked all and are finished, click Done. If you want to return to this at a later time, click Finish Later.

When you have reconciled your account, a message will be displayed offering you the opportunity to create a reconciliation report. Click Yes or No.

1. If you choose Yes, the Reconciliation Report Setup dialog appears.
2. Enter a title name.
3. Enter a date in the Show To Bank Balance As Of field.

4. Choose to create a report including All Transactions or Summary And Uncleared, which shows only the uncleared transactions and a summary of the cleared items.
5. Select Show Savings Goal Transactions if you choose to include them.
6. Click OK to open the Print dialog. You may choose to print the report to a paper printer or to the Quicken PDF printer.
7. If you choose No, you are returned to your account's Transaction List.

IN MY EXPERIENCE

As with banking and credit card statements, Quicken does not keep prior period reconciliation reports. The only way to save them is to print them. If you do not want to keep paper copies, use the Quicken PDF printer to create a "digitally" printed file that can be viewed with the free Adobe Reader program.

1. In the Print dialog, click the Printer drop-down list and choose Quicken PDF Printer, as shown next.
2. Click Print. A Save To PDF File dialog box appears.
3. In the Save In field, enter the name of the folder into which the report should be saved, or choose one using the drop-down arrow.
4. Name your file. Use a name that will mean something, perhaps something like Retirement Acct Reconciliation 9-30-11.
5. Click Save.
6. Your report is "printed" and saved to your selected folder and you are returned to the account's register or Transaction List.

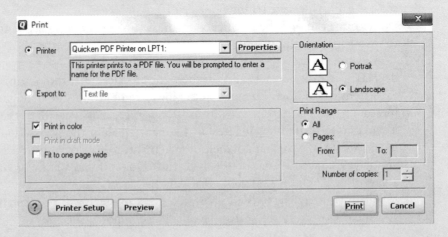

Also, if you have inadvertently turned off a message such as the "Don't Show Me This Screen Again" in the Reconciliation Report dialog, you can reset the message so that you see it again.

Click Edit | Preferences | Alerts | Warnings, and click Reset Quicken Warnings.

Adjusting Holdings

If the holdings amounts in Quicken don't match what you've downloaded, the Enter Transactions dialog can be used to adjust your holdings. Select the account you want to adjust from the Account Bar to open the account's Transaction List. Click the Enter Transactions button located under the name of the account.

From the Enter Transaction drop-down list, shown next, select the type of transaction you want. Fill in the information needed, and when you are finished, click Enter/Done. For additional information on using the Enter Transaction dialog, see Chapter 9.

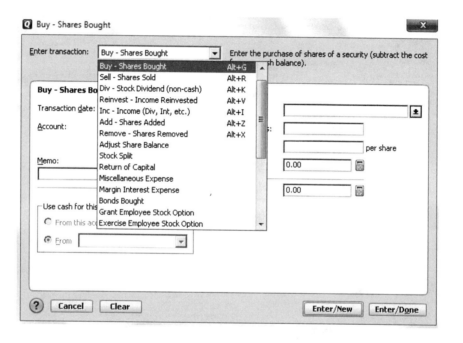

If you enter a transaction more than one year in the past to correct an account, you will see a warning message. If you are sure the information you are entering is correct, click Yes.

Exploring the Account Overview Window

When you download transactions from your financial institution, you also receive detailed account balance information. To review this information, select the account in the Account Bar to open the Transaction List. From the Account Actions menu, select Account Overview. The Account Overview window for this account appears as seen in Figure 10-2.

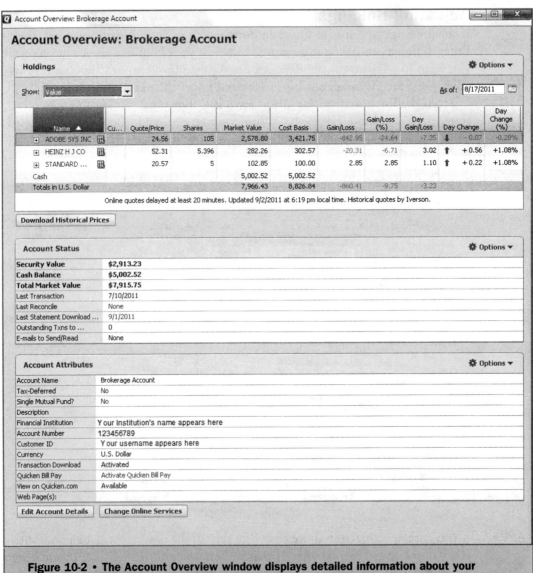

Account Overview: Brokerage Account

Holdings ⚙ Options ▾

Show: Value ▾   As of: 8/17/2011 📅

Name ▲	Cu...	Quote/Price	Shares	Market Value	Cost Basis	Gain/Loss	Gain/Loss (%)	Day Gain/Loss	Day Change	Day Change (%)
⊞ ADOBE SYS INC	📖	24.56	105	2,578.80	3,421.75	-842.95	-24.64	-7.35 ⬇	-0.07	-0.28%
⊞ HEINZ H J CO	📖	52.31	5.396	282.26	302.57	-20.31	-6.71	3.02 ⬆	+0.56	+1.08%
⊞ STANDARD ...	📖	20.57	5	102.85	100.00	2.85	2.85	1.10 ⬆	+0.22	+1.08%
Cash				5,002.52	5,002.52					
Totals in U.S. Dollar				7,966.43	8,826.84	-860.41	-9.75	-3.23		

Online quotes delayed at least 20 minutes. Updated 9/2/2011 at 6:19 pm local time. Historical quotes by Iverson.

Download Historical Prices

Account Status ⚙ Options ▾

Security Value	**$2,913.23**
Cash Balance	**$5,002.52**
Total Market Value	**$7,915.75**
Last Transaction	7/10/2011
Last Reconcile	None
Last Statement Download ...	9/1/2011
Outstanding Txns to ...	0
E-mails to Send/Read	None

Account Attributes ⚙ Options ▾

Account Name	Brokerage Account
Tax-Deferred	No
Single Mutual Fund?	No
Description	
Financial Institution	Your Institution's name appears here
Account Number	123456789
Customer ID	Your username appears here
Currency	U.S. Dollar
Transaction Download	Activated
Quicken Bill Pay	Activate Quicken Bill Pay
View on Quicken.com	Available
Web Page(s):	

Edit Account Details   **Change Online Services**

Figure 10-2 • The Account Overview window displays detailed information about your investment account.

Viewing Holdings

Your financial institution also sends you information about your individual holdings. You can review this information in the Account Overview window and compare it to the information in your portfolio. You can choose several ways of viewing your holdings, as seen here. Click the Show menu to see the options.

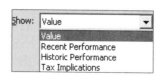

Some Quicken users prefer using the Portfolio view of the Investing tab to review their holdings.

- **Value** displays the following:
  - **Currency** is displayed if you have enabled multiple currencies.
  - **Quote/Price** as of the last time you downloaded.
  - **Shares** shows the number of shares you currently hold.
  - **Market Value** displays today's value of these shares.
  - **Cost Basis** shows what you paid for these shares when you bought them.
  - **Gain/Loss** displays your unrealized gain or loss as of the last time you downloaded.
  - **Day Gain/Loss** and **Gain/Loss %** indicates today's gain or loss based on the latest download prices in both dollars and percentages.
  - **Day Change** shows the trend for today for each security and the dollar amount of the change.
  - **Day Change %** displays the percentage of gain or loss for the day.
- **Recent Performance** shows the following:
  - **Market Value** shows today's (or as of the last download) information.
  - **Gain/Loss** shows the total gain or loss in dollars for today.
  - **Gain/Loss %** shows the total gain or loss in percentage for today.
  - **Gain/Loss 1-Month** shows the gain or loss in dollars for the past month.
  - **Gain/Loss 1-Month %** shows the percentage of the gain or loss percentage for the past month.
  - **Gain/Loss for % 3-Month and 12-Month** show the gain or loss percentage for these time periods.
- **Historic Performance** indicates the annual return for each security compared to its industry or category for the past one, three, and five years. It also displays the industry and/or category of each holding.
- **Tax Implications** displays tax information about each security. You may need to expand the security lot information by clicking the plus sign in the small square at the left of the security's name to see the tax implications for each lot. However, check with your tax professional for more information.

If you want to adjust your holdings, refer to the section "Adjusting Holdings" earlier in this chapter.

Seeing the Options

In the Holdings snapshot of the Account Overview, the Options menu allows you to do the following:

- **Preferences** opens the Portfolio View Options dialog. See Chapter 11 for further information about this dialog.
- **Show Closed Lots** is also discussed in Chapter 11.
- **Get Online Quotes** uses your Internet connection to update your holdings.
- **Go To Full Portfolio** takes you to the Investing tab's Portfolio view.

If you are using Quicken Premier edition and have chosen to update your quotes every 15 minutes, your holdings are automatically updated while Quicken is the active application. To turn on this useful feature, select Edit | Preferences | Investment Transactions, and select the Automatically Update Quotes Every 15 Minutes check box. Click OK or Close to close the Preferences dialog.

The Options menu in the Account Status snapshot offers the following:

- **Reconcile This Account** opens the Account Reconciliation dialog.
- **View All My Accounts** opens the Account List.

From the Account Attributes snapshot, the Options menu offers six more links or commands:

- **Create A New Account** opens the Add Account dialog.
- **View/Edit Comments** opens a comment dialog for this account.
- **Set Tax Attributes** opens the Tax Schedule Information dialog.
- **Set Web Pages** opens a dialog from which you can enter the web address to use as the Home Page, the Activity Page, and an Extra Page for this account.
- **Browse Web Pages** opens links to the pages you set in Set Web Pages.
- **Transaction Fee** opens the Transaction Fees dialog.

Checking Your Account's Status

As seen in Figure 10-2, the current status of your account is displayed in the center of the Account Overview window. It includes all of the following:

- The **Security Value** of this entire account

- The **Cash Balance** held in this account
- The **Total Market Value**

This snapshot also includes the Last Transaction, Last Reconcile, and Last Statement Download dates. You can also see any transactions that need to be compared, as well as any e-mails to the account's financial institution that you need to send or read from the Online Center.

From the Options menu in this section, you can choose to reconcile the account or view the Account List.

Reviewing the Account's Attributes

The bottom snapshot of the Account Overview window displays the account name, its tax-deferment status, and other information about your account. This includes your account number and user name, so be careful if you view this information in a public setting.

From this section's Option menu you can do the following:

- **Create a New Account**   Click this to open the Add Account dialog.
- **View/Edit Comments**   This option opens a dialog box in which you can add or edit comments about this account.
- **Set Tax Attributes**   This option opens the Tax Schedule Information dialog.
- **Set Web Pages**   You can enter the Home Page, Activity Page, and one additional webpage address for this account in this dialog.
- **Browse Web Pages**   After you have entered webpage addresses for this account, the next option displays a link to those pages.
- **Transaction Fee**   This dialog allows you to enter any fees associated with this account, as seen here.

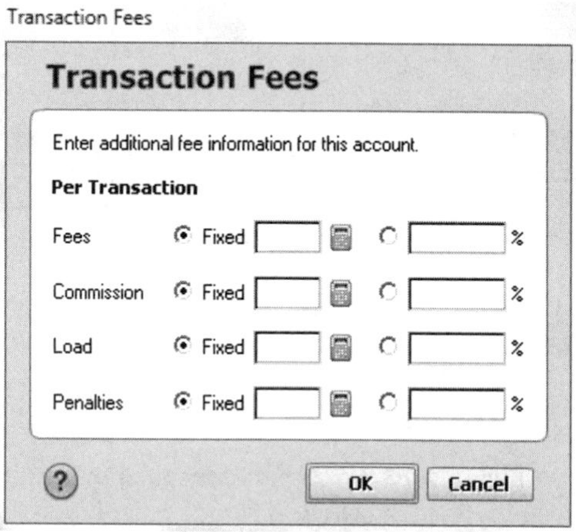

The Edit Account Details button at the bottom of the Account Overview screen opens the Account Details dialog at the General tab. The Change Online Services button opens the Account Details dialog at the Online Services tab.

Click Close to close the Account Overview.

Transaction Fees

Transaction Fees

Enter additional fee information for this account.

Per Transaction

Fees	⊙ Fixed	○ %
Commission	⊙ Fixed	○ %
Load	⊙ Fixed	○ %
Penalties	⊙ Fixed	○ %

(?)   OK   Cancel

Downloading Quotes and Investment Information

Quicken enables you to download up-to-date stock quotes, news headlines, and alerts for the securities in your portfolio and on your Watch List. You set up this feature once and then update the information as often as desired. You can even download historical price information so you can review price trends for a security that recently caught your attention.

Because the quote and investment information feature is built into Quicken, it doesn't rely on your brokerage firm for information. That means you can download quotes, headlines, and alerts even if your brokerage firm doesn't offer the downloading of transactions. All you need is an Internet connection.

Setting Up the Download

Before you can get quotes online, you must tell Quicken to download the information. Click the One Step Update symbol (the blue right-curling arrow) on either the Account Bar or the Tool Bar to open the One Step Update Settings dialog. Click the Download Quotes And Investment Information check box. Click the Select Quotes link to open the Security List, as seen in Figure 10-3. You can also open the Security List using the keyboard shortcut CTRL-Y.

Making Selections on the Security List

Using check boxes on the Security List, you may select the information you want to download for each of your securities. You may choose to

- Download quotes for each security.

Security ▲	Symbol	Type	Asset Class	Currency	Download Quotes	Watch List	Hide	
ADOBE SYS INC	ADBE	Stock	Large Cap Stocks	U.S. Dollar	☑	☐	☐	Edit Delete
Dow Jones Industrials	DJI	Market Index	Unclassified	U.S. Dollar	☑	☐	☐	
Fidelity Select Software & ...	FSCSX	Mutual Fund	Asset Mixture	U.S. Dollar	☑	☑	☐	
HEINZ H J CO	HNZ	Stock	Large Cap Stocks	U.S. Dollar	☑	☐	☐	
NASDAQ Composite	COMPX	Market Index	Unclassified	U.S. Dollar	☑	☐	☐	

New Security   Choose Market Indexes   ☐ Show hidden securities   Mark All

Done

Figure 10-3 • You can download information about your investment holdings at any time with your Internet connection.

- Include the security on your Watch List.
- Hide the security. However, even if you hide the security, Quicken does not uncheck the Download Quotes or Watch List check boxes.

The New Security button opens an Add Security To Quicken dialog with which you can enter a new security to the list. Review Chapter 9 for how to add a new security.

Creating a Watch List

To set up a group of securities you don't own but want to track, create a Watch List. Click Investing | Portfolio. Look in the Name column for the Watch List area, as seen here. If you do not see a Watch List in the Portfolio view you are using, you can click Customize, select the Account tab, and select Watch List in the list of accounts. Click OK to save the change and return to the Portfolio view.

Click the right-facing arrow to the left of Watch List, if necessary, to open your current list. By default, all of your current securities are shown on the list as well as any you have previously chosen to display. You may change the securities to include in the Watch List in the Security List, as discussed in "Making Selections on the Security List" earlier in this chapter.

Click the small newspaper icon to the right of a security name or symbol to display a link to the latest information about that security.

Viewing Downloaded Quotes

You can view information about your securities in two different ways:

- The Portfolio window, which is covered in greater detail in Chapter 11, displays quotes and news headlines for all securities you own or watch. To display this window, choose Investing | Portfolio, or press CTRL-U.
- The Security Detail View window displays information for individual securities or market indexes. See "Using the Security Detail View" next in this chapter. To open this window:
  1. From the Investing tab, click Portfolio.
  2. Click the name of the security or index you want to view from the list that displays. If the name does not show, click the right-facing arrow to

open the account, Watch List, or Indexes and click the name of the item you want to see. The Security Detail View dialog will appear as shown in Figure 10-4. You can also access the Security Detail View window from the Security List, which sorts the securities by name.

You can open the Security Detail View from the Security List by clicking the name of the security or the index.

Using the Security Detail View

The Security Detail View window (see Figure 10-4) offers the most detailed quote information. If you have been faithfully downloading quotes for your securities (or you have downloaded historical quotes, as discussed in the section titled "Downloading Historical Quote Information" later in this chapter), a chart of the

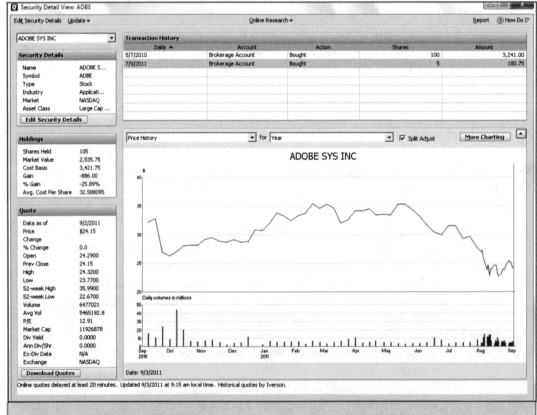

Figure 10-4 • The Security Detail View window shows information about a security.

price history appears in the body of the window. You can use the drop-down list in the top-left corner of the window to switch from one security to another.

The information found in the Security Detail View is extensive. As you can see in Figure 10-4, the left side of the window discusses the details about the security, your holdings, and the latest quotes. From this window you can edit the details of your security, download quotes, create additional charts, and do online research. (See "Using Online Research" later in this chapter for more information about online research.)

Working with the Security View Detail Menu Bar   The Security View Detail menu bar has five items from which you can learn more about the selected security:

- **Edit Security Details** opens the Edit Security Details dialog, as seen here. Use this dialog to make any changes in the security, including its ticker symbol, asset class, and security type. See "Downloading Asset Class Information" later in this chapter for additional information about that topic. You can tell Quicken if this is a tax-free security. Click Other Info to open the Additional Security Information dialog in which you can indicate how much income you expect from this security, your goal for this security, your broker's name and phone number, its rating, and any other comments.

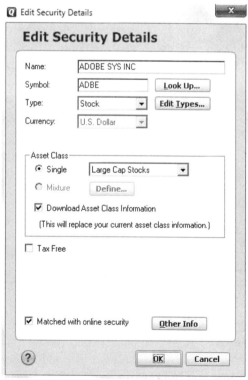

- **Update** opens a menu from which you can download quotes, send information to Quicken.com, download both asset classes and historical prices, and if necessary, edit the price history of this security.
- **Online Research** offers several tools, as discussed in "Using Online Research" later in this chapter.

- **Report** creates a security report that you can customize to fit your needs.
- **How Do I?** opens the Quicken Help window that discusses securities and security prices.

Viewing Price History   In the Investing tab's Portfolio view, downloaded quotes appear beside the security name or ticker symbol. Stock quotes are delayed 20 minutes or more during the trading day. Quotes for mutual funds are updated once a day by around 6:00 P.M. Eastern Standard Time. Prior to that, you'll see the previous day's prices with a small clock symbol icon beside the price (short for estimate), indicating that the price has not been updated since the previous trading day.

See the history of a security's prices by selecting the security in the Security Detail View window (double-click the security name in the Investing tab's Portfolio view). Choose Update | Edit Price to display the Price History window, which displays all of the recorded stock quotes for the security. Click Close to dismiss the Price History window.

It's quicker to right-click the security in the Portfolio view and select Price History from the context menu. If you do go from the Portfolio view to the Security Detail View window, you only need to single-click the security.

Viewing Security News

Quicken may display up to three icons in the Name column of the Portfolio view. Each icon displays pertinent information when you hover your mouse over the icon. If an information box includes a link, clicking the link uses your Internet connection to open a webpage with more information.

- An exclamation point icon displays alert information about the security, such as major price fluctuations and information about earnings announcements.
- A newspaper icon displays news headlines related to the security. Click the title to download the whole article.
- The H or L icon indicates that the security has reached a 52-week price high or low.

Downloading Historical Quote Information

Quicken enables you to download up to five years of historical quotes for any security you own or watch. Choose Investing | Update | Historical Prices. Quicken displays the Get Historical Prices dialog, shown next.

If you happen to own a security that is not publicly traded, you won't be able to download historical quote info for it. You could, however, import a price history file if you have a source of price data for the security.

Choose a time period from the drop-down list at the top of the dialog. Your choices are Month, Year, Two Years, and Five Years. Make sure check marks appear beside all securities for which you want to get historical quotes. (Click Mark All to get prices for all on the list.)

Some Quicken users have reported trouble when selecting five years of prices for many securities at the same time. Several have suggested that you request data for five years for a single security or one month for several securities.

Then click the Update Now button. With your Internet connection, Quicken retrieves the information you requested. When it's done, it displays the One Step Update Summary window. Click Close to dismiss the window.

Depending on your preference setting, you may not see the One Step Update Summary window unless there is an error.

Downloading Asset Class Information

For each security you own or watch, you can include asset class information. This enables you to create accurate asset allocation reports and graphs. Chapter 9 explains how to enter asset class information manually; Chapter 11 explains how you can use this information to diversify your portfolio to meet your investment goals.

The trouble is that most mutual funds consist of many investments in a variety of asset classes. Manually looking up and entering this information is time-consuming and tedious. Fortunately, Quicken automatically downloads this information for you, including your mutual funds.

However, you can change the information at any time. To do so, choose the Investing tab and click Tools | Security List. Click the security you want, and then click the Edit action button. This opens the Edit Security Details dialog seen earlier in this chapter. Make sure the Download Asset Class Information check box is selected, and close the dialog. The next time you update, asset classes are automatically updated.

Use Quicken.com for Updates

Using Quicken.com enables you to track your portfolio's value on the Web. Although you can do this without Quicken by manually customizing and updating the default portfolio webpage at Quicken.com, it's a lot easier to have Quicken automatically send updated portfolio information to Quicken.com for you.

To use the Quicken.com update feature, you must register Quicken. (Quicken will remind you if you haven't completed this step.) During the registration process, you will enter a member ID and password that you need to remember. The registration process sets up a private Quicken.com account for you to store your portfolio data.

Exporting Your Portfolio

In Quicken, choose Investing | Update | Update Portfolio On Quicken.com. The Preferences dialog, open to Quicken.com Portfolio, appears as shown next.

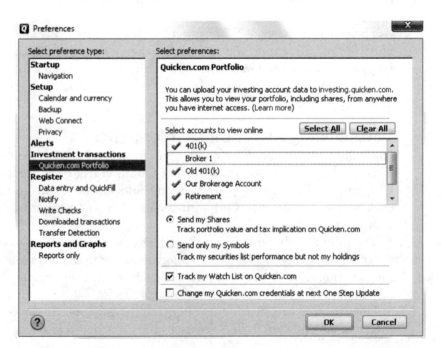

Click to place green check marks beside each account that you want to track on the Web. If you also want to track Watch List items on the Web, select the Track My Watch List On Quicken.com check box. Finally, select one of the following upload options:

- **Send My Shares** exports the ticker symbols and the number of shares of each security you own for your portfolio. This enables you to track both prices and portfolio values.
- **Send Only My Symbols** exports just the ticker symbols for your portfolio. This enables you to track prices but not portfolio values.

If you want to change your password or other information on Quicken.com, select the Change My Quicken.com Credentials At Next One Step Update check box.

When you've completed your selections, click OK. The next time you run One Step Update, your account will be updated.

To access your Quicken.com account, go to the Internet from any location. In the address bar of your browser, type **http://investing.quicken.com**. You are prompted for your Quicken.com registration member ID and password. Type the information and click Sign In. Your Investing Home page will appear as seen in Figure 10-5.

Utilizing Quote Lookup

The Quote Lookup feature in the Investing Home tab at Quicken.com enables you to look up stock ticker symbols. These symbols are required to use Quicken's Online Research feature for getting quotes and obtaining information about securities on the Web.

In each tab, type the ticker symbol for your security. If you don't know the symbol, or it does not appear on the pop-up list, click Lookup. Quicken displays the Symbol Lookup dialog in a Quicken browser window. Type all or part of the security name in the text box, and click Search. Quicken organizes the results by security type: Stocks, Mutual Funds, ETFs, and Indices. Click the tab of the security type you want, and examine the securities it found that matched the criteria you entered.

Since the Lookup feature opens another browser window, once you are done looking up symbols, close the new browser window to return to the browser window displaying your Quicken.com info.

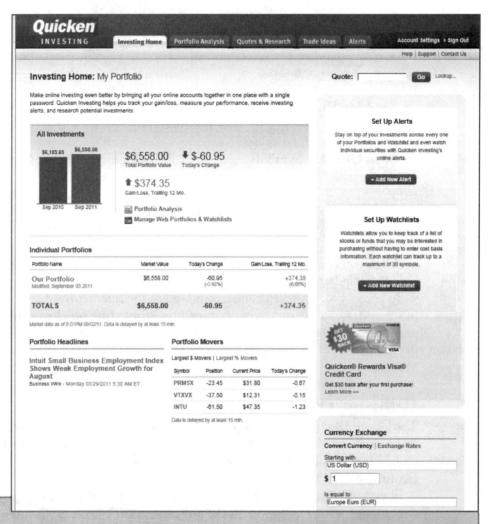

Figure 10-5 • After you have exported your portfolio, you can access it from anywhere with an Internet connection, using your member ID and password.

Using Online Research

Quicken offers access to a number of research tools at Quicken.com. You can use these tools to find and learn about securities before you invest.

This part of the chapter tells you a little about Quicken's online research tools so you can explore them. Most Quicken users find them valuable resources for making wise investment decisions. You can access online research information for a specific security from the Security Detail View window. Press CTRL-Y to open the Security List. Select a security, and from the Security Detail View menu bar, select Online Research to open a menu, as seen here.

You can access these tools as well from the Classic menu. Click View | Classic Menus to display the extended menu list. Choose Investing | Online Portfolio to open the Quicken.com login page.

Online Research ▾
Get full quote
News
Quotes and research
One-Click Scorecard
Set up Alerts
Stock Evaluator
Multiple security Charting

Get Full Quote and Quotes and Research

Both of these options open the Quicken Investing page to the Quotes & Research tab. From this page you see a wide variety of information about your company's price history, its industry position, and main competitors.

News

When you choose the News command, your Internet connection opens to the latest news about the security you selected. It can be information ranging from the company's board of directors announcement about a dividend or the latest press release from the company's media department.

One-Click Scorecard

One-Click Scorecard instantly displays reports that help you evaluate your security before you invest, using a variety of well-known analysis techniques and strategies.

When you have selected a security, as Quicken.com opens to the One-Click Scorecard section of the Quotes & Research tab, you'll see an analysis of its performance in a "scorecard" format, as seen here.

Robert Hagstrom	Geraldine Weiss

Hagstrom

NO INTEREST

These seven metrics are a snap to calculate, thanks to Quicken.com's One-Click Scorecard. Our goal with this tool is to help you evaluate potential investment candidates and eliminate those equities that aren't up to snuff. One-Click Scorecard won't do all the homework necessary for you to reach a decision, but it will help you develop a list of quality stocks to watch and study further.

Performed well consistently?	Fail
Avoids excess debt?	Fail
Converting sales to profits?	Fail
Shareholder's money handled rationally?	Pass
Increased shareholder value?	Pass
Consistently increased owner earnings?	Fail
Sells at 25% discount to intrinsic value?	Pass

Each of the scorecard items is explained, using charts, graphs, and analytical information.

Online Alerts

One of the advantages of exporting your portfolio to Quicken.com is the availability of setting alerts for price changes, volume movement, and any other news that might impact your portfolio. Choosing Set Up Alerts from the Online Research menu takes you to the Alerts tab on Quicken.com, from which you can create the type of alert that will most benefit your financial position.

Stock Evaluator

The Stock Evaluator command opens the Quotes & Research tab in Quicken.com to the Evaluator section. From this section, both growth trends and the financial health of your chosen security are graphed and explained. Another useful section of the Evaluator is the Management Performance assessment. This section includes price to earnings, price to sales, and price to earnings growth ratios.

Charting Multiple Securities

The final option in the Online Research menu allows you to chart the closing prices of up to five securities and include up to three indexes in your chart.

1. Click Multiple Security Charting to open the Multiple Security Charting dialog as seen in Figure 10-6.
2. Select the period of time you want to cover from the For What Period? drop-down list. The default is three months, but you can choose from seven more options.
3. Choose the securities you want to chart (up to five). To do so, click the name of the first security and hold down your CTRL key while choosing up to four more.
4. Select any indexes you want to include.
5. Click Go Online To Chart to complete your chart. Using your Internet connection and the Yahoo! Finance page, the chart displays information using the first security name (alphabetically) as its base.

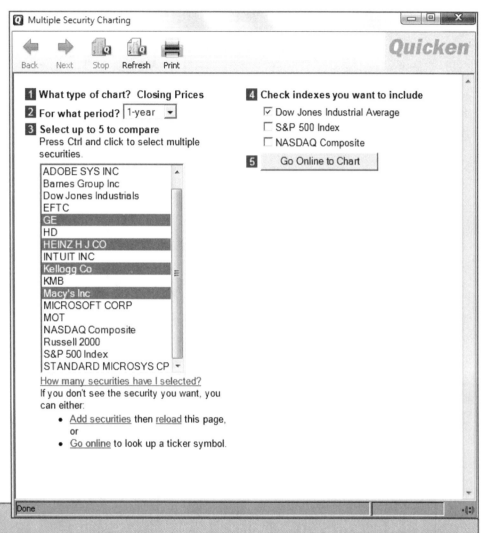

Figure 10-6 • **You can create charts that compare the closing prices of several different securities.**

Evaluating Your Position

In This Chapter:

- *Understanding the Portfolio view*
- *Studying your performance*
- *Exploring asset allocation*
- *Updating your investments*
- *Working with reports*
- *Utilizing Investment tab tools*
- *Using asset allocation*
- *Analyzing your portfolio*
- *Previewing your buy/sell decisions*
- *Estimating capital gains*
- *Setting investment alerts*

As you enter transactions into Quicken—whether manually or automatically via Transaction Download—Quicken builds a portrait of your investment portfolio and performance. If you're serious about investing, you can use this information to evaluate your investing position and fine-tune your portfolio to diversify and maximize returns.

Quicken's Investing tab offers a wide range of tools—including reports, graphs, alerts, analysis tools, and reference materials—that you can use to evaluate and strengthen your investment positions. This chapter takes a closer look at the features that can make you a better investor.

Using the Investing Tab

The Investing tab should be your first stop for evaluating your investment position. Each of its views includes snapshots with calculated information and links to more information on Quicken and Quicken.com features. Because the Investing tab always displays the most recent information it has, its windows are most useful immediately after downloading quotes, news, and research information, as discussed in Chapter 10. If you are using Quicken Premier or a higher version, you can tell Quicken to download quotes for you every 15 minutes.

Quicken must be the active window for this to work. If you are using another program or have minimized Quicken, Quicken will not update quotes until you make it the active window.

To open the Investing tab window, click the Investing tab near the top of Quicken's main window. The Portfolio view appears. Additional information is available in the views found by clicking the Performance or Allocations button as discussed later in this chapter.

If you have visited the Investment tab before, you may need to select the Portfolio view, as Quicken remembers the last view on the Investment tab you visited.

This part of the chapter takes you on a guided tour of Quicken's Investing tab so you know exactly how you can use it to monitor your investments.

Understanding the Portfolio View

The Portfolio view of the Investing tab (see Figure 11-1) displays all of your investments in one place. Information can be viewed in a wide variety of ways to show you exactly what you need to see to understand the performance, value, or components of your portfolio.

Open the Portfolio window by clicking the Portfolio button in the Investing tab or by pressing CTRL-U.

Using Portfolio View Options

You can quickly customize the Portfolio window's view by using the Show, Group By, and As Of drop-down lists right beneath the Portfolio, Performance, and Allocations buttons. There are many view combinations—far too many to illustrate in this book. Here's a brief overview so you can explore these options on your own.

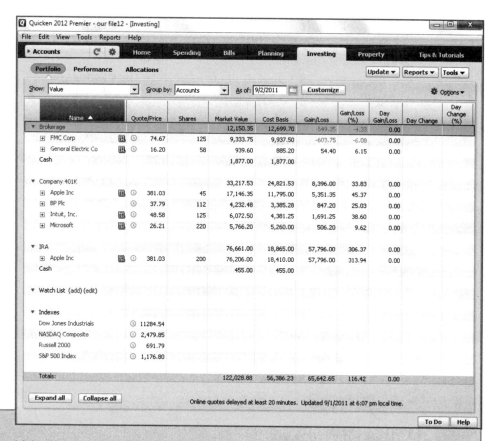

Figure 11-1 • Use the Investing tab's Portfolio view to see all of your investments in one place.

Using Show Options   The Show drop-down list enables you to specify the view that should be used to display the information. Each of the nine predefined views can be customized with the Customize Current View dialog, discussed later in this section. You can also create nine "custom" views to see data in ways most useful to you.

Using Group By Options   The Group By options enable you to select the order in which securities appear. The drop-down list offers six options: Accounts, Industry, Security, Security Type, Investing Goal, and Asset Class. These options correspond to information entered as part of a security's definition, either manually when you add the security to Quicken or automatically when you download asset information. Learn how to add securities to Quicken in Chapter 9 and how to download security information in Chapter 10.

Using Portfolio Date You can use the As Of box to set the date for which you want to view the portfolio. For example, suppose you want to see what your portfolio looked like a month ago, before a particularly volatile market period. Enter that date in the text box. Or you can click the calendar button beside the text box to display a calendar of dates, and then click the date you want to display. The view changes to show your portfolio as of the date you specified.

Customizing a View

Quicken offers an incredible amount of flexibility when it comes to displaying information in the Portfolio window. Not only does it come with nine preconfigured views that you can choose from the Show drop-down list, but it also enables you to create additional views to meet any need.

To customize a view, begin by using the Show drop-down list to choose the view you want to customize. Then click the Customize button to the right of the Show, Group By, and As Of drop-down lists. The Customize Current View dialog appears with the Columns tab displayed, as shown next. Set options as desired in the dialog, and click OK to change the view.

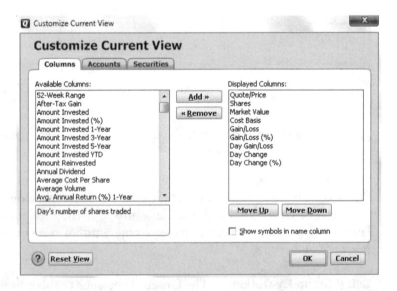

Selecting Columns to Show To display a column of information, select it in the Available Columns list and click the Add button beside it. To hide a column of information, select it in the Displayed Columns list and click the Remove button. You can change the order in which columns appear by selecting a column name in the Displayed Columns list and using the Move Up or Move Down button to change its order in the list.

Displaying Symbols Rather Than Names   To display a security's ticker symbol rather than its name, select the Show Symbols In Name Column check box.

Return to Default   Click the Reset View button to return this view to the default settings.

Selecting Accounts to Include   To specify which accounts should appear, click the Accounts tab, shown next. Toggle the check marks to the left of the account names in the Accounts To Include In This View list. Only those accounts that are selected will appear. You can change the order in which accounts appear by selecting an account name in the Accounts To Include list and clicking the Move Up or Move Down button.

Click Select All to include all of your accounts, or click Clear All to clear all of the check marks and start over. To include hidden accounts in the Accounts To Include In This View list, select the Show (Hidden Accounts) check box. To reset the view to the default settings, click the Reset View button.

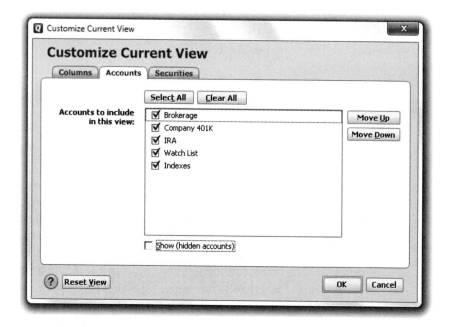

Selecting Securities to Include   Click the Securities tab to specify which securities should appear. Toggle the check marks to the left of the security names in the Securities To Include In This View list. Only those securities that are selected will appear. To include hidden securities in the Securities To Include list, select the Show (Hidden Securities) check box.

Click Select All to include all of your accounts, or click Clear All to clear all of the check marks and start over. To reset the view to the default settings, click the Reset View button.

When you have finished creating your new view, click OK to return to the Investing tab's Portfolio view.

Setting Portfolio View Options

Use the Options button at the far right of the Portfolio view to customize your views, as explained earlier, as well as to do the following.

Portfolio Preferences   This option enables you to specify the period for return calculations and the tax rate used in the Portfolio window, as shown here. Setting these options enables you to fine-tune the way Quicken makes Portfolio window calculations.

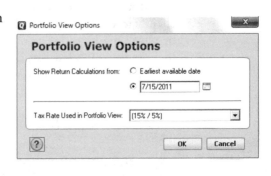

From the Investing tab Portfolio view, click Options | Portfolio Preferences to open the Portfolio View Options dialog.

The Show Return Calculations From area offers options for determining the period and tax rate for which Quicken calculates the return on investment:

- **Earliest Available Date**, the default, includes all periods for which you have entered transactions into Quicken.
- A blank field allows you to enter a starting date for calculations. All transactions between that starting date and the current date are included in the calculations. Alternatively, you can use the calendar icon to set the date.
- **Tax Rate Used In Portfolio View** allows you to choose tax rates that should be used in tax calculations for capital gains. If you are utilizing Quicken's Tax Planner, which is covered in Chapter 17, keep the default, Use Tax Planner Rate, selected. Otherwise, choose the rates that are appropriate for your financial situation. Check with your tax professional for further information about your specific situation. Click OK to save your changes and return to the Portfolio view.

Show Closed Lots   This option tells Quicken that you want to display lots that have been closed.

Studying Your Performance

If you are using Quicken's Premier (or higher) edition, the Performance button's view in the Investing tab (see Figure 11-2) displays graphs and tables of information about your investment performance. You can customize many of the

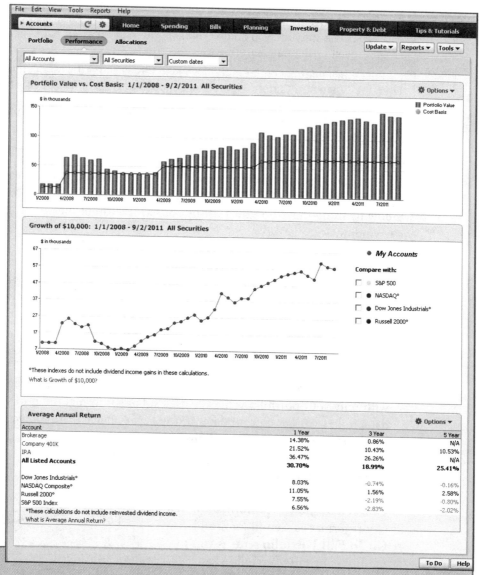

Figure 11-2 • The Performance view of the Investing tab shows you, at a glance, how your investments are doing.

IN MY EXPERIENCE

The Investment Performance reports the average annual return (AAR) for each investment. One of my clients thought this report presented the return on investment (ROI), which is a different calculation.

- To compute ROI you subtract the cost of an investment from the total gain and divide that result by the total cost.
- To calculate the AAR, you add the annual return percentage rates and divide that result by the number of years.

To see ROI information, from the Investing tab, click Portfolio | Customize. From the Customize Current View dialog, choose any of the five ROI calculations from the Available Columns list and add your choice(s) to the Displayed Columns list on the right side of the dialog. Click OK to display the information, which is shown in percentages.

---

snapshots that appear in the Performance view using commands on each snapshot's Options menu. You can further customize the Performance view window by using the drop-down list options at the top of the Performance view window.

Portfolio Value vs. Cost Basis

The Portfolio Value vs. Cost Basis graph uses a line graph and a bar graph to illustrate your portfolio's cost basis—what you've invested—and its market value. Ideally, you want the tops of the bars to appear above the line, indicating that your account is worth more than you spent to buy the securities.

The Options menu offers additional choices for this graph:

- **Go To Full Screen View Of This Graph** displays a graph (see Figure 11-3) with only your portfolio value versus cost basis information as of today's date, unless you set custom dates in the Performance Date Range drop-down list. In that case, the graph will display the ending date of the date range you chose, as shown here.
- **Show Value/Cost Basis Report** tells Quicken to show the information in a report format as seen in Figure 11-3.
- **Go To Full Portfolio** returns you to the Investing tab's Portfolio view.

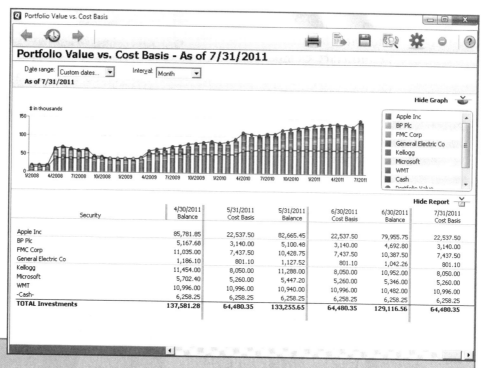

Security	4/30/2011 Balance	5/31/2011 Cost Basis	5/31/2011 Balance	6/30/2011 Cost Basis	6/30/2011 Balance	7/31/2011 Cost Basis
Apple Inc	85,781.85	22,537.50	82,665.45	22,537.50	79,955.75	22,537.50
BP Plc	5,167.68	3,140.00	5,100.48	3,140.00	4,692.80	3,140.00
FMC Corp	11,035.00	7,437.50	10,428.75	7,437.50	10,387.50	7,437.50
General Electric Co	1,186.10	801.10	1,127.52	801.10	1,042.26	801.10
Kellogg	11,454.00	8,050.00	11,288.00	8,050.00	10,952.00	8,050.00
Microsoft	5,702.40	5,260.00	5,447.20	5,260.00	5,346.00	5,260.00
WMT	10,996.00	10,996.00	10,940.00	10,996.00	10,482.00	10,996.00
-Cash-	6,258.25	6,258.25	6,258.25	6,258.25	6,258.25	6,258.25
TOTAL Investments	**137,581.28**	**64,480.35**	**133,255.65**	**64,480.35**	**129,116.56**	**64,480.35**

Figure 11-3 • You can obtain detail in both graphic and numeric formats about your portfolio's performance compared to your cost.

Growth Of $10,000

The Growth Of $10,000 chart illustrates how an investment of $10,000 in your portfolio has grown over the period you choose. You can select check boxes beside popular investment indexes to compare your investment performance to one or more indexes, as shown in Figure 11-2.

Average Annual Return

The Average Annual Return chart displays the one-year, three-year, and five-year return on each of your investment accounts. If the account has one or more securities in the one-, three-, or five-year period, there will be an average annual return reported for the account. If the account did not exist or no lots of the account's securities existed during the one-, three-, or five-year period, the average annual return will show as N/A.

The options for this section let you change the information's display, as seen here.

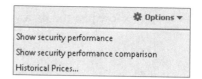

- **Show Security Performance and Show Security Performance Comparison** open a report, similar to the Portfolio view, showing how your securities have done as of a date you choose.
- **Historical Prices** opens the Get Historical Prices dialog, shown here, from which you can tell Quicken to download historical prices for one or more of your securities for the last month, year, two years, or five years. Place check marks in front of the name of each security for which you want

pricing. The Mark All and Clear All buttons can help you make your selections. Click Update Now to use your Internet connection to download the data. The One Step Update Summary dialog displays when the download is complete. Click Close to close the dialog and return to the Investing tab's Performance view.

If you have selected the Show This Dialog Only If There Is An Error check box at the lower-left corner of the One Step Update window, you may not see the One Step Update Summary.

Exploring Asset Allocation

The Allocations views of the Investing tab (see Figure 11-4) display a number of customizable graphs of your investment data, along with a few snapshots with links to other features. Each of the graphs that appear in the Allocations view can be customized using commands on the graph's Options menu. Buttons beneath each chart enable you to go to a full-sized graph in a report window or view a related report. You can further customize the Allocations view window by selecting one of the drop-down list options: All Accounts, Investing Only, Retirement Only, or one of your accounts. You can also select Customize to show just the data you prefer.

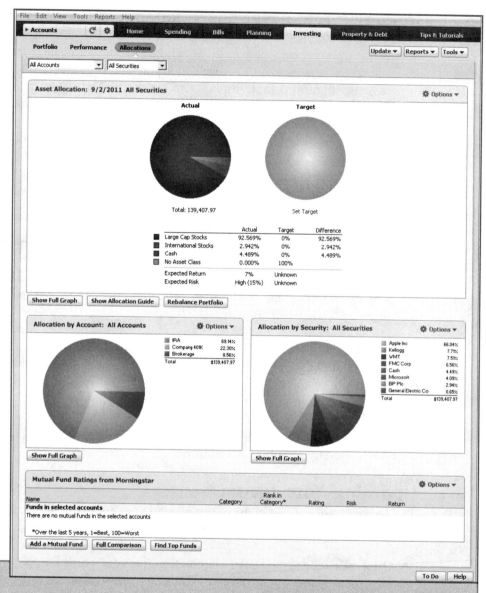

Figure 11-4 • The Allocations views of the Investing tab display pie charts of your investments.

Reviewing Your Asset Allocation

Asset allocation, which is covered in detail later in this chapter, refers to the way in which your investment dollars are distributed among different types of investments. It's a measure of how well your portfolio is diversified.

The Asset Allocation graph displays two pie charts: Actual Allocation and Target Allocation. Actual Allocation indicates your portfolio's current diversification. Figure 11-4 shows that the majority of the securities in this account are invested in large-cap stocks. Target Allocation is the allocation you set up with Quicken's Portfolio Rebalancer, which is discussed later in this chapter, in the section titled "Using the Portfolio Rebalancer." If you have not yet used the Portfolio Rebalancer, the Target Allocation pie won't have any slices.

Mutual Fund Ratings from Morningstar

If you use Quicken Premier or a higher version, Quicken displays up-to-date ratings from Morningstar, an investment research organization that rates mutual funds based on a variety of criteria. Ratings for mutual funds you track in Quicken are automatically downloaded with asset class and related information. The more stars, the higher the rating.

Allocation By Account

The Allocation By Account chart indicates how your portfolio's market value is distributed among the investing accounts you have entered into Quicken.

Allocation By Security

The Allocation By Security chart indicates how your portfolio's market value is distributed among the different securities.

Updating Your Investments

The Update button at the right of the Allocations view works with your Internet connection to keep your portfolio up to date:

- **Quotes** downloads the current quotations for your portfolio.
- **Historical Prices** opens the Get Historical Prices dialog discussed earlier in this chapter.
- **Update Portfolio On Quicken.com** opens the Preferences dialog for Quicken.com. Learn more about Quicken.com in Chapter 10, and learn more about Preferences in Appendix B.
- **One Step Update** opens the One Step Update Settings dialog from which you can tell Quicken which accounts you want to update.

Working with Reports

The Reports button's menu, shown here, offers a wide variety of reports, which can be customized to meet your needs. See Chapter 8 for customization options other than those included in each report.

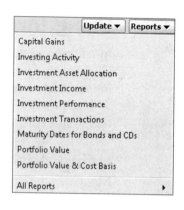

- **Capital Gains** reports can be for any date range you choose and can be subtotaled by Short- vs. Long-Term, Month, Quarter, Year, Account, Security, Security Type, Investing Goal, and Asset Class.
- **Investing Activity** reports display the activity, income (or loss), and capital gains for your accounts, based on the date range you set. This report is only available in Quicken Premier and higher versions.
- **Investment Asset Allocation** reports can be displayed both as graphs and reports. Use the Date Range drop-down list to tell Quicken the date range you want to display.
- **Investment Income** reports display the income and expenses related to your investments. These can be customized by date range and subtotals.
- **Investment Performance** reports show the return and average annual return on your accounts based on the date range and subtotal intervals you choose.
- **Investment Transactions** reports show complete data about your transactions for time periods you designate. You can subtotal in several different ways as well as customize the date range of the report to meet your needs.
- **Maturity Dates For Bonds And CDs** creates a detailed report of when your instruments will mature.
- **Portfolio Value** displays the total value of your holdings in both a graph and a report. This report can be customized by date range and subtotal intervals to show your information in the way you want to see it.
- **Portfolio Value & Cost Basis** reports show the cost and value of each of your securities as of the date and subtotal interval you specify.
- **All Reports** opens the same menu you see when clicking Reports on the menu bar.

Utilizing Investing Tab Tools

The Tools button's menu gives you access to the valuable estimators and guides provided by Quicken. See "Using the Asset Allocation Guide," "Previewing Your Buy/Sell Decisions," and "Estimating Capital Gains" later in this chapter.

Using Investment Analysis Tools

In addition to the Quicken.com-based investment research tools discussed in Chapter 10, Quicken offers a number of built-in tools that can help you learn more about investing and analyze your investment portfolio.

This part of the chapter introduces these analysis tools so you can explore them more fully on your own.

Using Asset Allocation

Many investment gurus say that an investor's goals should determine his or her asset allocation. If you're not sure what your asset allocation should be, Quicken can help. It includes a wealth of information about asset allocation, including sample portfolios with their corresponding allocations. You can use this feature to learn what your target asset allocation should be to meet your investing goals. Then you can monitor your asset allocation and, if necessary, rebalance your portfolio to keep it in line with what it should be.

Using the Asset Allocation Guide

The Asset Allocation Guide explains what asset allocation is, why it's important, and how Quicken can help monitor it in your portfolio. Choose Investing | Tools | Asset Allocation Guide. The Asset Allocation Guide window appears (see Figure 11-5).

To take full advantage of this feature, read the information on the main part of the window. You can click links within the text or in the left column to learn more about specific topics. If you're new to asset allocation, you may find the See Model Portfolios link especially useful. It shows suggested asset allocations based on risk and returns for a number of portfolios. Click Close to return to the Investing tab.

Monitoring Your Asset Allocation

To monitor the asset allocation of your portfolio, you must enter asset class information for each of your investments. You can do this in two ways:

- **Manually enter asset class information** Although this isn't difficult for stocks, it can be time-consuming for investments that have an asset class mixture, such as mutual funds.
- **Download asset class information** If you have a connection to the Internet, this is the best way to enter this information. With a few clicks, Quicken does all of the work in seconds. The information is complete and accurate. Learn how to download asset class information in Chapter 10.

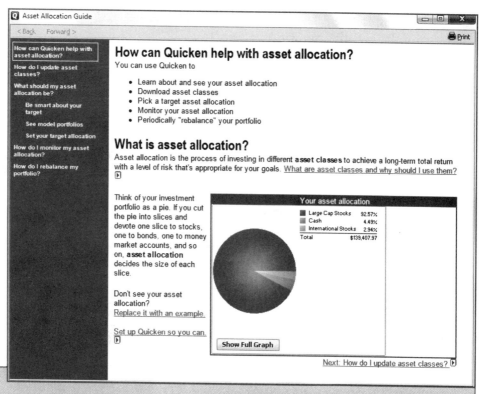

Figure 11-5 • The Asset Allocation Guide explains what asset allocation is and how it can help you meet your investment goals.

Viewing Your Asset Allocation

If you have chosen to display all of your accounts and all of your securities in the Asset Allocation graph in the Allocations view's Asset Allocation snapshot, the pie chart that appears in the Asset Allocation Guide window (see Figure 11-5) is the same chart as seen in Figure 11-4. To get more information about a piece of the pie, hover your mouse on a "pie slice" in either location. A yellow box appears, displaying the asset class, total market value, and percentage of portfolio value.

Setting Your Target Asset Allocation

If you know what you want your asset allocation to be, you can set up a target asset allocation. Quicken then displays your target in the pie chart beside the current asset allocation chart on the Investing tab's Allocations button's Asset Allocation window so you can monitor how close you are to your target.

Display the Allocations button's view of the Investing tab window (refer to Figure 11-4). Then choose Change Target Allocations from the Options menu in the button bar of the Asset Allocation snapshot. The Target Allocation dialog appears. Here's what it looks like with a sample allocation already entered.

Enter the desired percentages for each asset class. When the total of all percentages equals 100, click OK to save your settings. The Target chart in the Asset Allocation snapshot of the Investing tab window reflects your settings, as shown next.

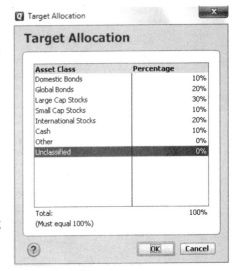

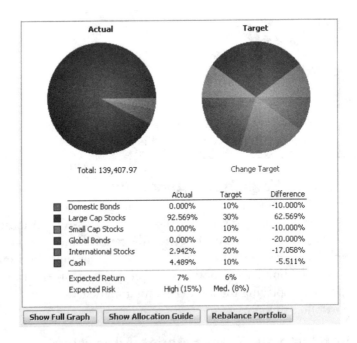

Using the Portfolio Rebalancer

If your current asset allocation deviates from your target asset allocation, you may want to rebalance your portfolio. This means buying and selling investments to bring you closer to your target asset allocation.

Keep in mind that brokerage fees and capital gains impacts often are related to buying and selling securities. For this reason, you should carefully evaluate your investment situation to determine how you can minimize costs and capital gains while rebalancing your portfolio. If small adjustments are necessary to bring you to your target asset allocation, you may not find it worth the cost to make the changes. Use this information as a guideline only! As always, consult your tax professional for additional information about your specific situation.

Quicken can tell you exactly how you must change your current asset allocation to meet your target asset allocation. In the Asset Allocation snapshot of the Investing tab's Allocations button, click Options | Rebalance Portfolio. The Portfolio Rebalancer window, shown in Figure 11-6, appears. It provides instructions and shows you how much you must adjust each asset class to meet your targeted goals.

Here's an example. Figure 11-6 indicates that $13,941 more needs to be invested in domestic bonds and $27,881 more invested in global bonds to meet the target asset allocation. If $41,822 of the large-cap investments were sold and reinvested in domestic and global bonds, the asset allocation would be closer to target, without changing the total value of the portfolio. Click Close to return to the Investing tab.

Analyzing Your Portfolio

Quicken's Portfolio Analyzer enables you to look at your portfolio in a number of ways. To display it, first turn on Classic menus by clicking View | Classic Menus. From the Classic menu, click Investing | Investing Tools | Portfolio Analyzer. You'll find these options on the left sidebar:

- **Performance** shows your portfolio's average annual rate of return. It also shows your five best and worst performers, so you can see how individual securities are doing.
- **Holdings** lists your investment accounts and then shows a pie chart of your top ten holdings. Because most experts recommend that no single security take up more than 10 percent of your portfolio, you may find the percentage distribution helpful when considering diversification.
- **Asset Allocation** displays your current actual and target asset allocation so you can see how close you are to your target. How to set up a target allocation was explained earlier in this chapter.
- **Risk Profile** shows how "risky" your portfolio is when compared to the risk associated with specific classes of investments.
- **Tax Implications** summarizes your realized and unrealized year-to-date (YTD) capital gains or losses. Capital gains and losses are broken down into two categories: short term and long term. For additional information about tax implications, consult your tax professional.

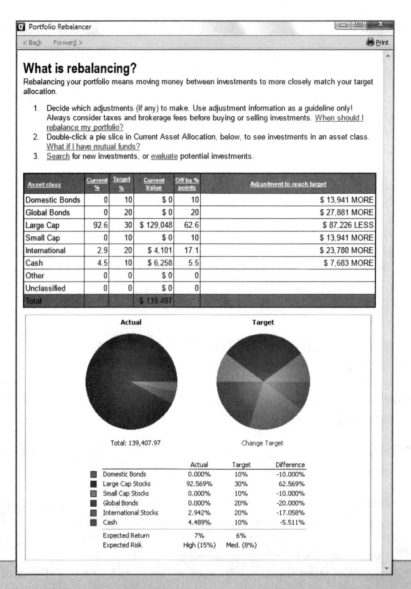

Figure 11-6 • The Portfolio Rebalancer window tells you what adjustments you need to make to bring your asset allocation closer to target.

What's great about the Portfolio Analyzer is that it provides tables and charts to show information about your portfolio, and then it explains everything in plain English so you know what the tables and charts mean. Using this feature regularly can really help you learn about the world of investing and how your portfolio measures up. To give it a try, choose Investing | Investing Tools | Portfolio Analyzer from the Classic menu. When you have finished reviewing the information, click Close to return to the Investing tab.

You may want to return to the Standard menus. If so, click View | Standard Menus.

Previewing Your Buy/Sell Decisions

Quicken Premier includes a feature called Buy/Sell Preview, which offers a quick and easy way to see the impact of a securities purchase or sale on your finances—including your taxes.

From the Investing tab, choose Tools | Buy/Sell Preview. In the top half of the Buy/Sell Preview window that appears, enter information about the proposed purchase or sale. Quicken automatically enters the most recent price information for a security you own or watch, but you can override that amount if necessary. When you're finished setting options, click Calculate. Quicken displays its results in the bottom half of the window.

The Buy/Sell Preview feature works with Quicken's Tax Planner, which is discussed in Chapter 17, to calculate the net effect of a sale on your expected tax bill or refund. Check with your tax professional for additional information. Click Done to close the Buy/Sell Preview window and return to the Investing tab.

Estimating Capital Gains

Quicken's Capital Gains Estimator enables you to estimate capital gains or losses and their related tax implications before you sell a security. The information it provides can help you make an informed decision about which security to sell.

Getting Started

Choose the Investing tab and click Tools | Capital Gains Estimator. The Capital Gains Estimator's welcome window appears. If you have used the tool before, you may see an info message about previous proposed sales holdings changes.

Start by reading the information in the main part of the window. It explains what the Capital Gains Estimator does and offers links for learning more about specific terms and topics. Then click each of the links in the left side of the window, in turn, to step through the process of setting up the Capital Gains Estimator for your situation. You'll be prompted to name and choose a scenario, select taxable investment accounts to include, set your tax rate, and enter capital loss carryover information. When you enter complete and accurate information, Quicken can provide a more accurate indication of tax impacts.

Deciding What to Sell

Quicken Premier users can tap into a feature in the Capital Gains Estimator that enables Quicken to help you decide which securities to sell. Follow instructions in the What Should I Sell? screen to tell Quicken your goals for the sale, and click the Search button at the bottom of the window.

A dialog appears while Quicken makes complex calculations to meet your goals. When it's finished, you can click the View Results button in the dialog to display a scenario with Quicken's recommendation and the results (see Figure 11-7).

Manually Adding Proposed Sales

If you prefer, you can manually indicate proposed sales in the Scenario window (refer to Figure 11-7). The Step 1 area shows all the securities you hold in the accounts you selected during the setup process. You can add a proposed sale in two ways:

- Click the name of the security you want to sell. Then enter the number of shares and sales price in Step 2. If you have multiple purchase lots for the security, this automatically sells the oldest lots first.
- If necessary, click the plus sign (+) to the left of the security that you want to sell to display the purchase lots. Then click the lot you want to sell. This enables you to specify exactly which lots are to be sold in the Proposed Sales area.

No matter which method you use, the sale is added to the Step 2 area of the window, which lists all of the proposed sales (see Figure 11-7).

To adjust the number of shares to be sold, click in the Shares To Sell field for the proposed sale (in the Step 2 area), and enter a new value. The value you enter must be less than or equal to the number of shares purchased in that lot.

You can set up proposed sales for up to three scenarios—just click the Scenario link on the left side of the window to see and set that scenario's options. You can mix and match any sales you like to reach your goal.

Reading the Results

When all the information has been entered, you can see the true power of the Capital Gains Estimator. It tells you about the proceeds from the sales, as well as the gain or loss. If you scroll down in the What If Scenarios screen (refer to Figure 11-7), you'll find more information about the proposed sale and its tax implications in the Step 3 area, including the gross profit and net proceeds from proposed sales. You can click links to view the results of additional calculations, such as the tax situation before and after executing the proposed sales and gain or loss on the proposed sales. Do the same for each scenario to see how they

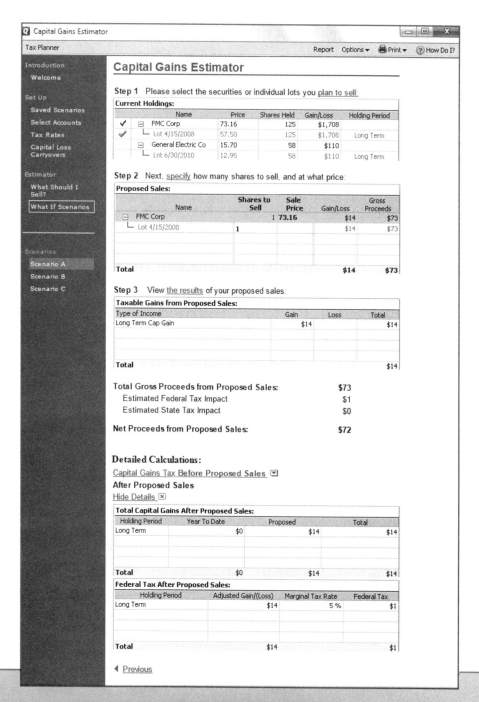

Figure 11-7 • Quicken displays its recommendations in the Capital Gains Estimator as a scenario.

compare—then make your selling decision. Click Close to return to the Investing tab.

Setting Investment Alerts

Investment alerts are downloaded automatically with quotes and news headlines, as discussed in Chapter 10. When you select a specific alert, or a group of alerts, they appear in the Show All tab of the Alerts Center. Ten investment alerts are available for your use:

- **Price And Volume** consists of three alerts. Price alerts notify you when a security's price rises above or falls below values you specify. Volume alerts notify you when the sales volume of a security exceeds a value you specify. News alerts give you the latest information about your securities, such as earnings announcements or analyst actions. The options for these are set on Quicken.com. Just click the link in the Preferences dialog, and your Internet connection opens to http://investing.quicken.com/alerts.

 You may be prompted for your Quicken user name and password to connect to Quicken.com.

- **Reminders** gives you the option to download two items from Quicken.com:
  - Quotes
  - Maturity Date, which reminds you when a CD or bond reaches its maturity date
- **Ratings And Analysis** lets you set two notifications:
  - When ratings and analysis information becomes available for stocks you track
  - When ratings and analysis information becomes available for mutual funds you track
- **Capital Gains/Losses** lets you set alerts for the following:
  - **Tax Implications On Sale** notifies you of your tax implications when you sell a security.
  - **Cap. Gains For The Year** notifies you if you exceed your capital gains limit for the year.
- **Tax Efficient Investments** provides you with information about investments that are more tax-efficient than those you already have.
- **Mutual Fund Distributions** provides you with information about mutual fund distributions.
- **Securities Holding Period** provides you with information about holding periods for securities you own.

Many Quicken users report the most useful alerts are Price And Volume, Maturity Date Reminder, Stocks Ratings And Analysis, and Cap. Gains For The Year. These alerts give timely information without information overload.

Setting Up Alerts   To set up investment alerts, click Tools | Alerts Center | Setup. Quicken displays the Setup tab of the Alerts Center window, as seen in Figure 11-8, which Chapter 8 discusses in greater detail. On the left side of the window, click the name of an alert you want to set, and then set options for the alert in the right side of the window. (You must set some alerts, such as the Price And Volume alert, on Quicken.com.) You can disable an alert by removing the check mark beside its name. When you are finished making changes, click OK to save them.

Deleting Alerts   To remove an alert, select Tools | Alerts Center, and click the Show All tab. Then check the alerts you wish to delete and click Delete. A warning message appears telling you the alert will be deleted. Click OK to confirm your deletion. If you want the alert to continue, click Cancel. Either choice returns you to the Show All tab of the Alerts Center.

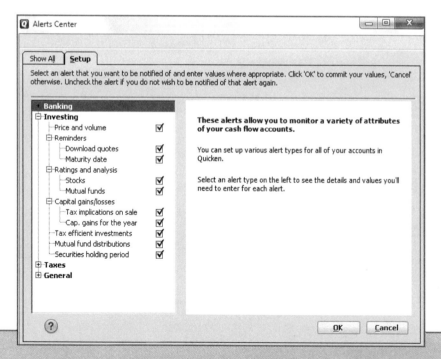

Figure 11-8 • Use Quicken's Alerts Center to set reminders for your various investing activities.

Tracking Your
Financial Position

This part of the book explains how you can use Quicken Personal Finance Software's Property & Debt features to keep track of your property and loans. It starts by covering assets, such as a car and home, and the loans that you may have used to finance them. Then it moves on to tell you how you can use the Property & Debt tab and other Quicken features to monitor expenses related to your assets and debt. This part of the book has two chapters:

Chapter 12:   Monitoring Assets and Loans

Chapter 13:   Keeping Tabs on Your Net Worth

Part Four

Monitoring Assets and Loans

Chapter 1

In This Chapter:

- *Understanding assets and debts*
- *Reviewing loans*
- *Creating asset and debt accounts*
- *Creating a loan*
- *Viewing loan information*
- *Modifying loan information*
- *Adding and disposing of assets*
- *Updating asset values*

Assets and debts (or liabilities) make up your net worth. Bank and investment accounts, which are covered in Chapters 4 and 9, are examples of assets. Credit card accounts, which are covered in Chapter 4, are examples of debts. But you may want to use Quicken Personal Finance Software to track other assets and debts, including a home, car, and recreational vehicle, as well as the loans related to those assets. By including these items in your Quicken data file, you can quickly and accurately calculate your net worth and financial fitness.

This chapter explains how to set up asset and debt accounts to track your possessions and any outstanding loans you used to purchase them.

The Basics

Before you begin, it's a good idea to have a clear understanding of what assets, debts, and loans are, and how they work together in your Quicken data file.

Understanding Assets and Debts

An asset is something you own. Common examples might be your house, car, camper, computer, television set, and patio furniture. Most assets have value—you can sell them for cash or trade them for another asset.

Although you can use Quicken to track every single asset you own in its own asset account, doing so would be cumbersome. Instead, you'll normally monitor high-value assets in individual accounts and lower-value assets in a group asset account. For example, you may create separate asset accounts for your home and your car, but group personal possessions, such as your computer, television, and stamp collection, in a single group asset account. This makes it easy to track all your assets, so you have accurate records for insurance and other purposes.

A debt is something you owe—often to buy one of your assets! For example, if you buy a house, chances are you'll use a mortgage to finance it. The mortgage, which is a loan that is secured by your home, is a debt. You can use Quicken to track all of your debts so you know exactly how much you owe at any given time.

Reviewing Loans

A loan is a promise to pay money. Loans are commonly used to buy assets, although some folks often turn to debt consolidation loans to pay off other debts—this is discussed further in Chapter 16.

Here's how it works. The lender gives the borrower money in exchange for the borrower's promise to pay it back. (The promise is usually in writing, with lots of signatures and initials.) The borrower normally pays back the loan to the lender with periodic payments that include interest on the loan balance, or principal. The amount of the loan is reduced after each payment. The borrower incurs interest expense, while the lender earns interest income.

While most people think of a loan as something you owe (a debt), a loan can also be something you own (an asset). For example, say you borrow money from your brother to buy a car. In your Quicken data file, the loan is related to a debt—money that you owe your brother. In your brother's Quicken data file, the loan is related to an asset—money that is due to him from you.

There are several types of loans, some of which are designed for specific purposes. Here's a quick summary of some of what's available, along with their pros and cons.

This list is not exhaustive. Financial institutions are always coming up with new loan products, and it's impossible to keep up with them here. If you're interested in a loan product that isn't mentioned in this chapter, consult the financial institution that is offering it to learn more about how it works and what it can do for you.

Mortgage

A *mortgage* is a long-term loan secured by real estate. In today's volatile climate, many mortgages require a down payment on the property of 10 to 20 percent or higher. Monthly payments are based on the term of the loan and the interest rate applied to the principal. The interest you pay on a mortgage for a first or second home is tax-deductible. If you fail to make mortgage payments, your house could be sold to pay back the mortgage.

A *balloon mortgage* is a special type of short-term mortgage. Rather than make monthly payments over the full typical mortgage term, at the end of the fifth, seventh, or tenth year, you pay the balance of the mortgage in one big "balloon" payment. Some balloon mortgages offer the option of refinancing when the balloon payment is due.

Home Equity Loans or Lines of Credit

A *home equity loan* or *second mortgage* is a line of credit secured by the equity in your home—the difference between the home's market value and the amount of outstanding debt. Your equity rises when you make mortgage payments or property values increase. It declines when you borrow against your equity or property values decrease. A home equity loan lets you borrow against this equity.

A home equity loan has two benefits: interest rates are sometimes lower than other credit, and the interest may be tax-deductible. For these reasons, many people use home equity loans to pay off credit card debt; renovate their homes; or buy cars, boats, or other recreational vehicles. But, as with a mortgage, if you fail to make your home equity payments, your house could be sold to satisfy the debt.

Reverse Equity Loans

A *reverse equity loan* (sometimes called a *reverse mortgage*) provides people who own their homes in full with a regular monthly income. Instead of you paying the lender, the lender pays you. This type of loan is attractive to retirees who live on a fixed income. The loan is paid back when the home is sold—often after the death of the homeowner.

Auto Loans

An *auto loan* is a loan secured by a vehicle, such as a car, truck, or motor home. Normally, you make a down payment and use the loan to pay the balance of the vehicle's purchase price. Monthly payments are based on the term of the loan and the interest rate applied to the principal. Interest on car loans is not tax-deductible.

Personal Loans

A *personal loan* is an unsecured loan—a loan that requires no collateral. Monthly payments are based on the term of the loan and the interest rate applied to the principal. You can use a personal loan for just about anything. Some people use them to pay off multiple smaller debts so they have only one monthly payment. Interest on personal loans is not tax-deductible.

Loan Considerations

When applying for a loan, a number of variables have a direct impact on what the loan costs you, now and in the future. Ask about all of these things before applying for any loan.

Interest Rate

The *interest rate* is the annual percentage applied to the loan principal. Several factors affect the interest rate you may be offered:

- **Your credit record** affects the interest rate offered, because a borrower with a good credit record can usually get a better rate than one with a bad credit record. Of course, if your credit record is really bad, you might not be able to borrow money at any rate.
- **The type of loan** affects the interest rate offered, because, generally speaking, personal loans have the highest interest rates, whereas mortgages have the lowest. From highest to lowest between these two types are a used car loan, a new car loan, and a home equity reserve or line of credit.
- **The loan term** affects the interest rate offered, because the length of a loan can vary the interest within a specific loan type. For example, for car loans, the longer the term, the lower the rate.
- **The amount of the down payment** affects the interest rate offered, because the more money you put down on the purchase, the lower the rate may be.
- **Your location** affects the interest rate offered, because rates vary from one area of the country to another.
- **The lender** affects the interest rate offered, because rates also vary from one lender to another. Certain types of lenders have lower rates than others.

Two kinds of interest rates can apply to a loan:

- **Fixed rate** applies the same rate to the principal throughout the loan term.
- **Variable rate** applies a different rate to the loan throughout the loan term. For example, the loan may start with one rate and, each year, switch to a different rate. The rate is usually established by adding a certain number of

percentage points to a national index, such as Treasury bill rates. A cap limits the amount the rate can change. Mortgages with this type of rate are referred to as *adjustable rate mortgages*, or *ARMs*.

Although ARMs usually offer a lower initial interest rate than fixed-rate mortgages, you should consider the overall economic conditions before deciding on one. For example, for a couple who purchased their first home in the mid-1980s when interest rates were high, they might have selected an ARM. When interest rates dropped, so did the rate on the mortgage. If they had selected a fixed-rate mortgage when they bought that home, they would have had to refinance to get the same savings. Rates were much lower in the late 1990s, so a fixed rate protected buyers from possible rate increases in the future.

Term

A loan's *term* is the period of time between the loan date and when the date payment is due in full. Loan terms vary depending on the type of loan:

- Mortgage loan and home equity reserve loan terms are typically 10, 15, 20, or 30 years.
- Balloon mortgage loan terms are typically 5, 7, or 10 years.
- Vehicle loan terms vary from 3 to 7 years.

Down Payment

A *down payment* is an up-front payment toward the purchase of a home or car. Most mortgages require at least 10 percent down; 20 percent is preferred.

Keep in mind that if you make only a 10 percent down payment on a home, you may be required to pay for the cost of private mortgage insurance (PMI). This protects the lender from loss if you fail to pay your mortgage, but it increases your monthly mortgage payments.

Application Fees

Most lenders require you to pay an application fee to process your loan application. This usually includes the cost of obtaining a property appraisal and credit report. These fees are usually not refundable—even if you are turned down.

Mortgage Closing Costs

In addition to the application fee and down payment, many other costs are involved in securing a mortgage and purchasing a home. These are known as closing costs. The Real Estate Settlement Procedures Act of 1974 requires that your lender provide a good-faith estimate of closing costs. This document summarizes all of the costs of closing on a home based on the mortgage the lender is offering.

Here's a brief list of the types of costs you may encounter. Because they vary from lender to lender, they could be a deciding factor when shopping for a mortgage. Note that most of these fees are not negotiable.

- **Origination fee** covers the administrative costs of processing a loan.
- **Discount or "points"** is a fee based on a percentage rate applied to the loan amount. For example, 1 point on a $250,000 mortgage is $2,500.
- **Appraisal fee** covers the cost of a market-value appraisal of the property by a licensed, certified appraiser.
- **Credit report fee** covers the cost of obtaining a credit history of the prospective borrower(s) to determine creditworthiness.
- **Underwriting fee** covers the cost of underwriting the loan. This is the process of determining loan risks and establishing terms and conditions.
- **Document preparation fee** covers the cost of preparing legal and other documents required to process the loan.
- **Title insurance fee** covers the cost of title insurance, which protects the lender and buyer against loss due to disputes over ownership and possession of the property.
- **Recording fee** covers the cost of entering the sale of a property into public records.
- **Prepaid items** are taxes, insurance, and assessments paid in advance of their due dates. These expenses are not paid to the lender, but are due at the closing date.

Tips for Minimizing Loan Expenses

Borrowing money costs money. It's as simple as that. But you can do some things to minimize the cost of a loan.

Shop for the Lowest Rate   This may seem like a no-brainer, but a surprising number of people simply go to a local bank and accept whatever terms they are offered. You don't have to use a local bank to borrow money for a home, car, or other major purchase. Check the financial pages of your local newspaper or go online to research what terms are available. And if you're shopping for a car, keep an eye out for low-interest financing deals. Sometimes, you can save a lot of money in interest by buying when the time is right. For example, suppose you have a choice of two five-year car loans for $20,000—one at 7 percent and the other at 7.75 percent. Over the course of five years, you'll pay $1,003 less if you go with the lower rate. That can buy a lot of gas—even at today's fuel prices.

Minimize the Loan Term   The shorter the loan term, the less interest you'll pay over the life of the loan. The savings can be quite substantial. For example, suppose you have a choice between two loan terms for a $200,000, 4.75 percent mortgage: 15 years or 30 years. If you choose the 15-year mortgage, you'll pay $80,018.80 in interest, but if you choose the 30-year mortgage, you'll pay a whopping $175,584 in interest—nearly $96,000 more! Neither option is appealing, but the shorter-term mortgage is certainly easier to swallow. The drawback? The monthly payment for the 15-year mortgage is $1,555.66 before taxes and insurance, while the payment for the 30-year mortgage is just $1,043.29, again before insurance and property taxes are added. Obviously, your monthly spending budget will weigh heavily into the decision.

Maximize the Down Payment   The less you borrow, the less you'll pay in interest—and the less your monthly payments will be. Take the loan term example just shown. Suppose your budget won't allow you to go with the shorter-term loan—you just can't make those monthly payments. But if you cashed in an individual retirement account (IRA) worth $30,000 and put that toward the down payment (talk to your tax advisor; you may be able to do this without penalty for the purchase of a first home), you could knock $233 per month off the 15-year loan's monthly payment, which might be enough to fit it into your budget—and save another $12,000 in interest!

Make Extra Loan Payments   If you can't go for a shorter-term loan, consider making extra payments toward the loan's principal. Paying just $50 or $100 per month extra can save thousands in interest over the life of the loan.

Clean Up Your Credit Before Applying for a Loan   Loan terms vary based on credit history. To get the best deal, your credit should be as clean as possible. If you think there might be problems in your credit report, get a copy—you can learn how by choosing the Tips & Tutorials tab and clicking Credit Score at the bottom of the page. Then do what you need to get things cleaned up, but be wary of services that promise to do this for you. Some may not help you.

When evaluating the dollar impact of different loan deals, use Quicken's Loan Calculator. It'll make complex loan payment calculations for you. Chapter 15 explains how to use Quicken's financial calculators, including the Loan Calculator and Refinance Calculator.

Create Property and Debt Accounts

To track an asset or debt with Quicken, you must set up an appropriate account. All transactions related to the asset or debt will be recorded in the account's register.

In this section, you'll read about the types of accounts you can use to track your assets and debts, and how to set up each type of account. Quicken offers the following Property & Debt account types for tracking assets and debts:

- **House** A house account is used for recording the value of a house, condominium, or other real estate. When you create a house account, Quicken asks whether there is a mortgage on the property. If so, you can have Quicken create a related debt account for you or associate the house account with an existing debt account. This makes it possible to set up both your house asset account and mortgage debt account at the same time.
- **Vehicle** A vehicle account is similar to a house account, but it's designed for vehicles, including cars, trucks, and recreational vehicles. Quicken asks if there is a loan on the vehicle; if so, it can create a related debt account or link to an existing debt account.
- **Other Asset** An asset account is for recording the value of other assets, such as personal property. For example, a Quicken data file might include asset accounts for horses and related equipment, art and antiques, or personal possessions.
- **Loan** A loan account is for recording money you owe to others. As mentioned earlier, when you create a house or vehicle account, Quicken can automatically create a corresponding loan account for you.
- **Other Liability (not a credit card)** You can create a debt account to record other debts that are not related to the purchase of a specific asset. Debt accounts are shown in the Account List as liabilities.

Creating Asset and Debt Accounts

You create asset and debt accounts with the same Add Account dialog you used to set up your banking accounts. Quicken offers a number of ways to open this dialog for an asset or debt account. The most straightforward way to open it for any type of account is to click Add An Account in the Account Bar, and then click the account type you want to add: either an asset, such as a house or vehicle, or a loan or other debt.

A loan is actually a debt account that has special Quicken features attached to it. Use this option to set up a debt associated with a compounding interest loan, like a mortgage or standard car loan, which is explained later in this chapter.

Chapter 3 explains how to use the Quicken Account Setup dialog to create new Quicken banking accounts. This section provides information about the kinds of data you'll have to enter to create asset and debt accounts.

Account Type

The Add Account dialog displays a list of asset types: House, Vehicle, or Other Asset.

Account Name

Give the account a name that clearly identifies the asset or debt. For example, if you have two cars and plan to track them in separate asset accounts, consider naming the account with the make and model of the car. Ford Focus and Dodge pickup do a better job identifying the cars than Car 1 and Car 2. When creating a debt account, you may want to include the word "mortgage," "loan," or "payable" in the account name so you don't confuse it with a related asset.

Starting Point Information

For a vehicle account, Quicken asks for the make, model, and year of the car, as seen in Figure 12-1. After you have created the account, Quicken stores this

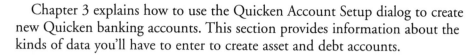

Figure 12-1 • Enter asset information for Quicken to store in the Account Details dialog.

information in the Account Details dialog for the asset. You can view and edit this information after the account has been created by right-clicking the account name in the Account Bar and choosing Edit/Delete Account.

Quicken is inconsistent about the first dialog you see when entering new accounts from different locations within Quicken. For example, Figure 12-1 shows the dialog you see when you click Add An Account from the Account Bar and choose Vehicle as the asset type.

If you want to add a new account from the Property & Debt tab, click the Property button. Click Property Options | Add A Vehicle Asset Account. The screen you see is the Add Account screen with the account name of "Car" ready for you to enter a new name. When you click Next from that screen, the Add Account dialog appears as described in "Starting Point Information," shown earlier.

To see the Account Details dialog for any account, you can also use CTRL-A to open the Account List.

For house and vehicle accounts, Quicken prompts you to enter information about the asset's purchase, including the acquisition date and purchase price. You can find this information on your original purchase receipts. Quicken also asks for an estimate of the current value. For a house, this number will (hopefully) be higher than the purchase price; for a car, this number will probably be lower. This is the amount that will appear as the asset account balance. For other assets and debts, Quicken prompts you for a statement date and balance. If you don't know how much to enter now, you can leave it set to zero and enter a value when you know what to enter. You will see how to adjust asset values later in this chapter.

With Quicken's Attachment feature, you can scan an asset's receipt and store this digital image with your Quicken data file.

Optional Tax Information

For other asset and debt accounts, you can click the Tax Schedule button on the Account Details dialog to enter tax schedule information for transfers in and out of the account. This is completely optional. Check with your tax professional to see if this information would benefit your tax position. Chapter 17 explains how to set up Quicken accounts and categories to simplify tax preparation.

Related Mortgage or Loan

When creating a house or vehicle account, Quicken asks whether there is a related mortgage or loan. You have four options, as shown next. Note that this

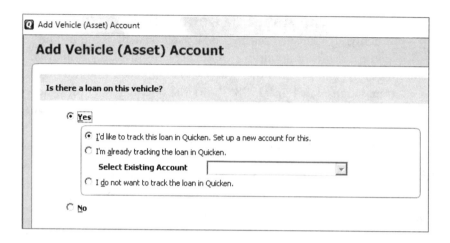

screen may appear differently if you started to add the account from another location, such as the Add An Account button in the Account Bar.

- **Yes. I'd Like To Track This Mortgage/Loan In Quicken. Set Up A New Account For This** This option tells Quicken that there is a related loan and that Quicken should create a debt account.
- **Yes. I'm Already Tracking The Mortgage/Loan In Quicken** This option enables you to select an existing debt account to link to the asset.
- **Yes. I Do Not Want To Track the Mortgage/Loan In Quicken** This option tells Quicken that there is a loan but you don't want to include it in your Quicken data file.
- **No** This option tells Quicken that there is no loan, so no debt account is necessary. (Lucky you!)

As you've probably guessed or noticed, the use of the word "mortgage" or "loan" in this dialog depends on whether you're creating a house or vehicle asset account. To select any of the Yes options, you must select the first Yes option and then choose one of the options beneath it. Otherwise, choose the No option.

Loan Information

If you indicated that Quicken should track a loan for a house or vehicle, it automatically displays the Loan Setup dialog, which you can use to enter information about the loan. If you set up a debt account, Quicken asks if you want to set up an amortized loan to be associated with the debt. See how to set up a loan later in this chapter, in the section "Creating a Loan."

Viewing the Asset or Debt Account Register

When you're finished setting up an asset or debt account (and related loans and loan payments, if applicable), Quicken automatically displays the account's register. Figure 12-2 shows what a house account might look like. The first transaction, dated 4/2/1998, shows the opening balance, which was the amount paid for the house. The next transaction, dated 1/1/2003, shows an adjustment automatically made by Quicken to increase the account's balance based on an estimate of its worth on the day the account was created.

The register in Figure 12-2 is shown with a two-line display. To change your display from the default one-line display, press CTRL-2.

All transactions that affect an asset or debt account's balance appear in the account register. Learn more about using account registers for asset and debt accounts later in this chapter, in the section "Other Asset Transactions."

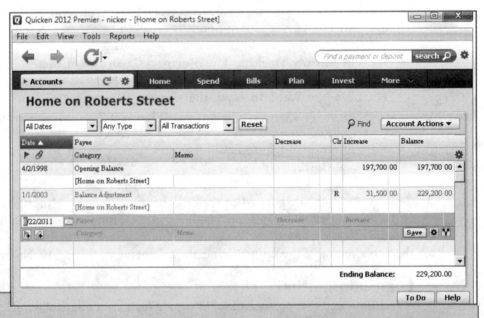

Figure 12-2 • Like other accounts in Quicken, assets and loans have their own account registers.

Loan Accounts in Quicken

Quicken makes it easy to track the principal, interest, and payments for a loan. Once you set up a loan and corresponding debt or asset accounts, you can make payments with Quicken using QuickFill and Scheduled Transactions (see Chapter 6) or Online Payments (see Chapter 5). The Loan feature keeps track of all the details, so you don't have to.

Before you see how to use the Loan feature, let's make something clear: a loan is not the same as an asset or debt account. A loan in Quicken is information that Quicken uses to calculate the amount of interest and principal due for each payment of an amortized loan, such as a mortgage or car loan. A loan must be associated with an asset account (if you are a lender) or a debt account (if you are a borrower), as well as an income or expense category to record interest income or expense. Loan transactions are recorded in the associated asset or debt account—not in Quicken's loan records. It's possible to delete a loan without losing any transaction data, as explained later in this section. But you can't delete an asset or debt account that has a loan associated with it unless the loan is deleted first.

Creating a Loan

You can set up a loan in the following ways:

- Create a house, vehicle, or debt account with a related mortgage or loan, as discussed earlier in this chapter. Quicken automatically prompts you for loan information.
- From the Account Bar, click Add An Account and choose Loan in the Property & Debt | Debt section.
- From the Property & Debt tab, click Debt | Loan And Debt Options | Add A New Loan.
- Also from the Property & Debt tab, click Property, click Property Options, and then click Add A New Loan.

Quicken displays the Loan Setup dialog seen here. It doesn't matter what the loan is for; the information you need to enter is basically the same. Here's what you can expect.

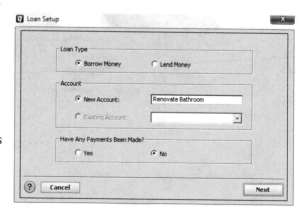

Loan Account Setup

The Loan Setup dialog starts by prompting you for a loan type. You have the following options:

- **Borrow Money** is for loans for which you're borrowing money from a lender, such as a car loan, mortgage, or personal loan. Quicken uses a debt account to record the loan.
- **Lend Money** is for loans for which you're the lender. Quicken uses an asset account to record the money owed from the borrower.

The Loan Setup dialog next prompts you to enter the account for the loan. Again, you have two options:

- **New Account** enables you to set up a brand-new account for the loan. Be sure to enter a name for the account.
- **Existing Account** enables you to select one of your existing debt accounts for the loan. If you're creating this loan as part of an asset creation process, the account will have already been created, named, and selected for you. Otherwise, this option is available only if you have already created a debt account that isn't linked to a loan.

The next section asks you if payments have been made. Either option takes you to the Loan Information section of the Loan Setup dialog. Here you are prompted for information about the loan creation, amount, and payments, as seen next. It's important to be accurate; get the dates and numbers directly from a loan statement or agreement if possible.

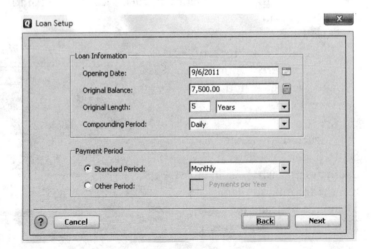

NOTE   While Quicken's default compounding period is Monthly, most financial institutions compound interest daily and post it to your account every month. Use the drop-down list to choose Daily if your lender compounds interest daily.

Click Next to continue. The dialog then asks you for balloon payment and regular payment information, as shown here. Quicken can calculate some of the values—such as the loan balance and monthly payments—for you. It does this automatically based on your answers to questions in the Loan Setup dialog. Keep in mind, however, that Quicken's calculated amounts may not match to the penny those calculated by your bank or finance company.

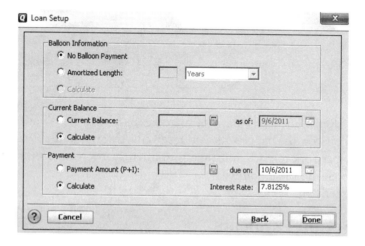

If you selected Calculate in the Current Balance and/or Payment section of this Loan Setup dialog, click Done to have Quicken estimate the amount of your loan payment, as shown next.

Click OK, and you are returned to the Loan Setup dialog showing the payment amount and first due date (based on the interest rate you entered), as shown next. Click Done. The Set Up Loan Payment dialog appears, as discussed in the next section.

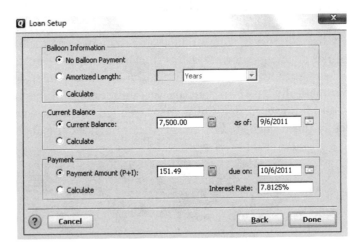

Remember, this may not match exactly with what your financial institution shows on the paperwork you received. Always use the financial institution's paperwork to enter information rather than relying on the Quicken calculations to ensure the amounts are exactly the same.

Set Up Payments

When you set up a loan, Quicken automatically prompts you to set up payment information by displaying the Set Up Loan Payment dialog, which is shown here.

If you see this dialog after using the Loan Setup dialog, the interest rate, principal and interest payment amount, payment type, next payment date, and interest category will be filled in for you. Otherwise, enter information in this dialog to set up the payment.

If the total payment should include additional amounts for property taxes, insurance, or other escrow items, click the Edit button. This displays the Split Transaction window, where you can enter categories, tags, memos, and amounts that must be added to the payment.

In the Transaction area of the dialog, you can specify the type and method for the transaction. For type, three options appear on the drop-down list:

- **Payment** is a transaction recorded in your account register only. You must manually write and mail a check for payment. This is covered in Chapter 4.
- **Print Check** is a transaction recorded in the Write Checks dialog and account register. You can use the Print Check command to print the check, and then you can mail it for payment. This is also covered in Chapter 4.
- **Online Payment** creates a payment instruction to be processed by your financial institution for use with online payment. This is covered in Chapter 5. This option appears only if at least one of your bank accounts is enabled for Quicken's Online Payment feature.

To indicate the method of payment, click the Payment Method button. The Select Payment Method dialog appears. This dialog offers the following three payment method options:

- **Scheduled Bill** is a transaction scheduled for the future. If you select this option, you must also choose options and enter values to specify how Quicken should enter the transaction, which account should be used to pay, and how many days in advance it should be entered and paid. This is covered in Chapter 6.
- **Memorized Payee** is a transaction memorized for use with QuickFill or Quicken's Calendar. This is also covered in Chapter 6.
- **Repeating Online Payment** is a recurring online payment instruction processed by your financial institution. If you select this option, you must also select a repeating online payment transaction from a drop-down list. If you have not already created a transaction to link to this loan payment,

select one of the other options and return to this dialog after you have created the required transaction. The procedure for recurring online payments is explained in Chapter 5.

- **Register Entry** is available only if you have selected Scheduled Bill in the top section of the dialog. You have two choices:
  - **Prompt Before Entering** tells Quicken to remind you before actually entering this scheduled transaction into the appropriate account register.
  - **Automatically Enter** tells Quicken to enter this transaction each time it becomes due without asking you.
- **Account To Pay From** lets you select the appropriate account from which this payment will be made.
- **Days In Advance** tells Quicken how many days before the due date to prompt you or to enter the transaction. The default is three days.

Click OK to return to the Set Up Loan Payment dialog. The information in the Transaction section of the Set Up Loan Payment dialog is as follows:

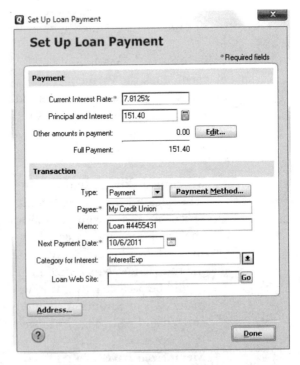

- **Payee** is a required field into which you must enter the name of the entity to whom you will be making the payments.
- **Memo** is an optional field where you can enter additional information. Many users choose to put their payee's assigned account number in this field. However, if you print checks from Quicken and use window envelopes to mail your bills, make sure the account number does not show through the window.
- **Next Payment Date** is filled in automatically if you've used the Loan Setup dialog. Otherwise, enter the date the next payment is due.

- **Category For Interest** is filled in automatically from the Loan Setup dialog if you've used it. Otherwise, enter the category you wish to use for the interest portion of each payment.
- **Loan Web Site** is an optional field in which you can enter the web site of the entity that holds your loan.
- **Address** can be used if your payment type is "Print Check" or "Online Payment." Clicking the Address button opens the Address Book so you can enter the mailing information for this payee. See Chapter 6 for more information about the Address Book.

When you have entered all of the information in the Set Up Loan Payment dialog, click Done. A message appears asking if this loan is to be associated with an asset, and if so, if you want to set up an account for that asset.

- Click Yes if you want to create an asset account for this loan. A Quicken Account Setup dialog appears with which you can set up an asset account for the full purchase price of the item you used the loan to buy. See the earlier section "Creating Asset and Debt Accounts" for directions on setting up the asset account.

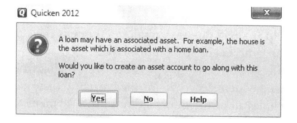

- Click No if there is no existing asset.

The Account Added window appears, at which point you can click Finish to close the dialogs.

Viewing Loan Information

All loans are associated with asset and/or debt accounts. However, you can use the View Loans dialog to edit information about your loans, as shown on the next page. You can open this window from any part of Quicken by pressing CTRL-SHIFT-H.

You can also open the View Loans dialog from the Account Bar by clicking the loan account to open the register for the loan. Then click Account Actions | Loan Details.

Button Options

Many of Quickens tools are icons on a toolbar at the top of a dialog or window. However, in the View Loans dialog, there are several buttons at the bottom offering options for working with loans:

- **Help** (a small question mark icon) opens the Quicken Help dialog with the Managing Loans section displayed.
- **Print** (a printer icon) opens the Print dialog from which you can print a loan payment schedule for the currently displayed loan. The printout includes all of the information in the Payment Schedule tab of the View Loans window, which is shown and discussed next.
- **New Loan** opens the Loan Setup dialog as explained earlier in this chapter.
- **Choose Loan** displays a menu of your current loans. Use it to choose the loan you want to display in the window.
- **Delete Loan** removes the currently displayed loan. If you click this button, a dialog appears asking if you want to save the associated account for your records. Click Yes to save the principal account information. For example, you might want this information for a net worth report. If you want to delete the entire loan account, click No. Of course, as with most dialogs within Quicken, you can always click the red X if you don't want to delete the loan at all.

Window Tabs

The tabs along the top of the window's information area enable you to view various pieces of information about a loan.

Loan Summary   By default, the View Loans dialog opens to the Loan Summary tab. As shown earlier, this tab's view summarizes the loan information.

Payment Schedule   Payment Schedule, shown next, displays a schedule of past and future payments. Click the Show Running Totals check box to display cumulative totals rather than individual payment information.

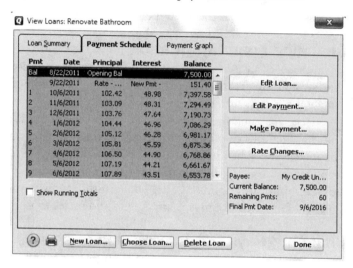

Payment Graph   Payment Graph, shown here, displays a graph of the loan payments. Where the two lines meet indicates the point at which you start paying more toward the loan principal than for interest. If you position your

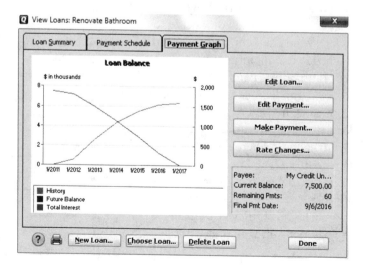

mouse cursor on a graph line, a magnifying glass tool appears displaying the dollar value at that point on the graph.

Modifying Loan Information

Once you've created a loan, you can modify it as necessary to record corrections, changes in the interest rate, or changes in payment methods. You can do all these things with buttons in the View Loans window.

Changing Loan Information

If you discover a discrepancy between the loan information in the View Loans window and information on statements or loan agreement papers, you can change the loan information in Quicken.

If necessary, click the Choose Loan button to choose the loan account's name from the menu to display the information for the loan you want to modify. Then, click the Edit Loan button. A pair of Edit Loan windows enables you to change just about any information for the loan. Modify values and select different options as desired. Click Done in the last window to save your changes. Quicken automatically makes any necessary entries to update the account.

Changing Payment Information

Occasionally, you may want to make changes to a loan's payment information. For example, suppose the real estate taxes on your property are reduced (you can always hope!) and the resulting escrow amount, which is included in the payment, changes. Or suppose you decide to switch your payment method from a scheduled transaction to a repeating online payment.

Select the loan account's name from the Choose Loan menu if the loan you want to modify is not already active. Then click the Edit Payment button. The Edit Loan Payment dialog, shown here, appears. Make changes as desired and click OK. Quicken updates the payment information with your changes.

Changing the Interest Rate

If you have an adjustable rate mortgage, you'll periodically have to adjust the rate for the loan within Quicken to match the rate charged by the lender.

If necessary, choose the loan account's name from the Choose Loan menu in the button bar to display the information for the loan whose rate you want to change. Then click the Rate Changes button.

The Loan Rate Changes window appears. It lists all the loan rates throughout the history of the loan.

To insert a rate change, click New in the window's button bar. The Insert An Interest Rate Change dialog appears, as shown here.

Enter the effective date and new rate in the appropriate text boxes. Quicken automatically calculates the new loan payment. When you click OK, the rate appears in the Loan Rate Changes window. Click the Close button to dismiss the window. Quicken recalculates the loan payment schedule for you.

Making a Loan Payment

Although it's usually more convenient to set up a loan payment as a scheduled transaction or repeating online payment instruction, as discussed earlier, you can also use the View Loans window to make a loan payment. This method is especially useful for making extra loan payments—payments in addition to your normal periodic payments.

If necessary, choose the loan account's name from the Choose Loan menu to display the information for the loan for which you want to make a payment. Then click the Make Payment button. A Loan Payment Type dialog appears, asking if you are making a regularly scheduled payment or an extra payment. Click the appropriate button.

Making a Regular Loan Payment If you click Regularly Scheduled Loan Payment, the Make Regular Payment dialog appears. Set options to specify the bank account from which the payment should be made, the type of transaction, the payee information, the date, and a memo for the transaction. If the Type Of Transaction drop-down list is set to Payment, you can enter a check number in the Number box or use one of the options on the Number drop-down list to set a number option. The Category and Amount fields are already set using values calculated by Quicken—you shouldn't have to change them. Click OK to enter the transaction.

Making an Extra Loan Payment   If you click Extra Loan Payment, the Make Extra Payment dialog appears, as seen next. This dialog is almost identical to the Make Regular Payment dialog, with two differences: the loan account is automatically set as the transfer account in the Category field, and the Amount field is left blank. Set options in the dialog to specify payment information, including the amount. Then click OK to enter the transaction.

Other Asset Transactions

Part of tracking assets is keeping track of their current values and modifying account balances when necessary. Like bank or investment accounts, which are discussed in Chapters 4 and 9, activity for an asset account appears in its account register.

The best way to open an asset's register is to click the name of the account in the Account Bar. The asset account's register appears.

In this section, you'll see how you can record changes in asset values due to acquisitions and disposals, improvements, market values, and depreciation.

Adding and Disposing of Assets

The most obvious change in an asset's value occurs when you add or remove all or part of the asset. For example, you may have a single asset account in which you record the value of all of your sports-related equipment. When you buy a new Jet Ski, it increases the value of the account. Similarly, if you sell one of your snowboards, it decreases the value of the account.

In many instances, when you add or dispose of an asset, money is exchanged. In that case, recording the transaction is easy: simply use the appropriate bank account register to record the purchase or sale, and use the asset account as a transfer account in the Category field.

If the asset was acquired without an exchange of cash, you can enter the transaction directly into the asset account using the Gift Received category (or a similar category of your choice) to categorize the income. Similarly, if the asset was disposed of without an exchange of cash, you can enter the transaction into the asset account register using the Gifts Given or Charity category (or other appropriate category) to categorize the write-off.

If you have completely disposed of the asset and no longer need the account, don't delete the account! Doing so will remove all income and expense category transactions and uncategorize all transfer transactions related to the account. Instead, consider hiding the account to get it off account lists, as explained in Chapter 3.

Updating Asset Values

A variety of situations can change the value of a single asset. The type of situation will determine how the value is adjusted. Here are three common examples.

Recording Improvements

Certain home-related expenditures can be considered improvements that increase the value of your home. It's important that you keep track of improvements, because they raise the property's tax basis, thus reducing the amount of capital gains you may have to record (and pay tax on) when you sell the house. Your tax advisor can help you determine which expenditures can be capitalized as home improvements.

Since most home improvements involve expenditures, use the appropriate spending account register to record the transaction. Be sure to enter the appropriate asset account (House, Condo, Land, and so on) as a transfer account in the Category field.

Adjusting for Market Value

Real estate, vehicles, and other large-ticket-item assets are also affected by market values. Generally speaking, real estate values go up, vehicle values go down, and other item values can vary either way depending on what they are.

IN MY EXPERIENCE
One of the most useful features of Quicken is the Account Attachments feature. This feature allows you to digitally attach copies of property tax statements, home improvement receipts, and other paper items that may add to the basis of your property. You can scan any of these documents and save the scanned copy in the same file with your Quicken data. See Chapter 4 for the explanation of the process.

To adjust for market value, click Account Actions | Update Balance at the top of the account register for the asset you want to adjust. The Update Account Balance dialog appears. Use this dialog to enter the date and market value for the asset. Then select a category or transfer account to record the gain or loss of value.

When you click OK, the entry is added to the account register as a reconciled transaction.

If you don't want the adjustment to affect any category or account other than the asset, choose the same asset account as a transfer account. When you click OK, a dialog will warn you that you are trying to record a transfer into the same account. Click OK again.

Recording Depreciation

Depreciation is a calculated reduction in the value of an asset. Depreciation expense can be calculated using a variety of acceptable methods, including straight line, sum of the year's digits, and declining balance. Normally, it reduces the asset's value regularly, with monthly, quarterly, or annual adjustments.

Depreciation is commonly applied to property used for business purposes, since depreciation expense on those assets may be tax-deductible. If you think depreciation on an asset you own may be tax-deductible, use Quicken to track the depreciation expense. Otherwise, depreciation probably isn't worth the extra effort it requires to track.

To record depreciation, create an entry in the asset account that reduces the value by the amount of the depreciation. Use a Depreciation Expense category to record the expense.

Keep in mind that you can set up monthly, quarterly, or annual depreciation transactions as scheduled transactions. This automates the process of recording them when they are due. See more about scheduled transactions in Chapter 6.

Keeping Tabs on Your Net Worth

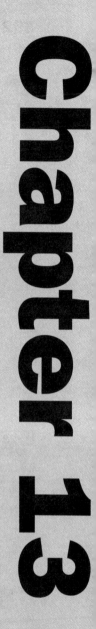

Chapter 13

In This Chapter:

- *Exploring the Net Worth button*
- *Using the Property button*
- *Creating alerts for Property and Debt accounts*
- *Opening the Debt button*
- *Accessing Property and Debt account registers*

When you create asset and debt accounts and enter related transactions into Quicken, as discussed in the previous chapters, Quicken summarizes your entries and calculates balances. It displays this information in a number of places: the Account Bar, the Property & Debt tab, account registers, and reports and graphs. You can consult Quicken's calculated balances and totals at any time to learn about your equity and the expenses associated with your debt and automobiles.

This chapter explains how to use Quicken's reporting features to keep tabs on your net worth. As you'll learn in these pages, a wealth of information about your net worth is just a mouse click away.

The Property & Debt Tab

Asset and debt account information, as well as an overview of your financial standing (net worth), are part of Quicken's Property & Debt tab. Open the Property & Debt section by clicking its tab near the top of Quicken's main window. Within the Property & Debt tab are three buttons that you can use to find information about your net worth: Net Worth, Property, and Debt.

If you don't see the Property & Debt tab, click View I Tabs To Show, and click Property & Debt.

Each of the buttons within the Property & Debt tab can display graphs and reports to help you understand your true financial position. An example is the Net Worth by Assets and Liabilities graph you see when you click the Net Worth button, as shown in Figure 13-1. Each of the other buttons displays additional information about your net worth accounts. Together, these charts paint a picture of your overall financial situation.

In this part of the chapter we'll take a closer look at the snapshots in the Property & Debt tab sections so you know both what you can find and how you can customize the information for your use.

Exploring the Net Worth Button

As you click the Net Worth button, you'll see two graphs: Net Worth by Assets and Liabilities and Net Worth by Account Type. Each of these graphs gives you good financial information and can be customized to meet your needs. However, there is much more available within the Net Worth button than first meets the

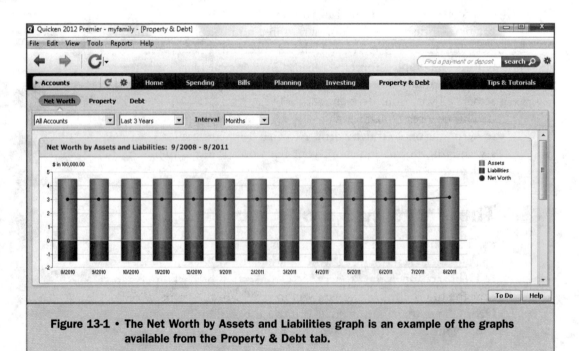

Figure 13-1 • The Net Worth by Assets and Liabilities graph is an example of the graphs available from the Property & Debt tab.

eye. At the top of the section are three drop-down lists with which you can customize any of the reports or graphs to meet your requirements, as seen here.

Accounts Drop-Down List   The first drop-down list displays the accounts you want to use for this graph. The default, as shown, is All Accounts. Click the downward arrow and choose Custom to open the Customize dialog. From this dialog you may

- Click the Select All button to include all of your accounts in the graph.
- Click the Clear All button to deselect all of your accounts.
- Select or clear the check box displayed by each account name to include it in the graph.
- Click the Show (Hidden Accounts) check box to include the accounts you have chosen to hide.

When you have completed your selections, click OK to close the dialog.

Time Period Drop-Down List   The second drop-down list in the Net Worth button allows you to set the time period to be included in your graph. As you can see here, you can choose from the following:

- Last 12 Months
- Last Year
- Last 3 Years
- Last 5 Years
- Last 10 Years
- Earliest To Date (the default time period)

With the Custom Date option, you can set the time period for which the graph displays information.

Intervals   The three choices on the Interval drop-down list are Month, Quarter, and Year. For example, if you want to see what your financial position has been for the last ten years, you might choose to display the information by quarter instead of months to see the general trend.

Net Worth by Assets and Liabilities

The first snapshot in the Net Worth button is the Net Worth by Assets and Liabilities, as shown in Figure 13-1. This graph uses a stacked column to indicate your net worth for the time period you choose. In our example, we have chosen to display the last three years' information at monthly intervals. As you can see in Figure 13-1, since we've opted to display monthly intervals, only the last 12 months display on our screen. The time period covered by the graph is shown above the display. We can change what appears on the graph by changing the interval represented.

The green bar represents your assets, the blue bar represents your debt, and the red line represents your net worth. If you're looking for a trend, ideally the green bars should get taller while the blue bars get shorter. The net effect would be a rise in the red line, as seen in Figure 13-2. If the red line is below the baseline of the graph, you're in some serious financial trouble because your debts exceed your assets.

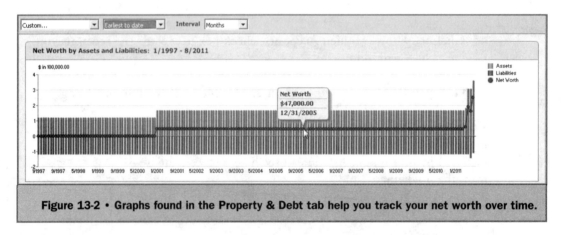

Figure 13-2 • Graphs found in the Property & Debt tab help you track your net worth over time.

When you position your mouse over a specific area on the net worth line of this graph, you see your net worth as of that date, as shown in Figure 13-2. Move your mouse to one of the green areas, and a similar report appears showing exactly what your assets were worth as of that date. Similarly, put your mouse in the blue area to see how much you owed at that date. Double-click a location to open another chart that displays your assets and liabilities in a pie chart as seen next. Click Done to close the chart.

Keep in mind that, by default, this graph represents all of your accounts in Quicken—including your banking and investment accounts. It's a true view of your net worth trend for the time period you choose. To set the various options within the graph, use the drop-down lists at the top of the section as described earlier.

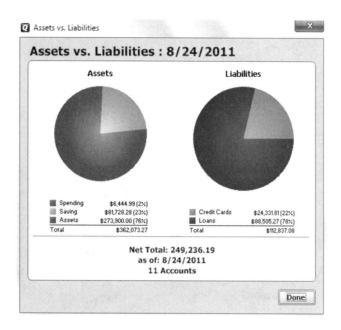

Net Worth Summary Report

Below the Net Worth by Assets and Liabilities graph, you'll see a button labeled Net Worth Summary Report. The report that appears when you click this button displays your information in both graphic and report format, as seen in Figure 13-3. (This report can also be displayed by selecting Reports | Net Worth & Balances | Net Worth.) As with any report or graph, the information is fully customizable. See Chapter 8 to review your many options when customizing reports.

Any accounts you have hidden in Quicken are not included in your Net Worth reports.

Net Worth by Account Type

The Net Worth by Account Type graph that appears in the lower portion of the screen when you select the Net Worth button in the Property & Debt tab shows the percentage of your net worth each of your account types represents. This is also a stack-type graph with each account type represented by a different color.

- Orange indicates your Spending accounts.
- Green indicates Investing accounts.
- Blue indicates Retirement accounts.
- Pink indicates Property & Debt accounts.
- Gray (kind of a blue-gray on my monitor) indicates Credit Card accounts.

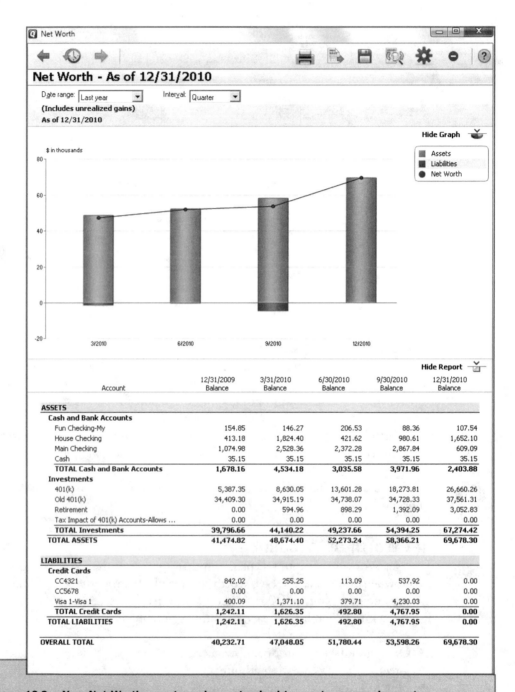

Figure 13-3 • Your Net Worth report can be customized to meet your requirements.

Account Balances Report

This button opens the Account Balances report with the settings that show the date range you have entered at the top of the Net Worth view. This report can also be opened by choosing Reports | Account Balances, but the resulting report when chosen in that location shows your balances from the earliest date entered in your Quicken account but no interval is set.

Using the Property Button

When you click the Property button in the Property & Debt tab, each of your assets and any associated liability are shown in a horizontal bar graph, as seen in Figure 13-4. If you have two current liabilities associated with one asset, as shown here in the House account, each liability is displayed with a different color.

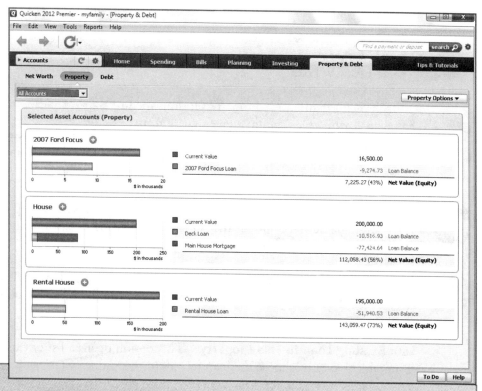

Figure 13-4 • The Property button shows a bar graph displaying both your assets and associated liabilities.

If you have refinanced an asset, such as your house, zeroed-out mortgages may appear to the right of the graph with their zero balance.

The drop-down list box at the top of the screen lets you select which of your accounts you want displayed in this graph. While All Accounts is the default choice, you may choose from several options:

- Personal Accounts Only
- One specific account (each shows by the account name)
- Custom (which opens a list of all of your asset accounts so you may choose two or more)

From the Property Options menu at the right side of the screen, you can choose among the following:

- Add A House Asset Account
- Add A Vehicle Asset Account
- Add Other Asset Account
- Add A New Loan

Each menu item on the Property Options menu has a small white plus sign in a green circle to its left, as seen here. You open the appropriate Add Account screen when you click that green circle icon or click the adjacent text.

 Creating a new account from the Property Options menu saves a step or two when adding a new account, as the Add Account dialog opens directly to the type of account you are creating.

Within the graph itself are similar icons to the right of each asset. Use these green circle icons to open a menu with which you can perform the following actions:

Link Existing Loan to This Property   This option opens a list of existing loans from which you can choose the loan to link to this property (asset).

Link an Existing Line of Credit to This Property   Choosing this option opens a small menu that displays all your current credit accounts from which you can choose.

Unlink Existing Liability from This Property When you choose this option from the menu, any current loans that have been associated with this asset are displayed. Click the one you want to unlink from this asset.

This option does not appear if there are no associated loans for this property (asset).

New Loan Selecting this option opens the Loan Setup dialog. Chapter 12 explains how to set up loans.

> ### IN MY EXPERIENCE
>
> The ability to link credit accounts with assets can be valuable. However, unless you have set up a line of credit as a "credit" account instead of a loan, Quicken does not make this information available as an "existing line of credit." Since you cannot change the account "type" after you have entered it, be cautious when creating your new accounts.
>
> If you have an existing line of credit that has been set up in Quicken as a loan, this account will usually be included with your House asset. See "Unlink Existing Liability from This Property" in this chapter to change that connection.

If a loan has never been associated with this property or asset, you will see only "New Loan." In addition, there will be a small "Add" button to the right of "No Loan" in the graph itself.

Creating Alerts for Property and Debt Accounts

While Chapter 6 introduced you to Quicken Alerts, there are some special alerts that relate directly to your property that are addressed here.

Setting Up Property and Debt Alerts

To set up an alert, begin by opening the Tools menu and clicking Alerts Center. Click the Setup tab and choose General. Click the name of the alert you want to set from the two options on the left side of the window to display its options on the right. Two alerts apply specifically to your property and so are addressed here:

- **Insurance Reappraisal** notifies you before an insurance policy expires so you can either reevaluate coverage or shop for a new policy, as seen on the next page.
- **Mortgage Reappraisal** notifies you before a mortgage changes from variable to fixed (or fixed to variable) so you can consider refinancing. Even if your mortgage doesn't convert, you can use this alert to remind you periodically to check for better mortgage deals.

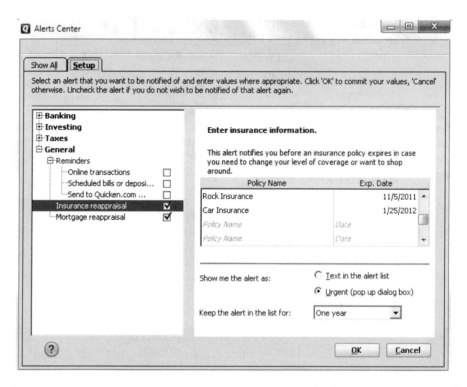

Both alerts work pretty much the same way. For each alert, enter a name and date in the right side of the window. For example, to set insurance policy expiration dates, click in the Policy Name field that contains the name of the policy holder with which you want to work. If you have not paid on a policy before, type the name of the policy holder (the insurance company). You'll see that your text appears on the right side of the box. Use your TAB key to move to the Expiration Date field. Enter the expiration date.

Select one of the options at the bottom of the window to indicate how you want the alert to appear: as text in the alert list, shown earlier, or as a pop-up dialog that appears when you start Quicken. Finally, use the drop-down list to specify the length of time the alert should remain in the list and click OK.

Repeat this process for each alert you want to set. When you're finished, click OK.

Working with Property and Debt Alerts

Once you have established property and debt alerts, you can manage them in several ways:

- Open the Alerts Center's Show All tab by clicking Tools and choosing Alerts Center. Select an alert and click the Delete button to remove an alert.

- In the Alerts Center's Setup tab, you can uncheck an alert category to prevent all the alerts in that category from being displayed in any way.

Opening the Debt Button

The Debt button displays two graphs that show your current debt position, as seen in Figure 13-5. Each graph portrays your liability information in a slightly

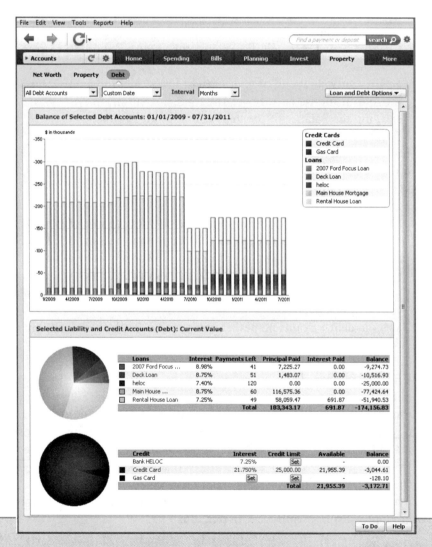

Figure 13-5 • The Debt button in the Property & Debt tab allows you to view your financial obligations in several ways.

different format. At the top of the graphs are several drop-down lists that let you select the accounts with which you want to work, the time period to cover, and the intervals to be displayed. A legend appears at the right of the section telling you what color the graph uses for each debt listed.

The first drop-down list lets you choose which accounts you want to use in the graph. You have your choice of the following:

- **All Debt Accounts** sets the graph to display all of your debts. This is the default setting.
- **Credit Cards Only** will display just the amounts you owe to credit card companies.
- **Loans Only** shows all of your current loans, including any mortgages. If you move your mouse cursor over any total, a small magnifying glass will appear showing the balance of the loan at that point in time.

 If you have designated a liability as "Other Liability" in the Add Account dialog, you may see an option for "Other Liabilities Only," which displays all of this type of account.

- **Custom** opens a Customize dialog that lets you choose which accounts to display. Click Select All to display all of your debts. Click Clear All and choose only the debts you want to display in your graph. Click the Show (Hidden Accounts) check box to include those debts that you have hidden in Quicken. Click OK to close the dialog and return to your graph.
- Specific debt account names let you create a graph that shows only one of your debt accounts.

The second drop-down list offers a variety of dates for which you can set your graphs. Most of the options are self-explanatory; however, when you click Custom Date, a dialog appears that you can use to set the time period for which you want the graph to display. Be aware that in this dialog, unlike most dialog boxes in Quicken, you have to click in the To field to change the date instead of using the TAB key to move to it. In this dialog, pressing the TAB key when you enter a date in the From field will move you to the OK button.

The third drop-down list lets you choose between three interval options for your graph's display: Months, Quarter, and Year.

Loan and Debt Options

At the top right of the Debt button's screen is a drop-down list offering two additional options as shown here:

- Add A New Loan
- Add A Credit Card

Both of these choices open the Add Account dialog with which you can quickly create a new account of the type you selected.

The small "i" inside the blue circle icon opens several different dialogs as described in the sections that follow.

Make a Payment and Loan Details   When you click the icon to the left of either Make A Payment or Loan Details, the View Loans dialog appears as discussed in Chapter 12. From this dialog you can view the payment schedule as both a list and a graph, edit the rate of interest, payment information, and the loan itself. And, as the menu item states, you can make a payment from this dialog.

Refinance and Loan Calculators   As you might guess, these menu options open a special dialog with which you can quickly calculate a refinancing plan or a new loan. Financial calculators are such useful items that we have devoted an entire chapter to working with them. See Chapter 15 to learn about their many benefits.

Balance of Selected Debt Accounts Graph

As seen in Figure 13-5, the first graph you see when you click the Debt button in the Property & Debt tab is a graph that displays a stack-bar graph showing your total debt by month for the year-to-date. This graph includes a legend explaining the color used for each credit card and loan account included in the graph.

Using the drop-down lists at the top of the screen, you can tell Quicken to show a wide variety of accounts, dates, and intervals to make the information meaningful to you.

Current Value Graph

The second graph in the Debt button's section of the Property & Debt tab displays the current value of the debt you selected in the first drop-down list at the top of the page. Each choice that you make displays the information in a slightly different way and includes somewhat different information.

The Selected Liability and Credit Accounts (Debt): Current Value graph displays information in both a pie chart and with columns of information, as seen in Figure 13-5. How you have chosen to display your debt accounts in the Debt button's first drop-down box will affect what shows on the Current Value graph. Depending on your choices, the information about the (nonhidden) accounts that you owe are shown in two sections: Loans and Credit.

Loans If you have selected All Debt Accounts or Loans Only in the first drop-down list, you will see the following:

- **Interest**, which displays the rate of interest for each loan.
- **Payments Left** to show you how many more payments you have on this loan through the date you chose in the drop-down boxes.
- **Principal Paid** shows the amount of principal you have paid on this loan since its inception through the date you chose in the drop-down boxes.
- **Interest Paid** totals the interest you have paid through the date you chose in the drop-down boxes. Remember, interest is the amount you pay to rent someone else's money.
- **Balance** shows what you still owe on this debt. It shows as a minus because it subtracts from your net worth. The balance displayed is as of the date you chose in the drop-down boxes.

Credit This section displays the credit cards or other loans you have entered into Quicken. As seen in Figure 13-5, the information is shown in pie chart form for the options you chose in the drop-down boxes. You see the following:

- **Interest**, which displays the interest rate being charged on each card. If it does not show, click the Set button to open the Interest Rate dialog. Enter the interest rate for the card as shown on your monthly statement, and click OK to close the dialog. You may also use this dialog to change the interest rate for the credit card.
- **Credit Limit** displays the credit limit of the card. This is not available if you have not entered the limit. Click the Set button to open the Credit Limit dialog. Type the amount of this card's credit limit, and click OK to return to the graph.
- **Available** displays the amount you can still charge on this card. It is your credit limit minus the current balance.
- **Balance** displays the amount you owe on this card to the credit card company as of the date you set in the drop-down boxes.

If you have not set the interest rate or the credit card limit on any of your credit accounts, you may adjust those items here.

1. Locate the account you wish to adjust and, in the proper column, click the Set button.
2. From the dialog that appears, as seen here, you may set an interest rate or a credit limit. Type in the appropriate information and click OK.

You may also adjust any number that is displayed in blue in the graph. For example, if our credit card company has complied with our request to lower our credit limit, we do the following:

1. Click the amount shown in blue in the credit limit column for the appropriate account.
2. At the Credit Limit dialog that appears, as seen here, type the new amount.
3. Click OK.

Accessing Property and Debt Account Registers

To learn more about the transactions and balances for a specific account, you can view the account's register.

- Click the name of an account in the Property button in the Property & Debt tab's screen.
- Click the name of the account from the Account Bar.
- Click the account's name from the Current Value graph in the Debt view of the Property & Debt tab.

With either method, the account's register will open. The register lists all transactions entered into that account, as well as the ending balance. As covered in Chapter 12, you can enter transactions directly into the register. Other transactions—such as principal payments for a mortgage or other loans—are automatically calculated and entered by Quicken.

Forecasting Your Financial Future

This part of the book tells you about Quicken Personal Finance Software's planning features, which you can use to plan for your retirement, major purchases, and other life events. It covers Quicken's built-in financial calculators, as well as features that can help you save money to make your dreams come true. You are introduced to the many tax tools that are available in Quicken to help you prepare for tax time. The four chapters are:

Part Five

Planning for the Future

Chapter 14

In This Chapter:

- *Planning your steps*
- *Setting plan assumptions*
- *Viewing plan results*
- *Setting "What If" options*
- *Using "What If" results*
- *Finding more planning tools*

To most of us, the future is an unknown, a mystery. After all, who can say what will happen tomorrow, next year, or ten years from now? But if you think about your future, you can usually come up with a few events that you can plan for: your marriage, the purchase of a new home, the birth of your children (and their education years later), and your retirement. (These are just examples—everyone's life runs a different course.) These events, as well as many unforeseen events, all have one thing in common: they affect your finances. This chapter tells you about planning for future events and how tools within Quicken Personal Finance Software can help.

Planning for Retirement

Throughout your life, you work and earn money to pay your bills, buy the things you and your family need or want, and help your kids get started with their own lives. But there comes a day when it's time to retire. Those regular paychecks stop coming, and you find yourself relying on the money you put away for retirement.

Retirement planning is one of the most important financial planning jobs facing individuals and couples. This section tells you about the importance of planning and offers some planning steps and suggestions.

Retired people live on fixed incomes. That's not a problem—if the income is fixed high enough to support a comfortable lifestyle. You can help ensure that there's enough money to finance your retirement years by planning and saving now.

Poor retirement planning can lead to catastrophic results—imagine running out of money when you turn 75. Or, envision making a lifestyle change when you're 66 or 67 to accommodate a much lower income.

Planning is even more important these days as longevity increases. People are living longer than ever. Your retirement dollars may need to support you for 20 years or more, at a time when the cost of living will likely be much higher than it is today.

With proper planning, it's possible to finance your retirement years without putting a strain on your working years. By closely monitoring the status of your retirement funds, periodically adjusting your plan, and acting accordingly, your retirement years can be the golden years they're supposed to be.

Planning Your Steps

Retirement planning is much more than deciding to put $2,000 in an IRA every year. It requires careful consideration of what you have, what you'll need, and how you can make those two numbers the same.

Assess What You Have

Take a good look at your current financial situation. What tax-deferred retirement savings do you already have? A 401(k)? An IRA? Something else? What regular savings do you have? What taxable investments do you have? The numbers you come up with will form the basis of your final retirement funds.

Be sure to consider property that can be liquidated to contribute to retirement savings. For example, if you currently live in a large home to accommodate your family, you may eventually want to live in a smaller home. The proceeds from the sale of your current home may exceed the cost of your retirement home. Also consider any income-generating property that may continue to generate income in your retirement years or that can be liquidated to contribute to retirement savings.

Determine What You'll Need

What you'll need depends on many things. One simple calculation suggests you'll need 80 percent of your current gross income to maintain your current lifestyle in your retirement years. You may find a calculation like this handy if retirement is still many years in the future and you don't really know what things will cost.

Time is an important factor in calculating the total amount you should have saved by retirement day. Ask yourself two questions:

- *How long do you have to save?*   Take your current age and subtract it from the age at which you plan to retire. That's the number of years you have left to save.
- *How long will you be in retirement?*   Take the age at which you plan to retire and subtract it from the current life expectancy for someone of your age and gender. That's the number of years you have to save for.

Develop an Action Plan

Once you know how much you need, it's time to think seriously about how you can save it. This requires putting money away in one or more savings or investment accounts. There are several options here, which are covered a little later in this chapter.

Stick to the Plan!

The most important part of any plan is sticking to it. For example, if you plan to save $5,000 a year, don't think you can just save $2,000 this year and make up the $3,000 next year. There are two reasons: first, you can't "make up" the interest lost on the $3,000 you didn't save this year, and second, you're kidding yourself if you think you'll manage to put away $8,000 next year.

If you consider deviating from your plan, just think about the alternative: making ends meet with a job bagging groceries when you're 73 years old.

Don't Wait! Act Now!

Most of us don't think about retirement planning or savings in our twenties or even thirties. However, the earlier we begin, the more enjoyable our retirement can be.

See for yourself. Table 14-1 shows how $2,500, $5,000, and $7,500 per-year contributions to a tax-deferred retirement account earning 5 percent a year can grow. (These calculations do not take into consideration tax benefits or inflation.)

Start Age	Years of Saving	Savings at Age 62		
		$2,500/year	$5,000/year	$7,500/year
60	2	$5,125	$10,250	$15,375
50	12	$39,793	$79,586	$119,378
40	22	$96,263	$192,526	$288,789
30	32	$188,247	$376,494	$564,741
20	42	$338,079	$676,159	$1,014,238

Table 14-1 • Regular Savings Can Make Your Money Grow

Getting Started with the Quicken Lifetime Planner

From the Planning tab (refer to Figure 14-1), you have access to all of Quicken's built-in planning features, including the Quicken Lifetime Planner's main plan assumptions and individual financial planners. Once you have set up your plan, the Planning tab provides an up-to-date view of how well your plan is working.

Here's how it works. You start by entering plan assumptions, which include information about you, your current finances, and your tax rate. Quicken makes calculations based on what you entered to display plan results. As you continue working with Quicken, entering transactions that affect your finances, Quicken updates the result of the plan.

Setting up Quicken Lifetime Planner assumptions can be time-consuming. However, the benefits of using this feature far outweigh the cost (in time) of setting it up. This is especially true if you're raising a family—Quicken can help you plan for the major events of your life so you're prepared for them. If you don't have the time to set up the Quicken Planner now, make time in the near future.

This section explains how to set assumptions for the planners within the Quicken Lifetime Planner and how to view the results of your plan in the Planning tab.

Setting Plan Assumptions

The easiest way to see what plan assumptions need to be made is to view the Plan Assumptions area of the Lifetime Planner. Click Planning | Lifetime Planner. When you first start out, the Plan: Results area may look like this illustration.

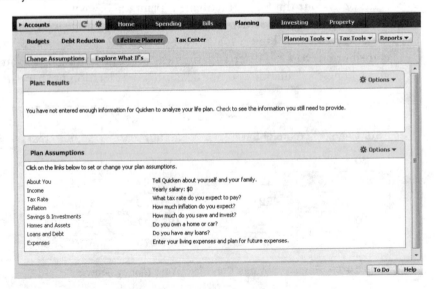

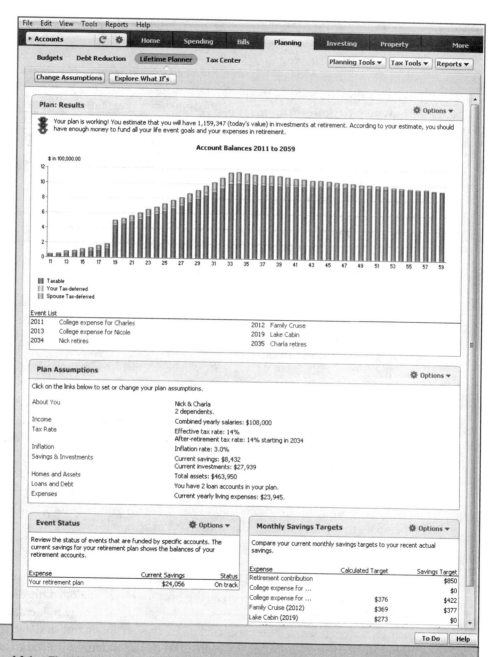

Figure 14-1 • The Lifetime Planner view in the Planning tab displays plan details and results.

To begin, start setting the details in the Plan Assumptions section. To set details for an assumption category, click its link. This displays a dialog you can use to enter information. Here's a look at each category.

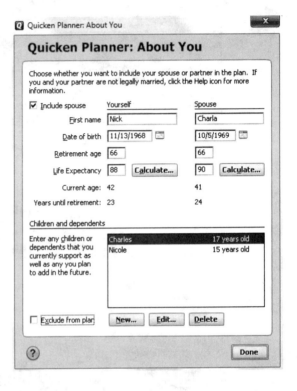

About You

Clicking the About You link displays the About You dialog, which is shown here. Its fields are pretty self-explanatory: your name and date of birth. When you're finished entering information in the dialog, click Done to save it.

Here are some less obvious things to consider when entering data into the About You dialog.

Include Spouse   If you turn on the Include Spouse check box, you can enter information into the Spouse column of the dialog. If you don't have a spouse or don't want to include him or her in your plan, leave that check box turned off.

Life Expectancy   You can either enter what you think might be your life expectancy or click the Calculate button to display the Calculate Life Expectancy dialog. Set options in the dialog, and Quicken tells you how long you may live. Of course, this is an estimate based on current research into life expectancy; you may or may not live to reach the age Quicken suggests.

Children and Dependents   To enter information about children or other dependents, click the New button at the bottom of the dialog. This displays the Add Child/Dependent dialog, in which you can enter the name and date of birth for a dependent. When you click OK, the person's name and age are added to the list. Repeat this process for each child or dependent you need to add. Once a child or dependent has been added, you can select his or her name and click the Edit button to change information about him or her, or click the Delete button to remove him or her permanently from the plan, or turn on the

Exclude From Plan check box so Quicken doesn't use him or her in its calculations. When you have finished making entries, click Done to close the About You dialog.

Income

Clicking the Income link displays the Income dialog, which is organized into three separate tabs of information. This is where you enter salary, retirement benefits, and other income information for you and your spouse.

Salary   The Salary tab, which is shown here, enables you to record information about current and future salary and self-employment income.

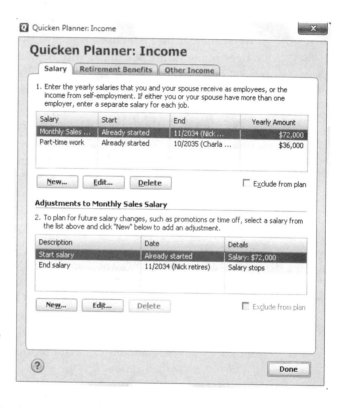

To add an income item, click the New button to display the Salary tab of the Quicken Planner. Then set options to enter information about the income item. As you can see in this illustration, the Salary dialog is extremely flexible, enabling you to enter start and end dates for a salary—which is useful for income from seasonal employment. If you don't need to enter specific dates, choose Already Started from the When Does This Salary Start drop-down list and one of the retirement options from the When Does This Salary End drop-down list. When you click OK, the item is added to the list.

For each item you add, Quicken automatically includes adjustments that specify when the item begins and ends. But you can add other adjustments if you know about changes that will occur in the future. Select the item in the top half of the dialog, and then click the New button at the bottom of the dialog.

Enter information in the Add Salary Adjustment dialog that appears and click OK. The information is added to the bottom half of the Salary tab of the Income dialog.

On the Salary tab, you can select any of the salary or adjustment items and click the Edit or Delete button to change or remove them. You can also select an item and select the Exclude From Plan check box to exclude its information from the Quicken Planner.

Retirement Benefits   The Retirement Benefits tab enables you to enter information about Social Security or pension benefits you are currently receiving or to estimate future benefits.

To estimate future Social Security benefits, enter the age at which you expect to begin collecting benefits and click the Estimate button. The Estimate Social Security Benefits dialog appears. You have two options:

- **Use Rough Estimate** enables you to select a salary range option to estimate benefits.
- **Use Mail-In Estimate From SS Administration** enables you to enter the amount provided by the Social Security Administration on your annual Social Security statement.

When you click OK, the amount is automatically entered in the Retirement Benefits tab.

To add a pension, click the New button at the bottom of the Retirement Benefits tab of the Income dialog. This displays the Add Pension dialog. Enter information about the pension, and click OK to add it to the Retirement Benefits tab. In that tab, you can select the pension and click Edit or Delete to change or remove it, or select the Exclude From Plan check box to exclude it from the Quicken Planner's calculations.

Other Income   The Other Income tab of the Quicken Planner: Income dialog enables you to enter income from other sources, such as gifts, child support, and inheritances. Don't use this tab to enter income from investments or rental properties; the Quicken Lifetime Planner provides other places to enter that.

From the Other Income tab, to enter an income item, click the New button. Enter information in the Add Other Income dialog. An interesting option in this dialog is the ability to specify how the money will be used: either saved and invested or used to pay expenses. The option you select determines how this income is used in the plan. If you're not sure what to select, leave it set to the default option. When you click OK, the item is added to the Other Income tab's list. You can edit, delete, or exclude the item from the plan as desired.

Click Done to close the Quicken Planner: Income dialog.

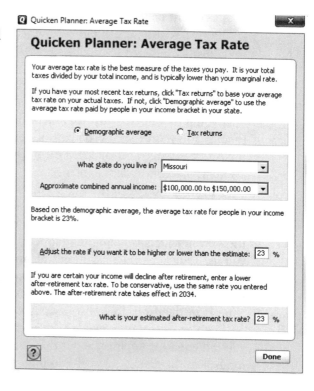

Tax Rate

Clicking the Tax Rate link in the Plan Assumptions area displays the Average Tax Rate dialog shown here. You have two options:

- **Demographic Average** enables you to estimate your tax rate based on where you live and what your income is.

- **Tax Returns** enables you to estimate your tax rate based on the total income, total federal taxes, and total state taxes from your most recent tax returns.

No matter how you estimate the tax rate, you can adjust it by entering a preferred value. You can also enter an estimate of your post-retirement tax rate, which may be lower. Click Done to close the Quicken Planner: Average Tax Rate dialog.

Inflation

Clicking the Inflation link displays the Estimated Inflation dialog, which includes a field you can use to enter the inflation rate you want to use for your plan. Quicken suggests an inflation rate of 3 percent, which is the average inflation rate since 1927, but you can enter any rate you think is correct in the text box. Click OK to save your estimate.

Savings & Investments

Clicking the Savings & Investments link displays the Savings And Investments dialog, which is organized into three tabs. Use these dialogs to enter information about current bank accounts, as well as contributions you make to investment accounts. Use the Return tab to enter the return you expect to earn on your investments.

Savings   Click the Savings tab to list all of the bank accounts you have set up in Quicken, along with their current balances.

If you have omitted any accounts from Quicken, now is a good time to add them if you want them to be part of your plan. Click the New button to display the Add New Account dialog. Learn how to use the Add New Account dialog to create new accounts in Chapter 3.

Quicken automatically assumes that each bank account will be used for general expenses. You can change this assumption by selecting an account and clicking the Details button. Choose a new purpose from the drop-down list in the Account Details dialog that appears and click OK. You may find that until you use Quicken's calculators and planners, general expenses is the only offered option. But if you have entered information into one of the Quicken Planners, such as college expenses in the Expenses Planner, an option for that expense appears in the drop-down list.

If you or your spouse makes regular contributions to one of your bank accounts, you can enter information about that contribution in the Savings dialog. In the top half of the dialog, select the account that receives the contribution. Then click the New button at the bottom of the dialog. Use the Add Contribution dialog that appears to indicate how much you contribute. The dialog will walk you through the process of entering information based on whether the contribution is a percentage of a salary or a base amount that increases each year. Click Done to close the Add Contribution dialog.

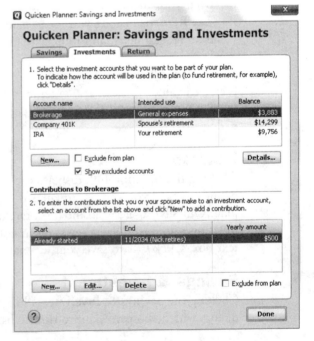

Investments   The Investments tab, shown here, lists all of the investment accounts you have set up in

Quicken, along with their current market values. Remember, since market value is determined by security prices, the market value is only as up-to-date as the most recently entered or downloaded security prices.

This link works just like the Savings tab. You can click the New button in the top half of the dialog to open the Add Account dialog to enter a new investment account. Choose an existing account, and click the New button in the bottom half of the dialog to enter regular contribution information for any selected investment account. You can also specify the intended use for any account by selecting the account name and clicking the Details button.

Return   The Return tab enables you to specify your expected rates of return for pre-retirement and post-retirement investments. If you turn on the check box near the top of the dialog, additional text boxes appear, enabling you to enter different rates of return for taxable and tax-deferred investments. At the bottom of the dialog, you can enter the percentage of the taxable return that is subject to taxes. This is normally 100 percent, but for your situation, the percentage may be different. Click Done to close the Quicken Planner: Savings And Investments dialog.

Homes And Assets

Clicking the Homes And Assets link displays the Homes And Assets dialog, which is organized into two tabs. This is where you can enter information about currently owned assets and assets you plan to purchase in the future.

Asset Accounts   The Asset Accounts tab, which is shown here, lists all of the asset accounts you have created in Quicken, including accounts for your home, vehicle,

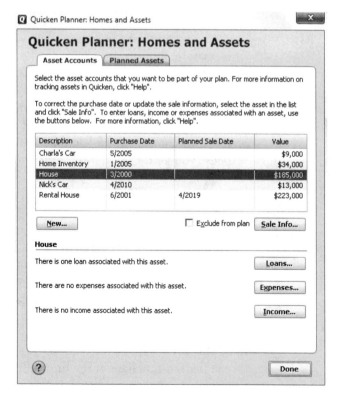

home inventory, and other assets. If you have additional assets that have not yet been entered in Quicken and you want to include them in your plan, click the New button and use the Add Account dialog that appears to create the new account. See how to add a new asset account in Chapter 12.

If you plan to sell an asset, you can enter information for that sale. Select the asset in the top half of the dialog, and then click the Sale Info button. You can enter a planned sale date that is before your purchase date if that is what you intend to do with a future purchase. A series of dialogs prompts you for information about the asset's purchase and sale date and price, as well as other information that affects how much money you can expect to receive and pay taxes on. This information is then added to your plan. Click Done to close the Sale Information dialog.

Three buttons at the bottom of the dialog enable you to associate loans, expenses, and income with a selected asset. This is especially important when working with assets you plan to sell, since the sale of the asset should also end associated debt, expenses, and income.

- **Loans** enables you to link existing loans to the asset or add new loans, including home equity loans. It also enables you to enter information about planned loans—for example, if you plan to use a home equity loan to build an addition on your house sometime next year. You can also enter information about planned payoffs—perhaps you're expecting a big trust fund check (lucky you!) and plan to use it to pay off your house.
- **Expenses** enables you to enter property tax information as well as other expenses related to the asset. For a home, this might include association fees, homeowner's insurance, and estimated maintenance and utility costs. For a car, this might include registration, fuel, service, and insurance. For each expense you add, Quicken prompts you for information about the expense, including how you expect to pay for it—with money in a specific bank account or with a loan. It even enables you to set up a monthly savings target to pay for the item.
- **Income** enables you to enter information about income you expect to earn from the asset. This is especially useful if you own rental property. The dialog that appears when you add an income item is almost the same as the Add Other Income dialog. It even allows you to specify how you plan to use the income: for investment or to pay expenses. Click Done to close the Loans, Asset Expenses, or Other Income dialogs.

Planned Assets The Planned Assets tab lets you enter information about any assets you plan to purchase in the future. For example, suppose you indicated in the Asset Accounts tab that you plan to sell your home or car on a specific date. If you plan to replace it with another home or car, this is where you'd enter information about the replacement. Quicken uses dialogs that walk you through the process of entering details about the future purchase. Once you've entered planned asset information, you can select the asset in the list and add loans, expenses, and income for it, as well as choose the accounts you plan to use to pay for it. Click Done to close the Quicken Planner: Homes And Assets dialog.

Loans And Debt

Clicking the Loans And Debt link in the Plan Assumptions area displays the Loans And Debt dialog, which is organized into three tabs. This is where you enter information about current and planned loans, as well as information from your debt reduction plan.

 If you have not yet set up your debt reduction plan, you will see only two tabs as shown next.

Loan Accounts   The Loan Accounts tab, which is shown here, displays information about current loans. This information comes from loans you have set up within Quicken. To add another loan that isn't already recorded in Quicken, click the New button to display the Loan Setup dialog, which is covered in Chapter 12. If you plan to pay off a loan before its last payment date, you can click the Payoff button to enter future payoff information.

Quicken Planner: Loans and Debt

Quicken Planner: Loans and Debt

| Loan Accounts | Planned Loans |

Enter any loans you currently have. For more information on tracking loans in Quicken, click "Help".

If you want to enter a loan associated with an asset, such as a home loan, go to the Homes and Assets section. If you plan to pay off a loan early, click "Payoff".

Description	Start Date	Length	Current Balance
House Mortgage	3/2000	30 Years	$144,723
Personal Loan fr...	5/1999	15 Years	$9,439

New...   ☐ Exclude from plan   Payoff...

Personal Loan from Folks

Original loan amount:	$25,000
Payment:	$239
Interest rate:	8%
Remaining payments:	47
Date of last payment:	6/2014

Done

Planned Loans   The Planned Loans tab enables you to enter information about loans you plan to make in the future. This does not include any loans you may have already planned in the Homes And Assets dialog discussed earlier in this chapter. Instead, this is for loans that are not associated with any particular asset, such as a personal loan you plan to pay for a really special vacation.

Existing Debt Plan   The Existing Debt Plan tab includes information from the Debt Reduction Planner, which is covered in Chapter 16. If you have credit card and other debt, it's a good idea to complete the Debt Reduction Planner as part of your overall planning strategy. Click Done to close the Quicken Planner: Loans And Debt dialog.

You can choose whether or not to include your Debt Reduction plan info in your Lifetime plan. If you choose to include your debt reduction here, you will need to exclude debt reduction plan accounts on the Loan Accounts tab.

Expenses

Clicking the Expenses link displays the Expenses dialog, which is organized into four tabs. This is where you enter information about your living expenses, as well as any adjustments to expenses and the expenses for college or other special events.

Living Expenses   The Living Expenses tab, which is shown here, enables you to enter your estimated living expenses using one of two techniques:

- **Rough Estimate** enables you to enter an estimate of your annual living expenses. Using this technique is quicker, but it may not be as accurate as using the Category Detail option.
- **Category Detail** enables you to have Quicken calculate an estimate of your

annual living expenses based on transactions already entered in your Quicken data file. This technique is more accurate than Rough Estimate, especially if you have been using Quicken for a while and have a good history of transactions. If you select this method, you can click the Details button that appears in the middle of the dialog to display the Living Expenses Category Detail dialog. Toggle check marks in the list of categories to include or exclude specific categories and enter monthly amounts as desired. When you click OK, Quicken annualizes the amounts and enters them in the Living Expenses tab.

> ### IN MY EXPERIENCE
>
> When working with the Living Expenses Category Detail dialog, you may see that each time you click the Details button and the Living Expenses Category Detail dialog appears, your "unchecked" categories are now checked again. To solve this frustration, when you clear a category so that it is not included in your totals, take the time to change the Monthly Amount to zero. The next time you open this dialog, your category monthly estimate will still be zero. Click OK to close the Living Expenses Category Detail dialog.

One thing to keep in mind here: don't include expenses that you may have already included for an asset. For example, if you included car insurance expenses in the Homes And Assets dialog as an expense associated with an automobile, don't include them again here. Doing so would duplicate the expense and overstate your annual expenses.

At the bottom of the dialog, you can enter a percentage of surplus cash—any cash left over after paying living expenses—that you want to put into savings.

Adjustments   The Adjustments tab enables you to enter any adjustments to your expenses that are related to planned changes in your life. For example, perhaps you plan to hire a nanny to take care of your child while you go back to work. You can add this planned expense as an adjustment for a predefined period. When you click the New button in the Adjustments tab, the Add Living Expense Adjustment dialog appears.

College Expenses   The College Expenses tab, shown next, enables you to plan for the education of your children—or yourself! Clicking the New button in this tab displays the Add College Expense dialog, which walks you through the process of entering expected college expenses for a plan member. You'll have to do a little homework to come up with realistic estimates of college costs, including tuition, room, board, books, and supplies. Remember, if you underestimate expenses, your plan won't be accurate. The dialog also prompts you for information about expected financial aid, student loans, and student contributions to cover all sources of financing. If you have a college fund—such as an educational IRA—already set up for the college expense, you can associate it with the expense to indicate how it will be paid for.

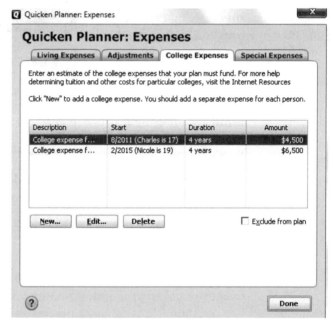

Special Expenses

The Special Expenses tab includes any expenses you may have already added in the Homes And Assets dialog and enables you to enter other one-time or annual expenses you expect to incur. Use this for items like a vacation, wedding, or large purchase. When you click the New button, Quicken prompts you for information about the expense, including the amount and how you expect to finance it. Click Done to close the Quicken Planner: Expenses dialog.

Reviewing and Changing Assumptions

You can review and modify your plan assumptions at any time. Quicken offers a number of ways to do this.

IN MY EXPERIENCE

Quicken even gives you help in finding outside funding for college expenses. Once you have created a plan that includes college expenses, follow these steps for some Internet links to help you or your student find college funding.

1. From the Planning tab, click the Lifetime Planner button.
2. In the Event List, choose College Expense For *nnn*, where *nnn* is the name of person.
3. The College Expense For *nnn* dialog appears. Choose College Cost | Tuition & Fees. From this section of the plan, there are several links that, with your Internet connection, open websites discussing college costs.
4. Click the X to close the plan.

The Plan Assumptions Area

Once you enter assumptions into the Quicken Planners, a brief summary of the assumptions appears in the Plan Assumptions area in the Planning tab (see Figure 14-1). To open this window, choose Planning | Lifetime Planner.

You can click links in the Plan Assumptions area to open the same dialogs discussed earlier in this chapter. Review and change plan assumptions as desired, and click Done or OK in the dialog to save them.

The Planning Assumptions Window

A better way to review plan assumptions is in the Planning Assumptions window, as seen next. To open this window, choose Planning | Lifetime Planner. You can access the Planning Assumptions window from the Options button in any of the four sections of the Lifetime Planner. Click Options | Review Or Change Plan Assumptions.

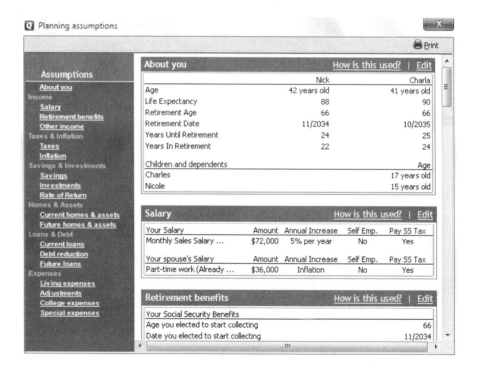

You can use links on the left side of the Planning Assumptions window to navigate quickly from one category of assumption to another. The details appear in the main part of the window. Each category of assumption offers two links:

- **How Is This Used?** explains how the information in that category of assumption is used in the plan.
- **Edit** enables you to edit the assumptions for that category, using the same dialogs discussed earlier in this chapter.

Saved Plans

Figure 14-1 shows the results of your saved plan, the plan assumptions, the status of any planned events, and your monthly savings targets. You can use this screen to review your savings plans and change them if you need or want to. Click a link to open the associated planner and change data as desired.

Viewing Plan Results

When Quicken has enough data about your assumptions to calculate plan results, it displays them graphically in the Plan: Results area of the Planning tab (see Figure 14-1).

As with the information displayed in the other Quicken tabs, you can print the Plan Results, Assumptions, Event Status, and Monthly Savings Targets by clicking File | Print Lifetime Planner.

The top of the Plan: Results area tells you whether your plan is working and how much you should have in investments at retirement. Amounts are in today's dollars; to view them in future dollars, choose Show Amounts In Future Value from the Options pop-up menu at the top-right corner of the Plan: Results area.

The graph beneath this summary shows your taxable and tax-deferred savings. The ideal shape of this graph shows a steady increase until the year you retire and then a gradual decrease. Hover your mouse pointer over a column to show a yellow box with the amount for that year. Clicking the column opens a Plan Summary dialog for that year showing income and expenses. You can use the <<Prev Year>> and <<Next Year>> buttons in the dialog to scroll through the years in the graph. This enables you to see the detailed numbers that make up the graph columns—very helpful! Plan results change automatically based on a variety of changes within your Quicken data file:

- When the account balances referred to in the plan change, the plan changes accordingly.
- When you change plan assumptions, the plan changes accordingly.

- When you use Quicken's planners to plan for major purchases, college, retirement, and other events that affect your finances, the plan changes to include these events.
- When you play "what if" with assumptions and save the changes as your plan, the plan changes accordingly. You'll see how to enter "what ifs" a little later in this chapter, in the section "The 'What If' Alternatives."

Viewing Event Status Items

Quicken also keeps track of your progress toward certain events and savings targets. It displays this information in the Planning tab of the Lifetime Planner window (refer to Figure 14-1).

The Event Status section displays information about events in your plan that are funded with specific accounts. From this section click Your Retirement Plan to open the My Retirement Plan window, seen in Figure 14-2, which looks a lot like the Plan Assumptions window. Click close to return to the Lifetime Planner.

Working with Your Future Expenses

The Monthly Savings Targets section of your Lifetime Planner displays information about your savings toward events in your plan, as seen next.

Q Income and Expenses Summary (2024)

<< Prev Year   Next Year >>   Print...   Close

Plan Summary (2024)
(All amounts are reported in today's value.)

Income Summary

Income	
Salaries	
Monthly Sales Salary	$92,451
Part-time work	$36,000
Total Salaries	$128,451
Pension Benefits	
My pension	$0
My pension: Survivor's Benefit	$0
Total Pension Benefits	$0
Social Security Benefits	
Self	$0
Spouse	$0
Total Social Security Benefits	$0
Withdrawals	
Your Tax-deferred	$0
Spouse Tax-deferred	$0
Total Withdrawals	$0
College Incomes	
Student Contribution for Charles	$0
Student Contribution for Nicole	$0
Total College Incomes	$0
Special Income	
Other income	$0

Monthly Savings Targets   ⚙ Options ▼

Compare your current monthly savings targets to your recent actual savings.

Expense	Calculated Target	Savings Target
Retirement contribution		$850
College expense for Charles (2011-2015)		$0
College expense for Nicole (2015-2019)	$291	$291
Family Cruise (2012)	$369	$377
Lake Cabin (2019)	$273	$0
Monthly total:	$933	$1,518
Savings last month:		$0
Average monthly savings (last 6 months):		$0

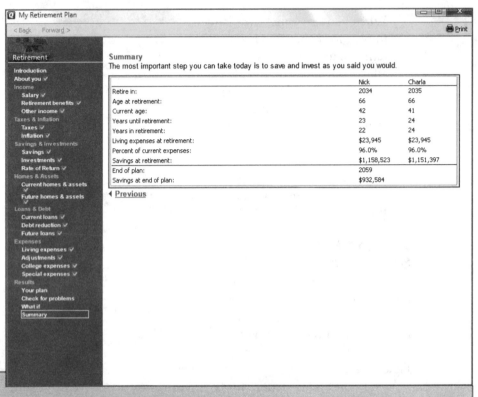

Figure 14-2 • The Summary section of the My Retirement Plan window shows the information you entered about your retirement plan.

Clicking any link for an expense displays the summary area for that expense in the Plan Assumptions window. You can review and modify event information in that window. When you are done reviewing the event, click Done or OK to return to the Lifetime Planner.

The "What If" Alternatives

Once you've entered assumptions, created plans for specific events, and viewed your plan results, you might wonder how a change in one or more assumptions would affect the plan. You can use the "What If" Event Scenarios feature to see how the changes would affect the plan without changing the plan itself.

Here's an example. Say you've been offered a job in another state. The job pays about the same salary that you make now, but you can move to a town where your living expenses would be greatly reduced. You can see how the job change would affect your financial plans for the future by playing "what if" to modify existing assumptions, and then see the old and new plan results side by side.

Setting "What If" Options

Each of the sections of the Lifetime Planner in the Planning tab has an Options button from which you can play What If. Click Options | What If I Did Something Different? to open the What If window seen in Figure 14-3. The first time you use it, the window displays the account balances shown in your plan results.

Choose a goal option from the drop-down list at the top-left corner of the window. Then click appropriate links on the left side of the window to open dialogs to change assumptions:

- Click Current Homes & Assets to add proposed sale information about your current home.

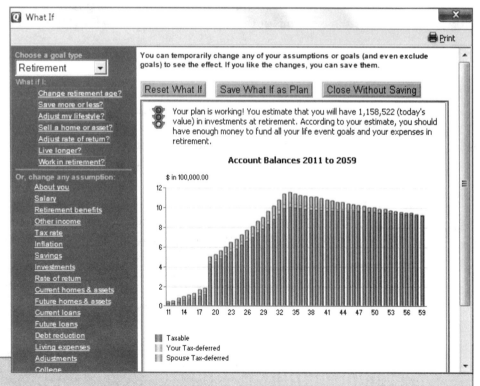

Figure 14-3 • You can use the What If window to play "what if" with your financial plans.

- Click Current Loans to record the proposed payoff of your mortgage when you sell your current home.
- Click Future Homes & Assets to add proposed purchase information about your new home and its associated mortgage.
- Click Adjustments to add a proposed adjustment for the reduced living expenses when you move to your new home.

See how that works? Each time you make a change, the Plan Comparison chart changes. The original plan is shown as an orange line and the change as a yellow line.

IN MY EXPERIENCE
When working with the Plan Comparison chart you may notice a slow response when applying the What If changes. Also, if you make a change that is too subtle, it may be hard to distinguish the lines.

Using "What If" Results

When you've finished changing assumptions and viewing results, you can click one of the three buttons at the top of the What If window:

- **Reset What If** clears all of the assumptions you changed while playing "what if." This enables you to start over.
- **Save What If As Plan** saves the assumptions you changed while playing "what if" as your actual financial plan. When the window closes, you'll see the results in the Planning tab change accordingly.
- **Close Without Saving** simply closes the window so you can continue working with Quicken. Your settings are not saved.

Finding More Planning Tools

Quicken offers additional tools found in the Planning tab. Budgets, which are covered extensively in Chapter 16, and financial calculation tools, which are found in the Planning Tools drop-down list. These tools are discussed at length in Chapter 15.

Using Financial Calculators

In This Chapter:

- *Learning about financial calculators*
- *Accessing the financial calculators*
- *Working with the Retirement Calculator*
- *Running the College Calculator*
- *Evaluating the Refinance Calculator*
- *Planning with the Savings Calculator*
- *Using the Loan Calculator*

Sometimes, the hardest part about financial planning is making the calculations you need quickly to determine the feasibility of a potential plan. For example, suppose you're thinking about refinancing your home because you can now get an interest rate that's lower than the rate you locked into six years ago. You know your monthly payment can decrease, but you're not sure if you'll save enough money to cover the fees involved in the refinancing. The calculations seem complex, and you're not sure what to do. That's where one of Quicken Personal Finance Software's financial calculators—the Refinance Calculator—can help. It can take raw data about your current mortgage and the one you're considering, and crunch the numbers in a flash to tell you whether it's worthwhile to take the next step.

This chapter tells you about each of Quicken's financial calculators. You'll find them handy tools for making the quick calculations you need to start the decision-making process with your financial plans.

A Look at Quicken's Financial Calculators

Quicken includes five financial calculators you can use to make quick financial calculations: the Retirement Calculator, the College Calculator, the Refinance Calculator, the Savings Calculator, and the Loan Calculator. These calculators make complex calculations simple.

Learning about Financial Calculators

All five of the financial calculators share the same basic interface. But although they are similar in appearance, each is designed for a specific purpose. It's important that you use the correct calculator to get the job done.

In most instances, you begin by telling the calculator what part of the formula you want to calculate. For example, when calculating a loan, you can calculate the loan amount or the periodic payment. Then you enter values and set other options in the calculator's dialog to give Quicken the information it needs to make its calculations. Clicking a Calculate button completes the process. Quicken is fast; the results appear as soon as you click Calculate—if not sooner.

Accessing the Financial Calculators

To view the financial calculators, click the Planning tab and choose Planning Tools. The five calculators appear at the bottom of the menu, as shown here.

If the Planning tab is not visible, click View | Tabs To Show | Planning on the menu bar. If you see Tools instead of Planning Tools, maximize your window to see Planning Tools.

Projected Balances
Savings Goals
Retirement Calculator
College Calculator
Refinance Calculator
Savings Calculator
Loan Calculator

Using the Financial Calculators

If you are ready to try Quicken's financial calculators, the rest of this chapter provides some detailed instructions for using each of them. All of the calculators open with one or more fields showing the text "CALCULATED" or "calculated." Click the Calculate button to change that text to the calculated number.

Working with the Retirement Calculator

The Retirement Calculator can help you calculate some of the numbers you need to plan for your retirement. To open it, choose Planning | Planning Tools | Retirement Calculator. The Retirement Calculator appears as seen in Figure 15-1.

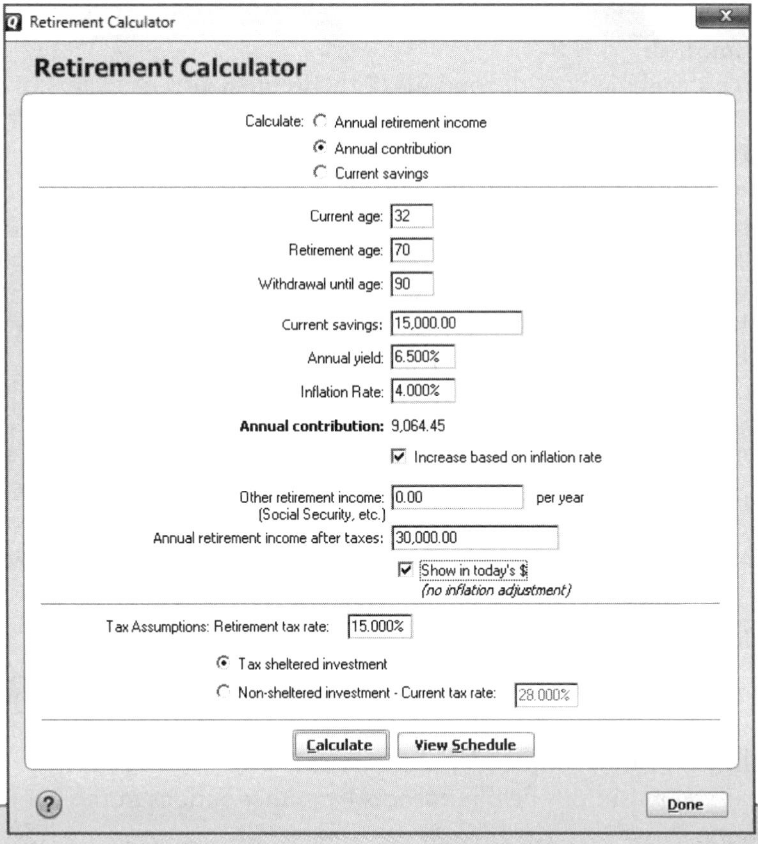

**Figure 15-1 • Use the Retirement Calculator for a quick overview of your income when
you retire.**

As you will note at the top of the calculator, you may calculate for three
different reasons:

- **Annual Retirement Income** calculates the annual amount of retirement
  income you'll have based on the values you enter.
- **Annual Contribution** calculates the minimum amount you should
  contribute to a retirement account to achieve the values you enter.
- **Current Savings** calculates the amount of money you should currently have
  saved to achieve the values you want when you retire.

Select an option, and then enter or select values and options throughout the
dialog. Most options are pretty straightforward and easy to understand. When

you're finished, click the Calculate button to see the results. Click Done when you're finished.

Here's a closer look at the options in the Retirement Calculator.

Retirement Information

Retirement Information options enable you to enter the values Quicken should use in its calculations. The values you must enter vary depending on the Calculate For option you select. For example, if you are 32 years old and plan on retiring at age 70 and want to know how much to save each year to achieve an annual income at retirement of $30,000 in today's dollars, calculate for the annual contribution, as seen in Figure 15-1.

Current, Retirement, and Withdrawal Until Age   Use these fields to enter your age today, the age at which you plan to retire, and your estimation of how long you will need to withdraw from this retirement fund.

Current Savings and Annual Yield   These fields are used to calculate how much you should have saved to meet the goals you set up. Enter the interest rate you are receiving to calculate the annual yield from those savings.

Inflation Rate   Inflation options make complex calculations to account for the effect of inflation on your savings dollars. Use this field to enter your best guess as to the future inflation rate, or use Quicken's default of 4 percent.

What you put in this field influences two other options in the Retirement Calculator:

- **Increase Based on Inflation Rate** makes calculations assuming that the annual contributions will rise with the inflation rate.
- **Show In Today's $** makes calculations assuming that the Annual Retirement Income After Taxes entry is in today's dollars and not inflated.

Tax Information   Tax Information options enable you to indicate whether your retirement savings are in a tax-sheltered investment or a non-sheltered investment. If you select the Non-Sheltered Investment option, you can enter your current tax rate and Quicken will automatically calculate the effect of taxes on your retirement income. In the example shown in Figure 15-1, if we changed the retirement investment from a tax-sheltered investment to a non-sheltered investment with a current tax rate of 28 percent, our 32-year-old would have to increase his annual contribution from $9,064.45 to $12.223.24. By experimenting with this feature, you can clearly see why it's a good idea to use tax-sheltered or tax-deferred investments whenever possible.

Calculate

Depending on the option you choose at the top of the Retirement Calculator, clicking the Calculate button does the computation for you. If you change the option, click Calculate a second time to see the results of your change.

View Schedule

Clicking the View Schedule button displays a printable list of deposits made and income withdrawn, with a running balance total, as seen next. Use the vertical scroll bar to view the theoretical balance in the retirement account as our subject reaches each age.

- Use the question mark to open Quicken's Help screen to answer questions about financial calculators.
- Select the printer icon to print a complete schedule by year.
- Click Done to close the Deposit Schedule window.
- Click Done to close the Retirement Calculator.

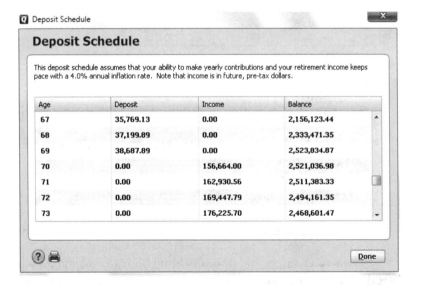

Deposit Schedule

This deposit schedule assumes that your ability to make yearly contributions and your retirement income keeps pace with a 4.0% annual inflation rate. Note that income is in future, pre-tax dollars.

Age	Deposit	Income	Balance
67	35,769.13	0.00	2,156,123.44
68	37,199.89	0.00	2,333,471.35
69	38,687.89	0.00	2,523,834.87
70	0.00	156,664.00	2,521,036.98
71	0.00	162,930.56	2,511,383.33
72	0.00	169,447.79	2,494,161.35
73	0.00	176,225.70	2,468,601.47

Running the College Calculator

The College Calculator enables you to calculate savings for the cost of a college education. Choose Planning | Planning Tools | College Calculator. The College Calculator shown in Figure 15-2 appears. The assumption in this calculator is that you will continue to save the entire time the student is in school.

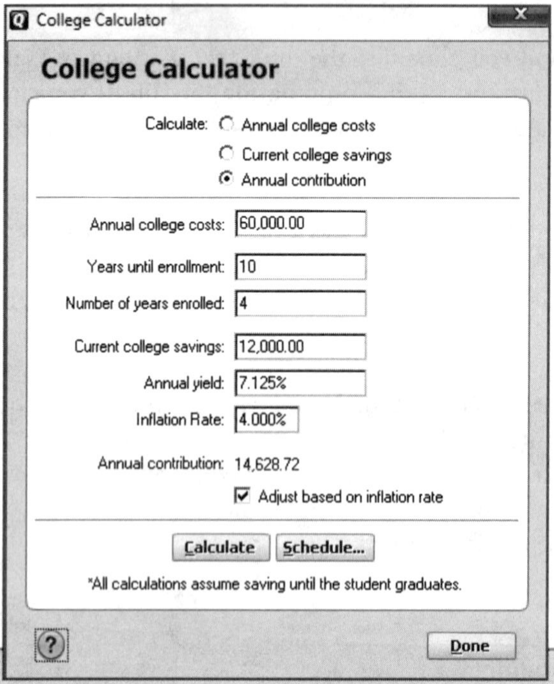

Figure 15-2 • Planning ahead for college costs can eliminate stress for you and your student.

Select a Calculate option from these choices at the top of the Calculator:

- **Annual College Costs** calculates the annual tuition you'll be able to afford based on the values you enter.
- **Current College Savings** calculates the amount of money you should currently have saved based on the values you enter.
- **Annual Contribution** calculates the minimum amount you should contribute to college savings based on the values you enter.

Then enter values and options throughout the dialog. As with the other calculators, the available options are straightforward. When you click Calculate, Quicken calculates the results. When you are finished, click Done.

Annual College Costs   You can use this field to enter your best guess at the cost of college per year when the person for whom you are saving enrolls in school.

Years   Both the Years Until Enrollment and Number of Years Enrolled fields will influence the outcome of the calculations. If you have an eight-year-old who, you assume, will be attending college for only four years, enter that information as shown in our example in Figure 15-2.

Current College Savings   This field shows either what you have already saved for this person's education or, when used as the calculate field, what you should have saved to date to meet the other college goal requirements. Entering the yield you currently receive and your best guess at the inflation rate helps Quicken show you more realistic numbers.

Calculate
The Calculate button computes the requested value.

Schedule
Clicking the Schedule button displays a printable list of deposits made and money withdrawn for tuition, with a running balance total. The last four years of the schedule will show the withdrawals. Click Done to close the Schedule, and click Done once again to close the Calculator.

Evaluating the Refinance Calculator
If you own a home and are thinking about refinancing, you can try the Refinance Calculator to see whether refinancing will really save you money and, if so, how much. Choose Planning | Planning Tools | Refinance Calculator. The Refinance Calculator appears.

Enter values for your current mortgage and proposed mortgage in the various fields to calculate your monthly savings with the new mortgage. When you are finished, click Done. Here's a closer look at the entries seen in Figure 15-3.

Existing Mortgage
Existing Mortgage options enable you to enter your current total monthly mortgage payment and the amount of that payment that is applied to property taxes and other escrow items. Quicken automatically calculates the amount of principal and interest for each payment. If you already know the principal and interest amount, you can enter that in the Monthly Payment box and leave the Impound/Escrow Amount box empty. The result is the same.

Proposed Mortgage
Proposed Mortgage options enable you to enter information about the mortgage that you are considering to replace your current mortgage. The Principal Amount may be the balance on your current mortgage, but it could be more or less, depending on whether you want to refinance for more or less money.

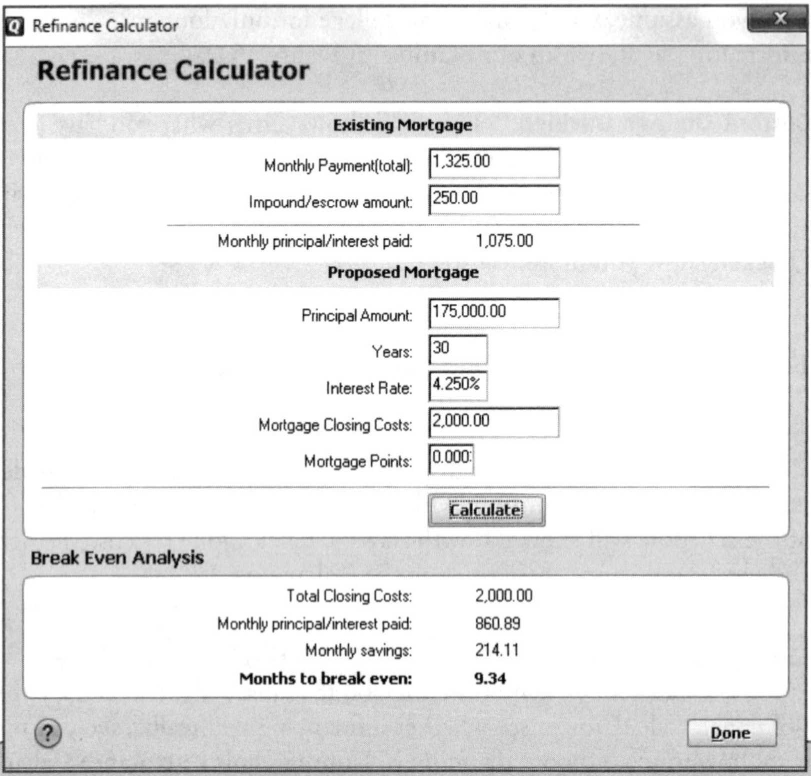

Figure 15-3 • Quicken's Refinance Calculator helps you to see the savings you would realize from refinancing your home.

(Refinancing often offers a good opportunity to exchange equity for cash or to use cash to build equity.)

If you would have to pay closing costs or points to complete the refinancing, enter them in the appropriate fields. This will help Quicken compute a more accurate break-even point.

Break-Even Analysis

Break Even Analysis options are optional. If you enter the closing costs and points for the proposed mortgage, Quicken will automatically calculate how long it will take to cover those costs based on your monthly savings. As you can see in Figure 15-3, after closing costs, the break-even point for this refinance is only nine and a half months. Click Done to close the Calculator.

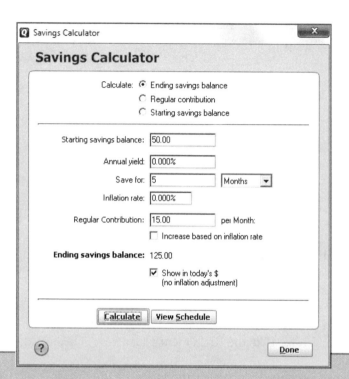

Figure 15-4 • **The Savings Calculator can show how contributing regularly to your savings can help you achieve your goals.**

Planning with the Savings Calculator

The Savings Calculator enables you to calculate savings, that is, periodic payments to a savings account or investment. Choose Planning | Planning Tools | Savings Calculator. The Savings Calculator appears, as shown in Figure 15-4.

As with the other calculators, this calculator offers three options:

- **Ending Savings Balance** calculates the total amount saved at the end of the savings period based on the values you enter.
- **Regular Contribution** calculates the minimum amount you should regularly contribute to savings based on the values you enter.
- **Starting Savings Balance** calculates the amount of money you should currently have saved based on the values you enter.

Save For

The Save For drop-down box offers several options in which to enter values for Quicken to use in its calculations. Enter what you have today, the interest rate you are receiving, and the period of time you want to save. The drop-down list offers four options from which Quicken will calculate:

- Years
- Quarters
- Months
- Weeks

IN MY EXPERIENCE

If you have youngsters, this is a great way to teach them how to save. Perhaps your ten-year-old wants a new bike. The bike she wants costs $125.00, and she has saved $50.00 of her birthday money, meaning she must save an additional $75.00. If she believes she can save $15.00 each month from her $20.00 per month allowance, she can see that she can buy her new bike in five months as seen in Figure 15-4.

Inflation

Inflation options make complex calculations to account for the effect of inflation on your savings dollars. Enter your best estimate at the future inflation rate. Quicken will use this entry to determine the end result of the option you chose at the top of the Savings Calculator screen.

When you have entered all of the information, click Calculate to show the outcome. As with other calculators, use the View Schedule button to see the result of the calculations. Like the Retirement Calculator Schedule, this schedule can be printed.

After you have completed your calculations, click Done to close the Deposit Schedule, and click Done again to close the Savings Calculator.

Using the Loan Calculator

Quicken's Loan Calculator can quickly calculate the principal or periodic payment for a loan. Choose Planning | Planning Tools | Loan Calculator to open the Loan Calculator, as shown here.

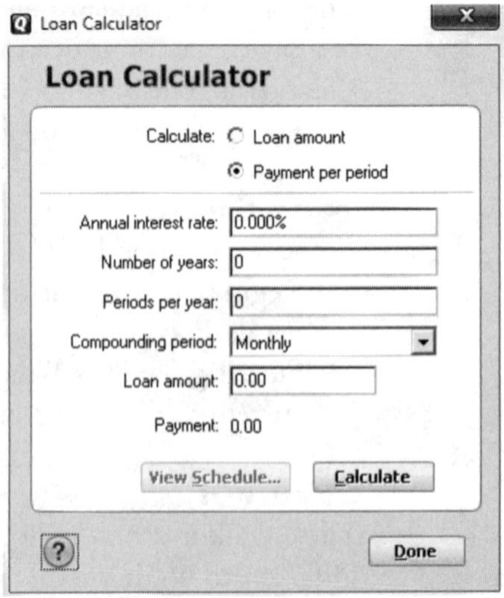

This handy tool will calculate the total loan amount if you enter the payments, interest, and other requested information. Its more common use is to calculate the total payment per period—usually a monthly payment.

Select one of the options, enter information in the remainder of the dialog, and click Calculate. Getting the answer is a lot quicker and easier with the Loan Calculator than using one of those loan books or creating formulas in an Excel spreadsheet to do the job. When you're finished, click Done.

You may calculate for two different options:

- **Loan Amount**, which calculates the amount of the total loan, given the interest rate, number of years, how many payments per year, and the interest rate on the loan.
- **Payment Per Period** calculates how much your payment would be each month (or other period) to pay off the loan amount you enter, given the interest rate, number of years you would have to pay back the loan, and how many times a year you would make payments.

Loan Information

Loan Information options enable you to enter values for Quicken to use in its calculations. The information you must enter varies depending on the Calculate option you select.

Annual Interest Rate   Enter the interest rate for this loan in the Annual Interest Rate field.

Number of Years, Periods Per Year, and Compounding Period   This tells Quicken how many years the loan is for and the number of times per year you will be paying on this loan. While 12 payments per year is the norm, you may choose any number. The number you choose impacts the Calculator's computations, so choose wisely.

Although the default entry in the Compounding Period is Monthly, most financial institutions compound daily and enter the total to your account at the end of each month.

View Schedule

Clicking the View Schedule button displays a printable amortization table that lists the payment number, the amount of the principal and interest paid at each payment, and the ending balance for the loan. Click the Print button at the top of the schedule to open the Print dialog and choose a printer. Click Print from the Print dialog to create your paper copy.

Calculate

The Calculate button at the bottom of the calculator performs the calculation based on your choices and the information you have entered.

Reducing Debt and Saving Money

Chapter 16

In This Chapter:

- *Taking control*
- *Using the Debt Reduction Planner*
- *Meeting Quicken's automatic budget*
- *Creating your own budget*
- *Organizing categories into groups*
- *Forecasting for your future*
- *Understanding why we save*
- *Saving strategically*
- *Seeing what's available*
- *Using Savings Goals*

As we face a different future from that of our parents and grandparents, the importance of saving money and reducing debt is becoming more apparent. The best way to prepare for life events is to build up your savings. Saving money is an important part of financial management. Savings enable you to take vacations and make major purchases without increasing debt, help your kids through college, handle emergencies, and have a comfortable retirement.

This chapter tells you about saving money and how tools within Quicken Personal Finance Software can help. If you're in debt and can't even think about saving until you dig your way out, this chapter can help you, too. It starts by covering Quicken tools for reducing your debt.

Reducing Your Debt

Consumer credit is a huge industry. It's still easy to get credit cards—even with the new regulations. And it's a lot easier to pay for something with a piece of plastic than with cold, hard cash. The "buy now, pay later" attitude has become an acceptable way of life. It's no wonder that many Americans are deeply in debt.

Those credit card bills can add up, however. And making just the minimum payment on each one only helps the credit card company keep you in debt—and paying interest—as long as possible. If you're in debt, don't skip this part of the chapter. It'll help you dig yourself out so you can build a solid financial future.

Taking Control

It's not easy to save money if most of your income is spent paying credit card bills and loan payments. If you're heavily in debt, you might even be having trouble keeping up with all your payments. But don't despair. There is hope! Here are a few simple things you can do to dig yourself out of debt.

Breaking the Pattern

Your first step to reducing debt must be to break the pattern of spending that got you where you are. For most people, that means cutting up credit cards. After all, it's tough to use a credit card if you can't hand it to a cashier at the checkout counter.

Before you take out the scissors, however, think about this: you may not have to cut up all of your credit cards. Leave yourself one or two major credit cards for emergencies, such as car trouble or unexpected visits to the doctor. The cards that should go are the store and gas credit cards. They can increase your debt, but they can be used in only a few places.

Here's the logic behind this strategy. If you have nine credit cards, each with a credit limit of $2,000, you potentially could owe $18,000, just on those credit cards. If the minimum monthly payment for each card is $75, before you even start each month, that's $675 for which you are obligated. If you have only two credit cards, each with a credit limit of $2,000, you can get yourself into only $4,000 of debt. Based on the same assumptions, you start your month owing only $150 in minimum payments.

Reducing Your Credit Limits

Sure, it's a great temptation to use your credit cards to spend just a little more every month—especially when you're not even close to your credit limit. But high credit limits are a trap. The credit card company or bank flatters you by offering to lend you more money. What they're really doing is setting you up so you'll owe them more—and pay them more in monthly finance and interest fees.

The next time your credit card company tells you they've raised your credit limit, do yourself a favor: call them up and tell them to reduce it right back to where it was—or lower!

Shopping for Cards with Better Interest Rates

Yes, it's nice to have a credit card with your picture on it. Or one that's gold, platinum, or titanium. Or one with your college, team, club, or association name on it. However, the purpose of a credit card is to purchase items on credit. That means you are renting the money from a credit card company or bank at a certain amount of interest. If you do not pay off the balance of a credit card at the end of each billing period, you pay the interest on that balance. The balance and interest rate determine how much it costs you to have that special picture or name on a plastic card in your wallet. Is it worth 19.8 percent a year? Or 34 percent?

Here's a reality-check exercise: Gather together all of your credit card bills for the most recent month. Now add up all the monthly finance fees and interest charges. Multiply that number by 12. The result is an approximation of what you pay in credit card interest each year. Now imagine how nice it would be to have that money in your hands the next time you go on vacation or need a down payment on a new car or home.

Low-interest credit cards are still widely available; try a web search. But before you apply for a new card, read the terms carefully. Many offer the low rates for a short, introductory period—usually no longer than 6 or 12 months. Some offer the low rate only on new purchases, while others offer the low rate only on balance transfers or cash advances. Be sure to find out what the rate is after the introductory period.

Here are two strategies for using a low-interest card:

- Consolidate your debt by transferring the balances of other credit cards to the new card. For this strategy, select a card that offers a low rate on balance transfers. When you transfer the balances, be sure to cut up the old cards so you don't use them to add more debt to your load.
- If you must use credit, use the low-interest card to make purchases. Even better, make the new card your emergency credit card and pay cash for everyday items. Be sure to cut up your old emergency card so you don't wind up using both of them.

And if you really like that special picture or name on the card in your wallet, call the credit card company and ask if they can give you a better interest rate.

In many instances, they can—especially when you tell them you want to close your account.

Consolidating Your Debt

Consolidating your debt may be one way to dig yourself out. By combining balances into one debt, whether through balance transfers to a single credit card or a debt consolidation loan, you're better able to pay off the balances without causing financial hardship. This is sometimes the only option when things have gotten completely out of control and you can't meet your debt obligations. However, make sure you have cut up the old cards so you don't add new debt to the older, consolidated amount.

If you do choose to use a debt consolidation company, investigate them thoroughly before you give them any money.

Although this can be a risky way to handle your debt, if you own a home, you might consider a home equity loan to consolidate your debt. The interest rate is usually lower than any credit card or debt consolidation loan, and the interest may be tax-deductible. There's more about home equity loans in Chapter 12.

Using Charge Cards, Not Credit Cards

There's a difference between a credit card and a charge card:

- **Credit cards** enable you to buy things on credit. If each month you pay less than what you owe, you are charged interest on your account balance. Most major "credit cards" are true credit cards. MasterCard, Visa, and Discover are three examples. Most store "charge cards" are also credit cards.
- **Charge cards** enable you to buy things on credit, too. But when the bill comes, you're expected to pay the entire balance. You don't have to pay any interest, but if you don't pay the entire balance on time, you may have to pay late fees and finance charges. One American Express plan is an example of a charge card.

The benefit of charge cards is that they make it impossible to get into serious debt. How can you owe the charge card company money if you must pay the balance in full every month? Using these cards prevents you from overspending. Every time you use the card to make a purchase, a little accountant in the back of your head should be adding the charge to a running total. You should stop spending when that total reaches the limit of your ability to pay.

Chapters 4 and 5 explain how you can use Quicken to track credit and charge card balances either manually or online. If you use Quicken to keep track of expenditures, you won't need that little accountant in the back of your head.

If you don't want an American Express card (for whatever reason), use another major credit card as a charge card. Just pay the entire balance each time you get a bill. If you don't carry a balance, you can't be charged interest. However, be aware that, with new banking regulations, many financial institutions are changing the way they deal with credit cards. Some have instituted fees and other charges. Be sure to read any literature that comes from your bank regarding their practices. Also, check out the financial institution's website for specific information on their credit practices.

If You Can't Stop Spending, Get Help

Many people who are deeply in debt may have a spending problem. They can't resist buying that fifth pair of running shoes or that trendy new outdoor furniture. They don't need the things they buy, but they buy them anyway. There's nothing wrong with that if your income can support your spending habits, but if your net worth is less than $0, it's a real problem—one that might require counseling to resolve.

The next time you make a purchase, stop for a moment and think about what you're buying. Is it something you need? Something you can use? Something you can justify spending the money on? If you can't answer yes to any of these questions, don't buy it. If you have to buy it anyway, it's time to seek professional help.

Living Debt-Free

It is possible to live debt-free—and you don't have to be rich to do it. Just stop relying on credit to make your purchases and spend only what you can afford.

Imagine how great it would feel to be completely debt-free. It's worth a try, isn't it?

Using the Debt Reduction Planner

Quicken's Debt Reduction Planner is a tool for helping you reduce your debt. You enter information about your financial situation, and Quicken develops a debt reduction plan for you. The Debt Reduction Planner is thorough, easy to use, and an excellent tool for teaching people how they can get out of debt as quickly as possible, saving hundreds (if not thousands) of dollars in interest charges.

If you're in serious debt—actually having trouble making ends meet because you can't seem to get any of your debts paid down—a pair of scissors, a telephone, and the Debt Reduction Planner are probably your three best tools for getting things under control.

First, use the scissors to cut up most, if not all, of your credit cards. Next, use the telephone to call your credit card companies and try to get your interest rates reduced. (The answer is always no until you ask!) Then use the Debt Reduction Planner to come up with a solid plan for reducing your debt.

Here's what the Debt Reduction Planner can help you do that you might not be able to do on your own:

- Objectively look at your debts and organize them by interest rate. The debts with the highest interest rate (that cost you the most) are the ones that are paid off first, thus saving you money.
- Show you the benefit of using some of your savings to reduce the balances on your most costly debt.
- Help you set up spending limits, with alerts, for the categories on which you spend too much money.
- Create an itemized plan based on real numbers that you can follow to reduce your debt.
- Show you, in dollars and cents, how much money you can save and how quickly you can become debt-free by following the plan.
- Help you to stop dreading the daily mail and its package of bills. Use the Debt Reduction Planner to get things under control.

Note that the Debt Reduction Planner is designed to create a plan to pay off your credit card debt first. While you can track and include all of your debt in the plan, Quicken suggests you begin with the debt that costs you the most (the debt with the highest interest rate). That means setting up accounts for your credit cards rather than simply tracking monthly payments as bills paid. Chapters 3 and 4 discuss the two different ways to track credit cards in Quicken.

NEW IN QUICKEN 2012

In Quicken 2012 the Debt Reduction Planner has been streamlined and is even easier to use than in previous versions. It is integrated with the Planning tab and provides Quicken users with a step-by-step method to eliminate debt.

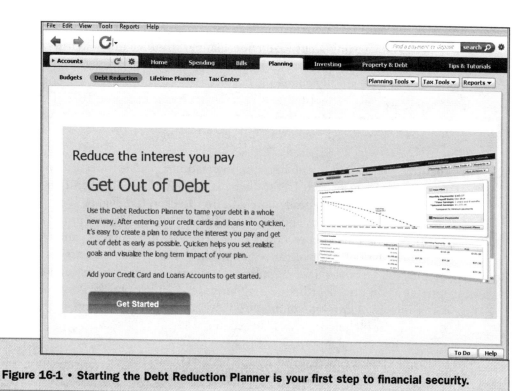

Figure 16-1 • Starting the Debt Reduction Planner is your first step to financial security.

NOTE

The wording on the initial debt reduction plan view is a little different depending on which accounts you have already set up. If you have not created any accounts, there is a line just above the Get Started button that says "Add your Accounts to get started." If you have created accounts other than credit cards and loans, the line will say "Add your Credit Card and Loans Accounts to get started."

Using the Debt Reduction Planner with Your Currently Entered Debt Accounts

To get started with the Debt Reduction Planner, from the Planning tab, choose the Debt Reduction button. The Debt Reduction Planner appears with its Get Started button as seen in Figure 16-1. What you see next depends on whether you have entered information about your debt into Quicken.

- If you have not yet entered any credit card or other debt into Quicken, you are prompted to do so after you click the Get Started button. The Add Account dialog appears so that you can enter your credit card. See Chapter 3 if you need to review how to enter a new account in Quicken. See the section "Starting Debt Reduction Planner from Scratch" later in this chapter to work with new accounts in the Debt Reduction Planner.

- If you have already entered debt information, you will see a dialog that reflects your current (entered) balances, as seen in Figure 16-2. The balance of this example assumes at least some of the information about what you owe is already entered into Quicken.

Identify Your Debts   The first step in creating a plan is to recognize what you owe. In the Identify Your Debts dialog you see the credit card and loan information you have already entered into Quicken (see Figure 16-2). Note that your current credit cards appear on the left side of the Planner in the Accounts To Include In This Plan section. Other debt accounts, such as your mortgage, appear on the right side of the screen in the Other Debt Accounts section. By default, the Debt Reduction Planner is designed to help you decrease high-interest credit card debt before long-term debt, which Quicken assumes to have lower interest. However, you may add any of these debt accounts to the Accounts To Include In This Plan section.

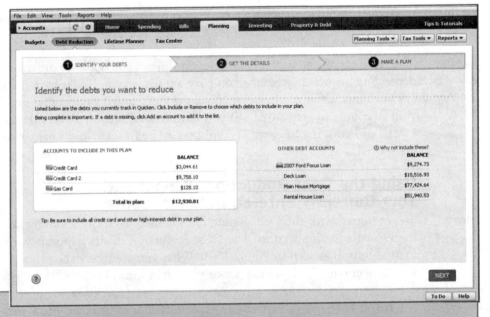

Figure 16-2 • Your first step in decreasing debt is identifying the debts you want to reduce.

1. To add an account to the plan:
   a. Position your mouse cursor to the left of the account you want to add to the Planner.
   b. Click Include. The account now appears as part of your plan.
2. To remove an account from the plan:
   a. Position your mouse cursor to the right of the account.
   b. Click Remove. The account is not included in the plan and appears in the Other Debt Accounts section of the Planner dialog as seen here.

ACCOUNTS TO INCLUDE IN THIS PLAN			OTHER DEBT ACCOUNTS		⑦ Why not include these?
	BALANCE				**BALANCE**
Credit Card	$3,044.61		2007 Ford Focus Loan		$9,274.73
Credit Card 2	$9,758.10		Deck Loan		$10,516.93
Gas Card	$128.10	Remove	Main House Mortgage		$77,424.64
			Rental House Loan		$51,940.53
Total in plan:	**$12,930.81**		Include	Store Account	$951.22

Tip: Be sure to include all credit card and other high-interest debt in your plan.

3. After you have chosen all the accounts you want to include in your plan, click Next.

Get the Details   The Get The Details dialog of the Debt Reduction Planner appears as seen in Figure 16-3. Here is where you enter the current interest rates and the minimum payments for each of the accounts you've included in your plan. If you have not yet entered this information into Quicken, you can find this information on your latest credit card statement or from the financial institution's website. If the current interest rate or minimum payment amounts are different than shown here, do the following:

1. Enter the actual interest rate in the Interest Rate field for each account. Click in the field, and any existing information is highlighted. Type in the correct rate.
2. Click in the minimum payment field for each account. If there is an existing amount, it will be highlighted and you can type in the proper amount. If you enter a minimum payment that does not meet the minimum based on the interest rate you entered, you'll see a warning message as shown on the next page.

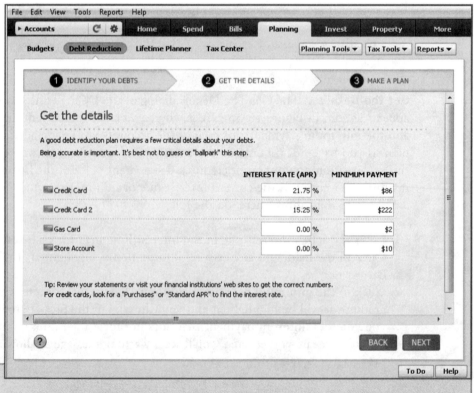

Get the details

A good debt reduction plan requires a few critical details about your debts.

Being accurate is important. It's best not to guess or "ballpark" this step.

	INTEREST RATE (APR)	MINIMUM PAYMENT
Credit Card	Based on this Interest Rate your minimum payment must be at least $86	
Credit Card 2		22
Gas Card	0.00 %	$2
Store Account	0.00 %	$10

You will not be able to continue until you make any necessary corrections. When the corrections are made, the Next button becomes available. Click Next to continue.

Figure 16-3 • Enter the interest rate and minimum payment amounts for each credit account to be included in your debt reduction plan.

Make Your Plan   The Make A Plan dialog is the workhorse section of the Debt Reduction Planner. You'll see that Quicken first calculates the plan based on your current payment amounts, as seen in Figure 16-4. There are several areas of information in this dialog with which you can work to create a plan that gets you out of debt sooner.

1. Your Debt Plan is shown at the upper-left corner of the Make A Plan dialog. As you start your planning, the amount displayed shows how much interest you will be paying if you continue paying just the minimum monthly payments. Below the minimum payment information is a chart showing when you will be debt-free making just the minimum payment on each outstanding account. The Your Debt Plan summary may appear anywhere along the slider above the chart, depending on the accounts and minimums in your plan.

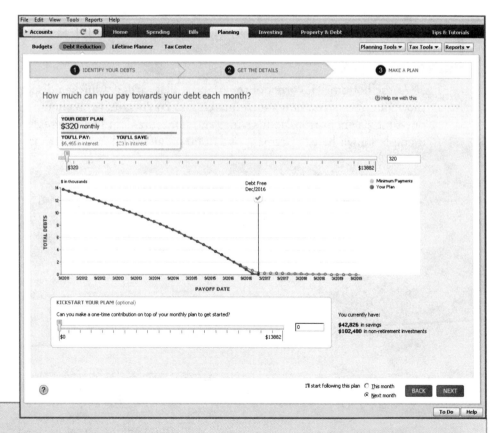

Figure 16-4 • Quicken shows you how long you'll be paying when you make only minimum monthly payments on your credit cards.

2. Move the slider or enter a new amount into the field to the right of the chart to see how much you will save by paying more than the minimum payment each month, as shown here. In our example, paying only $130 more each month results in a savings of nearly $3,000 over the next three years.

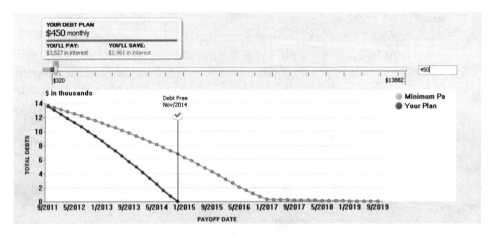

At the bottom-left corner of the Make A Plan dialog, Quicken displays another slider that shows you how much interest you could save if you choose to make a one-time payment from your savings and nonretirement investments. In the example shown here, a payment of $1,000 today would save even more in interest.

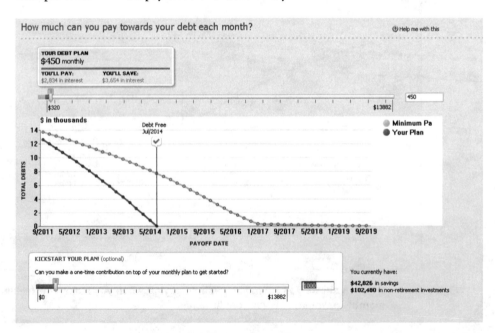

The Help Me With This link at the upper-right side of the Make A Plan dialog offers suggestions to help with your plan.

Once you have entered your plan amounts, you can finish your Debt Reduction Planner session by telling Quicken when you plan on starting the new payment schedule:

- Click This Month if you intend to pay more than minimum payments starting with this month's payments.
- Click Next Month if you've already paid the minimum for this month and want to start paying more than the minimum next month.

If you are satisfied with your plan, click Next to see your completed plan as seen in Figure 16-5.

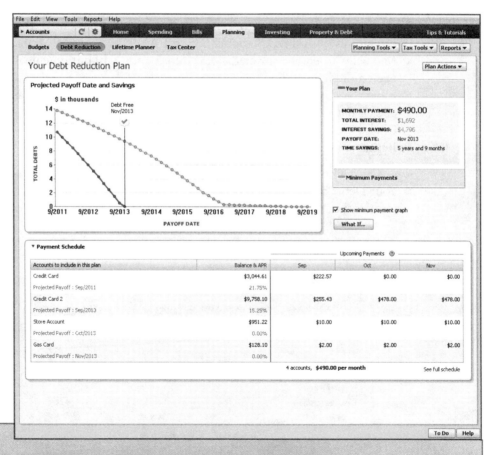

Figure 16-5 • Your completed debt reduction plan shows the result of the decisions you made.

In your Debt Reduction Plan dialog, you can make comparisons, tell Quicken how to display your plan, create What If alternatives, and see a schedule of your upcoming payments. You can use each section of the Debt Reduction Plan screen to learn more about your completed plan. See "Modifying Your Plan" later in this chapter for more information.

Starting Debt Reduction Planner from Scratch

If you have not entered any of your credit cards into Quicken, the Debt Reduction Planner will prompt you to do so. To get started, from the Planning tab, choose the Debt Reduction button. The Debt Reduction Planner appears with its Get Started button as seen in Figure 16-1.

1. Click the Get Started button. The Add Account dialog appears.
2. From the Add Account dialog, select Credit Card and click Next.
3. Enter your financial institution's name or select it from one of the lists. You can also use Advanced Setup, choosing I Want To Enter My Transactions Manually, to enter your credit card information without downloading. If you need more help adding your accounts, review Chapters 3 and 4.
4. Enter the date of your latest credit card statement, and enter the balance as of that date.
5. Click Next to complete the setup of your credit card.
6. Repeat steps 1 through 5 for each credit card with a balance.

Once all of your cards are entered, they will be reflected on the Identify Your Debts dialog in the Debt Planner as shown next. Once all of your information is complete, click Next to continue.

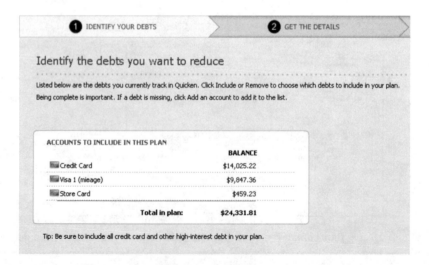

7. In the Get The Details dialog, enter the interest rate shown on your credit card statements for each item. You can move between the fields with your TAB key. Quicken will automatically enter the correct minimum payment based on the interest rate you enter.
8. Click Next to open the Make A Plan dialog. Follow the directions described in the "Make Your Plan" section shown earlier.

Modifying Your Plan

Once you have created your plan to reduce debt, you can adjust it at any time. To review the plan, go to the Planning tab and choose the Debt Reduction button. Your current plan appears.

Click the Plan Actions button and choose from one of the menu options:

- Click Explore Other Plan Options to open the Experiment With Other Plan Options dialog as described in "Use the What If Option" later in this chapter.
- Click Delete This Plan to delete your current plan and start over.
- Choose Edit Your Plan from the drop-down menu, as seen here, to work with your current plan.

Editing Your Plan   When you choose Edit Your Plan you are returned to the Identify Your Debts dialog, where you can remove or include any of your accounts. Once you have made changes, click Next to continue.

1. In the Get The Details dialog, make any necessary changes to interest rate and/or minimum payments. Click Next to open the Make A Plan dialog.
2. Make any changes in the Make A Plan dialog. Perhaps you've decided to pay an additional $50 per month to reduce debt faster. Or you've decided to take more money from savings. Whatever the choices, indicate as appropriate and click Next to complete your modifications. Click the Back button to return to an earlier dialog.

Once you have clicked Next in the Make A Plan dialog, you can't click Back. You'll need to edit the plan again to go back.

Once your current plan appears, you can click in several places to see current information.

3. Position your mouse cursor and click any "tick" on the Projected Payoff Date and Savings graph lines to see how much you will owe at a specific date. The

yellow line shows your debt as of a specific date paying minimum payments, while the green line shows the total projected debt at that date using your current reduction plan, as seen here.

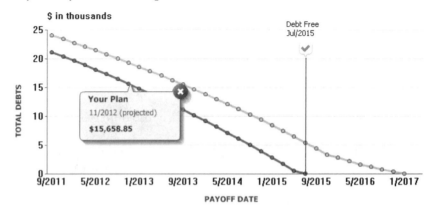

 You can choose to hide the minimum payment graph by clearing the Show Minimum Payment Graph check box.

Your plan displays the monthly payment, total interest you will pay, the interest savings, the payoff date, and how much time you will save over paying just minimum payments. Click the yellow bar to toggle and show the same information paying just the minimum required, as seen here.

Your Plan	
MONTHLY PAYMENT:	**$587.00**
TOTAL INTEREST:	$5,456
INTEREST SAVINGS:	$3,747
PAYOFF DATE:	Jul 2015
TIME SAVINGS:	1 years and 6 months

Minimum Payments

4. Click the downward-pointing arrow to the left of Payment Schedule to hide the Payment Schedule display. This choice also hides the Upcoming Payments information. If you click the arrow, the Payment Schedule section rolls up and the arrow points right.

5. Click See Full Schedule at the bottom-right corner of the Pay Schedule section to open the My Payment Schedule window, as seen next. This schedule includes currently due payments and displays any one-time payments, along with the projected balances after the payments are made. It shows the schedule for the entire life of the plan until you have paid off all the accounts you've included in the Debt Reduction Planner.

6. Click Print 6 Month Plan to open the Print dialog from which you can preview or print the payment schedule for the next six months. This schedule also shows the projected balance for each account after the plan's payment schedule is met.
7. Click Print 12 Month to print or preview the scheduled payment plan for the next year.
8. Click Done to close the schedule and return to your plan.

Use the What If Option

You may be pleased with your debt reduction plan as it stands but curious about what would happen if you applied your income tax return to your debt, or increased or decreased the monthly payment amounts. The What If option allows you to see these changes without really changing the plan. To see your options, select the What If button to open the Experiment With Other Plan Options dialog, as seen in Figure 16-6.

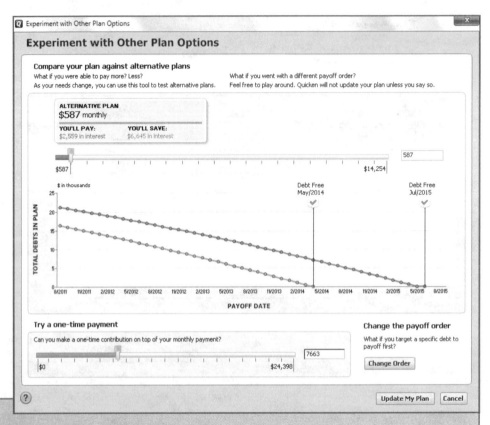

Figure 16-6 • You can experiment with different payment schedules without changing your plan in the Experiment With Other Plan Options dialog.

Change Your Monthly Payment   Either use the sliders or type a new amount directly in the payment field in the Experiment With Other Plan Options dialog. Position your mouse key on a tick on each graph line to see the total due at that point in time, as seen on the top of the next page.

Note that the second graph line in this dialog is blue, indicating your possible alternative plan.

Try a One-Time Payment   Considering selling that gas-guzzling second car? Did you win the sports pool at work? If you come into some extra cash, think about applying those funds directly to your debt load. Enter the amount in the payment field or use the slider to see how those extra funds would lessen your debt load.

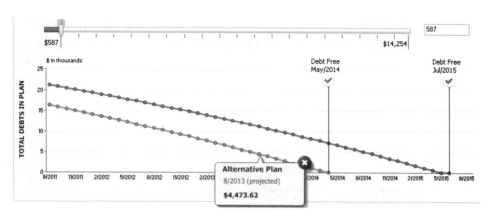

Change Payoff Order   By default, Quicken maximizes your interest savings by selecting the order in which you pay off your credit card debt. You can use another method if you choose. Click the Change Order button to open the Change Payoff Order dialog as seen next. From this dialog you can

- See the default order, which maximizes your interest savings.
- Use the Debt Snowball method.
- Choose the order yourself.

Select the Custom Order option to tell Quicken the order in which you plan to pay off your cards. When you select that option, small blue up and down arrows appear to the left of each card, as seen next. Click the upward-pointing arrow to move a card up in the list and the downward-pointing arrow to move it down.

⊙ **Custom order** (you choose)

Payoff order		Accounts in your plan	Balance & APR	Monthly Payment
1		Store Card	$459.23	$13.00
	▼	Projected Payoff : Apr/2016	21.45%	
2	▲	Visa 1 (mieage)	$9,847.36	$257.00
	▼	Projected Payoff : Jul/2016	19.25%	
3	▲	Credit Card	$14,025.22	$347.00
		Projected Payoff : Aug/2016	17.65%	

Click OK to save any changes to the Change Payoff Order dialog, or click Cancel to return to the Experiment With Other Plan Options dialog.

At the Experiment With Other Plan Options dialog, click Update My Plan if you have made changes you want to keep. If you are satisfied with your current plan, click Cancel to return to your Debt Reduction Plan screen.

IN MY EXPERIENCE

One of the suggested methods of paying off credit card debt is the Debt Snowball method. Using this method, a person starts by paying as much as possible on the card with the lowest balance while paying minimum payments on the rest of their credit cards. Then, when the first card is paid off, they apply the same method to the card with the next lowest balance and so on. The main advantage to this system is a feeling of accomplishment; one debt is paid off and gone.

While this method may not save the debtor as much interest as when paying off the card with the highest interest rate first, it is often used when one has a very high debt load and is feeling overwhelmed.

You can decide what method, or combination of methods, works the best for your financial situation. The main goal is to get out of debt and then stay away from the credit card debt merry-go-round.

Budgeting with Quicken

When money is tight and you're interested in meeting financial goals, it's time to create a budget and monitor your spending. But if you're serious about managing your money, consider creating a budget before you need one. Although Quicken's categories give you a clear understanding of where money comes from and where it goes, budgets enable you to set up predefined amounts for each category, thus helping you to control spending.

Budgets also make it easier to create forecasts of your future financial position. This makes it possible to see how much cash will be available at a future time—such as next summer for your vacation or when your child graduates from high school and wants to go to college.

The idea behind a budget is to determine expected income amounts and specify maximum amounts for expenditures. This helps prevent you from spending more than you earn. It also enables you to control your spending in certain categories. For example, say you realize that you go out for dinner a lot more often than you should. You can set a budget for the Dining category and track your spending to make sure you don't exceed the budget. You'll eat at home more often and save money.

If you don't like the word "budget," consider it as a "spending" or even a "making better use of our money" plan.

This section explains how Quicken works with budgets, and how you can use the budgeting tools to set up a budget and use it to keep track of your spending. Hopefully you'll see that budgeting is a great way to keep spending under control.

Meeting Quicken's Automatic Budget

Quicken automatically generates a budget for you based on past transactions. You can edit the budget it creates to meet your needs, or you can create a budget from scratch.

The quickest and easiest way to create a budget is to let Quicken do it for you based on your income and expenditures. For Quicken to create an accurate budget, however, you must have several months' worth of transactions in your Quicken data file. Otherwise, the budget may not reflect all regular income and expenses.

For our example, we've started a small checking account with only a few expenses, as seen in Figure 16-7. As you can see, it spans only five months of activity and uses only three expense categories.

Figure 16-7 • Quicken uses your entries to create an automatic budget.

To get started, choose the Planning tab and click the Budgets button. Click the Get Started button to open the Create A New Budget dialog as seen here. Quicken assigns the default name of Budget 1. If you wish to change the name, highlight it and type in your own.

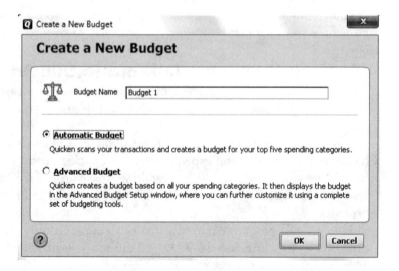

Click OK to continue. Your automatic budget appears as seen in Figure 16-8. Since we created this budget from very few transactions, you see only three expense categories. Normally, the automatic budget graphs the top five expenses and puts all of the other expenses into the Everything Else category.

Understanding Quicken's Automatic Budget

Quicken creates its budget based the amount you spent on each category and the total number of months in which you spent money in that category. In our example, we spend a total of $91.00 on car washes for the time period in which we entered transactions. From the example in Figure 16-7, you can see that we spent the following:

$$\$12.00 \text{ in April} + \$14.00 \text{ in May} + \$23.00 \text{ in June} +$$
$$\$23.00 \text{ in July} + \$19.00 \text{ in August}$$

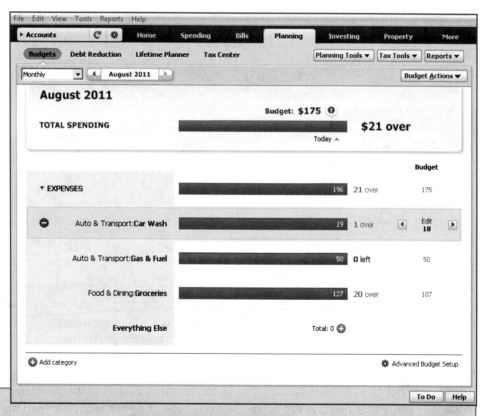

Figure 16-8 • The automatic budget is based on your spending.

This adds up to $91.00 for the five months in which we entered transactions. $91.00 divided by the five months is an average of $18.20 per month, which Quicken rounds to the nearest dollar. Thus, $18 is displayed in the Budget column of our automatic budget. Since we spent $19.00 in the month of August, we are $1 over the "budgeted" average amount computed by Quicken.

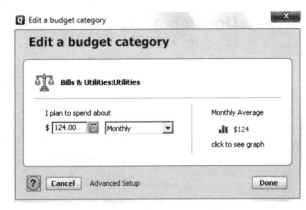

If you want to adjust the "budgeted average" displayed by Quicken, click the word Edit in the Budget column to open the Edit A Budget Category dialog, seen here. As you can see, the monthly average is displayed in the dollar field.

You can type any number in the dollar field to tell Quicken how much to budget for this category. Then, from the drop-down list, tell Quicken how often you plan on spending this amount. You may choose from

- Monthly
- Daily
- Weekly
- Every Two Weeks
- Twice A Month
- Every Two Months
- Quarterly
- Twice A Year
- Yearly

Click the Monthly Average amount at the right of the dialog to display a graph of your spending in this category, as seen next. There are two tabs within this graph. The History tab shows how much you've spent for this category over the time period in your budget. Note that the average, in this case $18, is portrayed by a red line through the spending columns.

Click any of the bars displayed in the monthly budget graph to open a columnar graph that displays the average monthly spending for each month. This columnar graph is not available in time periods other than the monthly budget.

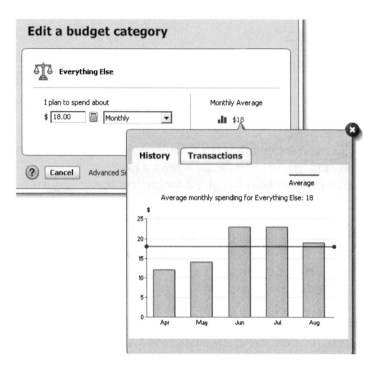

The Transactions tab displays a list of each transaction during the time period of your budget. When you are done reviewing the information displayed in the graph, click the X in the gray circle at the upper-right corner to close the graph, and click Done in the Edit A Budget Category dialog to return to your budget.

 You can also press ESC on your keyboard to close the spending graph.

Click the colored area of the Total Spending bar in the budget's bar graph to see both your total spending and how much you are over budget for the currently selected month, as shown here.

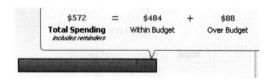

As you see in Figure 16-8, the default time period for Quicken's automatic budget is Monthly. The date drop-down list displays your options:

- Last 3 Months
- Last 6 Months
- Quarter To Date
- Last Quarter

- Year To Date
- Last Year
- All Time (this option includes all entries you have made to your spending accounts, and depending on how long you've been entering data into Quicken and the speed of your computer, it may take a moment or two to create)

The current month is the default entry, but you can move between months by using the left- or right-facing arrows. However, you can only go backward to earlier months. For example, if the current month is October, you can go back to any earlier month, but you cannot go forward to November.

If you go back a month, the drop-down list options are:

- Use Current Budget-Results Based On Current Budget
- Use Historical Budget-Results Based On Budget Settings In Place On (name of the month)

Use the Current Month's Results   If you choose to use the current month's results, the drop-down list changes to Use Current Budget. Using the current month's results compares what you spent in the previous month to the average budget amount computed in the current month. In our example, since we spent $23.00 for car washes in July, we would be $5.00 over the "budgeted" amount calculated in August. Since we spent $14.00 in the same category in May, the budget would show that we had $4.00 "left" or "under-budget" as seen here.

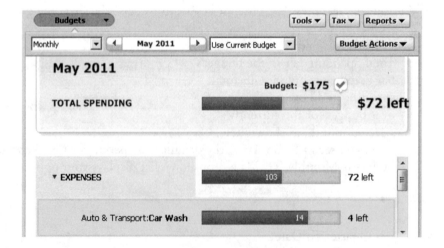

The Total Spending computation at the top of the page compares all of your spending to the monthly average. If any of your expenses are "over budget," meaning over the calculated average for the month, a small warning icon appears. This icon, a white exclamation point in a gold triangle, contains a message warning you of the fact, as seen next.

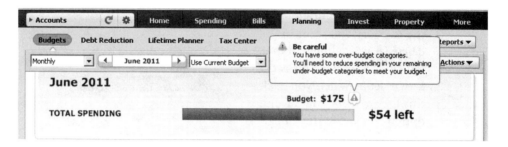

In addition to the white exclamation point in the gold triangle, you may see two other icons in the same location. A green check mark indicates you have not gone over budget (over average in the automatic budget) for the current month. A white exclamation point in a red circle warns that you have exceeded your budget for the selected time period.

Using Historical Results   If you have chosen Use Historical Budget-Results Based On Budget Settings In Place On (name of month), the drop-down list changes to Use Historical Budget and the selected month field moves to the left. You can only change to a historical budget when you are in the Monthly view.

As an example, let's say you have a food and dining budget of $500 in July. When August comes around, you decide to lower the budget to $400. With the historical budget settings, July will continue to have a food and dining budget of $500, and August will be $400. This setting only affects what Quicken shows you when you are *reviewing* a budget; it has no effect on setting a budget.

Since your budgets are based on information that has already transpired, you cannot edit any of the budget amounts in the Budget column in earlier months.

Adding Categories   To add a category to the budget, click the Add Category button at the bottom of the Budget window. This displays the Add A Budget Category dialog. Choose a category from the drop-down list, and click Next.

You are asked how much you plan on spending per month in this category. Enter the amount you plan on spending and, if the amount is annual, quarterly, or for any time period other than monthly, click the drop-down list arrow to choose from its several options.

If you are unsure about what to enter as your planned spending, click the Monthly Average graph to see what you have spent over the last few months.

Click Done to close the dialog.

Removing Categories Click the category you want to delete. A white line within a red circle appears. This is the Delete icon. When you click this Delete icon, you have the option to remove this category from this budget, as seen here.

Budget Actions The Budget Actions button at the right of your budget screen opens a menu, as seen here. The actions you can perform with this menu are as follows:

- **Advanced Budget** opens the Advanced Budget Setup dialog. See "Creating Your Own Budget" later in this chapter.
- **Edit Budget Name** opens the Edit Budget Name dialog with which you can change the name of the current budget.
- **Budget Reports** opens a submenu where you can see a report of your budgets on either a monthly or a comparison basis.
- **Delete This Budget** allows you to delete the current budget. The Delete Budget dialog appears and explains that all information will be deleted. You may choose the Delete button to delete the budget or Cancel to return to the current budget.

IN MY EXPERIENCE

When working with Quicken budgets, occasionally there may be one-time items you do not want to include, such as a large down payment on a new car. Normally this expense would be categorized as an Auto & Transport expense, but would certainly skew your budget if the amount were included. You might consider creating a subcategory under Auto & Transport entitled Down Payment and then excluding that item from your budget. See "Creating Your Own Budget" in this chapter to understand how to exclude a category or subcategory from a budget.

- **Duplicate This Budget** opens a dialog with which you can duplicate this budget and give your duplicate budget a new name.
- **Create New Budget** opens a dialog with which you can create a budget. See "Creating Your Own Budget" later in this chapter for directions.

Creating Your Own Budget

While Quicken's automatic budget is great for a quick overview of your spending, creating your own budget allows you to carefully look at each category to estimate your future expenses.

If you have not yet created a budget, the easiest way to get started is to choose the Planning tab and click the Budgets button. This opens the Get Started screen as described in "Meeting Quicken's Automatic Budget" earlier in this chapter. Click the Get Started button, which opens the Create A New Budget dialog. However, this time, choose the Advanced Budget option and click OK. The Advanced Budget Setup dialog appears as seen in Figure 16-9.

If you have created a budget with the Automatic Budget setup, open that budget and choose the Advanced Budget Setup link at the bottom-right corner of the Automatic Budget window.

As you can see, the Advanced Budget Setup dialog shows the information about your expenses in a slightly different manner than the automatic budget.

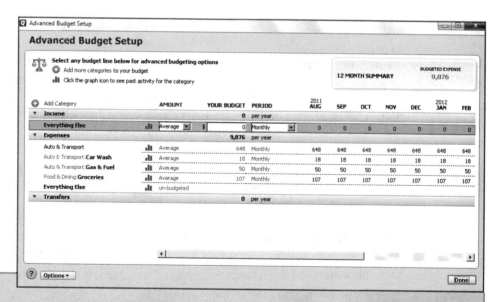

Figure 16-9 • Using the Advanced Budget Setup dialog can help you create a workable spending plan.

Using the Advanced Budget's Options

At the bottom left of the Advanced Budget Setup dialog is the Options button. From here you can do the following:

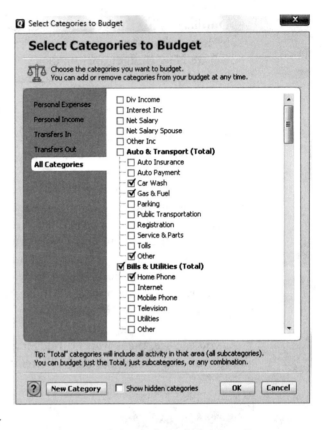

- **Select Categories To Budget**   Click this option to open the Select Categories To Budget dialog. From this list, shown here, you can check the categories you want to include in your budget. If you choose a main category with (Total) included in its title, you may choose to budget the entire main category or just its subcategories or any combination of the two. At the bottom of the dialog, click New Category to create a new category. You can immediately include this new category in your budget. If you want to include categories you have hidden in your budget, click Show Hidden Categories check box. Click OK to close the Select Categories To Budget dialog and return to your budget.

You may use the Add More Categories icon (a white plus sign in a green circle) at the top of your budget or the Add More Categories link to add one or more new categories to your budget

- **Assign Category Groups**   This option opens the Assign Category Groups dialog. See "Organizing Categories into Groups" later in this chapter for more information.

Setting a Budget Item's Options   You can modify the budget for a category by modifying its settings. If you'd like an idea of what has happened in the past, click the small blue graph icon next to the Amount column for each item.

- **Amount**   By default, the amount displayed in each item's amount field is the average amount you have spent over the number of months you have been using Quicken. The number appears in each month's amount as seen in Figure 16-9. However, you have to move the horizontal scroll bar to the right to see other months. This average appears in the Your Budget column.
- **Your Budget**   If you have opted to enter a specific amount for each month of the next 12 months, this column is not available. If you choose Average in the Amount column, this field becomes available for you to enter an amount.
- **Period**   When you choose to use an average amount, the Period column becomes available. After you have entered an amount in the Your Budget column, click the Period drop-down list to choose from the several options. Quicken will automatically average the amount over the next 12 months. In our example shown here, we've chosen to budget an annual amount of $96, which Quicken averages and shows as $8 in each month's column

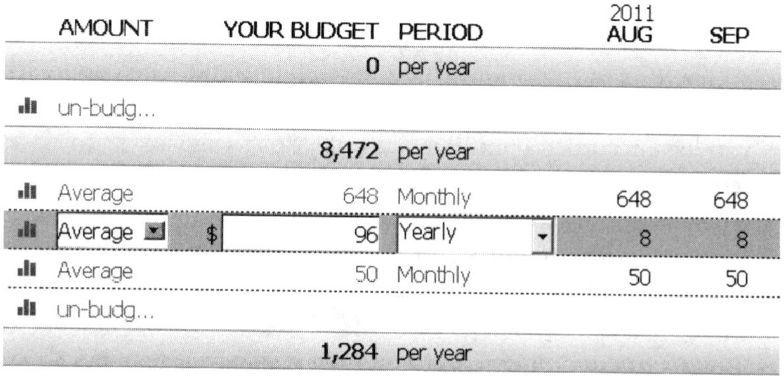

AMOUNT	YOUR BUDGET	PERIOD	2011 AUG	SEP
	0	per year		
un-budg…				
	8,472	per year		
Average	648	Monthly	648	648
Average ▾ $	96	Yearly ▾	8	8
Average	50	Monthly	50	50
un-budg…				
	1,284	per year		

- **Month**   Each of the next 12 months is shown with its own column so that you may enter specific information or view Quicken's calculated averages.

When you have completed setting each of your budget options, click Done to close your advanced budget. You are returned to the Budgets section of the Planning tab.

Viewing a Specific Budget   If you have created more than one budget, you can choose to work with just one. From the Planning tab, click Budgets. Click the name drop-down list to see your choices. Click the budget you want to use, as seen here.

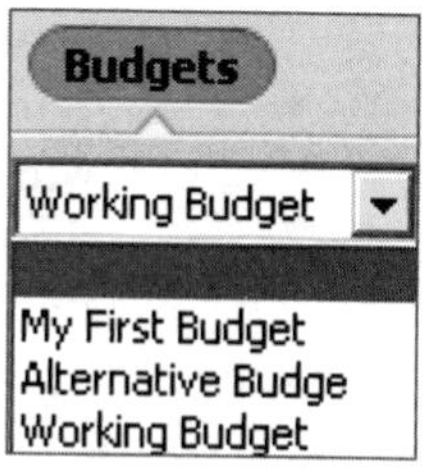

Budgets

Working Budget ▾

My First Budget
Alternative Budge
Working Budget

To edit a budget's name, select the budget name and click the Budget Actions button at the upper-right corner of the budget window. Select Edit Budget Name from the drop-down list. Enter a name in the Edit Budget Name dialog that appears, and click OK.

Deleting a Budget To delete a budget, select the budget name. From the Budget Actions menu, choose Delete This Budget. The Delete Budget dialog appears, as shown here. Click Delete to eliminate this budget or Cancel to close the dialog.

Comparing a Budget to Actual Transactions

Once you have created a budget you can live with, it's a good idea to periodically compare your actual income and expenditures to budgeted amounts. Quicken lets you do this in a number of different ways.

There's one important thing to keep in mind when comparing budgeted amounts to actual results: make sure your comparison is for the period for which you have recorded data. For example, don't view a year-to-date (YTD) budget report if you began entering data into Quicken in March. Instead, customize the report to show actual transactions beginning in March. Details about creating and customizing reports and graphs are in Chapter 8.

Budget Reports and Graphs The Budget Reports option in the Budget Actions menu offers two reports for comparing budgeted amounts to actual results:

- **Budget Report** displays actual and budgeted transactions.
- **Monthly Budget Report** displays the actual and budgeted transactions by month as well as a graph

IN MY EXPERIENCE

Quicken builds both the Automatic Budget and the Advanced Budget by using the most recent 12 months of transactions in all spending accounts. If you do not have a complete 12 months of transactions, Quicken uses the period in which you have entered transactions. For example, if you have nine months of transactions, with the first month having no transactions before the 20th of the month and a last month with no transactions after the 10th of the month, Quicken will use the middle seven months to calculate the average by summing up all the transactions in a category minus any significantly large transactions that are considered anomalies, and dividing by the number of good months, in this case, seven.

that shows if the result was favorable or unfavorable. This means your spending was within your budget (favorable) or exceeded your budgeted amount (unfavorable). An example is shown in Figure 16-10.

Chapter 8 explains how to customize reports and graphs.

Budget Comparison Graph   You can display your budget graph in a custom view of the Quicken Home window. This feature enables you to keep an eye on the budget categories and groups that interest you most.

To use this feature, switch to the Home tab and click Customize. Use the Customize View dialog as instructed in Appendix B. A Budget snapshot is found under Planning that provides a connection to your budget information.

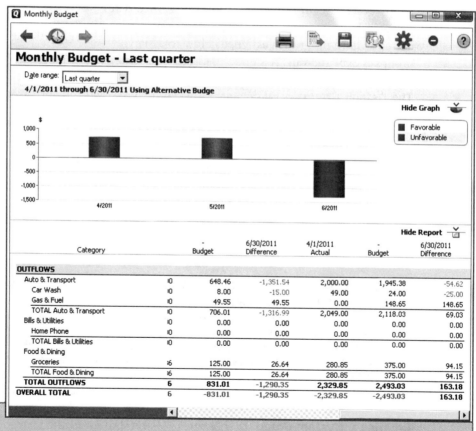

Figure 16-10 • A budget report compares actual and budgeted amounts.

Organizing Categories into Groups

Budgets are based on transactions recorded for categories and subcategories. (That's why it's important to categorize all your transactions—and not to the Miscellaneous category!) Quicken also enables you to organize categories by customizable category groups. Although you don't have to use the Groups feature when creating your budget—it's entirely optional—grouping similar categories together can simplify your budget.

Choose Tools | Category List to display the window. (You can also open the Category List by pressing SHIFT-CTRL-C.) If the Group column does not appear in your list, choose Show Category Group from the Options menu at the bottom of the window to display it, as shown. By default, Quicken assigns nearly every category to either the Personal Income or Personal Expense group. Your bank and investment accounts have no groups assigned. How to assign groups is explained in "Assigning a Group to a Category," later in this chapter.

Options ▼
✓ Show Category Usage
Show Description
✓ Show Category Group
✓ Show Type
✓ Show Tax Line Item
Assign category groups
Manage Categories

The Default Groups   By default, Quicken includes two category groups that it assigns to the categories it creates when you first set up your Quicken data file:

- **Personal Income** is for earned income, such as your salary, and miscellaneous income items, such as interest, dividends, and gifts received.
- **Personal Expenses** are all of your personal expenses, items you pay for and record in your account registers.
- **Transfers** are for transfers between existing accounts. You may not see this available until you have added several accounts to your Quicken file.

IN MY EXPERIENCE

In addition, if your Quicken data file includes business-related categories, Quicken includes Business Income and Business Expenses groups to track the income and expenses from your business.

To create a Business Income or Business Expense group, you must have created either an income or expense category and assigned it to a business tax schedule in the Tax Reporting tab of the New Category setup.

Creating a Custom Group   To create a custom group, in the Category List window, click Options and choose Assign Category Groups. The Assign Category Groups dialog appears, as seen in Figure 16-11.

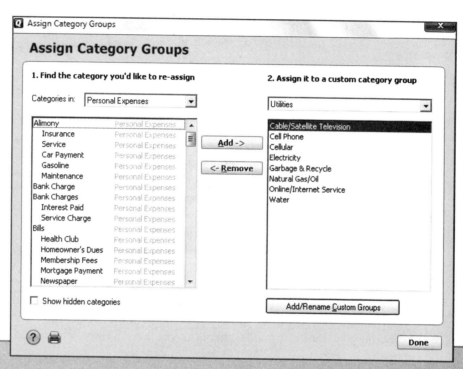

Figure 16-11 • You can assign category groups and create new groups to better organize your transactions.

If this is the first custom group you are creating, the Assign Category Group dialog will display a message that you have not created any custom groups, as seen here.

Click the Add Custom Groups button (or if you have already added a custom group, click the Add/Rename Custom Groups button) to open the Custom Category Groups dialog. When it appears, click New to open the Create Custom Group dialog. Type the name of your custom group and click OK.

The new group appears in the Custom Category Groups dialog as seen on the next page. Click Done to close the Custom Category Groups dialog and return to the Assign Category Groups dialog.

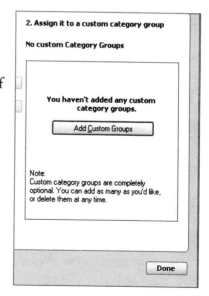

To add categories to your new group, select a category from the list on the left side of the dialog and click Add. It will appear on the right side of the dialog in the 2. Assign It To A Custom Category Group column. Continue through the list of categories until you have finished selecting the categories you want to include in this group.

You can add more than one item at a time by choosing the first item in a group of categories in the left column, holding down your SHIFT key, and choosing several categories in a row. You can select categories from several locations in the list on the left side as well. To do this, hold down your CTRL key and while continuing to hold it down, click the items you want. If you have to scroll, keep holding down the CTRL key until you have selected (clicked) all the categories you want to include. Then, release the CTRL key and click the Add button. All of your selected items will appear in the right column.

Should you want to include categories you have hidden, click the Show Hidden Categories check box.

If you want to remove a category, select it from the list in the right column and click Remove. It will once again appear in the left column.

After you have completed your choices for this custom group, click Done to close the Assign Category Groups dialog and return to the Category List.

Assigning a Group to a Category

You can assign a standard or a custom group to a new category. In the Category List window, click New to create a new category. The Set Up Category dialog appears. Enter the category name and whether it is an income or an expense item. Click the arrow next to the Group box to display the drop-down list and choose a group from the list.

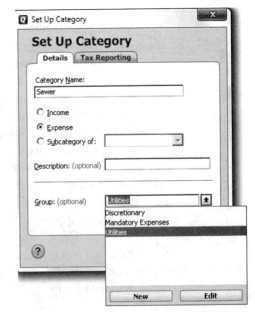

You can create a new group directly from this dialog by clicking the New button, or edit an existing group by clicking Edit. (Chapter 2 discusses creating new categories in more detail.) After you have selected the group, click OK to include the group with this category and save your new category to the Category List.

If you have not yet created any custom category groups, you will not see the Group field in the Set Up Category dialog. Return to the Category List, click Options | Assign Category Groups, and create at least one custom category group.

To add a group to an existing category, select the category, and, from the Action column, click Edit to open the Set Up Category dialog. Click the arrow next to the Group box to display the Group drop-down list. If the category is one of the default Quicken categories, the Personal Expenses group may appear in the Group box, although it is not an option in the group list. Simply click the group to which you want this category assigned, and click OK. The custom group is now assigned to this existing category.

Modifying the Custom Category Group list   You can modify or delete custom category group names. From the Category List, click Options | Assign Category Groups, and click Add/Rename Custom Groups. The Custom Category Groups dialog appears. Select a group name, and click Rename to rename an existing group. To delete a custom category group, select the group name and click Delete.

After you have made your changes, click Done to return to the Assign Category Groups dialog. Click Done one more time to close the Assign Category Groups dialog and return to the Category List.

Where Does Your Money Go?

As you work with the various planners and reports available in Quicken, you are probably getting more comfortable understanding just where your hard-earned dollars are going. If you've used the Debt Reduction Planner and created a budget, you may also be thinking about the future and how your financial situation will be improving. Quicken offers several tools that help you understand where you will be spending your funds. Using Quicken's Projected Balances tool will help you to understand what expenditures are coming up in the near future. Then, in the second part of this section, we'll discuss saving your money.

Remember when you got your first piggy bank? It may not have looked like a pig, but it had a slot for slipping in coins and, if you were lucky, a removable rubber plug on the bottom that made it easy to get the coins out when you needed them. Whoever gave you the bank was trying to teach you your first financial management lesson: save money.

As an adult, things are a little more complex. See the section entitled "Understanding Why We Save," which explains why you should save, provides some saving strategies, and tells you about the types of savings accounts that make your old piggy bank obsolete.

Forecasting for Your Future

Forecasting uses known and estimated transactions to provide a general overview of your future financial situation. This "crystal ball" can help you spot potential cash flow problems (or surpluses) so you can prepare for them. Quicken helps you to see your projected balances and can also help you create savings goals.

Projected Balances

Quicken helps you keep up with what your account balances will be in the future with the Projected Balances report. This report can be found in the Bills tab, as a link from the Stay On Top Of Monthly Bills section in the Main View of the Home tab, and by choosing the Planning tab and then Planning Tools | Projected Balances.

You can set the range for the Projected Balances report for the next 7 days, next 14 days, next 30 or 90 days, or the next 12 months, or even customize a range that suits your requirements. See Figure 16-12 for an example of the Projected Balances report for the next 12 months. See Chapter 6 for more information on Projected Balance.

Understanding Why We Save

Most people save money so there's money to spend when they need it. Others save for a particular purpose. Still others save because they have so much they can't spend it all. Here's a closer look at why saving makes sense.

Saving for "Rainy Days"

When people say they are "saving for a rainy day," they probably aren't talking about the weather. They're talking about bad times or emergencies—situations when they'll need extra cash.

For example, suppose the family car needs a new transmission. Or your beloved dog needs eye surgery. Or your daughter manages to break her violin three days before the big recital. In the "rainy day" scheme of things, these might be light drizzles. But your savings can help keep you dry.

If your paychecks stop coming, do you have enough savings to support yourself or your family until you can get another source of income? On the

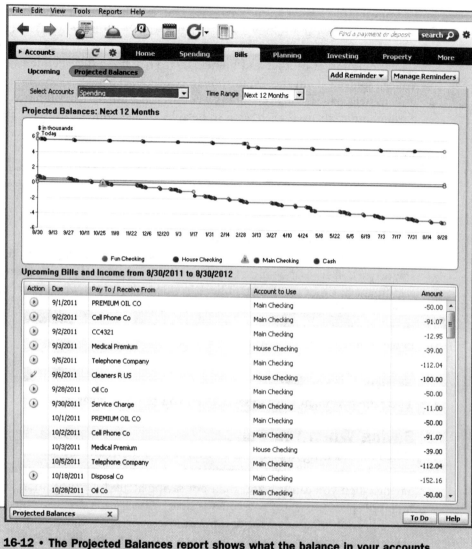

Figure 16-12 • The Projected Balances report shows what the balance in your accounts may be for a selected time period.

"rainy day" scale, this could be a torrential downpour. Your savings can be a good umbrella.

Saving for a Goal

Planning for your future often includes planning for events that affect your life—and your wallet. Saving money for specific events can help make these events memorable for what they are, rather than what they cost.

For example, take a recently engaged couple, Maxine and Jack. They plan to marry within a year and buy a house right away. Within five years, they plan to have their first child. That's when Maxine will leave her job to start the more demanding job of mother and homemaker. They hope their children will go to college someday, and they want to help cover the expenses. They also want to be able to help pay for their children's weddings. Eventually, they'll retire. And throughout their lives, they want to be able to take annual family vacations, buy a new car every six years or so, and get season tickets for their local football team's games.

All of these things are major events in Maxine's and Jack's lives. Saving in advance for each of these events will make them possible—without going into debt.

Saving for Peace of Mind

Some people save money because events in their lives showed them the importance of having savings. Children who lived through the Depression or bad financial times for their families grew up to be adults who understand the value of money and try hard to keep some available. They don't want to repeat the hard times they went through. Having healthy savings accounts gives them peace of mind.

Saving Strategically

There are two main ways to save: when you can or regularly.

Saving When You Can

When money is tight, saving can be difficult. People who are serious about saving, however, will force themselves to save as much as possible when they can. Saving when you can is better than not saving at all. One suggestion given by financial specialists is to "pay yourself first." This means that you consistently take a portion of any income and put it into a savings account. The amount really doesn't matter; it is the consistency that creates the habit.

Saving Regularly

A better way to save money is to save a set amount periodically. For example, consider putting away $25 every week or $200 every month. Timing this with your paycheck makes sense; you can make a split deposit for the check. A savings like this is called an annuity, and you'd be surprised at how quickly the money can accumulate.

Seeing What's Available

There are different types of savings accounts, each with its own benefits and drawbacks. Here's a quick look at them.

Keep in mind that all the accounts discussed in this chapter (except where noted) should be insured by the FDIC (Federal Deposit Insurance Corporation). This organization covers savings deposits up to $250,000 per entity (person or company) per bank, thus protecting you from loss in the event of a bank failure. (The $250,000 insured amount is true through December 31, 2013.)

Standard Savings Accounts

All banks and credit unions offer savings accounts, and most accommodate any balance. Savings accounts pay a small amount of interest on your balance and allow you to deposit or withdraw funds at any time.

Payroll Savings

If your company offers it, consider having a small portion of each paycheck deducted directly and deposited into your savings account. This is a great feature for people who have trouble saving money, because the money comes out of their paychecks before they can see and spend it. It's as if the money never existed, when in reality, it's accumulating in an interest-bearing account. In case you're wondering, the withdrawn funds are included in your taxable income.

Certificates of Deposit

A certificate of deposit, or CD, is an account, normally with a bank, that requires you to keep the money on deposit for a specific length of time. Your earnings are based on a higher, fixed-interest rate than what is available for a regular savings account. The longer the term of the deposit and the more money deposited, the higher the rate. At the CD's maturity date, you can "roll over" the deposit to a new account that may have a different interest rate, or you can take back the cash. If you withdraw the money before the CD's maturity date, you pay a penalty, which can sometimes exceed the amount of the interest earned.

Money Market Accounts

There are two types of money market accounts. A money market deposit account held at a regularly chartered bank is insured up to $250,000 through December 31, 2013. (At this writing, the amount will revert to $100,000 as of January 1, 2014, but future legislation could change that.) A money market mutual account is actually a form of investment, but it should be included here because some banks offer it. It has a higher rate of return than a regular savings account but is not insured by the FDIC. It is considered a conservative investment and can be treated just like a savings account for depositing money. There may, however, be restrictions on the number of withdrawals you can make each month.

Interest-Bearing Checking Accounts

Some institutions offer interest-bearing checking accounts. They usually have minimum balance requirements, however, forcing you to keep a certain amount of money in the account at all times. Some banks offer rewards or incentives of higher interest rates to encourage you to keep higher balances in your checking accounts.

Using Savings Goals

Quicken's Savings Goals feature helps you save money by "hiding" funds in an account. You set up a savings goal and make contributions to it using the Savings Goals window. Although the money never leaves the source bank account, it is deducted in the account register, thus reducing the account balance in Quicken. If you can't see the money in your account, you're less likely to spend it.

Getting Started

Open the Savings Goals window by choosing Planning | Planning Tools | Savings Goals. Figure 6-13 shows what the window looks like with one savings goal already created.

The top half of the Savings Goals window seen in the figure lists the savings goals you have created with Quicken. The bottom half shows the progress for the

---

IN MY EXPERIENCE

Kind of sounds silly, doesn't it? Using Quicken to transfer money from your checking account to another account that doesn't even exist?

But don't laugh—the Savings Goals feature really works. A friend used a similar technique. She simply deducted $10 or $20 from her checking account balance, thus giving the illusion that she had less money in the account than was really there. This helped her save money by making her think twice about writing a check for something they really didn't need. It prevented her from bouncing checks during the time when the needs of her growing family caused her to keep a dangerously low checking account balance. When her daughter graduated from high school, there was enough money in this "secret" account to pay for a new laptop as the girl went off to college!

Give it a try and see for yourself!

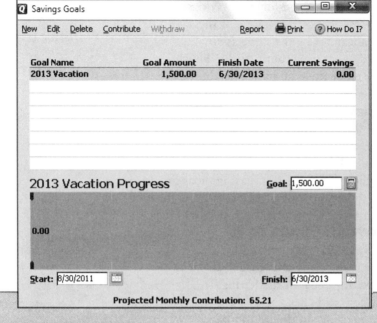

Figure 16-13 • Use Savings Goals to help meet future needs.

selected goal. The amount you have to put away each month is shown at the bottom of the window. Use the buttons to work with the window's contents:

- **New** enables you to create a savings goal.
- **Edit** enables you to modify the selected savings goal.
- **Delete** removes the selected savings goal.
- **Contribute** enables you to contribute funds from a Quicken account to the selected savings goal.
- **Withdraw** enables you to remove funds from a savings goal and return them to a Quicken account.
- **Report** creates a report of the activity for savings goals.
- **Print** prints a report of savings goal details.
- **How Do I?** displays the Quicken Personal Finances Help window with instructions for using the Savings Goals feature.

Creating a Savings Goal

To create a savings goal, click the New button in the Savings Goals window. The Create New Savings Goal dialog, which is shown next, appears.

Enter the information for your savings goal in the text boxes. The name of the savings goal cannot be the same as any Quicken category or account. In the Finish Date field, enter the date by which you want to have the money saved. For example, if you're using a savings goal to give your parents a 50th wedding anniversary party, the finish date should be shortly before the date you've planned for the party. When you've finished, click OK to add the savings goal to the list in the Savings Goals window.

Contributing Funds to a Savings Goal

To contribute funds to a savings goal, select the savings goal in the Savings Goals window and click the Contribute button on the button bar. The Contribute To Goal dialog, shown here, appears.

Select the account from which you want to transfer the money from the drop-down list. The balance and name of that account appear in the bottom of the dialog. Then enter the amount of the transfer in the Amount box. By default, Quicken suggests the projected monthly contribution amount, but you can enter any amount you like. When you've finished, click OK.

Quicken creates an entry in the account register of the account from which the money was contributed. It also updates the progress bar and information in the Savings Goals dialog.

When you create a savings goal, Quicken creates an asset account to record the goal's transactions and balance. To automate contributions to the goal, you can create a scheduled transaction to transfer money periodically from one of your bank accounts to the savings goal asset account. Scheduled transactions are covered in Chapter 6.

Meeting Your Goal

Once you have met your savings goal, you can either withdraw the funds from the savings goal so they appear in a Quicken account or delete the savings goal to put the money back where it came from.

Withdrawing Money   In the Savings Goals window, select the savings goal from which you want to withdraw money. Click the Withdraw button on the button bar. The Withdraw From Goal dialog, which works much like the Contribute To Goal dialog, appears. Use it to remove funds from the savings goal and put them back into the account from which they were contributed. Click OK to close the Withdraw From Goal dialog.

Deleting a Savings Goal

In the Savings Goals window, select the savings goal you want to delete, and click the Delete button on the button bar. A dialog appears, explaining that this choice will return all funds to the source accounts:

- Click Remove It From Quicken Completely to eradicate any record of the savings goal.
- Click Keep It As A Zero Balance Asset Account For My Records to keep a record of the goal.
- Click OK to delete the savings goal.

Planning for Tax Time

Chapter 1

In This Chapter:

- *Including tax information in accounts*
- *Connecting tax information with categories*
- *Using TurboTax*
- *Working with the Tax Planner*
- *Creating scenarios*
- *Minimizing taxes by maximizing deductions*
- *Utilizing the Itemized Deduction Estimator*
- *Exploring the Tax Withholding Estimator*
- *Understanding the Tax Center*

Tax time is no fun. It can force you to spend hours sifting through financial records and filling out complex forms. When you're done with the hard part, you may be rewarded with the knowledge that you can expect a refund. But it is more likely that your reward will be the privilege of writing a check to the federal, state, or local government—or worse yet, all three.

Fortunately, Quicken Personal Finance Software can help. Its reporting features can save you time. By using the tax planning and monitoring tools that are available through Quicken, the next tax season may be a little less stressful. This chapter will show you how.

Tax Information in Accounts and Categories

As discussed briefly in Chapter 3, Quicken accounts and categories can include information that will help you at tax time. This section explains how you can set tax information in accounts and categories.

Including Tax Information in Accounts

You enter an account's tax information in the Tax Schedule dialog for the account. Choose Tools | Account List or press CTRL-A to display the Account List window. Select the name of the account, and click the Edit button that appears to the right of the account name. The Account Details dialog will appear. At the bottom of the Account Details dialog, click the Tax Schedule button. The Tax Schedule Information dialog, shown here, appears.

Use the Transfers In and Transfers Out drop-down lists to map account activity to specific lines on tax return forms and schedules. When you're finished, click OK. Repeat this process for all accounts for which you want to enter tax information.

Keep in mind that if you use the Paycheck Setup feature to account for all payroll deductions, including retirement plan contributions, you may not have to change the settings for many of your accounts. (That's another good reason to set up your regular paychecks in Quicken.) Chapter 6 explains how to set up a paycheck in Quicken. However, as with all things tax-related, check with your tax professional.

Remember, when working with accounts and categories, and especially subcategories, you cannot use names that contain the characters :}/{|^.

Connecting Tax Information with Categories

Quicken automatically sets tax information for many of the categories it creates. You can see which categories are tax-related and which tax form lines have been assigned to them in the Category List window (refer to Figure 17-1). (If this information does not appear, choose Options | Show Tax Line Item at the bottom of the window.) Concentrate on the categories without tax assignments; some of these may require tax information, depending on your situation.

You can use the Set Up Category dialog to enter or modify tax information for a category. Choose Tools | Category List to open the Category List window. Select the category for which you want to enter or edit tax information. Then click the Edit button in the Action column to display the Set Up Category dialog and choose the Tax Reporting tab.

You can also open the Category List by pressing SHIFT-CTRL-C.

If the category's transactions should be included on your tax return as either income or a deductible expense, select the Tax Related Category check box. Then use the Tax Line Item For This Category drop-down list to choose the

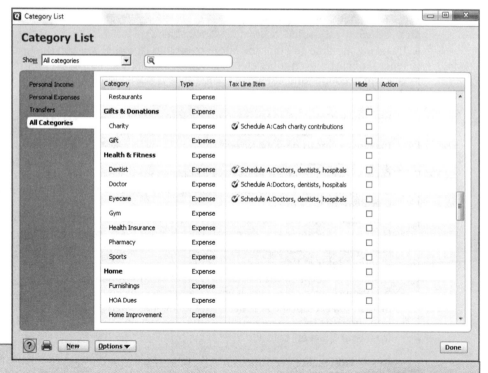

Figure 17-1 • The Category List window shows the tax information provided for each category.

form or schedule and line for the item. (You can expand this list by selecting the Extended Line Item List option.) A description of the tax-line item you chose appears at the bottom of the dialog, as seen here. Click OK to return to the Category List. The tax-line item you chose appears on the same line as your category. Repeat this process for all categories that should be included on your tax return. Keep in mind that you can also enter tax information when you first create a category, as explained in Chapter 3.

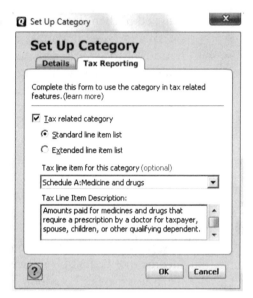

You can also select the Tax Related Category check box and leave the tax line item blank if the category is tax related but there is not a specific line item that applies. A red circle with a white check mark will appear by the category in your Category List without a specific tax line.

Tax Reports

Quicken offers several tax reports that can make tax time easier by providing the information you need to prepare your taxes. All of these reports are based on the tax information settings for the accounts and categories in your Quicken data file. You can learn more about Quicken's reporting feature in Chapter 8.

To create a report, select Reports | Tax from the menu bar. Choose the name of the report from the menu:

- **Capital Gains** summarizes gains and losses on the sales of investments, organized by the term of the investment (short or long) and the investment account.
- **Tax Schedule** summarizes tax-related transactions, organized by tax form or schedule and line item.
- **Tax Summary** summarizes tax-related transactions, organized by category and date.

And, if you are using Quicken Premier edition, you have three additional options, all of which allow you to print reports from which you can enter information directly into the appropriate federal income tax schedules:

- Schedule A – Itemized Deductions
- Schedule B – Interest and Dividends
- Schedule D – Capital Gains and Losses

Online Tax Tools

Click the Planning tab, and then click Tax Tools to access the Online Tax Tools submenu, as shown here. This menu offers access to some tax-related features

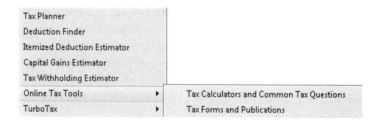

and information sources on the TurboTax.com website that can help you with your taxes. All you need to take advantage of these features is an Internet connection.

Here's a quick look at the online tax tools. The next time you're thinking about taxes, be sure to check these out.

Tax Calculators and Common Tax Questions

With your Internet connection, the Tax Calculators option displays the TurboTax Free Tax Calculators And Money Saving Tax Guides page. You can find links to various online tools for making tax and other financial calculations on this page. You can also follow links to get tax tips and learn more about TurboTax.

Tax Forms and Publications

With your Internet connection, choosing Tax Forms And Publications opens another TurboTax page from which you can link to both federal and state returns as well as other official IRS forms.

When you click a federal form link you are taken to the IRS site for federal forms, from which you can download each form. The form is downloaded as an Acrobat PDF file that appears in either a web browser window or an Adobe Acrobat Reader window. (You must have the freely distributed Adobe Acrobat Reader software to open and use these forms.) Print the form to fill it out manually.

If you choose a state link, you are taken to that state's website, from which you can download your forms. Most states offer additional information and publications on their sites as well as the tax forms. As with the federal forms you download from the IRS page, most state forms download as Acrobat PDF files.

Adobe Reader is often included with computers you purchase "off-the-shelf." Click Start | All Programs to see if it is already on your computer.

About TurboTax

If you're tired of paying a tax preparer to fill out your tax return for you, but you're not quite confident enough about your tax knowledge to prepare your own return by hand, it's time to check out TurboTax online tax-preparation software. It's a great way to simplify tax preparation.

TurboTax works almost seamlessly with Quicken to prepare your taxes. Just follow the instructions in this chapter to set up your accounts and categories with tax information. Purchase the TurboTax program at your local store or online. Then, from TurboTax, import your Quicken data. TurboTax takes you through an easy interview process to make sure you haven't left anything out—much like the interview you might go through with a paid tax preparer. TurboTax then calculates the bottom line and enables you to either print your returns or file them electronically.

Using TurboTax

Intuit offers several versions of TurboTax, which you can access online. You can learn more about them by opening the Planning tab and selecting Tax Tools | TurboTax | File Your Taxes With TurboTax. With your Internet connection, the link takes you directly to the TurboTax Personal Tax Products And Services page.

There are several options from which you can choose, from the most basic returns, which you can prepare online, to the TurboTax Home & Business edition, with which you can file both personal and small-business returns.

All online editions featured on this page require no payment until the return is filed. Of course, you can also purchase either a downloadable or a CD version of each program directly from this site.

- **TurboTax Basic Edition** is for taxpayers with basic tax preparation needs. It includes just the 1040EZ form.
- **TurboTax Deluxe** can perform tax calculations for taxpayers who own a home, make donations, or have childcare or medical expenses. In other words, most people.
- **TurboTax Premier** offers all of the functionality of TurboTax Deluxe and adds tax calculations for taxpayers who own stocks, bonds, mutual funds, or rental properties.
- **TurboTax Home & Business** offers all of the functionality of TurboTax Premier and adds tax calculations for small businesses, such as sole proprietorships or single-owner LLCs.
- **TurboTax Business** (found in the Small Business Taxes tab on the TurboTax website) provides tax preparation for corporations, partnerships, and multimember LLCs while maximizing business tax deductions. It does not include the means to prepare your personal taxes.

Import TurboTax File

Click Tax Tools | TurboTax | Import TurboTax File to import last year's TurboTax information and start this year's tax return.

Export TurboTax Reports

The last two links in the TurboTax submenu are used in conjunction with TurboTax to quickly send both the Tax Schedule and Capital Gains reports into the TurboTax program.

Planning to Avoid Surprises

One of the best reasons to think about taxes before tax time is to avoid surprises on April 15. Knowing what you'll owe before you owe it can help ensure that you pay just the right amount of taxes up front—through proper deductions or estimated tax payments—so you don't get hit with a big tax bill or tax refund.

You may think of a big tax refund as a gift from Uncle Sam. Well, it isn't. It's your money that Uncle Sam has been using, interest-free, for months. When you overpay your taxes, you're giving up money that you could be using to reduce interest-bearing debt or earn interest or investment income. Making sure you don't overpay taxes throughout the year helps you keep your money where it'll do *you* the most good.

Quicken Personal Finance Software's tax planning features, like the Tax Planner and Tax Withholding Estimator, can help you avoid nasty surprises. Other built-in tax tools, like the Deduction Finder and Itemized Deduction Estimator, can save you money and help you make smarter financial decisions. All of these features can be found in the Tax Tools menu in the Planning tab, which is full of options to help you plan and monitor your tax situation.

Quicken offers built-in tax planning tools that you can use to keep track of your tax situation throughout the year. The Tax Planner helps you estimate your federal income tax bill for the 2011 and 2012 tax years. You can add up to three additional scenarios to your planner to help plan for possible changes in your life. In addition, Quicken provides several estimating tools to help you with your taxes. For example, the Tax Withholding Estimator helps you determine whether your withholding taxes are correctly calculated. Finally, the Tax Center in the Planning tab summarizes your tax situation with a number of useful snapshots. Here's a closer look at each of these features.

If it is still 2011 when you first open the Tax Planner and you try to project values for tax year 2012, you may see a message stating that Quicken cannot display projected tax values for a future year. When your computer's calendar changes to 2012, you will be able to use both years for the Projected Value scenario. This does not apply to other scenarios that you can create.

Working with the Tax Planner

Quicken's Tax Planner includes features from Intuit's TurboTax tax preparation software to help you estimate your federal income tax bill for the 2011 and 2012 tax years. While this can help you avoid surprises, it can also help you see how various changes to income and expenses can affect your estimated tax bill.

Opening the Quicken Tax Planner Window

To open the Tax Planner, open the Planning tab and choose Show Tax Planner. You can also click Tax Tools | Tax Planner. (If you don't see Tax Tools, expand your screen.) Read the introductory information to get a clear understanding of what the Tax Planner can do for you and how it works.

You can also add an icon for the Tax Planner to the Quicken Tool Bar. Learn more about adding icons to the Quicken Tool Bar in Appendix B.

Viewing the Tax Planner Summary

To see what data is already entered in the Tax Planner, click the Tax Planner Summary link in the navigation bar on the left side of the Tax Planner window. A summary of income tax–related data, as well as the calculated tax implications, appears as shown in Figure 17-2.

Entering Tax Planner Data

Data can be entered into the Tax Planner from three different sources:

- TurboTax data can be imported into Quicken. In the main Quicken application window, from the Planning tab, choose Tax Tools | TurboTax | Import TurboTax File. Then use the dialog that appears to locate and import your TurboTax data. This information can be used to project current-year amounts in the Tax Planner.

You can also open the TurboTax import dialog by clicking File | File Import | TurboTax File.

- User Entered data can override any automatic entries. Use this to enter data that isn't entered any other way or that has not yet been entered into Quicken—such as a tax-deductible item you paid with cash.
- Quicken Data is automatically entered into the Tax Planner if you have properly set up your tax-related Quicken categories with appropriate tax

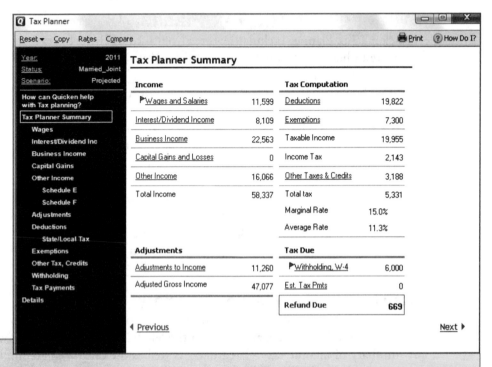

Figure 17-2 • The Tax Planner Summary screen displays a summary of currently entered tax-related information.

return line items, as discussed in "Tax Information in Accounts and Categories" earlier in this chapter.

Here's how it works. Click a link in the navigation bar on the left side of the Tax Planner window or in the Tax Planner Summary screen (refer to Figure 17-2) to view a specific type of income or expense. Then click a link within the window for a specific item. Details for the item appear in the bottom of the window, as shown in Figure 17-3. If the detail information doesn't show, click Show Details to expand the window and show the details. If desired, change the source option and, if necessary, enter an amount.

The options you can choose from vary depending on whether TurboTax data is available or the item has transactions recorded in Quicken. For example, in Figure 17-3, TurboTax data is not available, but transactions have been entered in Quicken. You can either select the User Entered option and enter a value in the Annual Total column or select the Quicken Data option and enter an adjusting value in the Adjustment column, as shown. This makes it easy to

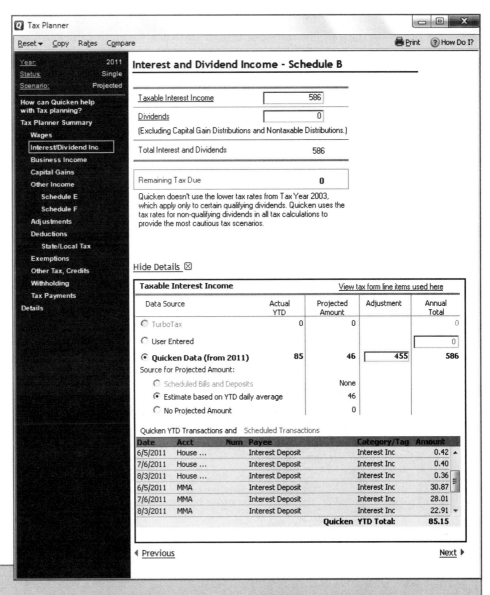

Figure 17-3 • The Tax Planner shows both totals and detailed information.

manually override any automatic entries created by the data you have entered into Quicken.

Repeat this process for any Tax Planner items you want to check or change. The Tax Planner automatically recalculates the impact of your changes.

To reset values quickly to amounts automatically entered by Quicken, choose Reset on the Tax Planner's button bar and click Reset To Quicken Default Values.

Creating Scenarios

The Scenarios feature of the Tax Planner enables you to enter data for multiple scenarios—a "what if" capability that you can use to see tax impacts based on various changes in entry data. For example, suppose you're planning to get married and want to see the impact of the additional income and deductions related to your new spouse. You can use a scenario to see the tax impact without changing your Projected Value scenario.

To use this feature, click the Scenario link in the upper section of the navigation bar on the left side of the Tax Planner window (refer to Figure 17-2). The Tax Planner Options screen, which is shown next, appears. Click the Scenarios down arrow to choose a different scenario from the drop-down list.

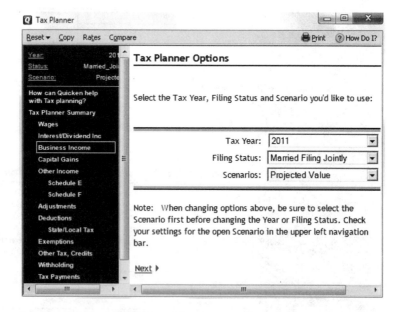

If Quicken asks whether you want to copy the current scenario to the scenario you chose, click Yes if that new scenario hasn't yet been created. Choose options from the Tax Year and Filing Status drop-down lists to set the scenario options. Then click the Next link at the bottom of the window to return to the Tax Planner Summary window. If necessary, change the values in the new scenario.

When creating or editing a scenario, you must choose the scenario first before you change the tax year or filing status.

To compare one scenario to another, click the Compare button in the Tax Planner window's button bar. A Tax Scenario Comparisons dialog appears, showing the results of each scenario's calculations. When you're finished viewing the comparative information, click OK to dismiss the dialog.

Finishing Up

When you're finished using the Tax Planner, click the Close button on the title bar. This saves the information you entered and updates the Projected Tax calculations in the Tax Center. (Learn about the Tax Center later in this chapter, in the section "Understanding the Tax Center.")

Meet the Estimators

Some of the most useful tips to aid your tax planning are found under the Tax Tools button in the Planning tab. From helping you find and itemize your tax deductions to helping you determine your tax refund (or payment), each tool can help you make your tax situation clearer. The more you know about taxes that you must pay, the better you will be able to manage your money to ensure there are funds to pay them.

Minimizing Taxes by Maximizing Deductions

One way to minimize taxes is to maximize your deductions. While Quicken can't help you spend money on tax-deductible items—that's up to you—it can help you identify expenses that may be tax-deductible so you don't forget to include them on your tax returns.

Quicken offers two features to help maximize your deductions. The Deduction Finder asks you questions about expenditures to determine if they are tax-deductible. The Itemized Deduction Estimator helps make sure you don't forget about commonly overlooked itemized deductions.

Deduction Finder

The Deduction Finder uses another TurboTax feature to help you learn which expenses are deductible. Its question-and-answer interface gathers information from you and then provides information about the deductibility of items based on your answers.

Working with the Deduction Finder Window

To open the Deduction Finder, open the Planning tab and choose Tax Tools | Deduction Finder. An Introduction dialog may appear. Read its contents to learn more about Deduction Finder and then click OK.

Figure 17-4 shows what the Deductions tab of the Deduction Finder window says about the costs of operating your car if you are an employee.

Use the buttons to work with the Deduction Finder window:

- **See Introduction** displays the Introduction window so you can learn more about how Deduction Finder works.
- **Clear Checkmarks** removes the check marks from items for which you have already answered questions.
- **Print** prints a summary of deduction information about all the deductions for which you have answered questions.
- **How Do I?** opens the Quicken Personal Finances Help window, where you can find additional information about using the Deduction Finder.

Finding Deductions

As you can see in Figure 17-4, the Deductions tab of the Deduction Finder window uses clearly numbered steps to walk you through the process of selecting deduction types and deductions, and then answering questions. It's easy to use. You need only choose the type of deduction from the drop-down list at number 1, as shown in the figure. As you see, Employee is the first option. You don't have to answer questions about all the deductions—only the deductions you think may apply to you. When you've finished answering questions about a

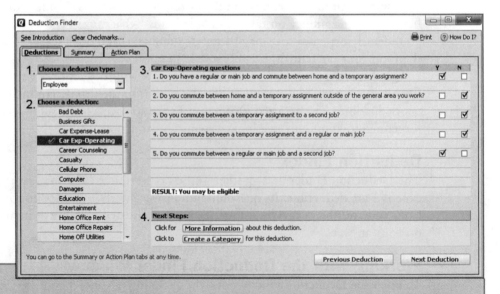

Figure 17-4 • The Deduction Finder helps you identify expenses that may be tax-deductible.

deduction, the result appears near the bottom of the window. You can then move on to another deduction.

The Summary tab of the window summarizes the number of deductions available in each category, the number for which you answered questions, and the number for which you may be eligible to take deductions based on your answers to the questions.

When you've finished answering questions, you can click the Action Plan tab, as seen next, to get more information about the deductions and the things you may need to do to claim them. Although you can read the Action Plan information on-screen, if you answered many questions, you may want to use the Print button on the button bar to print the Action Plan information for reference.

When you have completed your entries and printed your Action Plan, click the Close button to close the Deduction Finder.

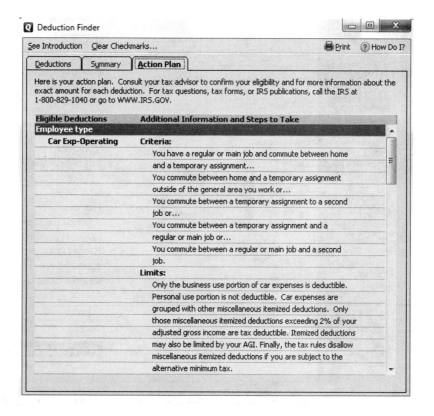

Utilizing the Itemized Deduction Estimator

The Itemized Deduction Estimator feature, which is available in the Quicken Premier edition, helps make sure you don't overlook any itemized deductions, specifically the deductions on Schedule A of your tax return, for which you might qualify. It does this by guiding you through a review of deduction ideas and providing the information you need to know whether you may qualify.

To get started, open the Planning tab and choose Tax Tools | Itemized Deduction Estimator. The How Can I Maximize My Deductions? window appears, as shown in Figure 17-5.

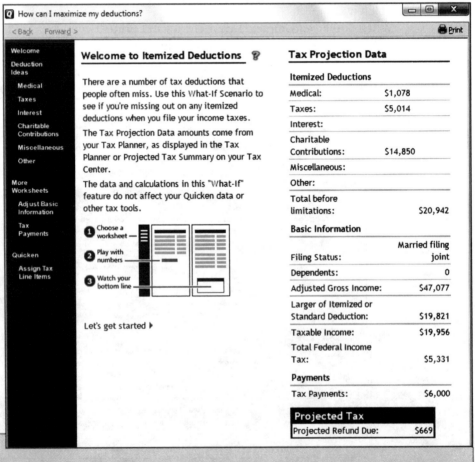

Figure 17-5 • Use the Itemized Deduction Estimator to help you find all of your Schedule A deductions.

Read the information and follow the instructions in the middle column of the window. You'll be prompted to enter information related to itemized deductions for medical expenses, taxes paid, interest paid, charitable contributions, and other items. The instructions are clear and easy to follow. Each time you enter information that can change your taxes, the Projected Refund Due or Projected Tax Due amount in the lower-right corner of the window changes. Your goal is to get a projected refund due amount as high as possible or a projected tax due amount as low as possible.

Again, none of the entries you make in the Itemized Deduction Estimator feature will affect your Quicken data or any other tax planning feature within Quicken. Make changes and experiment as much as you like. When you are done, click Close.

Exploring the Tax Withholding Estimator

Quicken's Tax Withholding Estimator feature, also available in Quicken Premier, helps you determine whether your W-4 form has been correctly completed. It does this by comparing your estimated tax bill from the Tax Planner to the amount of withholding tax deducted from your paychecks.

Using the Tax Withholding Estimator Feature

To get started, in the Planning tab, choose Tax Tools | Tax Withholding Estimator. The Am I Under Or Over Withholding? window appears.

Read the information and follow the instructions in the middle column of the window. You'll be prompted to enter information related to withholding taxes. Since the instructions are clear and easy to follow, they're not repeated here. Each time you enter data, the Projected Refund Due or Projected Tax Due amount in the lower-right corner of the window changes, as shown here. If a refund is due, you will see a message telling you that you may be over-withholding. Consider increasing the deductions you claim on your W-4 at work if the refund number is sizeable.

Projected Tax	
Projected Refund Due:	$669
You may be over withholding.	

None of the entries you make in the Tax Withholding Estimator feature will affect your Quicken data or any other tax planning feature within Quicken, so don't be afraid to experiment.

Acting on the Results of Tax Withholding Estimator Calculations

What do you do with this information once you have it? Well, suppose your work with the Tax Withholding Estimator feature tells you that you should change your

W-4 allowances from 1 to 2 to avoid overpaying federal withholding taxes. You can act on this information by completing a new W-4 form at work. This will decrease the amount of withholding tax in each paycheck. The result is that you reduce your tax overpayment and potential refund.

In some states, changing your federal withholding allowances with the W-4 changes your state withholding as well. Be careful you do not end up under-withholding your state taxes if you change your federal withholdings.

Periodically Checking Withholding Calculations

If you are entering all of your information into Quicken, including your paycheck information, consider using the Tax Withholding Estimator feature every three months or so to make sure actual amounts are in line with projections throughout the year. Whenever possible, use actual values rather than estimates in your calculations. And be sure to act on the results of the calculations by filing a new W-4 form, especially if the amount of your projected refund due or projected tax due is greater than you anticipated.

Capital Gains Estimator

If you are tracking your investments in Quicken, the Capital Gains Estimator can help you calculate the taxable consequences of selling an investment. This tool is explained in detail in Chapter 11.

See the sections "Online Tax Tools" and "About TurboTax" earlier in this chapter, which discuss the other items in the Tax Tools menu.

Understanding the Tax Center

Quicken summarizes all information about your tax situation in the Tax Center (see Figure 17-6). Here's a quick look at what you can find in the Tax Center window.

Projected Tax

The Projected Tax snapshot provides a summary of your upcoming projected tax return, including the amount that you'll have to pay or get back as a refund. If some items in the Projected Tax section need to be completed, a small flag will appear to the left of the item.

The information in this snapshot is based on the Tax Planner's Projected scenario, discussed earlier in this chapter.

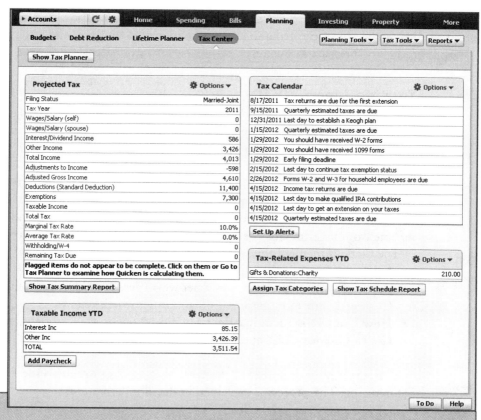

Figure 17-6 • The Tax Center window displays specific information about your tax situation.

From the Options menu in the Projected Tax section of the Tax Center you can

- Open the Tax Planner.
- Create a Tax Summary Report. This report can also be created by clicking the Show Tax Summary Report button at the bottom of the Projected Tax section of the Tax Center.

Tax Calendar

The Tax Calendar section warns you of upcoming IRS tax deadlines. From here you can create Tax Alerts from either the Options menu or the Set Up Alerts button at the bottom of the section.

While quarterly estimated taxes are due on January 15, April 15, June 15, and September 15, if those dates fall on a holiday or a weekend, the actual payment is due the next working day.

Taxable Income YTD

The Taxable Income YTD snapshot summarizes all of your year-to-date tax-related income. Quicken calculates these totals based on the transactions you enter throughout the year. All income categories that are marked "tax-related" and have transactions appear in this snapshot. If you have chosen to enter your net paycheck and have not told Quicken that this amount is tax related, nothing will appear in this list except a link to set up your paycheck.

If you have any non-paycheck-related taxable income, such as dividend income from investments, the Taxable Income YTD snapshot will not be blank.

The Options menu of this section of the Tax Center offers the following options:

- **Report My Net Worth** creates a net worth report as of the current date. See Chapter 13 for more information about net worth reports.
- **How Does This Income Affect My Taxes?** opens the Tax Planner.
- **Go To Category List** opens the Category List.

The Add Paycheck button at the bottom of the section opens the Paycheck Setup dialog. The process is explained in detail in Chapter 6.

Tax-Related Expenses YTD

The Tax-Related Expenses YTD snapshot summarizes all of your year-to-date tax-related expenses. Quicken automatically calculates this information based on the transactions you enter throughout the year. All expense categories that are marked "tax-related" and have transactions appear in this list.

The Options available from this section are as follows:

- **Find Other Deductions** opens the Deduction Finder, explained in the section "Deduction Finder" earlier in this chapter.
- **How Will These Deductions Affect My Taxes?** opens the Tax Planner.
- **Create A Tax Schedule Report** opens a report for the current tax year showing information for Form 1040. The report contains Schedule A and B entries for tax-related categories if you are using Quicken Premier edition.
- **Link Categories To Tax Forms** opens the Category List so that you can associate categories with specific tax-line items as explained in "Including Tax Information in Accounts" earlier in this chapter.
- **Go To Category List** opens the Category List.

The Assign Tax Categories button at the bottom of this section opens the Category List. The Show Tax Schedule Report button opens the report described earlier.

Tax Alerts

Tax alerts are only visible in the Alerts Center. This is also where you go to set alerts related to your tax situation. You can access the Tax Alerts feature through the Options menu in the Tax Calendar or from the menu bar by choosing Tools | Alerts Center | Setup. In the Setup dialog you have three options related to taxes, as shown here:

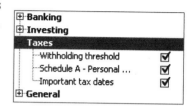

You can also see tax alerts in the Alerts snapshot that can be added to your Main View on the Home tab or into another view you create on the Home tab. If necessary, click the plus sign to the left of the Taxes item in the Alerts Center's Setup tab to expand the tax-related alerts.

- **Withholding Threshold** enables you to set a value of dollars withheld from your paycheck to alert you if your payroll withholding is too much or not enough. This alert only works when you set up your paycheck in Quicken.
- **Schedule A – Personal Deductions (Schedule A Reminder)** displays information about the types of personal deductions you can claim on Schedule A of your tax return.
- **Important Tax Dates** notifies you in advance of tax calendar events, such as estimated tax due dates and extension deadlines.

Learn more about setting alerts in Chapters 8.

Appendixes

This part of the book provides some additional information you may find helpful when using Quicken Personal Finance Software. These three appendixes explain how to work with Quicken data files, how to customize Quicken, and answer some of your questions when you are converting from Microsoft Money.

Part Six

Managing Quicken Files

In This Appendix:

- *Creating a data file*
- *Opening, saving, and copying Quicken data files*
- *Setting backup preferences*
- *Backing up your data*
- *Restoring data files*
- *Protecting a data file*
- *Working with passwords*
- *Importing files into Quicken*
- *Exporting Quicken files*
- *Working with additional file operations*
- *Using keyboard shortcuts*

All the information you enter in your Quicken Personal Finance Software is stored in a Quicken data file. This file includes all account and category setup information, transactions, and other records you enter into Quicken. Technically speaking, your Quicken data file consists of a single file with the QDF extension.

Commands under Quicken's File menu enable you to perform a number of file management tasks, such as creating, opening, backing up, restoring, password-protecting, importing and exporting, and copying portions and years of data files, as well as validating and repairing your data files. This appendix discusses all of these tasks.

Working with Multiple Data Files

Chances are, you won't need more than one Quicken data file other than the one you create as part of the Quicken Setup process, covered in Chapter 2. However, if you need to keep financial records for someone else, such as your local community group or an aging relative, you can easily create a new Quicken file.

Creating a Data File

Start by choosing File | New Quicken File. A dialog appears, asking whether you want to create a new Quicken file or a new Quicken account, as shown here. (Some users confuse the two and try to use the File menu's New command to create a new account. You learn how to create an account in Chapter 2.) Select New Quicken File and click OK.

A Create Quicken File dialog, like the one shown next, appears. Use it to enter a name for the data file. Although you can also change the default

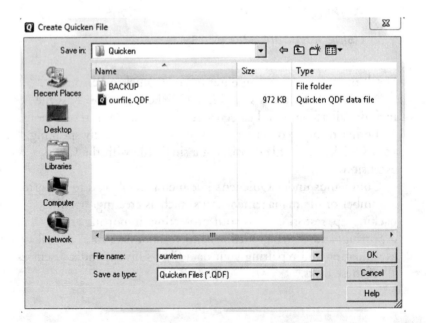

directory location, it's easier to find the data file if it's in the Quicken subdirectory of your Documents (or Documents And Settings) folder with other Quicken data files. It is also easier to find the Quicken file if it is renamed with no spaces or other special characters. Click OK.

Consider making your filename eight characters or less. While most modern programs can use longer filenames, there are occasional issues if the filename is longer than eight characters.

Quicken's Setup appears next. Create your first account and continue setting up your new file as you did your first Quicken file. Refer to Chapter 2 for step-by-step instructions or to refresh your memory.

Opening, Saving, and Copying Quicken Data Files

The first options on the File menu help you work with your Quicken files. Use these commands to create a new file, as discussed earlier, open an already existing Quicken file, determine the location, and save a copy of your current file.

Opening a Different Data File

If you have more than one Quicken data file, it's important that you enter transactions into the right one. You can see which data file is currently open by looking at the filename in the application window's title bar as shown here. Note that the title bar shows the version of Quicken that you are using, the file in which you are working, and even the current view. In our example, we are using Quicken 2012 Premier, in AuntEm's file in the Main View of the Home tab.

🄌 Quicken 2012 Premier - AuntEm - [Home]

To open a different data file, choose File | Open Quicken File, or press CTRL-O, and use the Open Quicken File dialog that appears to select and open a different file. Only one Quicken data file can be open at a time. In the example shown here, there are two files from which to choose.

In the illustration shown on the next page, you'll also note a folder named "Backup." See "Backing Up Your Quicken Data File" later in this chapter to learn more about Quicken Backup files and folders.

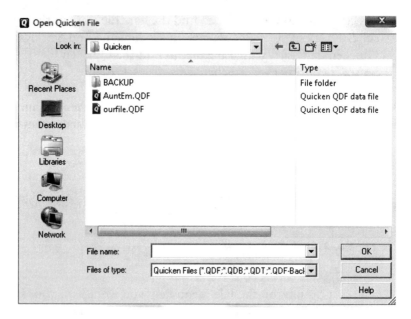

Save A Copy As

Click this menu command to open a dialog with which you can save an exact copy of your current file to another location. This other location can be a flash (sometimes called a "thumb") drive, another location on your network, or an external hard disk. If you have a CD or DVD burner on your computer, you can use the CD or DVD writing software on your computer to copy the file to a CD or DVD.

Quicken makes it easy for you to copy your currently open file.

1. Click File | Save A Copy As, as shown next. The Copy Quicken File dialog appears. (This dialog looks similar to the Create Quicken File and Open Quicken File dialogs shown earlier.)

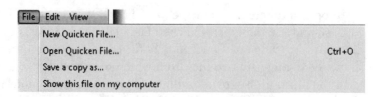

2. Choose the folder into which you want to save this Quicken file by clicking the drop-down list arrow in the Save In: field as shown next.

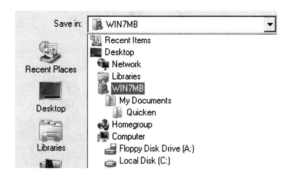

3. Select the location for your copied file, give it a new name such as "myfilecopy" to distinguish it from your original file, and click OK. Your file is now copied to the other location.

4. A message appears stating that your file has been copied successfully and showing the name you gave it. You are asked if you want to open the copied file, as shown here. If you click Yes, you see an additional prompt asking if you want to close the current file. To return to your currently open Quicken file, click No.

Show This File
On My Computer

You can immediately find where your current file is located by choosing File | Show This File On My Computer. When you click this command, Quicken opens a Windows Explorer window showing where the currently open file is located on your computer, as seen next.

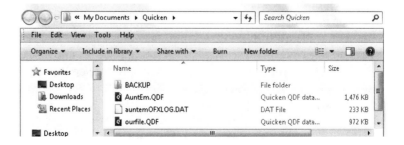

Backing Up Your Quicken Data File

Imagine this: You set up Quicken to track all of your finances, and you record transactions regularly so the Quicken data file is always up-to-date. Then one evening, when you start your computer to check your e-mail or enter a cash transaction into Quicken, you find that your hard drive has died. Not only have your plans for the evening been ruined, but your Quicken data file is also a casualty of your hard drive's untimely death.

Throughout this book, you've been encouraged to back up your data files. If you back up your Quicken data as regularly as you update its information, the loss of your Quicken data file will be a minor inconvenience, rather than a catastrophe. In this section, you'll learn how to back up your Quicken data file and how to restore it if (or when) the original data file is lost or damaged.

Setting Backup Preferences

By default, Quicken reminds you to run a backup every third time you leave your Quicken program. However, you can change this prompt in Quicken Preferences. The Backup Preferences dialog also allows you to tell Quicken how often to automatically save a copy of your files. Open the Backup Preferences dialog by clicking Edit | Preferences | Setup | Backup. The dialog appears as seen in Figure A-1.

About Automatic Backups

Quicken creates a Backup folder in the same location where your data files are stored. Every fifth time you open your Quicken file, Quicken creates a backup file of your information and stores that record in the Backup folder. While this is useful if your data file becomes corrupted or there is a software or hardware

> ## IN MY EXPERIENCE
>
> One of the points I stress to clients and students alike is that eventually all hard drives will fail. The only way to circumvent this fact is by having a current backup of your data. By far, the most secure backup file is the one that resides someplace other than near your computer. If your computer is stolen or damaged in a tornado, fire, or other disaster, your backup disks might also be lost.
>
> For a small fee, Quicken Online Backup can help protect your data by making it easy to back up your data to a secure server far from your computer and other backup files. This service is fully integrated with Quicken. Just use Quicken's Backup command to back up your data file using Quicken Online Backup.
>
> If your Quicken data is important to you, check out this feature. Click the Learn More link in the Quicken Backup window to get the details on this useful service. You can test it for free for the first 30 days, and the service's interface is easy to use.

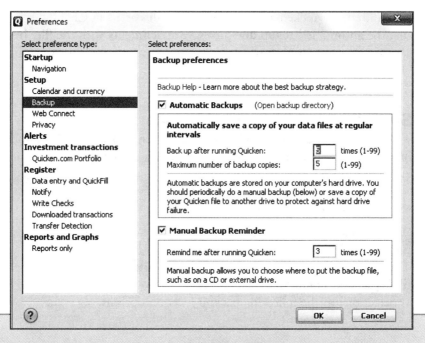

Figure A-1 • Backups can be automated in Quicken by using Quicken Backup Preferences.

error, storing the file on your hard drive does not protect you against hard drive failures.

As seen in Figure A-1, you can change both the number of times Quicken saves your file to this folder and the number of copies maintained in that folder. Enter any number between 1 and 99 to change from the default of 5. Each file is saved with the following format:

QData-YYYY-MM-DD.aphh.mm.QDF-backup

(Data filename - four-digit year - two-digit month - two-digit day - AM or
   PM - two-digit hour - two-digit minute.QDF-backup)

Name	Size	Type	Date modified
🅠 auntem-2011-08-15.AM06.35.QDF-backup	1,476 KB	Quicken QDF backup dat...	8/15/2011 6:35 AM

If you use the Quicken attachments feature discussed in Chapter 4, be aware that the automatic backup does not save attachments with the file. In order to save attachments, you must use the manual backup procedure described in "Backing Up Your Data" in this appendix.

Setting Manual Backup Reminders

The Preferences setting tells Quicken how often you want to be reminded to back up. A manual backup allows you to tell Quicken the location for your backed up file.

Backing Up Your Data

While you are using Quicken, you begin the backup process by choosing File | Backup And Restore | Backup Quicken File or by pressing CTRL-B at any time. This displays the Quicken Backup dialog for the currently open Quicken data file, as seen in Figure A-2.

Select one of the following backup location options.

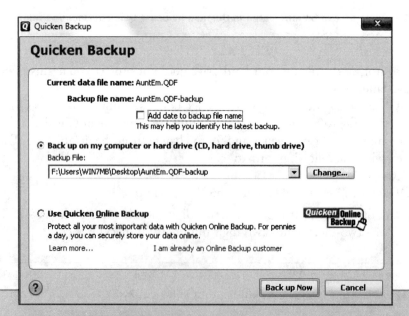

Figure A-2 • Use the Quicken Backup dialog to ensure you can recover your data in case of a hard disk failure.

Back Up On My Computer Or Hard Drive (CD, Hard Drive, Thumb Drive)

This option enables you to back up to another disk, either on your computer or on one that's accessible via a network. If you select this option, you can use the Change button to locate and select a backup disk and directory. It's a good idea to alternate between two disks for backup purposes. This means you'll always have two versions backed up, in case one version is corrupt. It's a good idea to choose a backup location other than your hard disk, such as a thumb drive (for small files) or an external hard disk. (Backing up to your computer's internal hard disk defeats the purpose of backing up!) If you want to automatically append the current date to the backup filename, select the Add Date To Backup File Name check box. (These instructions assume you have selected Back Up On My Computer.) Keep in mind that your computer may not be able to write directly to a CD-R or DVD-R. If you choose to back up to an optical disk, you might have to back up to your hard disk and then burn the resulting file to disk.

1. Select Back Up On My Computer Or Hard Drive (CD, Hard Drive, Thumb Drive).
2. The folder into which your backed up file will be saved is displayed. To back up to another folder or location, click Change.
   a. Select the drive, folder, and location into which you want to save your backed up files.
   b. Click OK.
3. Click Back Up Now. Your Quicken data file disappears momentarily and a small message appears telling you that Quicken is backing up your data.
4. When the backup is complete, the data file's windows reappear and a dialog informs you that the file was backed up successfully, as shown here. Click OK to dismiss the dialog.

Quicken and the folks at Intuit do not recommend storing your Quicken file on a network drive and working with your file across your network. While backing up to a network drive can work effectively for many, it's a good idea to store your actual Quicken data file in the Quicken subfolder in your Documents folder on your computer.

IN MY EXPERIENCE

Students and clients have shared a common backup issue, whether it be to CDs, DVDs, or flash drives. The issue is "my Quicken data did not back up properly." In addition, there seem to be as many error messages as there are different CD/DVD burning programs available. Many of these errors are due to formatting issues. In most cases, one way to solve the question is as follows:

1. To back up to a CD or DVD, create a folder on your desktop.
   a. Right-click a blank area on your desktop.
   b. Click New | Folder. Name your folder and press ENTER.
2. Back up your file to that folder.
3. Burn the backed up file to your CD or DVD following the manufacturer's directions.
4. After you have verified that the backed up file is on your external device, find the backed up file icon on your desktop and delete it. An example of a backed up file icon is shown here.

AuntEm.QDF -backup

Remember that some CD/DVD programs will not accept filenames longer than 31 characters. This is another good reason to keep your filenames short!

Try following the same procedure if Quicken does not back up to your flash drive. Occasionally, flash drives are formatted by the manufacturer and can cause some of the same issues as CD or DVDs.

Do check the amount of space available on your CD or DVD. If, for some reason, your Quicken data file is too large to fit on the available space, the file will not back up. Since many CD and DVD programs determine the backed-up file size, if there is a question in your mind, you're better off to burn to a new, blank disk.

Remember that files burned to a CD or DVD may be "read-only," meaning you cannot work with files on that optical device directly. For this reason, it is a good idea to use external devices for backup and store your active Quicken data file on your computer's hard drive.

Use Quicken Online Backup

Choose this option to back up to a server on the Internet, using Quicken's Online Backup service, which is available for a nominal fee. You can learn more about this service by selecting Learn More in the Use Quicken Online Backup section to connect to the Quicken Online Backup website.

If you have an online backup account, click the I Am Already An Online Backup Customer link to enter your account ID and password.

- When working with online backup through Quicken, there have been issues with some firewall hardware and software. Refer to the documentation that came with your product to forestall any problems.

- Make sure you keep a record of your Quicken Online Backup account ID and password. If you forget it, you'll have to contact Quicken Support to complete your backup.
- Antivirus and non-Quicken backup programs can interfere with Quicken Online Backup.
- Quicken Online Backup cannot access files stored on CDs, DVDs, flash drives, or Zip drives.

Restoring Data Files

In the event of loss or damage to your data file, you can restore from a recent backup. You can restore from an external file or one on your hard drive. Each process works in a similar way.

Start the restoration process by opening Quicken and clicking File | Backup And Restore | Restore From Backup File. You may restore from one of Quicken's automatic backups, a backup file that you created, or from an online backup as shown here.

1. To restore from one of Quicken's automatic backups, select the file you want to restore and click Restore Backup. If the file you want to restore is the currently opened file, you are prompted to write over the current file or to create a copy of the file as shown here.

2. To restore a backup file that you have created, ensure the device on which the file is stored is connected to your computer.

3. Click Restore From Your Backup | Browse to locate and select the appropriate backup file.

4. Click Restore Backup. If a file by the name of the file you are trying to restore exists, you'll see a message asking what you want to do. If you are restoring your backed up file over the current file, choose Overwrite The Existing File With the Restored File. Overwriting a file means replacing all the information that is in the current file. This cannot be reversed, so make very sure that is what you want to do!

5. If you choose to create a copy of the backed up file, click Create A Copy. You see a message that the file was restored and are asked if you want to open the restored file as shown here.

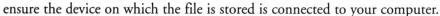

6. To restore a file from your online backup, choose Restore From Online Backup to log into Quicken Backup. You see a list of the last 90 days of backups.

7. Select the file you want to restore. After Quicken has restored your files, click OK to close the confirmation message.

8. To open your restored file, click File | Open.

IN MY EXPERIENCE

As you can see, restoring your files from most locations is pretty straightforward. However, there may be some additional steps when restoring a file from a CD or DVD. The most common issue when restoring from your CD is a message that Quicken cannot find a file or access the disk in Drive "D" (where "D" is the name of your DVD or CD drive). The easiest way to solve this is as follows:

1. Create a new folder on your desktop and name it "Restored Files" or some similar name.
2. Use Windows Explorer to copy the file from your CD or DVD into the folder you just created.
3. Restore the file as described in "Restoring Data Files" earlier in this appendix.
4. For some files, you may have to change the properties of the file from its read-only state. To do this:
   a. Right-click the file you've just copied to the new folder on your desktop.
   b. Click Properties to open a dialog as seen here.
   c. Clear the Read-Only check box.
   d. Click Apply to close the dialog.

You can then proceed with the restoration as described in "Restoring Data Files."

Moving a Quicken Data File Between Two Computers

Intuit's technical support staff is often asked how to move a Quicken data file from one computer to another. In fact, this question is so common that we are including it here.

The best way to move a data file from one computer to another is with the Backup and Restore Backup File commands. Begin by opening the file in Quicken on the computer on which it resides. Then follow the instructions in this appendix to back up the file to removable media, such as a thumb (or flash) drive, CD, DVD, external hard drive, or to a network drive (preferably

---

IN MY EXPERIENCE

Many computer users are confused about the difference between backing up their files and copying their files. When should you back up and when should you copy? In today's computing world, that's a great question. When personal computers first came into general use, the storage devices, such as floppy disks, held much less information than today's spacious devices. Saving data was no less important in 1990, but the media held much less information. The 3½-inch floppy disks that were often used held only 1.44MB of information. Today's flash (or thumb) drives (those small storage devices about 3 inches × 0.75 inches), measure their capacity in gigabytes. (When you remember that 1,024MB is 1GB, you get an idea of the storage capacity of a flash drive.) In order to efficiently and safely save data, earlier backup programs compressed the information to fit on the small media. One had to use the same program to restore the information back to the hard disk.

Today, all Quicken files, including the backups, are encrypted for security. When you run the Quicken Backup utility, Quicken appends the word "backup" to each file during the process. This tells Quicken that the file is not the current working file.

With today's large external hard disks, saving space may not be as important as easy retrieval of your data. If that is the case, consider using either of the two Copy commands offered by Quicken. These commands copy the information rather than save it as a backed up file. While Quicken recommends the Backup and Restore utility when moving data files from one place to another, the Copy options are available and with them, you can easily retrieve your data and get back to work.

---

one that the other computer is connected to). Then fire up Quicken on the other computer and follow the instructions in this appendix to restore the backup copy. When you're finished, the Quicken data file is ready to use on the new computer.

It's important to remember that once you begin making changes to the file on the new computer, the file on the old computer will no longer be up-to-date. This means that if you want to use the file on the old computer again, you need to complete the backup and restore process to move the file back to that computer. As you can imagine, if you often move the file from one computer to another and back, it can be difficult to keep track of which version of the file is the most up-to-date.

Although you can make your Quicken data file "portable" by keeping it on removable media so you can access it from any computer, this is not the recommended method. Flash drives, CDs, and DVDs are all more susceptible to data loss and damage than an internal or networked hard disk. Quicken users have reported numerous problems using this technique; don't add your own problems to the list. A networked drive may not be a good place to store your file either, at least if you are going to keep it networked while you work on it.

Password-Protecting Quicken Data

Quicken offers two types of password protection for your data: file passwords and transaction passwords. This section shows how these options work.

Protecting a Data File

When you password-protect a data file, the file cannot be opened without the password. This is the ultimate in protection—it prevents unauthorized users from even seeing your data.

Setting Up the Password

Choose File | Set Password For This Data File to display the Quicken File Password dialog, which is shown here. Enter the same password in each text box, and click OK.

Read the suggestions from Quicken about secure passwords. And, one more thing: no password is secure if it is written on a sticky note and affixed to your monitor.

Opening a Password-Protected Data File

When you open a data file that is password-protected, the Enter Quicken Password dialog, which is shown next, appears. You must enter your password correctly and then click OK to open the file. As mentioned in the dialog, passwords are "case-sensitive." That means if you've used capital letters when setting your password, you must enter your password with capital letters.

Changing or Removing a Password

Choose File | Set Password For This Data File to display the Quicken File Password dialog. Enter the current password in the Old Password box, and then enter the same new password in the two boxes beneath it. (To remove a password, leave the two bottom boxes empty.) Click OK.

Protecting Existing Transactions

When you password-protect existing transactions, the transactions cannot be modified unless the password is properly entered. This prevents unauthorized or accidental alterations to data.

Setting Up the Password

Choose File | Set Password To Modify Transactions to display the Password To Modify Existing Transactions dialog, shown here. Enter the same password in the top two text boxes. Then enter a date through which the transactions are to be protected, and click OK. This is an

especially useful tool when you have completed entering all of your transactions for the year and are ready to run your reports for your income tax return. Protecting your transactions through the end of the year will ensure that you don't inadvertently change a number that might affect your return.

Modifying a Password-Protected Transaction

When you attempt to modify a transaction that is protected with a password, the Transaction Password dialog, shown here, appears. You must enter your password correctly and then click OK to modify the transaction.

Changing or Removing a Password

Choose File | Set Password To Modify Transactions to display the Change Transaction Password dialog. Enter the current password in the Old Password box, and then enter the same new password in the two boxes beneath it. (To remove a password, leave the two bottom boxes empty.) Click OK.

Working with Passwords

Here are a few things to keep in mind when working with passwords:

- Passwords can be up to 16 characters in length and can contain any character, including a space.
- Passwords are case-sensitive. That means, for example, that "PassWord" is not the same as "password."
- If you forget your password, you will not be able to access the data file. Write your password down and keep it in a safe place.
- Your data file is only as secure as you make it. Quicken's password protection can help prevent unauthorized access to your Quicken data files.

Password Error Messages

After you have established your passwords, you may see error messages when trying to open a file or change a transaction. Before you call Quicken Support, consider these possibilities:

- Is your CAPS LOCK key on? If you have inadvertently pressed the CAPS LOCK key on the left side of your keyboard, you may be typing in all caps. Remember your passwords are case-sensitive.
- Is your NUM LOCK key off? When your password contains numbers and you enter those numbers from the ten-key pad at the right side of your keyboard, you may be entering symbols instead of numbers if you have turned off the NUM LOCK key.
- Are you in the right data file? If you have more than one data file on your computer, you may have opened the wrong one by mistake.
- Try another password. Many of us have several passwords that we use, and you may just be entering the wrong password.
- If you have recently changed your password and have just restored from a backup copy, you may have restored a file with an old password. Try that old password.

Quicken's Password Removal Service

If all else fails, Quicken offers a (currently) free service to remove the password from your file. According to current information, this is usually completed in one or two business days.

You will need to send a copy of your file to Quicken. Their process is secure and confidential. Your first step is to contact Quicken Support via their website.

1. Type **Password Removal** into the Search box. From the list that appears, choose Password Removal Service.
2. You'll need to give them your e-mail address, your phone number, the version and release of Quicken that you are using, and the name of your file. The website will show the versions of Quicken that the Password Removal Service is currently supporting.
3. Respond to the e-mail sent by Quicken, or log onto the website as instructed.
4. Enter the case number, your e-mail address, and your PIN in the appropriate fields as shown here.
5. Click the I Have Read And Agree To The Terms Of Service check box, and click Submit.
6. A dialog appears that prompts you to add the file you want fixed. Locate it and click Start Upload.

Customer Login

Please use the case number and PIN provided by your support agent.

* Required

Case: *

E-mail: *

PIN: *

☐ I have read and agree to the Terms of Service.

Submit

7. Once your file has been uploaded, you're done. Quicken will remove the password and return your file within one business day. Download your file to your hard drive, and you will be able to access your data once more.

Additional File Procedures

In addition to the processes discussed earlier, there are several other tasks you can perform from the File menu.

Importing Files into Quicken

Importing information into Quicken can make your financial life much easier. From downloading information from your financial institution, as discussed in

Chapter 6, to converting from Microsoft
Money, as discussed in Appendix C, importing
data saves you time.

    From within Quicken, click File | File
Import to open the submenu that shows your
options, as shown here. As you can see, several
types of files can be imported:

> Web Connect File...
>
> QIF File...
>
> Quicken Transfer Format (.QXF) File...
>
> Import security prices from CSV file...
>
> TurboTax File...
>
> Microsoft Money® file...

- **Web Connect Files** are those files created by financial institutions that do
  not have Direct Connect availability. You download these files onto your
  hard drive and then import them into your Quicken data file. See Chapter 6
  for detailed information about Web Connect files.
- **QIF Files** are Quicken Interchange Format files that have been created in a
  third-party program for importing into Quicken. While not all programs
  support this format, many financial programs do.
- **Quicken Transfer Format (.QXF) Files** are files that permit the exchange
  of banking data with other Quicken data files, such as Quicken Essentials
  for Mac.
- **Import Security Prices From CSV File** allows you to utilize security price
  reports in this format.
- **TurboTax Files** can be imported into Quicken for tax planning.
- **Microsoft Money Files** can be quickly converted into Quicken data files.
  See Appendix C for detailed instructions.

Exporting Quicken Files

Several types of files are shown on the File Export menu. These file types are
used to transfer information between Intuit products, such as Quicken Essentials
for Mac, as well as the Windows versions of Quicken:

- QIF files are used to
  export Quicken data
  from one Quicken
  account to another
  Quicken account or to
  another Quicken file. To
  export a file, click File |
  File Export | QIF File.
  The QIF Export dialog
  appears, as shown next.

> ### NEW IN QUICKEN 2012
>
> One enhancement in Quicken 2012 is the
> ability to import and export .qxf files from
> Quicken Essentials for Mac as well as other
> Quicken Windows programs. QXF files are
> Quicken's financial interchange files that are
> used to exchange information between Intuit
> programs. You may notice when using Web
> Connect from your financial institution that the
> files are formatted as .qxf.

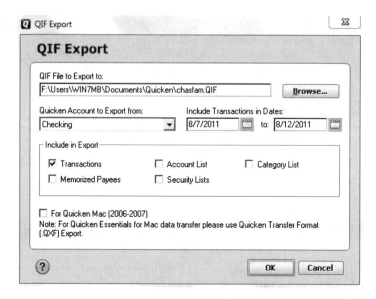

- Quicken Transfer Format (.QXF) files, as explained earlier, are Quicken financial data files used to transfer data files from Quicken for Windows to Quicken Essentials for Mac. Click File | File Export | Quicken Transfer Format to open the Export To Quicken Transfer Format dialog. By default, the file with which you are working is the filename you will export. Click Save. You will see a message box when the export file is created successfully. You will then need to import this .qxf file into your Quicken Essentials file.
- Export TurboTax Tax Schedule Report and Export TurboTax Capital Gains Report allow you to transfer TurboTax files (.txf) into other programs.

Working with Additional File Operations

Four options are listed as file operations in the File menu. Each is discussed here.

Copying the Current Data File

This copy command enables you to copy all or portions of the current data file to a different disk or save a copy with a different name. While similar to the Save A Copy As command discussed earlier in this appendix, this command gives you choices regarding what time period to include in the copied file, as well as a choice to include uncleared and investment transactions. It also may clear unused space in the Quicken file.

When you choose File | File Operations | Copy, the Copy File dialog, shown next, appears. Click Browse to choose a location for your file if you want the copied file stored in a location other than the current folder. The new filename will be the same as the current file, but will have "Cpy" at the end of the filename. You can change the name if you choose. Select the date range that is to be included in the copy, and clear the check box if you do not want to include earlier, uncleared transactions. While you may choose to clear the Include All Prior Investment Transactions, consider keeping them for a more complete record of your investment transactions. Click OK to make the copy.

If there is already a Quicken file with the same name in your Quicken folder, you will receive a prompt to give a new name to the file copy. Type a new name for this second file copy, and click OK.

When the copy is finished, a dialog asks if you want to continue working with the original data file or the new copy. Select the appropriate option, and click OK to continue working with Quicken.

The process does not change the original file in any way. Perhaps you want to copy categories, scheduled transactions, and memorized payees to a new file without the transactions. Or, perhaps there is a date range in which you had some major changes in your financial life and want to review those transactions.

Making a Year-End Copy of a Data File

The Year-End Copy command creates two special copies of your data file. Choose File | File Operations | Year-End Copy to display the Create A Year End Copy dialog, shown here, and set options for the two files.

Current Data File   The Current Data File section allows you to set options for the file you will continue working with in Quicken.

Do Nothing. My Current Data File Will Remain Unchanged   This option simply saves a copy of the current data file as-is.

I Only Want Transactions In My Current Data File Starting With This Date
This option enables you to enter a starting date for the files in the data file you will continue to use. For example, if you enter 1/1/2012, all transactions prior to that date will be removed from the data file.

Archive Data File   The Archive Data File section allows you to set options for creating an archive copy of the file. An archive is a copy of older transactions saved in a separate file. You can set two options:

- Enter a complete path (or use the Browse button to enter a path) for the archive file.
- Enter the date for the last transaction to be included in the file. For example, if you enter 12/31/2011, the archive file will include all transactions in the current file, up to and including those transactions dated 12/31/2011.

Creating the Files   When you click OK in the Create A Year End Copy dialog, Quicken creates the two files. It then displays a dialog that enables you to select the file you want to work with: the current file or the archive file. Select the appropriate option (normally Current File), and click OK to continue working with Quicken.

> ### IN MY EXPERIENCE
> Many Quicken users do not use the Create A Year End Copy utility. With today's large hard disks and fast machines, large Quicken data files are not an issue like they may have been when hard disks were small and computers didn't run at warp speed.

Checking the Integrity of a Data File
The Validate And Repair command facilitates checking the integrity of a Quicken data file. This command is particularly useful if you believe that a file has been damaged. It is a good idea to copy your file to an external device, such as a CD or external hard drive, before you perform the Validate And Repair function—in other words, perform a backup before working with this utility!

When you choose File | File Operations | Validate And Repair, the Validate and Repair Your Quicken File dialog appears, as shown next. By default, the current file is selected, but you may click Browse to select another file to check if you choose.

There are four specific operations that affect your data in different ways:

- **Validate File** should be run when you feel your data might be corrupted. Ensure you have performed a backup on your file before you run this process.
- **Rebuild Investing Lots** reviews your investing information. Current valuation amounts could change if this file has errors. Ensure you have performed a backup on your file before you run this process.
- **Delete Investing Price History** attempts to repair any data damage in your investing files. After the prices are deleted, only prices within the last five years will be replaced. Ensure you have performed a backup on your file before you run this process.
- **Reset All Quicken Printer Settings** simply fixes any issues with your printer setup. You may have to reset the check and report print settings after this procedure is complete, but none of your financial information is affected.

Click OK to start each selected process. After each process completes, Quicken displays a text file that tells you whether the file has any problems, as seen here.

 Some Quicken users use this process and add one more step. If you hold down the CTRL and the SHIFT keys when clicking OK, you perform an additional validation step called a Super Validate. This additional step may find more errors in a damaged file. As always, before you perform any function that may impact your financial transactions, do a backup!

Using Keyboard Shortcuts

If you have been working with computers for a long time and are comfortable with your keyboard, Quicken has a number of keyboard shortcuts that can save time. When you see a keyboard combination to the side of a menu command, it means that you can press that combination of keys and achieve the same result as when you click that command on the menu. For example, by choosing Open Quicken File on the File menu, you see the keyboard shortcut CTRL-O. Hold down the CTRL key on your keyboard, press the o key, and release both keys to open an existing Quicken file. Note the CTRL-P keyboard shortcut by the Print Checks command on the File menu. Many views in Quicken are available for you to print.

DATA_LOG.TXT - Notepad

File   Edit   Format   View   Help

```
[Mon Aug 15 21:25:07 2011]

File: "F:\Users\WIN7MB\Documents\Quicken\myfamily"

QDF:
Validating your data.
No errors.

QEL:
No read errors.

QEL:
All internal consistency checks passed.

[Mon Aug 15 21:25:13 2011]
Some Transactions corrected

[Mon Aug 15 21:25:13 2011]
Deleted price history.

[Mon Aug 15 21:25:13 2011]
Rebuilt price history.

[Mon Aug 15 21:25:14 2011]
Updated quotes.

[Mon Aug 15 21:25:15 2011]
Rebuilt investing lots.
Validation has completed.
```

IN MY EXPERIENCE

One additional thought when working with files you suspect have been damaged: try uninstalling and then reinstalling your Quicken program. Often, it is something within the program itself that can cause your files to appear damaged. Just remember to back up before you uninstall the program.

 Since printing is covered in each appropriate chapter of this book, we do not cover the print options in this appendix.

Quicken Keyboard Shortcuts

Quicken lets you access many of its features directly from the keyboard with one or a combination of keys. Table A-1 lists some of these shortcuts, which are also mentioned throughout the book.

Quicken Keyboard Command	Result
CTRL-A	Opens Account List
CTRL-B	Opens Quicken Backup dialog
CTRL-F	Opens Quicken Find dialog
CTRL-G	Opens Go To Date dialog
CTRL-H	Opens Find And Replace dialog
CTRL-J	Opens Bill And Income Reminders dialog
CTRL-K	Opens the Quicken Calendar
CTRL-L	Opens the Tag List
CTRL-M	Opens the Memorized dialog (from within a register transaction)
CTRL-N	Opens the Customize View dialog (from the Home tab)
CTRL-O	Opens the Open Quicken File dialog
CTRL-P	Opens the Print dialog
CTRL-S	Opens the Split dialog
CTRL-T	Opens the Memorized Payee dialog
CTRL-U	Opens the Portfolio view of the Investing tab
CTRL-W	Opens the Write Checks dialog
CTRL-Y	Opens the Security List
CTRL-SHIFT-A	Opens the Account Attachments dialog
CTRL-SHIFT-C	Opens the Category List
CTRL-SHIFT-E	Opens the Account Details dialog (when an account is selected in the Account Bar or you are working in an account's register)
CTRL-SHIFT-H	Opens the View Loans dialog
CTRL-SHIFT-O	Opens the Account Overview window (when an account is selected in the Account Bar or you are working in an account's register)
CTRL-SHIFT-P	Opens the Print screen
ALT-F or ALT-SHIFT-F	Opens the File menu
F1	Opens Quicken Help
F11	Toggles between your regular display and a full-size screen

Table A-1 • Quicken Keyboard Shortcuts

Customizing Quicken

In This Appendix:

- *Creating custom Home tab views*
- *Re-creating the Summary view*
- *Crafting an Analysis & Reports View*
- *Customizing the Tool Bar*
- *Telling Quicken your preferences*
- *Converting your older Quicken files to a new computer*
- *Changing multiple transactions*
- *Using the Emergency Records Organizer*

Once you've worked with Quicken Personal Finance Software for a while, you may want to fine-tune the way it looks and works to best suit your needs. Many of these options are discussed elsewhere in this book. Other customization options—like customizing the Tool Bar—are less commonly used. This appendix will explain many of the customization options available for Quicken and provide cross-references to other chapters in the book where you can learn more about the features they work with.

Customizing Quicken's Interface

Quicken offers a number of ways to customize its interface to best meet your needs. This part of the appendix explains how to customize the Home tab and the Quicken Tool Bar.

Creating Custom Home Tab Views

As discussed in Chapter 1, the Home tab offers customizable views of your Quicken data. You can use this tab to create multiple Home tab views, each of which shows the "snapshots" of summarized financial information that you want to display. Figure B-1 shows an example.

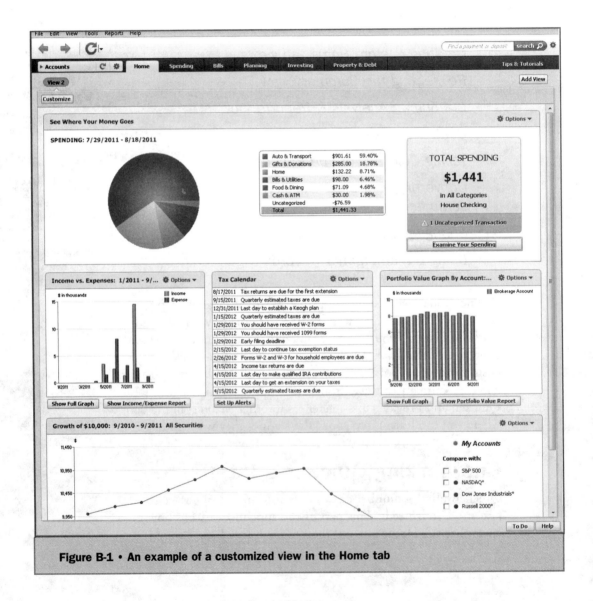

Figure B-1 • An example of a customized view in the Home tab

The Home tab was known as My Pages in some previous versions of Quicken. If you've upgraded to Quicken 2012 from an earlier version, you may already have custom views of the Quicken Home page set up in your Quicken data file. You'll get access to these views on the Home tab, where you can switch from one to another, modify them, and delete them, as discussed in this section.

Displaying the Home Tab Views

To get started, click the Home tab near the top of the Quicken window. Quicken displays the Main View button. Before you customize this view, it displays three snapshots: See Where Your Money Goes, Stay On Top Of Monthly Bills, and Track Spending Goals To Save Money. Once you've customized the Home tab, it displays the snapshots you added to it (refer to Figure B-1).

Modifying the Current View

You can modify the current view with the Customize button. This button opens the Customize View dialog, which is shown next. Make changes as desired, and click OK to save them.

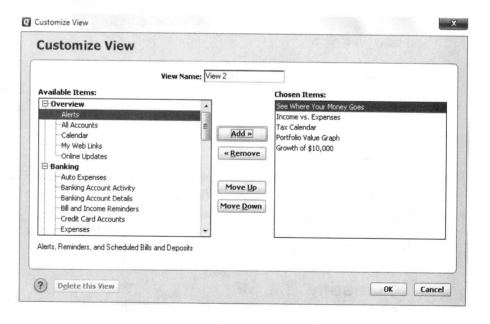

Adding an Item   Items are organized by type in the Available Items list, making it easy to find the one you want. To add an item to the view, select it in the Available Items list and click Add. Its name appears in the Chosen Items list.

You can include more than 40 items in the view; however, rather than have a great number of items that crowd your window, it's better to create separate views with fewer items in each view.

Removing an Item   To remove an item from the view, select it in the Chosen Items list and click Remove.

Rearranging Items   To rearrange the order of items in the Chosen Items list, select an item and click Move Up or Move Down. Repeat this process until the items appear in the order you want.

Creating a New View

By creating multiple views, you can make several versions of the Home tab window, each with a specific set of information. You can then quickly switch from one view to another to see the information you want.

In the Home tab window, click the Add View button (refer to Figure B-1). The Customize View dialog, which is shown earlier, appears.

Enter a name for the view in the View Name box. Then follow the instructions in the previous section to add items to the view, and click OK. A new Quicken Home tab window view is created to your specifications and appears on-screen.

Switching from One View to Another

If you have created more than one view for the Quicken Home window, each view has its own menu button at the top of the Home tab window, as shown in Figure B-1. To switch from one view to another, simply click its button.

Deleting a View

To delete a view, select the button for the view you want to delete. Click Customize to open the Customize View dialog. Then choose Delete This View from the menu. Click Yes in the confirmation dialog that appears. The view is deleted. You must have at least one view in the Home tab, meaning you cannot delete the "last" view.

Re-creating the Summary View

In earlier versions of Quicken, a Summary view displayed a number of snapshots with useful information about your banking accounts. If you liked this view, as many did, you can easily create it, as described next.

1. Open the Home tab, and click Add View. The Customize View dialog appears. In the View Name field, type **Summary View**. If any information appears in the Chosen Items list, click the first item, hold down your SHIFT key, and click the bottom item to select the entire list. Then, click Remove to remove these items. You are only removing them from the Chosen Items list in the current view. They are still available in the Available Items list on the left.

2. Start by selecting Alerts in the Available Items list, and click Add. You will note that all of the items are in this order within the six sections: Overview, Banking, Investing, Property & Debt, Planning, and Tax.

3. Add the following from the Banking section of the Available Items list: Spending And Savings Accounts, Credit Card Accounts, and Bill And Income Reminders, in that order. When you click OK, you'll see a Summary View, similar to the one that was in previous Quicken versions, as shown in Figure B-2.

In your new Summary View, all snapshots include an Options menu and buttons that you can use to work with that snapshot. For example, the Alerts snapshot at the top of the view has both buttons and Options menu commands for showing, setting up, and deleting alerts. Many of these options are discussed throughout this part of the book; you can explore the others on your own.

Here's a brief summary of each snapshot in your new Summary View.

Alerts

The Alerts snapshot lists alerts you have set up. You can click blue links to go to the account or other items the alert applies to. See how to set up and use banking-related alerts in Chapter 6.

Spending And Savings Accounts

The Spending And Savings Accounts snapshot lists all of your checking, savings, and cash accounts, along with their ending balances. Remember, the *current balance* shows the net of all of the deposits and checks through today's date. The *ending balance* includes any checks or deposits you have entered that will occur on future dates. You can click links to view the account register, set up balance alerts, and set interest rates.

Credit Card Accounts

The Credit Card Accounts snapshot lists all of your credit card accounts along with their current and ending balances. You can click links to view the account register, set the credit limit, and specify the interest rate.

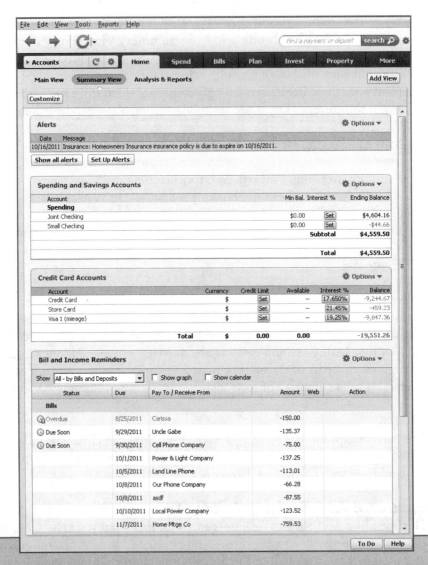

Figure B-2 • The Summary View includes useful information about your current balances and planned spending.

Bill And Income Reminders

The Bill And Income Reminders snapshot lists all of your bills, deposits, and other scheduled transactions. It may also display a list of transactions that Quicken thinks you may want to schedule. Buttons beside each selected item enable you to enter, edit, or skip a scheduled transaction, or to schedule or ignore a suggested transaction. See more about working with scheduled transactions in Chapter 6.

Crafting an Analysis & Reports View

Another popular view can be created easily in Quicken 2012. This Analysis & Reports view includes both graphs and reports that explain your current financial position.

1. From the Home tab, click Add View to open the Customize View dialog. Type **Analysis & Reports View** in the View Name field. Remove any items in the Chosen Items list.
2. Add the following from the Available Items list: Expenses, Income vs. Expenses, and Budget, in that order. When you click OK, you'll see an Analysis & Reports View, as shown next.

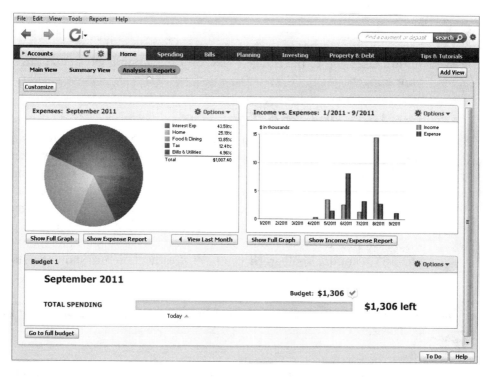

The Analysis & Reports View includes snapshots that summarize and help you analyze entries in your banking accounts. Most of these snapshots give you a glimpse of Quicken's extensive and highly customizable reporting features, as discussed in Chapter 8.

Here's a quick look at the snapshots in the Analysis & Reports View.

Expenses

The Expenses snapshot displays a pie chart of your expenses for the current or previous month.

Income vs. Expenses

The Income vs. Expenses snapshot displays a column chart of your year-to-date income and expenses.

Budget

The Budget snapshot displays information from your budget. To use this snapshot, you must set up a budget using Quicken's budgeting feature, as discussed in Chapter 16. Otherwise, this area in the Analysis & Reports view will display a link to the Budget section of Quicken.

If you have not yet set up a budget, you will see the Track Spending Goals To Save Money snapshot with the Get Started button. Clicking the Get Started button takes you to the Budgets view on the Planning tab so you can set up your budget.

Customizing the Tool Bar

The Quicken Tool Bar is an optional row of buttons along the top of the screen, just beneath the menu bar. These buttons offer quick access to Quicken features.

You can customize the Tool Bar by adding, removing, or rearranging buttons, or by changing the display options for the buttons. You can do all this with the Customize Toolbar dialog, which is shown on the top of the next page. To open this dialog, open the View menu and click Show Toolbar. With the Tool Bar displayed, position your mouse anywhere on the Tool Bar, right-click, and choose Customize Toolbar. (If you have already chosen to show the Tool Bar, you can click View | Customize Toolbar as well.)

You can also customize the Tool Bar by clicking the small gear icon at the right end of it.

To customize the Tool Bar, make changes in this dialog and click OK. The Tool Bar is redrawn to your specifications.

Adding Buttons

To add a button, select it in the Available Toolbar Buttons list and click Add. Its name appears in the Your Toolbar Buttons list. If you want more items to choose from, click the Show All Toolbar Choices check box to display all the possibilities. The list expands to show approximately three times as many items.

You can include as many buttons as you like on the Tool Bar. If the Tool Bar includes more buttons than can fit within the Quicken application window, a More button (a green down arrow) appears on the Tool Bar, as shown next. The More button may appear on the Tool Bar when you resize your Quicken window to make it smaller. Click this button to display a menu of buttons; choose the name of the button you want.

Adding Saved Reports to the Tool Bar

To add a saved report to the Tool Bar, click the Add Or Remove Saved Reports button in the Customize Toolbar dialog. Then select the In Toolbar check box beside each saved report you want to add to the Tool Bar. Click OK to save your changes. Learn more about the Manage Toolbar Reports dialog in Chapter 8.

Removing Buttons

To remove a button, select it in the Your Toolbar Buttons list and click Remove. Its name is removed from the Your Toolbar Buttons list, but is still available on the Available Toolbar Buttons list should you want to include it at another time.

Rearranging Buttons

You can rearrange the order of buttons on the Tool Bar by changing their order in the Your Toolbar Buttons list. Simply select a button that you want to move, and click Move Up or Move Down to change its position in the list.

Changing the Appearance of Buttons

Two Show options determine how Tool Bar buttons are displayed:

- **Icons And Text** displays both the Tool Bar button and its label, as shown here.

- **Icons Only** displays just the Tool Bar icon. When you point to an icon, its label appears.

The Global Search field appears on the Quicken Tool Bar by default. You can remove it from the Tool Bar by clearing the Show Global Search check box in the Customize Toolbar dialog.

Editing Buttons

You can also create custom keyboard shortcuts for the buttons on your Tool Bar. From the Customize Toolbar dialog, select the item you want to edit. Click Edit Shortcut Or Label to open the Edit Shortcut Or Label dialog, as shown here. Change the label name, create a shortcut key combination, or both, and then click OK.

You can now open that item from your keyboard using the keystrokes shown in the Edit Shortcut Or Label dialog. However, if you remove the button from the Tool Bar, the keystroke combination no longer works for that item. Also, the label change does not appear in the Your Toolbar Buttons list, but it does appear on the Tool Bar when you save your customized settings.

Restoring the Default Tool Bar

To restore the Tool Bar back to its "factory settings," click the Reset To Default button in the Customize Toolbar dialog. Then click OK in the confirmation dialog that appears. The buttons return to the way they appear when Quicken is first installed.

Setting Preferences

The Preferences menu gives you access to dialogs for changing Quicken Preferences settings. Many Preferences settings have been discussed throughout other chapters in this book, but this section reviews all of the options you can change and tells you where you can learn more about the features they control.

Telling Quicken Your Preferences

As the name suggests, Preferences control Quicken's general appearance and operations. To access these options, open the Edit menu and choose Preferences to open the Preferences dialog, as seen in Figure B-3. It lists a variety of categories, each of which is discussed next.

Startup

Startup preferences enable you to specify what should appear when you start Quicken. Use the drop-down list to select Home (the default setting), one of the tabs (Home, Bills, Planning, and so on), a specific account register, the Transaction List, or one of the views within the tabs.

You can choose what you want Quicken to do when it starts, such as download transactions or require a password, and also choose one of the predefined color schemes for the Quicken program: blue (the default), green, purple, or tan. You can also choose to have non-active (disabled) windows dimmed. Use the slider to determine how much or how little "dimming" should occur.

Depending on your monitor settings, sometimes changing the color scheme can make Quicken easier for you to read. Also, you can make the font easier to read by selecting View | Use Large Fonts.

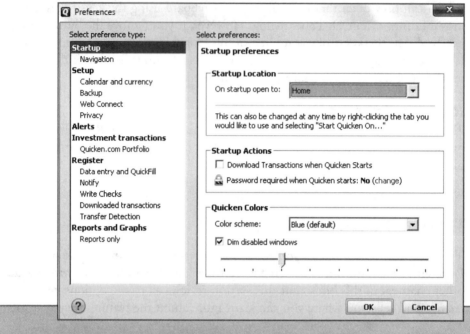

Figure B-3 • Use the Preferences dialog to make Quicken your own.

Navigation   Startup Navigation allows you to choose how you want to get around Quicken:

- **Main Navigation** lets you choose to use the Classic menus (those used prior to 2010). If you choose Classic menus, you also have an option to turn off the display of the tabs.
- **Account Bar** lets you select where to place the Account Bar and whether to display cents in the Account Bar balances.
- **Other Options** lets you choose whether to show the Quicken Tool Bar. If you have a widescreen monitor, you may choose to dock the side bar permanently on the right side of your monitor.

Setup

Setup options control basic Quicken operations, such as the following:

- **Keyboard Mappings** enables you to change what certain standard Windows keyboard shortcuts do. In most Windows programs, the CTRL-Z, CTRL-X, CTRL-C, and CTRL-V shortcut keys perform commands on the Edit menu.

In Quicken 2012, these keyboard shortcuts are set to the Windows standard. See Appendix A for more information about keyboard shortcuts.

- **Turn On Quicken Sounds** turns on Quicken sound effects. You may want to leave this check box off if you use Quicken in an environment where sounds might annoy the people around you.
- **Turn On Animation**, which is turned on by default, activates the Quicken animation effects that appear when you complete certain actions.
- **Automatically Minimize Pop-up Windows** automatically minimizes a Quicken window—such as a report window or the Category List window— to the Quicken task bar when you click outside that window. (This is the window behavior in some older versions of Quicken.) With this option turned off, you can have multiple Quicken windows open at once and can manually minimize each one.

Calendar and Currency   The folks at Intuit realize that not everyone manages their finances on a calendar-year basis or in U.S. dollars alone. The Calendar and Currency options enable you to customize these settings for the way you use Quicken:

- **Working Calendar** enables you to choose between two options: Calendar Year is a 12-month year beginning with January, and Fiscal Year is a 12-month year beginning with the month you choose from the drop-down list.
- **Multicurrency Support** assigns a "home" currency to all of your current data, placing a currency symbol beside every amount. You can then enter amounts in other currencies by entering the appropriate currency symbol. It is not necessary to set this option unless you plan to work with multiple currencies in one Quicken data file.

Backup   The Backup options, illustrated on the next page, enable you to customize the way Quicken's Backup feature works. Click Backup Help to open Quicken Help to the section explaining backing up.

You can choose to have Quicken automatically do backups on your computer's hard drive, as well as choose to be reminded to do manual backups on any drive you want. Besides allowing you to turn these two forms of backup on or off, you also have these settings:

- **Back Up After Running Quicken** *NN* **Times** tells Quicken to automatically back up (make a copy of) your Quicken data on your normal hard drive after you have run Quicken the specified number of times.
- **Maximum Number Of Backup Copies** is the number of backup copies Quicken should automatically keep. The higher the value in this text box,

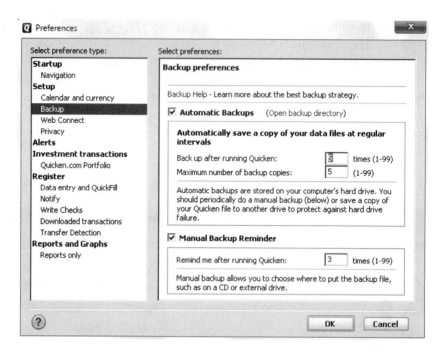

the more backup copies of your Quicken data are saved. This enables you to go back further if you discover a problem with your current Quicken data file. You learn more about backing up data in Appendix A.

- **Remind Me After Running Quicken *NN* Times** enables you to specify when you want to be reminded to manually back up your Quicken data file. If you also have automatic backups turned on, use the manual backup to back up your data to a location other than your regular hard drive.

Web Connect   The Web Connect options enable you to customize the way Quicken's Web Connect feature works. Web Connect, as discussed in Chapter 5, is a method for downloading transaction information from your financial institution into your Quicken data file.

- **Give Me The Option Of Saving To A File Whenever I Download Web Connect Data** displays a dialog after a Web Connect session that enables you to save the downloaded Web Connect information to a file.
- **Keep Quicken Open After Web Connect Completes** tells Quicken to keep running after Web Connect completes a download from the Web.

Privacy   This option opens Privacy Preferences, as shown next. A link allows you to learn more about Quicken's privacy policies, and another link opens the

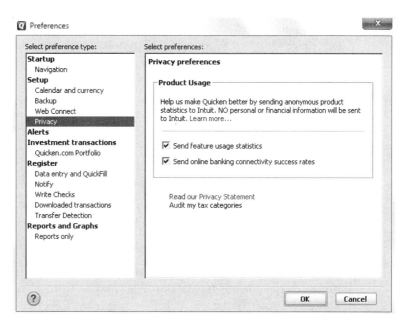

Intuit Consumer Group Privacy Statement. In addition, you have two other options:

- **Send Feature Usage Statistics to Quicken** anonymously sends statistical data to Quicken citing the number of times you use a specific feature within the program.
- **Send Online Banking Connectivity Success Rates** tells Quicken the number of times you successfully connect to a financial institution from Quicken.

 You may see an additional item that looks like a link but is not. If you see a sentence that says "Audit My Tax Categories," understand this is not a working link. As Quicken sends future updates, this sentence should disappear.

Alerts

Alerts preferences enable you to set the lead time for calendar notes to appear in Alerts snapshots. Learn about alerts in Chapter 6. This does not affect the lead time for scheduled transactions or Billminder.

- **Billminder** is explained in detail in Chapter 6. You can select a lead time period from the drop-down list; timing options range in periods from Last Month to Next Month.

- **Warnings** allow you to change all Quicken warnings back to their default. Click Reset Quicken Warnings, and a message appears that all warnings are reset.

Investment Transactions

Investment Transactions options let you customize the way the Investment Transaction list looks and works. Learn about the Investment Transaction list in Chapter 9.

- **List Display** determines whether transactions should appear with one or two lines in the list.
- **Sort Choice** determines whether transactions should be sorted in ascending or descending order by date.
- **Show Hidden Transactions** displays hidden transactions in the list.
- **Show Attach Button** displays the Attach button beside the Edit and Delete buttons for the current transaction. You may want to turn off this check box if you do not use the Image Attachment feature. Chapter 4 explains how to attach images to transactions.
- **Automatically Update Quotes Every 15 Minutes** updates your stock portfolio with your Internet connection every 15 minutes. This feature comes with Quicken Premier and higher editions.

Quicken.com Portfolio As explained in Chapter 10, http://investing.quicken .com is an online site where you can track your investment information from any location with Internet access.

- **Select Accounts To View Online** tells Quicken what accounts to view online at Quicken.com and how to send information. You can pick and choose which accounts to use, or use the Select All button to select all of your accounts, or click Clear All to clear your choices and start over.
- **Send My Shares/Send Only My Symbols** tells Quicken what information about your holdings to track.
- **Track My Watch List On Quicken.com**, if cleared, stops Quicken.com from keeping track of the items you've included in your security Watch List.
- **Change My Quicken.com Credentials At Next One Step Update** tells Quicken you want to update or amend your online credentials the next time you connect with Quicken.com through One Step Update.

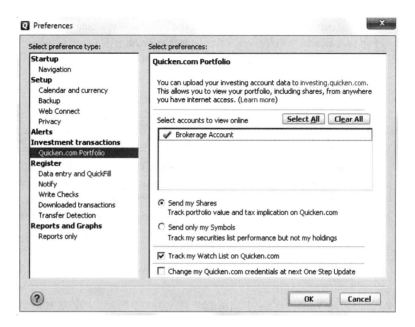

Register

Register preferences enable you to fine-tune the way the account register works. Five groups of settings appear in addition to the Register preferences themselves. Account register windows are discussed throughout this book, but details for using them are provided in Chapter 4.

Register Preferences   Register options, shown next, affect the way the transactions you enter appear in the account register window:

- **Show Date Before Check Number** is the default setting for your registers. Clear this check box to have the check number appear in the first column.
- **Show Memo Before Category** puts the Memo field before the Category field in your account register.

Transaction Entry
- **Automatically Enter Split Data** turns the OK button in the Split Transaction window into an Enter button for entering the transaction.
- **Use Automatic Categorization** uses the Automatic Categorization feature to "guess" which category should be assigned to a transaction based on a database of company names and keywords stored within Quicken. This applies both to transactions you enter and those that you download.

- **Automatically Place Decimal Point** automatically enters a decimal point two places to the left when entering dollar figures in Quicken or using Quicken's built-in calculator. For example, if you enter 1543 in the calculator, Quicken enters 15.43.

Register Appearance

- **Gray Reconciled Transactions** displays all reconciled transactions with gray characters rather than black characters.
- **Remember Register Filters After Quicken Closes** remembers any register filter settings you may have made when you close Quicken so those settings are in place the next time you start the program.
- **Use Pop-Up Registers** opens registers in separate windows, allowing you to have several different windows with a variety of information open at the same time.
- **Fonts** displays a dialog you can use to select the font and size for register windows.
- **Colors** displays a dialog you can use to select colors for register windows.

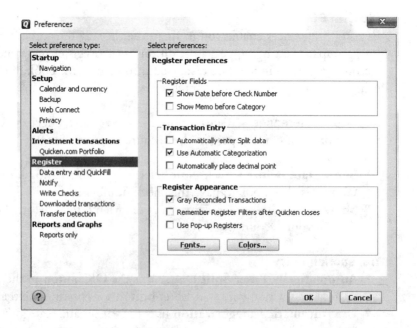

Data Entry and QuickFill   Data Entry and QuickFill options allow you to fine-tune the way Quicken's QuickFill feature works. Learn more about QuickFill in Chapter 6.

Data Entry

- **Use Enter Key To Move Between Fields** enables you to use both the ENTER and TAB keys to move from field to field when entering data.
- **Complete Fields Using Previous Entries** enters transaction information using the information from previous entries.
- **Recall Memorized Payees** uses memorized payees to fill in QuickFill entries. This option is not available if the Complete Fields Using Previous Entries option is disabled.
- **Provide Drop-Down Lists On Field Entry** automatically displays the drop-down list when you advance to a field with a list.
- **Capitalize Payees And Categories** automatically makes the first letter of each word in a payee name or category uppercase.
- **Show Buttons On QuickFill Fields** displays drop-down list buttons on fields for which you can use QuickFill.

QuickFill and Memorized Payees

- **Automatically Memorize New Payees** tells Quicken to automatically enter all transactions for a new payee to the Memorized Payee List.
- **Automatically Include On Calendar Payee List** tells Quicken to automatically add memorized payees to the Calendar window. This option is turned on by default. You can display the Memorized Payee List by choosing Show Memorized Payee List from the Options menu on the Calendar's button bar.
- **Add Address Book QuickFill Group Items To Memorized Payee List** tells Quicken to add entries from the Address Book to the Memorized Payee List so they automatically fill in address fields when writing checks.
- **Remove Memorized Payees Not Used In Last *NN* Months** tells Quicken to remove memorized payees that have not been used within the number of months you specify. By default, this feature is turned on, with the number of months set at 14. By entering a value of 6 (for example), Quicken memorizes only the payees you entered in the past six months, thus keeping the Memorized Payee List manageable. Using this feature with a lower value (for example, 3) can weed one-time transactions out of the Memorized Payee List. Changing this option does not affect transactions that have already been entered. Chapter 6 discusses memorized transactions.

Notify   Notify options affect the way you are notified about problems when you enter transactions in the register:

- **When Entering Out-Of-Date Transactions** warns you when you try to record a transaction for a date more than a year from the current date.

- **Before Changing Existing Transactions** warns you when you try to modify a previously entered transaction.
- **When Entering Uncategorized Transactions** warns you when you try to record a transaction without assigning a category to it.
- **To Run A Reconcile Report After Reconcile** asks if you want to display a Reconcile Report when you complete an account reconciliation.
- **Warn If A Check Number Is Re-used** warns you if you assign a check number that was already assigned in another transaction.
- **When Changing The Account Of An Existing Transaction** notifies you when you change the account of a transaction you have already entered.

Write Checks   Write Checks preferences affect the way the checks you create appear when printed when using the Write Checks window:

- **Printed Date Style** enables you to select a four-digit or two-digit date style.
- **Spell Currency Units** tells Quicken to spell out the currency amount in the second Amount field.
- **Allow Entry Of Extra Message On Check** displays an additional text box for a message in the Write Checks window. The message you enter is printed on the check in a place where it cannot be seen if the check is mailed in a window envelope.
- **Print Categories On Voucher Checks** prints category information, including splits and tags, on the voucher part of voucher checks. This option affects only voucher-style checks.
- **Change Date Of Checks To Date When Printed** automatically prints the print date, rather than the transaction date, on each check.

Downloaded Transactions   Downloaded Transactions preferences, which are shown next, control the way Quicken handles transactions downloaded into it from your financial institution. You learn more about downloading transactions into Quicken in Chapter 5.

- **Automatically Add To Banking Registers** saves manually reviewing and accepting each banking transaction, and possibly leaving an unaccepted transaction out of Quicken reports and graphs.
- **Automatically Add To Investment Transaction Lists** saves you time by entering your downloaded transactions to your investment account "registers" rather than having to manually review and accept each transaction.

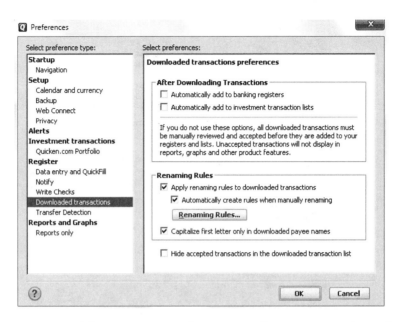

Renaming Rules   The Renaming Rules options allow you control over how Quicken deals with the differences between the payee names in your records and those of the bank's.

- **Apply Renaming Rules To Downloaded Transactions** turns on Quicken's renaming feature, which is discussed in Chapter 5.
- **Automatically Create Rules When Manually Renaming** tells Quicken to create renaming rules automatically based on transactions you rename manually.
- Click **The Renaming Rules** button to open the Renaming Rules dialog, which you can use to create, modify, and remove renaming rules.
- **Capitalize First Letter Only In Downloaded Payee Names** capitalizes just the first letter of a payee name for a downloaded transaction.
- **Hide Accepted Transactions In The Downloaded Transaction List** does not display transactions that have already been accepted in the Downloaded Transactions list.

Transfer Detection   This option tells Quicken to review each downloaded transaction to see if is matched with another transaction. If you select this option, when Quicken finds matched transactions, you have two options:

- **Automatically Create Transfer When Detected** makes the transfer from the one account to the other automatically and enters the transaction in both registers.

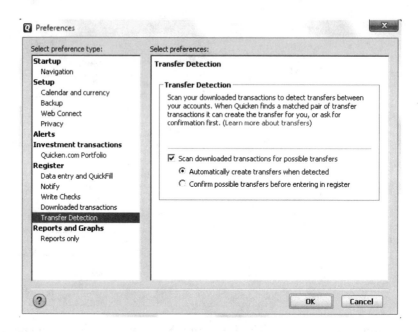

- **Confirm Possible Transfers Before Entering In Register** directs Quicken to ask you whether the transaction is, indeed, a transfer.

Reports and Graphs

Reports And Graphs preferences include two categories of options for creating reports and graphs. Creating reports and graphs is discussed in detail in Chapter 8.

Reports And Graphs Preferences   Reports And Graphs options enable you to set your own default options for creating reports and graphs:

- **Default Date Range** and **Default Comparison Date Range** enable you to specify a default range for regular and comparison reports. Choose an option from each drop-down list. If you choose Custom, you can enter exact dates.
- **Customizing Reports And Graphs** options determine how reports and graphs are customized and what happens when they are. Customizing Creates New Report Or Graph, which is the default setting, creates a subreport based on the report you customize. Customizing Modifies Current Report Or Graph changes the report you customize without creating a subreport.

- **Customize Report/Graph Before Creating** tells Quicken to offer to customize a report or graph when you choose one.

Reports Only   This group of options, which is shown next, applies only to reports:

- **Account Display** and **Category Display** enable you to set what you want to display for each account or category listed in the report: Description, Name, or Both.
- **Use Color In Report** tells Quicken to use color when displaying report titles and negative numbers.
- **QuickZoom To Investment Forms** tells Quicken to display the investment form for a specific investment when you double-click it in an investment report. With this check box turned off, Quicken displays the investment register transaction entry instead.
- **Remind Me To Save Reports** tells Quicken to ask whether you want to save a customized report when you close the report window.
- **Decimal Places For Prices And Shares** enables you to specify the number of decimal places to display for per-share security prices and number of shares in investment reports.

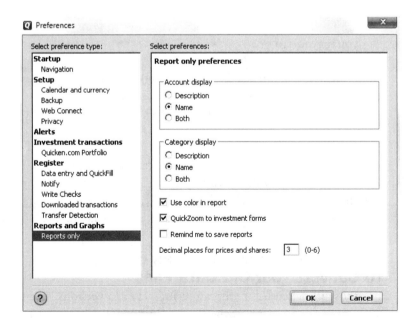

Useful Tips

While most Quicken users find the program exactly to their liking after they use some of the customization features mentioned earlier, others have questions about some specific how-tos.

Converting Your Older Quicken Files to a New Computer

After using the Quicken program for a number of years on a desktop computer, you may get a new laptop and want to upgrade to Quicken 2012. Depending on the version you are running, the best way to do this is as follows:

1. Do a backup of your old files before you start anything else.
2. On the "old" computer, choose File | Validate And Repair to ensure your old files are in the best shape possible.
3. Install Quicken 2012 on your "old" computer.
4. Open your Quicken data file, and let Quicken update all of your current files.
5. Install Quicken 2012 on your new computer. You may install up to three copies of your Quicken program onto computers within your own household.
6. Copy the files from your "old" computer to your "new" computer, and you're ready to go.

Because the file format in Quicken versions prior to 2010 was different from the single file format today, it is best to convert your old data before transferring it to your new computer. That way, you will only have one data file on your new computer.

When you are installing Quicken, you may see an option asking if you are a new Quicken user. If you inadvertently choose that option, you can still access your data files. Click File | Open Quicken File, and choose the data file you want to use. Your data will be converted to use with Quicken 2012.

Using Intermediate Versions of Quicken to Convert Your Old Data Files

For those Quicken users who are using very old versions, you may need to use an intermediate version of the program to convert your files to use with Quicken 2012. Here are some suggestions:

- **Quicken for DOS** users will need to update to Quicken 8 for DOS and from there convert to Quicken 2004, which is an intermediate program for Quicken 2005 and later.
- **Quicken 1 (through Quicken 5) for Windows** users must install Quicken 6 and update their files to Quicken 6 for Windows, from which they can convert to Quicken 2004, which is an intermediate program for Quicken 2005 and later.

There is a website from which you can read more information about converting from older versions of Quicken. With your Internet connection, type **http://quicken.intuit.com/support/help/GEN82211** into the address bar of your browser. From there you can even download the intermediate programs required to complete your conversion.

Changing Multiple Transactions

As companies merge and life changes, you may have a recurring transaction that needs to be changed. While you can edit the payee, category, tag, or memo for current month and future transactions in the Bills and Reminders tab, as explained in Chapter 6, you may want to change all of the previous transactions as well. It is not a difficult task to do so; however, as always when making any changes to your data, perform a backup before making those changes.

The process shown here assumes that the transactions are all from the same account. In our example, we're changing the name of a payee from Account Maintenance Fee to Service Charge.

1. Create a backup of your data file.
2. Open the account in which you posted the transactions.
3. Sort by the name of the item you want to change—in this example, it is the Payee.
4. Click the first item on the list and, holding your SHIFT key down, click the last item on the list. Each of the items will be highlighted, as seen here.

Date	Check #	Payee ▲		Payment
		Category	Memo	
3/14/2011	Check #	Account Maintenance Fee		12 00
		Fees & Charges	Download from	
7/15/2011		Account Maintenance Fee		12 00
		Fees & Charges	Download from	
8/12/2011		Account Maintenance Fee		12 00
		Fees & Charges	Download from	

Depending on your monitor and the color preferences you have set for your register, the highlighting may be hard to distinguish.

5. Right-click one of the highlighted selections to open a context menu.
6. From the context menu choose Edit Transactions.
7. The Find And Replace dialog appears as seen here.
8. In the With field, enter the new name, as seen next. Keep in mind that if you are changing something other than the payee, you will need to select the appropriate field in the Replace drop-down list.

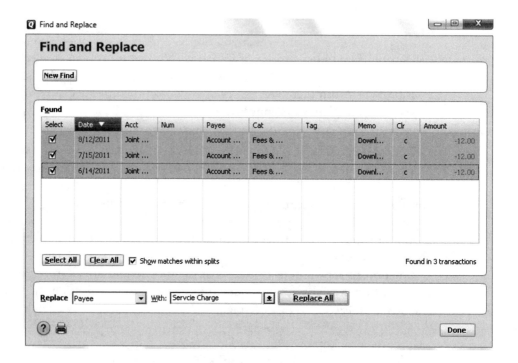

9. Click Replace All to replace the payee name.
10. A Renaming Rule dialog appears. Choose to create this renaming rule, or tell Quicken not to show this Renaming Rule message again. Click OK. (You do not see the Renaming Rule dialog if you are replacing a field other than Payee.)
11. You are returned to the Find And Replace dialog. Click Done.
12. You are returned to the register where your new payee name is now showing. (Remember, you've sorted in alphabetical order, so if your new name starts with a different letter, you will have to scroll down the register to see it.) See the following illustration for an example.

Date	Check #	Payee ▲	Payment
► 🗑 ✎		Category	
6/14/2011		Service Charges	12 00
		Fees & Charges:Bank Fee	
7/15/2011		Service Charges	12 00
		Fees & Charges:Bank Fee	
8/12/2011		Service Charges	12 00
		Fees & Charges:Bank Fee	

You can perform this same process using any register field, including Amount, Category, Memo, and Tag, as well as Check Number, Cleared Status, and Date. However, be sure to run a backup before starting the process just to ensure your data's safety.

Quicken Emergency Records Organizer

Earlier versions of Quicken included an organizational tool in which users could maintain important information about emergency contacts, personal and legal documents, mortgage and investment information, and so on. While the Attach Document utility has taken over much of the necessity of using this tool, many Quicken users still rely on the data that can be kept.

You can still install the Emergency Records Organizer in Quicken 2012. To do so, first run a backup of your data file. If you are comfortable working with Windows folders, this is an easy process.

1. Right-click the Start button.
2. Click one of the following, depending on your version of Windows:
   - In Windows 7, click Open Windows Explorer.
   - In Windows Vista, click Windows Explorer.
   - In Windows XP, click Explore.
3. Locate your Quicken installation folder.
   - In Windows 7 (32-bit), Vista, and XP, it is located in C:\Program Files\Quicken.
   - In Windows 7 and Vista (64-bit) computers, you'll find it in C:\Program Files (x86)\Quicken.
4. Once in the folder, scroll to Emergency Records Organizer.exe, as shown next. Depending on your computer's settings, you may not see the "exe" file extension, just EmergencyRecordsOrganizer.

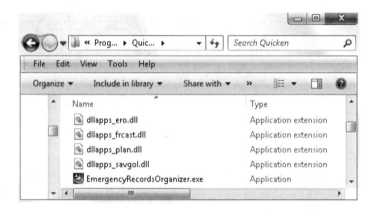

5. Double-click the .exe file. A message may appear asking if you want to let this program make changes to your computer. Click Yes.

6. You see a Quicken message asking if you want to add "Emergency Records Organizer" to Quicken. If so, click Yes.

7. The program is installed. You may see a message saying it has been included with Quicken. Click OK to dismiss the message telling you the Emergency Records Organizer was successfully installed.

Using the Emergency Records Organizer

After you have installed the Emergency Records Organizer, you must be using Classic menus or add the Emergency Records Organizer as a button to the Quicken Tool Bar to access it.

1. Click View | Classic Menus.

2. Click View | Tabs To Show to ensure Property & Debt has a check mark.

3. From the menu bar, click Property & Debt.

4. See the Emergency Records Organizer at the bottom of the menu, as shown here.

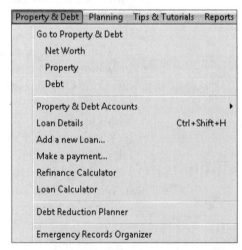

To enter information in the Emergency Records Organizer:

1. Click Property & Debt from Classic menus, and then click

Emergency Records Organizer. The Emergency Records Organizer window opens.

2. Click the Create/Update Records tab.

3. Click the Select An Area down arrow, and click one of the 11 areas in which to enter information.

When you first open the Emergency Records Organizer and select Accounts, all of the accounts you currently have set up in Quicken are included in the Topic List. No new accounts can be added to this list through the Emergency Records Organizer. However, as you add new accounts, you can use the generic Other Accounts or add the new record to an existing account.

4. Click an option under Select A Topic. The records pane on the right will display text boxes to enter information pertaining to that topic.

5. Enter the relevant information in each field. Press TAB to move between fields.

6. Click Save to save the record when finished.

7. Click New Record to add another record in this topic.

The Notes area can hold up to 199 characters, including spaces.

Creating Reports in the Emergency Records Organizer

One of the best uses of the Emergency Records Organizer is to create reports that may be needed by various professionals in case of an emergency.

1. With the Emergency Records Organizer displayed, click the Reports tab, click the Report Type down arrow, and choose which report you want.

2. Click Sort By Family Members to include all information about each family member separately. Otherwise, it will be displayed by area.

3. Click Print Topics With No Data Entered to show that data has not been entered about this topic as yet.

4. Click Print to print the report. The report goes directly to the printer. If you need more than one copy, you must click Print for each copy.

5. Click Close to exit the Emergency Records Organizer.

Converting from Microsoft Money

In This Appendix:

- *Preparing to convert from Microsoft Money to Quicken*
- *Converting your Money files*
- *Taking your first steps in Quicken*
- *Exploring the Bills tab*
- *Working with your account registers*
- *Creating reports*
- *Planning with Quicken*
- *Surveying the Investing tab*
- *Understanding Quicken's backup procedures*

Welcome to Quicken, Microsoft Money user! This document will help explain some of the similarities and a few differences as you start using Quicken. We'll talk about what you are used to seeing in Microsoft Money and what the same process looks like on your Quicken screen. Along the way, you'll see the many features that Quicken offers.

Converting Your Data Files from Money to Quicken

As you prepare to convert your Money data files to Quicken, there are a few things you can do in Money to make the conversion easier. Review your files as shown here, and ensure that all of your Money records are complete and up to date.

If you are converting Money data files to versions of Quicken prior to Quicken 2010, see the information Intuit has available at http://quicken.intuit.com/ support, and type **Microsoft Money** into the Search box.

Preparing to Convert from Microsoft Money to Quicken

To ensure a smooth transition, first review your Money data files. Performing each of the following actions will improve the chances of a good conversion:

- Clean up your Payee list to ensure there are no duplicate names because of mistyping. It's a lot easier to do this before you convert than to take the time afterward.
- Review your Category List and remove any that are unused.
- Review your online recurring payments and calendar to ensure you have stopped them. You'll be setting them up again in Quicken.
- Check that your financial institution can download into Quicken (most can) and how that download is accomplished. To see what download types are provided by your financial institution, go to http://web.intuit.com/ fisearchbasic and choose your financial institution from the list.
- Reconcile all of your accounts prior to converting.
- Ensure that all of your downloaded transactions are complete and up to date.
- Review your account names in Money to ensure they are less than the Quicken maximum character length (40 characters), and change them if necessary.
- Ensure that none of your account or category names include the characters [ ] / | ^. These characters are prohibited in Quicken and will be replaced. Here is an example of what you might see if you downloaded a file that contained one of those characters in either the account or category name.

> **Item Renamed (Illegal Characters)**
> Category or account name contained one or more of the following prohibited characters ": [ ] / | ^" in Quicken. Prohibited characters were replaced: Income-Interest

- Ensure that none of your Money accounts have the same name as your Money categories. For example, if you have a Money bank account called "Savings," ensure that there is not a category in Money called "Savings" as well. Consider calling the bank account "Family Savings" or changing the name of the category. In some rare cases, Quicken has seen the duplicate names and made the account a category or the category a bank account.
- Consider running a repair on your Money file before you start the conversion to ensure that no problems exist in your file.

Your Money category names, payee names, and notes and memos do not have this same 40-character limit, so the Quicken file converter will truncate filenames if needed, as seen in "Warning Messages" later in this appendix.

Both Quicken and Money are, by default, installed in the Program Files folder on your main hard drive (usually the "C" drive). However, you can keep your data files in whatever folder you choose, as discussed in Chapter 1. After you have installed Quicken, it is time to convert your files (those with the file extension .mny) from Microsoft Money to Quicken.

In order to convert your .mny files, you must have both Quicken and Microsoft Money installed on the same computer.

You should have no problem converting all of your bank transactions and your checking, savings, credit card, and investment accounts. Likewise, your category and other name information should also convert cleanly after you have made any necessary changes to the number of characters in each name. Remember that any recurring payments you have set up in Money, such as monthly insurance payments, will have to be canceled in Money and reset in Quicken.

Converting Your Money Files

Quicken 2012 can convert Microsoft Money Plus Sunset and Money 2008 files. If you have an earlier version, as of the date of this writing, Microsoft has made a Sunset version of the program that can be downloaded from their website. There are specific instructions and explanations on that website regarding the download.

As all online and support services ended in January 2011, the Sunset version allows Money users to keep their data and enter new items manually. This link is to the Microsoft Download Center, where you can download this version: www.microsoft.com/downloads/en/confirmation.aspx?FamilyID=60302e1e-207e -4710-ac80-d19c22e47488&displaylang=en. (You may be able to access this website through a search engine by typing in **Microsoft Money Plus Sunset** as well.)

Convert your older Money data files to either Money 2008 files or Microsoft Money Plus Sunset, and convert those files into Quicken. Before you start your conversion, verify the balances in each of your Money accounts. Print a list of these balances to compare with your Quicken balances after the conversion. To print the list:

1. In Money, click Account List. Ensure that each of your accounts is displayed.
2. Click File | Print to print the report.

Then, check these account balances after the conversion to ensure the information has come across cleanly.

Begin the Conversion

To begin converting your .mny files:

1. Install and launch Quicken. The Welcome To Quicken window appears.
2. From the three choices available, choose I Want To Import My Data From Microsoft Money, and then click the Get Started button.
3. A blank Quicken Home page opens. Quicken will locate your .mny file and start the conversion automatically.

> **IN MY EXPERIENCE**
>
> It is a good idea to remove any file passwords, including the Windows Live password, from your Money file before you convert this file. You can reset passwords in Quicken once the conversion is complete and your new file is functional.
>
> To remove your Windows Live password from your Money file:
>
> 1. Disconnect from the Internet.
> 2. Open Money and sign in while you are still offline.
> 3. Remove the Windows Live ID from your Money file.
> 4. Close your Money file and reconnect to the Internet.

NOTE You must have an empty Quicken file in which to import your Microsoft Money data.

4. Quicken starts to convert the .mny file on this computer. If you have more than one Microsoft Money file, you will be asked to choose the proper file. If the conversion does not start immediately, click File | File Import | Microsoft Money file, as seen in Figure C-1.
5. A message box appears showing the progress of the file being imported.
6. After the files have been converted, a message box appears telling you that your Microsoft Money data file has been imported, as seen next.

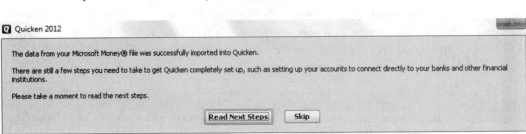

Quicken 2012

The data from your Microsoft Money® file was successfully imported into Quicken.

There are still a few steps you need to take to get Quicken completely set up, such as setting up your accounts to connect directly to your banks and other financial institutions.

Please take a moment to read the next steps.

[Read Next Steps]   [Skip]

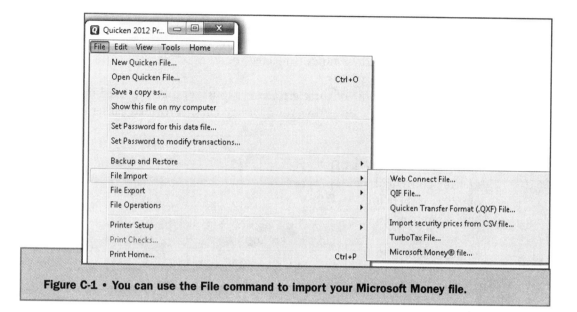

Figure C-1 • You can use the File command to import your Microsoft Money file.

7. Click Read Next Steps to open the Help window that explains what you need to do next. See "Taking Your First Steps in Quicken" later in this appendix for information on each step.
8. Print the Help for future reference, if you choose.
9. Click Close to close the Help dialog. Your converted file opens to the Home tab's Main View.

You import your Money data files into a new, empty Quicken file. Do not try to convert Money data files into an existing Quicken file with data in it. If you try to do this, you will see a message warning you that you'll have to create a new, empty file. Click Create File to do so.

If you see warning or error messages during the conversion process, you can visit the Quicken site at this link—http://quicken.intuit.com/support/help/GEN82752.

Warning Messages

During the conversion process, you may see the following warning messages:

- WARNING: One or more accounts in Money is in the middle of a reconciliation.
- WARNING: Account bank name truncated to: …

- WARNING: Transaction memo truncated to: …
- WARNING: Payee memo truncated to: …
- WARNING: Address notes truncated to: …

As you can see, some of these errors refer to issues that you fixed if you followed the tips in "Converting Your Money Files," provided earlier in this appendix.

Using the View Log

After the conversion is complete, if there are some discrepancies, Quicken may display a message asking you to view a log file of the differences. Click View Log, if it displays, or click Help | Log Files | Microsoft Money: File Import Results to see the list and explanation, as seen in Figure C-2. You can see this file at any time from within Quicken.

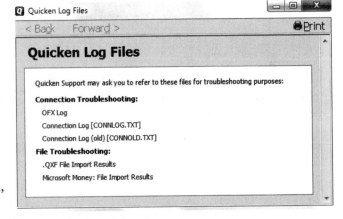

Taking Your First Steps in Quicken

After you have completed your successful conversion, there are a few steps you should complete before continuing:

- Review your account and payee names to ensure they converted properly. Because of the slight differences between the two programs in maximum character length and permitted characters, you may need to change the names of some of your payees or accounts.
- Set up your accounts for Transaction Download and Online Bill Pay. Any instructions you had in Money may need to be reset in Quicken. For more information on activating your accounts for online services, see Chapter 5.
- Set your recurring payments as described in Chapter 5. If you stopped them as described in "Converting Your Data Files from Money to Quicken" earlier in this appendix, there won't be any duplicate payments.

- **Investment account balances.** In Quicken, the balances of your investment accounts might not match the balances you had in Money because of differences in how the two programs report balances. Money includes the linked cash account in the balances of its investment accounts. Quicken does not.

- **Total account balance.** If you have an investment watch account, the total account balance you see in Quicken might not match the total account balance you saw in Money. This is because Money excludes watch accounts in its total balance, while Quicken includes them.

- **Issues with the way your data was imported.** If Quicken noted any issues with the way your data was imported, they are recorded below. Please read the Summary and the Details section to understand exactly how your data was impacted.

Note: Please print this document. It will get overwritten if you import your Microsoft Money file again.

Print

More information about your imported data and how to handle it is available online at Quicken.com.

Summary of Issues

At the bottom of this page is a section called "Details of Your Money File Import", which lists all the issues Quicken discovered while importing your data from Microsoft Money. The following summary explains what the messages in the Details section mean.

Errors

In some cases, we were not able to import certain data from your Money file. Please read these explanations to understand what will be missing from your Quicken file.
To find out exactly what part of your data was affected, scroll down to the Details section of this document and review any message that contains the same phrase as the header for the explanation listed in this section. Go to Details

Security Not Imported
Quicken was not able to import at least one of your securities. To identify the security that was not imported, look for a message in the Details section that says "Failed to convert security X to Quicken", where X is the name of the security.

Balloon Amortization
Your Money file included at least one balloon loan. Money stores the balloon amount, whereas Quicken stores the balloon amortized length. When Quicken imported the loan, it estimated the length. However, this estimation could be incorrect. Please check the

http://qw.quicken.com/cgi-bin/qd.cgi/w/2012/MnyCvtr2

Figure C-2 • Quicken explains any discrepancies found after importing your Money data files.

- Check your account's balances. There are some differences between how the two programs record information. As an example, Quicken separates the cash portion of your investing account into a banking account, while Money included this linked cash account in the investing total.

Remember that if you had two separate files in Money, you will need two separate files in Quicken. For example, if you had a file called Family Business and another file named Home Accounts in Money, you will have two files in Quicken as well. You cannot combine the two during the conversion.

- Review, and if necessary adjust, information on loans with balloon payments. Money stores the amount of the balloon payment, while Quicken stores the balloon amortized length and will try to estimate the length during the conversion.
- Create a new retirement plan and, if necessary, a new budget using the tools found in Quicken. See Chapter 14 for information about planning with Quicken and Chapter 16 to create a budget. The information you created in Money does not transfer into Quicken.
- If you were using Microsoft Money Home and Business, all of your accounts, categories, transactions, payees, and scheduled bills will be quickly converted into Quicken Home & Business edition. However, some of the more specific information, such as inventory, project, and customer data, does not carry over.
- Your Quicken accounts are shown on the Account Bar at the left of the Quicken window. You can also see them in the Account List. Open the Account List by pressing CTRL-A or click Tools | Account List from the Quicken menu bar.

To show two lines in your banking register, from any account register, click Account Actions and click Two-line Display as shown here. To toggle between one- and two-line display for Investment Transaction lists, use Edit | Preferences and select Investment Transactions in the Select Preference Type pane. In the List Display drop-down menu, select One Line or Two Line.

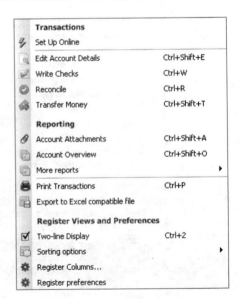

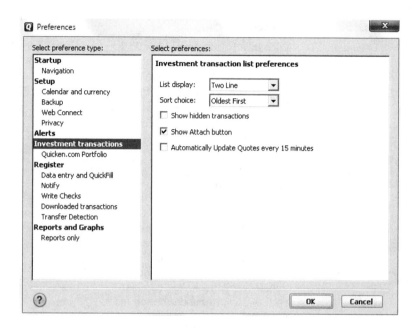

- After you have converted your Money file, remember to download your transactions from your financial institution into Quicken rather than Money. You cannot import individual transactions, only Money files, into Quicken.

Exploring the Bills Tab

The Bills tab in Quicken provides all of your bill information in one location. All of the bills you have scheduled appear on the list, and you can add new reminders with a simple click. Table C-1 gives some comparisons to what you see in Microsoft Money.

Viewing the Projected Balances

Quicken can tell you what the projected balances of any (or all) of your accounts will be based on the transactions you have scheduled, as seen in Figure C-3. In the Bills tab, click Projected Balances, and select the account and time range you want to see. This is similar to the Forecast Cash Flow feature in Money.

Look in the Quicken Home tab's Main View in the Stay On Top Of Monthly Bills section after you have worked with your Bill Reminders. There is a direct link to the Projected Balances graph. You can also customize views that include the Projected Balances graph. Look in Appendix B for directions on customizing views in the Home tab.

Description	Quicken	Money
Calendar	Click Bills | Upcoming | View As | Calendar to see a colorful and complete calendar. (You can also press CTRL-K to see the Calendar.) Double-click a day with upcoming expenses, select the expense, and click Enter to enter the transaction.	Click Bills | Bills Summary | Show Calendar | Enter In Register to open the Record Payment window into an account.
Recurring payments	In Quicken, recurring payments are called reminders. To set up a new reminder, simply right-click a transaction in an account's register. From the context menu that appears, click Schedule Bill Or Deposit to open the Add Reminder dialog, as discussed earlier in this book. You can also click the Add Reminder button in the Bills tab button bar.	Switch to Advanced Bills, and click the Bills tab. From the Bills Summary page, click New | Transaction Type. Complete the Create A Recurring Bill dialog, and click OK.
Printing checks	From any account's register, select a transaction. From the Check # drop-down list, select Print Check. Click File | Print Checks to open the Select Checks To Print dialog and print the check.	Click Banking | Account List *account name*. Right-click in the Num field, and then choose Print This Transaction | Enter. Click File | Print Checks.
Online payments	Activate online payments through your bank or Quicken Bill Pay service. From the Account Bar, right-click the account name. Choose Edit | Delete Account to open the Account Details dialog. Choose the Online Services tab. If your financial institution offers it, click Activate Bill Pay. See Chapter 5 for more information about setting up online payments.	Set up through your bank, MSN Bill Pay, or another bill-paying service. Click Banking | Account List | Common Tasks | Manage Online Services.

Table C-1 • Reviewing and Paying Bills in Quicken versus Microsoft Money

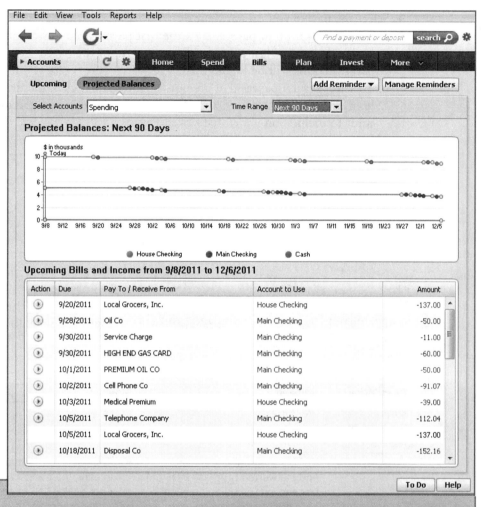

Figure C-3 • The Projected Balances view in the Bills tab displays a graph of your future account balances.

Working with Memorized Payees

When your Money file is converted, all of your payees are included in the Memorized Payee List by default. To delete payees or transactions you may not want to include:

1. Always perform a backup before any process with which you are deleting or moving data.
2. Press CTRL-T to open the Memorized Payee List.

3. Select the payees you do *not* want on your list.
   a. To select a group of payees, click the first payee, hold down your SHIFT key, and click the last payee in the group. All of the payees between your two selections will be highlighted.
   b. To select several payees that are not listed together, click the first payee, hold down your CTRL key, and click the rest of the payees you do not want to include on your Memorized Payee List. All of the payees you select will be highlighted.

4. Right-click any highlighted item, and choose Delete from the context menu that appears. You will see a dialog asking if it is okay to delete the *n* (number) of items, as seen here.
5. Click OK to delete the payees from the list.

Working with Your Account Registers

The Account Actions menu in each account register gives you the tools you need to update your transactions, write and print checks, transfer funds from one account to another, run reports, and change your register views, as described in Table C-2.

Description	Quicken	Money
Move through the account register	Press TAB.	Press TAB.
ENTER key	If you are entering a transaction and inadvertently press ENTER, the transaction will be automatically entered into the register, even if you have not completed the entry. To return to the transaction, simply click it to make any necessary changes. You can also set your Preferences to use the ENTER key to move between the register fields. From the menu bar, click Edit | Preferences | Register | Data Entry And Quickfill. Select Use Enter Key To Move Between Fields.	If you press ENTER without completing the transaction, a dialog appears asking you to complete the information or click OK to enter the transaction as-is. To return to the transaction, double-click to open the transaction form dialog, from which you can make changes, additions, or deletions.

Table C-2 • Working with Transactions in Your Account Registers

> ### IN MY EXPERIENCE
>
> If your account balances seem awry, check the following:
>
> - Try clicking the date field to ensure the date of your latest transaction is in the line at the bottom of the list. Since you can filter by any of the column headings, this is often where problems arise with balances. You can get your register sorted by other than date order and see strange balances, or you can filter your register using date, transaction type, or reconciliation status and get weird-looking balances. Or maybe you have both a sort and a filter applied and that is what's causing the issue.
> - If the values in the Account Bar seem strange, it may be that Quicken is displaying the ending balance, which includes any future transactions that you have scheduled and entered into the register. For example, if you have entered a property tax payment that will come out at the end of the month, that payment is included in Quicken's ending balance. To see your current balances in the Account Bar, right-click in the Account Bar, and choose Show Current Balance In Account Bar.
> - Consider waiting for your next paper statement to reconcile your accounts manually the first time after you have converted from Microsoft Money to Quicken.

You can also adjust which columns appear in your register. Click the small gear icon above the vertical scroll bar in the register to choose the columns you want displayed. You can also make your selection by choosing Account Actions | Register Columns.

Account Bar

The Account Bar displays a list of all of your accounts. As described in Chapter 1, the accounts are grouped into three areas:

- **Banking**, which includes those accounts you use for spending, such as your checking and cash accounts, savings, and credit card accounts
- **Investing**, which includes all of your brokerage, 401(k), IRAs and Keogh accounts, and any 529 Plan accounts
- **Property & Debt**, which includes all of your asset and liability accounts

Just as you would do in Microsoft Money, simply click any of the account names to open its register or, for investing accounts, its Transaction List.

Account Details

The Account Details dialog, shown next, shows the financial institution where the account is held, what you have set as the minimum balance (useful if your institution offers free checking if you maintain a minimum balance), the interest rate for the account if there is one, and other useful information.

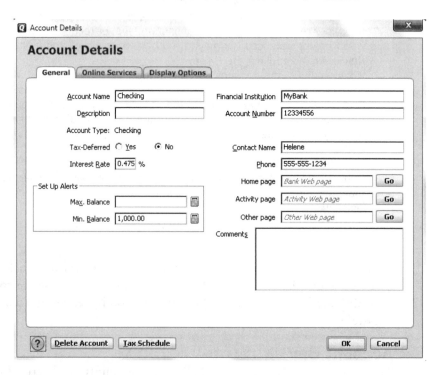

If you set Money to automatically place a decimal point in all transactions, you can accomplish the same task in Quicken by choosing Edit | Preferences | Register | Transaction Entry | Automatically Place Decimal Point. For example, if you enter 12345, Quicken will enter it as 123.45. Otherwise, Quicken will enter this transaction as 12,345.00.

Downloading Transactions

In Money, many users posted future transactions into account registers and then downloaded information from the bank and reconciled these entries. In Quicken, you may schedule recurring transactions in much the same way. However, you must tell Quicken to enter those transactions before you download. Otherwise, the scheduled transactions will show as past due and may be duplicated by the download from your financial institution. After you have downloaded your transactions, carefully review the download to ensure that what the bank paid and the scheduled transaction you entered earlier are the same amount. Ensure as well that you have not told Quicken to automatically enter downloaded transactions. To ensure this feature is turned off, click Edit | Preferences | Register | Downloaded Transactions, and, if necessary, clear the Automatically Add To Banking Registers check box. See Chapters 5, 6, and 10 for more information about downloaded transactions.

You can move a transaction in Quicken in a similar way to moving one in Money. Right-click any transaction in an account's register, and from the resulting context menu, choose Move Transaction. (You can also do this with multiple transactions. Either hold down the SHIFT key and choose a group of transactions, or hold down the CTRL key and choose transactions from several dates. This highlights the transactions). The Move Transaction(s) dialog appears. From the Move To Account drop-down list, select the account to which you want to move the transaction (or transactions). Click OK to close the dialog.

Creating Reports

Quicken includes robust reporting capabilities. You can create a report for any period, using any information you choose. If you are accustomed to using Advanced Reports in Microsoft Money, you'll feel very comfortable with Quicken reports.

You can see a menu for all Quicken reports by choosing Reports | Reports & Graphs Center to open the Reports and Graphs Center as seen in Figure C-4. In addition, several of the tabs have a Reports button that directs you to specific reports for that section. See Chapter 8 for a complete discussion of reports in Quicken.

The Reports and Graphs Center gives you options for colorful graphs that are sometimes easier to read than a report full of numbers, as seen in the example shown next.

IN MY EXPERIENCE

Quicken's customizable reports can help you create reports to answer many of your financial questions. A recent student wanted quarterly reports for each of her teen-aged children showing what each child spent each quarter and in what category. She created a tag for each child and used the Cash Flow By Tag and set the time period for the last quarter.

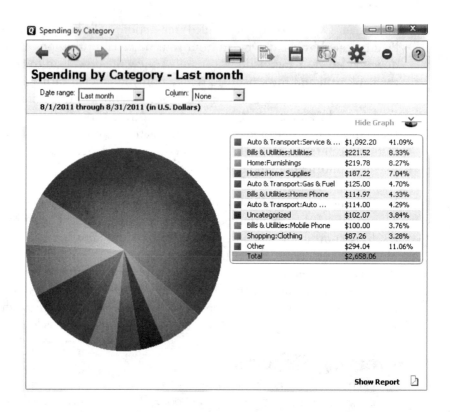

Planning with Quicken

The Quicken Planning tab places all of your budget and forecasting tools in one location. This tab is a combination of the Planning, Budget, and Tax tabs you used in Microsoft Money. In one screen you access all of the tools, calculators, and reports that help you plan your financial life. For example, in the Lifetime Planner view, you can tell Quicken facts about yourself and your family to plan for major expenses in your life, as seen in Figure C-5.

Along with your budget tools, the Planning tab includes a number of tax tools, as shown here. These include online tax calculators and links to common tax questions.

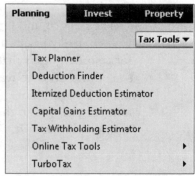

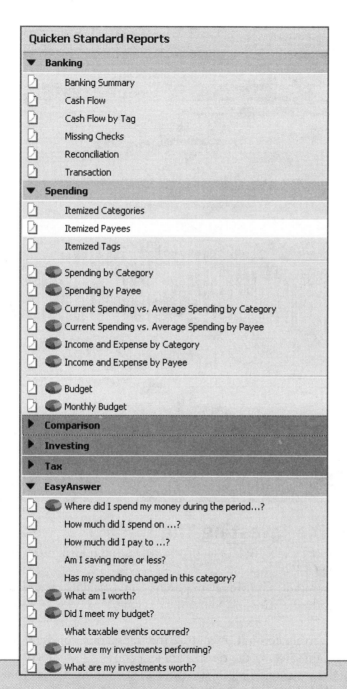

Figure C-4 • Quicken's graphs and charts help you understand your financial information in easy-to-read formats.

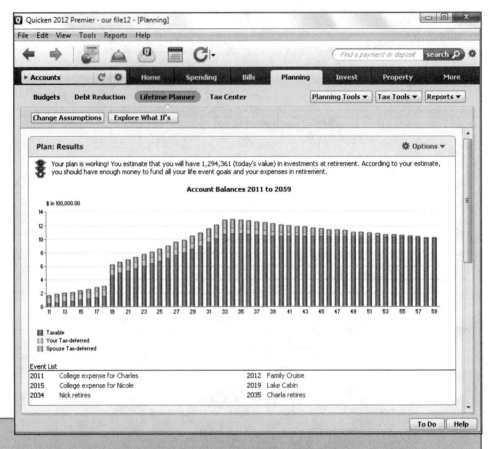

Figure C-5 • Quicken helps you to keep track today and plan for tomorrow with its
Planning tab utilities.

Surveying the Investing Tab

The Quicken Investing tab displays all of your investing information, as
described in Table C-3.

If you created reminders in Money to purchase investments on a regular
schedule, you can do the same in Quicken.

1. From your investing account, memorize the transaction you want to
   schedule by right-clicking the transaction and choosing Memorize
   Investment Transaction. You can also press CTRL-M to memorize your
   transaction. A dialog will appear letting you know this payee is about to
   be memorized. Click OK.

Description	Quicken	Money
Retirement accounts	Does not allow cash accounts to be linked to retirement accounts. Cash accounts are shown separately.	Allows linked cash accounts.
Investing information	Click the Investing tab and then choose Portfolio to see the current standing of your investing and retirement accounts.	Click the Investing tab and then choose My Investing Tools | Portfolio Manager to view just your account information.
Investing tools	Choose View | Classic Menus. Then click Investing | Investing Tools from the menu bar to access several tools.	The Investing tab opens a window with investing tips, the Investing Advisor, and several other tools. You see other information by clicking the Investing bar at the left of the window.

Table C-3 • The Different Activities on the Investing Tab

If you memorize more than one transaction for the same security, you will see a warning that the transaction is already memorized. You can click Replace, Add, or Cancel. One Quicken user used the Add option to create three memorized investment transactions for the same security with different memos for her employee 401(k) contribution, the employer match, and the catch-up contribution.

2. Press CTRL-J to open the Manage Bill & Income Reminder dialog. From that menu, click Create New | Scheduled Transaction Group. The Create Transaction Group dialog appears, as seen here.

3. Enter a name for your group, the account you want to use, the next due

date, and the frequency. Choose Investment and check the items you want to remember.

4. Click OK to close the dialog.

Understanding Quicken's Backup Procedures

If you've been working with financial software for any length of time, you know how important a good, current backup can be. Quicken's backup procedures are just a bit different, but aim for the same goal: current, accurate backups. The differences between backing up in Quicken and Money are shown in Table C-4.

Quicken	Money
From the menu bar, click File | Backup And Restore. Choose Back Up Quicken File, or from anyplace in Quicken, hold down CTRL and press B.	From the menu bar, click File | Backup, and type a name for the backup file.
Either accept the default location for your backed-up file or select a new one. You can even enter today's date to distinguish this file from others in the same location.	Click Save.
Click Back Up Now. The backed-up file is saved in your selected location. A message box appears telling you the file has been backed up successfully.	The backed-up file is saved in the selected folder.

Table C-4 • Backup Procedures in Quicken versus Money

It is always a good idea to save your backup data to someplace other than your main hard drive. Choose an external hard drive, a flash (thumb) drive, a recordable CD or DVD, or an online backup service such as Quicken Online Backup.

These are just some of the Quicken screens, windows, and dialogs with which you'll be working as you transition from Microsoft Money. As you continue to work with Quicken, you'll find that it is intuitive and helpful. Again, welcome to Quicken!

Index

D

Q

S

AUG 21 2012